Biblical Truths

Biblical Truths

The Meaning of Scripture
in the Twenty-first Century

DALE B. MARTIN

Yale

UNIVERSITY PRESS

New Haven and London

Yale University Press books may be purchased in quantity for
educational, business, or promotional use. For information, please e-mail
sales.press@yale.edu (U.S. office) or sales@yaleup.co.uk (U.K. office).

Set in Minion type by Newgen North America.
Printed in the United States of America.

Library of Congress Control Number: 2016948023
ISBN 978-0-300-22283-8 (hardcover : alk. paper)

A catalogue record for this book is available from the British Library.

This paper meets the requirements of ANSI/NISO Z39.48–1992
(Permanence of Paper).

10 9 8 7 6 5 4 3 2 1

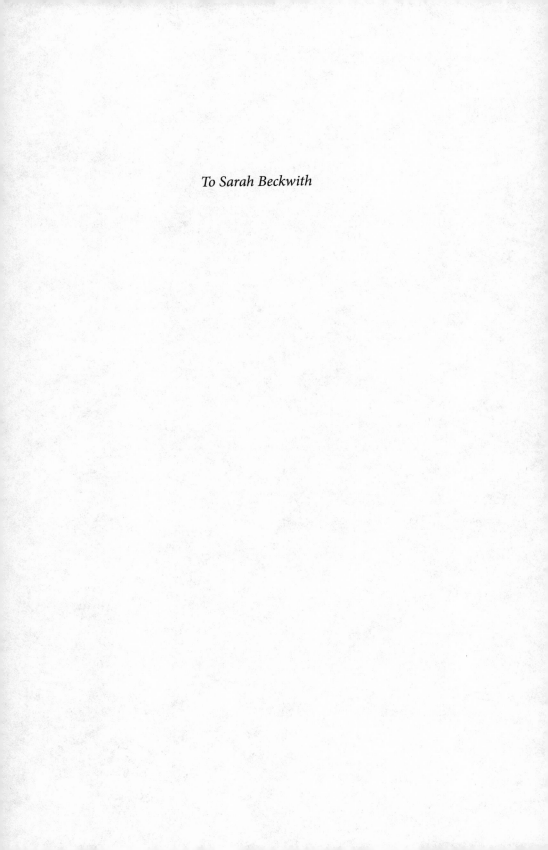

To Sarah Beckwith

Contents

Acknowledgments   ix
List of Abbreviations   xi

Introduction   1
1. Knowledge   38
2. Scripture   71
3. God   111
4. Christ   169
5. Spirit   221
6. Human   262
7. Church   311

Bibliography   353
Subject Index   369
Author Index   378
Scriptural Citations Index   380

Acknowledgments

I can unfortunately not name everyone—in churches, schools, and other audiences—who has offered encouragement and remarks on the writing of this book, but I really must thank the following for quite explicit feedback and concrete suggestions for improvements: Kathy Ehrensperger, Kathryn Greene-McCreight, Samuel Loncar, Frank Matera, David Wheeler Reed, Kari Wheeler Reed, Andrew Steffan, Michael Thate, Graham Ward, Michael Zimm, and my sister, Ferryn Martin. I especially thank the students in the course "Theology and the New Testament," taught at Yale University and Yale Divinity School in 2015, and my co-teacher for the course, Kathryn Tanner. I wish to thank the Department of Theological Studies at St. Louis University for supporting me as the Danforth Visiting Professor of Theological Studies during the final stages of preparing the book for publication. Thanks are due also to my research assistant in the same department, Michael Trotter, for compiling the author and scripture indexes. The book is dedicated to Sarah Beckwith, a wonderful and close friend of long standing and one of my best theological dialogue partners.

Abbreviations

CBQ	*Catholic Biblical Quarterly*
HTR	*Harvard Theological Review*
JB	Jerusalem Bible
JBL	*Journal of Biblical Literature*
JRS	*Journal of Roman Studies*
JSNT	*Journal for the Study of the New Testament*
JTS	*Journal of Theological Studies*
K	C. G. Kühn. *Claudii Galeni Opera omnia.* Paris: De Boccard, 2003; reprint of edition 1821–23.
KJV	King James Version
LCL	Loeb Classical Library
LSJ	*A Greek-English Lexicon.* Compiled by Henry George Liddell and Robert Scott. Revised and augmented by Henry Stuart Jones, with the assistance of Roderick McKenzie. With a Supplement 1968. Oxford: Clarendon, 1968.
LXX	The Septuagint
NEB	New English Bible
NIV	New International Version
NOAB	*The New Oxford Annotated Bible: with the Apocryphal/ Deuterocanonical Books.* 3d ed. Edited by Michael D. Coogan. Oxford: Oxford University Press, 2001.
NRSV	New Revised Standard Version
NTS	*New Testament Studies*
par.	parallels (of similar passages in different Gospels)
PG	Patrologia Graeca, edited by J.P. Migne
RSV	Revised Standard Version
TDNT	*Theological Dictionary of the New Testament*
ZKTh	*Zeitschrift für katholische Theologie*

Biblical Truths

Introduction

Around 1800 a genre of theological scholarship arose that proposed to instruct modern Christians about how they should interpret their Bibles. Variously known as "biblical theology," "theology of the Old Testament," "New Testament theology," or some variation on those terms, such books told people—or at least sufficiently "modern" people—what were good and what were bad ways of reading the Bible, showing how to interpret the Bible looking for its history but ultimately for its theology. The purpose of this introductory chapter is to tell the story of that genre and to critique it. The purpose of the rest of the book is to offer an alternative.

Before modernity, Christians read their scriptures as if the text were the voice of God speaking directly to them. When the Apostle Paul refers to a scriptural text, for example, he simply says, "the writing says" or, to translate a bit more piously, "scripture says."[1] Scripture is simply its own voice, contemporaneous to Paul himself. Augustine similarly reads the Psalms as if they are speaking directly to him. He reads, "Let your anger deter you from sin" (Ps 4:4) and takes it to be a direct message from God, through "David," of course, to Augustine and his fellow Christians.[2] Although these premodern Christians knew that biblical texts had human authors, they read the texts not for what some author "behind" the text might have "meant" but for what

---

1. See Rom 4:3; 10:11; 11:2. But other New Testament authors do the same (John 7:42; 19:37; Acts 1:16). See the discussion below in the chapter titled "Scripture." All quotations from the Bible are my translations unless otherwise noted.

2. *Confessions* 9:10. See fuller discussion in Martin, *Pedagogy*, 56–60.

the words of the text "said." They acknowledged that David was the author of the Psalms (they thought, usually, that he was the author of all of them), that Solomon was the author of Proverbs and a few other books, and that Paul was the author of the letters that bore his name, but for ancient or medieval Christians, the *main voice* of the text was the text itself. The text was its own agent and had its own voice. People considered that the text was what was speaking, not a historically "reconstructed" author *behind* the text.

These premodern Christians also believed that the text spoke doctrinally and ethically, not just historically. In other words, they didn't feel the need to ascertain what the text *meant* in its historical context before they could ascertain what it *meant* for themselves.[3] They believed they could take the text at face value to give them Christian doctrine *directly,* which was also taught by the church. When they read the stories of the texts, they took them to be "true." Granted, they didn't mean true in the way modern people have often meant true—as being "just like history" or "just like science." They knew that scripture could speak symbolically or allegorically. In those cases, the "truth" of the text's narratives needed spiritual insight to gather its "truth" from any possible misleading historical, literal, or scientific error. But correctly perceived, the text of scripture itself told stories that were "true." The "truth" of the story was in the story itself.[4]

In a sense, what I'm saying is that, before modernity, theology and biblical scholarship were the same thing. Medieval education in dogma and theology was fashioned around the reading of scripture. Scripture was assumed to be itself theology. And biblical writers were assumed to be speaking directly to the needs of the church in the year 500, or 1000, or 1300.

Though I'm greatly simplifying a complex historical development, I think it is fair to say that things began to change around 1800, at first, admittedly, only among scholars but eventually among many lay Christians in the pews. Beginning around 1800 the idea started gaining ground that a *historical* account of the meaning of the text of the Bible must precede—and furnish the basis for—a theological or doctrinal statement of Christian belief. As I will tell the story below in more detail, scholars began dividing up the duties of scholarship into two different tasks or even disciplines. First, they argued, scholars had to explain what the biblical texts *meant* in their ancient contexts, what they meant to their ancient authors, what they likely meant

3. I allude here to the famous essay by Krister Stendahl, "Biblical Theology, Contemporary."
4. The allusion here is to Hans Frei's famous book *Eclipse of Biblical Narrative.*

to their original readers or auditors. Only after the *ancient* meaning was established could scholars then *apply* those ancient meanings to modern Christian uses. In the modern world of theology and biblical studies, scholars began believing that they had to establish first the ancient "meaning" of the text and only after that ask what doctrine, theology, or ethics modern Christians should derive from those ancient texts today.

In thinking about biblical texts as occupying two different worlds—the ancient and the modern—modern scholars also, probably without realizing it, shifted their attention from the words of the texts themselves to the human author behind the text or the event the text was supposed to be describing. The meaning of the text increasingly became not "what is the meaning of the words of the text as they would be read by a competent reader?" but, instead, either "what happened?" or "what did the human author intend to say?" This was such a subtle shift that most modern readers failed to discern it, assuming, instead, that *the meaning* of a text is *necessarily* what the *author meant*.[5] But that has never been the only way human beings have read texts. Throughout human history, texts have been read in many different ways, and the "intention of the author" has been only one among many other "tools" human beings have used to establish "the meaning" of a text. In modern biblical scholarship, however, a shift occurred in people's minds: whereas Christians used to perceive scriptural texts to mean in many different ways (verbally word by single word, by sentence, typologically, allegorically, symbolically, anagogically, to name only some of the options), modern scholars insisted that at least the primary, or foundational, meaning of the text was a meaning we could imagine as the original author's "intention." Thus the ultimate goal of interpreting scripture shifted in the modern world from a concentration on the text itself to an imagined authorial intention or past event. The meaning was now not "in" the text but "behind" the text, usually in the author.

It is no accident that this change in theology and biblical studies happened around the same time as the rise in the authority of modern historiography. There had always been something like "history," some telling of stories that purported to represent past events. But in the last couple of centuries people developed an increased sense that "the modern world" was

---

5. The most well known representative of this position is Hirsch, *Validity in Interpretation*, but it has been widely assumed throughout the twentieth century, only to be almost universally rejected by philosophers and theorists of textual interpretation since around 1980. See my discussion below in the chapter "Scripture."

vastly different from all eras before us.[6] The divide between "the ancients" and "the moderns" came to dominate much of intellectual life and even popular culture. The rise of modern historiography worked with assumed or stated rules. To name just a few: the closer a witness (textual, archeological, whatever) was to an event, the better; the use of "primary sources" was preferred to the use of "secondary sources"; God, gods, or other "supernatural" beings could not be taken into consideration as agents or causes of events of "history"; different persons or events in history had to be treated analogically in comparison to similar persons or events (that is, no one or no thing could be incomparably unique in history).

Beginning around 1800, therefore, theologians began applying this kind of historical consciousness to their study of the biblical texts. The different documents of the Bible came from many different historical periods and different geographical locations. If we were to understand these texts correctly, we had to read them as *historical* documents, which is here just to say, as documents created by human beings in the ancient worlds of the Near East or the Greek and Roman Mediterranean. Most theologians continued to believe that these texts would still be meaningful, even "truthful," to us modern Christians, but the *primary* meaning of the texts had to be arrived at by means of philological, and especially historiographical, methods. The rise of what came to be known as "historical criticism" of the Bible—to put it simply, reading biblical documents for what we imagine their meaning would have been for their original authors and readers—corresponded with the rise of the hegemony in many academic disciplines of history.

Thus proceeded the development within the larger discipline of theology of the subfield "Theology of the Bible," or, as I will narrow the topic for my purposes in this book, "Theology of the New Testament." The genre—and the way biblical studies have been taught to most theological students throughout the twentieth century and now into the twenty-first—operates on the assumption that the "first" meaning of a biblical text must be arrived at by using methods of modern historiography. Theological applications of the meanings of those texts are supposed to "depend on" or be "founded on" the primary *ancient* meaning of the text. History has become something like the most important handmaiden to Christian theology—or, one might say, the governor needed to orient or control theological speculation.

6. For one description of the sense of the "different worlds," see Volf, *Captive to the Word*, 5–6.

Although I was myself initiated into modern historical criticism of the Bible and biblical theology during my own theological education at a very modern Princeton Theological Seminary and then more deeply in my doctoral program at Yale University, I gradually came to be dissatisfied with the reigning control such historical methods attempted on Christian interpretation of scripture. I came to believe that theological students were not being adequately taught how to think theologically and how to read Christian scripture for creative *theological* purposes rather than *historical* purposes.[7] Priests, pastors, and ministers were also therefore not well-equipped to help laypeople in their churches read the Bible in ways truly helpful for their lives and for more mature ways of thinking about "what they were supposed to believe." Biblical interpretation seemed increasingly to me to be cut off from a mature faith and understanding of Christian doctrine.

I also realized that through decades of being a biblical scholar but also reciting the creeds Sunday after Sunday, I had, without often thinking about it, developed my own ways of "thinking theologically." I had developed ways of being true to "the facts and history" of the Bible, recognizing that little of the Bible stands up to the standards of modern "history," that more of the Bible was "mythology" than anything related to either science or history, and yet I came to such knowledge while remaining a Christian who accepted the traditional doctrines of orthodox Christianity. How had I done that? How had I held in one life and one mind faith in radically premodern confessions and teachings while nonetheless working as a modern and very critical scholar? I have written this book in an attempt to work that out and to illustrate how I, no longer content with the genre Theology *of* the New Testament, might yet practice "theology *with* the New Testament."

Most of this book, therefore, contains my own experiments in theological interpretation of Christian scripture that use but are not subservient to historical methods and historical criticism. It is organized along the lines of (at least one version of) systematic theology, with the major chapters addressing seven "usual suspects" of systematics: from epistemology to ecclesiology. Indeed, apart from my beginning with the theological topics of epistemology and theology of scripture, the remaining chapter topics are taken from traditional systematic theological templates, especially those of Protestant theology. I chose such traditional subjects for chapter organization because

7. My research confirming this, along with my suggestions for changes in theological curriculum, can be found in Martin, *Pedagogy.*

I was intentionally setting for myself constraints: I wanted to demonstrate that innovative (at least from the modernist point of view) methods of biblical interpretation could nonetheless take place within traditional theological categories and concerns. Before moving into my own interpretations, I will further illustrate the biblical theology of modernism by means of explaining the history of its rise and describing and critiquing three major examples of the genre.

Johann Philipp Gabler

Most accounts of the history of biblical theology point to an academic address delivered by Johann Philipp Gabler in 1787 as providing a convenient beginning point for the genre, or at least the fundamental ideas that led to the production of biblical theologies.[8] Some scholars have noted that the significance of the occasion may be obvious to scholars more in hindsight than when Gabler spoke. Gabler delivered the lecture as his official inaugural speech upon appointment as professor at the University of Altdorf. It was no doubt published in some form at the time, though the original seems to be lost.[9] It was delivered in Latin and seems to have had little effect on either biblical studies or theology until many years later. Apparently, not until 1836, almost fifty years after it was delivered, did a scholar refer to the speech as a significant turning point in the discipline. Indeed, it may have been the case that the text was available for wider use only after it was published after the death of Gabler by his sons in 1831 in a volume of Gabler's collected writings.[10] Regardless of the immediate impact of Gabler's lecture, it has come to be cited by most histories of biblical theology as an important inauguration of the subdiscipline. At any rate, an analysis of Gabler's speech may serve as a suitable entrée into a description of the modern genre of biblical theology.

Gabler begins with the problem posed by the existence of one Bible but many different interpretations: how can scripture provide a "secure sanctu-

---

8. Examples are practically endless, but one may consult at least the following: Ladd, *Theology of the New Testament*, 14; Boers, *What Is New Testament Theology?*; Sandys-Wunsch and Eldredge, "J. P. Gabler," 149; Guthrie, *New Testament Theology*, 21–28; Adam, *Making*; Esler, *New Testament Theology*, 2, 12–20; Matera, *New Testament Theology*, xix–xx.

9. See Sandys-Wunsch and Eldredge, "J. P. Gabler." I have depended on the English translation provided there and also on the commentary by Sandys-Wunsch that accompanies the translation. It is on that commentary that I depend for this historical overview of the publication and impact of the speech in its own time.

10. Ibid., 149.

ary" for sacred knowledge when there is such "ambiguity and vicissitude of human knowledge" among different individuals and "the various sects" of Christianity? Gabler begins, therefore, with a stated need for epistemological security amid different interpretations of the Bible. He admits that one reason for such differences is that some people simply "read into" the text their own ideas and prejudices. But he adds that the confusion arises also because people don't recognize the difference (a) between "religion" and "theology" and (b) between biblical theology and dogmatic theology. Most of the rest of his lecture is dedicated to explaining these differences and advocating that scholars treat each of these topics separately rather than confusing them.

"Religion" refers to the simple teachings of scripture about "what each Christian ought to know and believe and do in order to secure happiness in this life and in the life to come." Religion is "everyday, transparently clear knowledge" (136). "Theology," on the other hand, is complex, subtle, and must be taught and learned. Theology refers to the teachings of the Bible elaborated by interaction with other disciplines, especially philosophy and history.

Theology is then itself divided into biblical theology and dogmatic theology. Biblical theology is what we have when we try simply to describe what ancient authors believed and taught about their religion, and this is to be produced using the philological and historical tools developed in the Humanist and Renaissance movements, but especially in the Enlightenment of the eighteenth century, toward the end of which Gabler is speaking. Biblical theology, therefore, is a straightforward description of the theology "contained in" the Bible but not elaborated by modern needs of dogmatics. Once the philologian or historian has established, for example, what Paul believed about some theological topic and has compared Paul's teachings to those derived from other biblical authors, it is the duty of the dogmatic theologian (today we would probably prefer some term such as "systematic" theologian) to bring in issues from other disciplines, especially philosophy, to show how that biblical theology may be used in our own, very different, historical situation. Dogmatic theology, for Gabler, is to be derived from biblical theology and then elaborated for modern consumption.

It is important to notice that each pair—religion versus theology and biblical theology versus dogmatic theology—is structured so that the first item is "simple" and the second "complex." Moreover, for Gabler, the second item in each pair must be built on the foundation of the first item: theology is founded on the simplicity of religion, and dogmatic theology is founded on the relative simplicity of biblical theology. Both sides of each of these pairs is necessary for modern Christian theology. The tasks move from simple to complex. They also move from historical construction of ancient ideas to modern elaboration of those ancient ideas for systematic theology for modern Christians. Moreover, much that we find in the Bible will be particular to its own historical setting and not usable for modern Christians. It is the job of the scholar to ascertain the universal and eternal truths by separating them from the historically contingent particulars of the ancient text. As John Sandys-Wunsch put it, "The result of Gabler's theology, then, is to postulate a double biblical theology, one setting out biblical religion as it appeared in history and the other setting out God's eternal truths enclosed in this historical shell."[11]

In spite of my observation that Gabler's speech may not have been seen at the time as revolutionary or of supreme historical significance, it does offer an opportunity for analyzing the development of modern historical criticism of the Bible. Gabler insists, for example, on recognizing the vast difference between ancient historical times and ours: the worldviews, mythological ideas, and assumptions of ancient authors cannot be taken as doctrine for us moderns. The Mosaic laws, he insists, were appropriate for their time but not for Christian observation. Paul was expressing a contingency of his own culture when he urged the veiling of women (1 Cor 11). For Gabler it is self-evident that such teachings have no universal or eternal relevance or truth.[12] Our consciousness of the difference between the ancient and the modern is a central theme of modern biblical scholarship. We simply cannot transfer the ancient world into ours, and we must also be careful not to impute our own ideas to the ancient text. Rather, we must carefully discern what in the ancient text is applicable for us—and what not.

Other themes of modern historical criticism can be found in Gabler's text. He insists, for instance, that the different authors of the Bible and the different texts differ from one another, even in significant ways. They should not be hastily harmonized (140). He warns against allegorical or "spiritual" interpretation.[13] He insists on the use of only proper, modern philological and historical methods. Gabler also recognizes that "revelation" within the Bible developed over time (see commentary at 153). Recognizing what is spe-

---

11. Ibid., 157.

12. Ibid., 142.

13. The word Gabler uses here is "trope," but, as the translators point out, this was in Gabler's context a technical term referring to allegorical or similar methods of interpretation: 140n4.

cific to different historical periods of the Bible helps the modern scholar recognize "what was meant for all times" (154). These are all important themes of modern biblical criticism taught to just about every seminary or divinity student to this day.

The most important aspect of Gabler's method for my purposes, however, is how he structures the different tasks of biblical theology. The first, the one that is of first importance, is to do the work of history: what is religion in the Bible and what is theology? What is the biblical theology of the different ancient authors and texts? Only once those descriptive tasks have been accomplished, carefully using the tools of modern philology and historiography, can the modern theologian provide the more elaborated system of doctrine necessary for a mature theology for modern churches. The historical task provides the epistemological foundation, the basis, for the secondarily elaborated modern theological application. This is the cardinal rule for almost all "theologies of the Bible" produced in the nineteenth and twentieth centuries: history first, theological application second.[14]

Most of the biblical theology attempted throughout the nineteenth and twentieth centuries, at least that of the more critical bent, generally followed, theoretically if not in actual practice, Gabler's insistence that theological systems must be founded on historical research. Gabler's arguments became even more significant after they were updated and promoted by William Wrede in 1897.[15] Though beginning with Gabler and claiming that much of what Gabler called for was by Wrede's time "self-evident" to most scholars, Wrede actually goes further than Gabler and insists that the goal of New Testament theology should not be refining theology or dogma at all, but describing the pure "history" of early Christian belief and practices.[16] At any rate, the positing of New Testament theology on a historical "base" has been the dominant quest for most practitioners of the genre for the past two hundred years.

---

14. Again, see Stendahl, "Biblical Theology, Contemporary."

15. Wrede, *Über Aufgabe und Methode.* For English translation, see Morgan, *Nature of New Testament Theology.* Morgan translates the title of Wrede's work as "The Tasks and Methods of 'New Testament Theology,'" but that deemphasizes Wrede's designation of the genre as "*so-called* New Testament theology" (my emphasis).

16. For the "self-evident" statement, see "Tasks and Methods," 68. For discussion, see Adam, *Making Sense,* 63–76.

Martin Kähler

This general "base/superstructure" of "history/theology" was significantly challenged in the last decade of the nineteenth century by the writings of Martin Kähler, especially in his famous lecture, first published in 1892, *Der sogenannte historische Jesus und der geschichtliche, biblische Christus* (The so-called historical Jesus and the historic, biblical Christ).[17] Admittedly, Kähler's concern was with nineteenth-century "Life of Jesus" proposals, but as I shall clarify shortly, the arguments Kähler here proposes for historical Jesus research are just as applicable for any attempt to "base" modern Christian theology on some indispensable "historical foundation," even when that is a construction of the "historical" meaning of a biblical text read in its original context.

Kähler begins by insisting that "we do not possess any sources for a 'Life of Jesus' which a historian can accept as reliable and adequate."[18] Scholars had come to realize that the Gospels are themselves theological documents, that we have no eyewitnesses to Jesus's life and ministry, and that no ancient "sources" rise to the level of adequate "records" in the sense needed by modern biographers. But the more devastating critique laid out by Kähler centers on what it is that constitutes Christian faith in the first place. Is Christian faith the belief that "Jesus the man" or "Jesus in the flesh" existed? Isn't it rather that Jesus is "the Word become flesh"? Even unbelievers can accept that Jesus of Nazareth existed and was "flesh." What makes Christian faith Christian is "the Word" (God!) part of the formula, or perhaps we could say, the combination of the flesh *and the Word*. The historical details of the "flesh" part of that formula are (1) insufficient for faith and (2) relatively unavailable to us.[19]

Kähler insists also that belief in the miraculous resurrection of Jesus is an indispensable part of Christian faith: "The risen Lord is not the historical Jesus *behind* the Gospels, but the Christ of the apostolic preaching, of the *whole* New Testament" (65). Moreover, "to confess him as Christ is to

17. Kähler, *So-Called Historical Jesus.* The English translation is based on the second edition, published in 1896. For the particulars of publications, see the introduction by Braaten, esp. 9n17.

18. Kähler, 48 (all citations are to the English translation).

19. This is all in the long Enlightenment intellectual tradition inspired by Lessing, that "Accidental truths of history can never become proofs of necessary truths of reason." Lessing, "On the Proof of the Spirit and of Power," 53. Or, as Søren Kierkegaard famously put it, "How can something of a historical nature be decisive for an eternal happiness?," *Concluding Unscientific Postscript,* 86.

confess his unique, supra-historical significance for the whole of human-ity" (65). The apostles and other disciples did not go out preaching about a mere man. Inspired by their "experience" of the resurrection and his glory, they preached about a person who was much more than any merely histori-cal man. This leads to what is perhaps Kähler's more famous slogan: "*This real Christ is the Christ who is preached. The Christ who is preached, how-ever, is the Christ of faith.*" The merely "historical" (*historische*) Jesus, a con-stantly variable product of modern scholars, is not the object of Christian faith; we believe rather in the Jesus Christ whose incarnation, ministry, and resurrection changed people then and changes people still, the "historic" (*geschichtliche*) Christ.[20]

Kähler's work strongly influenced both systematic theologians and biblical scholars after him.[21] Some have credited his arguments, coupled with Albert Schweitzer's *Quest of the Historical Jesus* (1906), with causing a hiatus in historical Jesus research until the revival of such interests in the 1950s and 1960s. At any rate, his work exerted powerful influence certainly on Karl Barth and Rudolf Bultmann, the former considered by many the most sig-nificant systematic theologian and the latter occupying that role in biblical studies of the twentieth century. Neither Barth nor Bultmann entertained any interest in the historical Jesus. Yet what they took from Kähler for the historical Jesus was definitely not absorbed with regard for their views of the use of historical criticism in the interpretation of the New Testament. In fact, both of them, when writing about the meaning of New Testament texts, often assume that the historical construction of the ancient meaning of the text remains normative for modern interpretations of it.[22] To demonstrate this and to illustrate the problems of the twentieth-century genre of Theol-ogy of the New Testament, I turn to Barth's commentary on the Epistle to the Romans.

Karl Barth

Barth's commentary, *Der Römerbrief,* was first published in 1918 and famously caused a stir, primarily because it seemed more a theological treatise than

20. For explanation of Kähler's rather idiosyncratic use of these two German words (even he would not be consistent in maintaining this difference in all his writings), see the introduction by Braaten, 20–21.

21. See the introduction to Kähler by Braaten.

22. As I point out in note 30 below, this is true for Barth in his commentary on Ro-mans, though less so in his later writings.

the usual modern historical-critical scholarly commentary and because it was correctly seen as a radical rejection of the German liberalism that had so ruled German theology before the First World War. The commentary went through six editions, Barth writing new prefaces for each. In fact, reading the different prefaces itself provides insight into what Barth thought he was doing. For example, in his preface to the English translation, published in 1933 and based on the sixth edition, Barth shows that he felt stung by readers of his commentary who took him to be offering more a "spiritual" reading of Romans. He insists, on the contrary, that his "sole aim was to interpret Scripture," to "*ex*-plain the text." "I shall not be impressed in the least by general propositions concerning the value or lack of value of my 'spiritual outlook,' or of my 'religious position,' or of my 'general view of life.' My book deals with one issue, and with one issue only. Did Paul think and speak in general and in detail in the manner in which I have interpreted him as thinking and speaking? Or did he think and speak altogether differently?"[23] Since Barth explicitly rejects the label "spiritual" interpretation, I assume he would agree that the criteria for ascertaining what Paul "thought" and "spoke" were normal historiographical criteria, that is, through what I have been calling historical criticism. Therefore it is by those standards that I intend to evaluate Barth's interpretation of Paul's letter to the Romans: does it work adequately with the methods and criteria of modern historiography?

Barth himself says that the meaning of Romans can be summed up in a few short sentences: "Where the faithfulness of God encounters the fidelity of men, there is manifested His righteousness. There shall the righteous man live. This is the theme of the Epistle to the Romans" (42). But this characterization is woefully inadequate for the huge, complex commentary supplied by Barth. In order to analyze what Romans is about for Barth, we must illustrate the complexity of his interpretation. And though what I provide here is itself only a short and too simple description of the book, some such description is necessary in order to comment on the nature of Barth's exegesis.

Romans, for Barth, is a story of human predicament and the radical means God offers for the way through death to life, through imprisonment to freedom. "Men" find themselves to be "slaves and puppets of things, of 'Nature' and of 'Civilization,' whose dissolution and establishing by God they have overlooked."[24] The history of religions is a history of men trying

---

23. Barth, *Epistle*, ix–x.

24. This is offered as an interpretation of Rom 1:23–25. Ibid., 51. I use the terms "men" and sometimes "Man" or "man," because it is Barth's terminology but also because it helps us keep in mind that his theology is universalistic in that all human beings come to God

to achieve God's approval (111), get God's reward, or escape the ultimate meaninglessness of their existence. Men through religion seek to save themselves. Religion, however, even at its best, can take man only so far. Barth often castigates "religion" (and he does seem to believe that there is such a thing as "religion" in general and universally). "All religions either *reckon* that human achievements in this world—some concrete human behavior or disposition—constitute a claim to the favour of God and must be rewarded by Him (ii. 6); or else they *reckon* that human achievements are themselves the reward of God, since they are the tangible and recognizable products of a transformation of human behaviour that has been wrought by God. . . . In all religions it is therefore possible to disregard or to escape from the paradox of faith."[25] The church is also thus indicted. In fact, the church seems for Barth to be merely the best form of religion he can conceive. The church, even at its best, comes up short. The church is "a living witness in history that men have exhausted every human possibility" (338). The church has done, though, some positive work in history. Commenting on Rom 7:22–25, Barth says, "We have seen at last the reality of religion; we have recognized what men are. How vast a gulf separates the nineteenth-century conquering-hero attitude to religion from that disgust of men at themselves, which is the characteristic mark of true religion!" (269). Note that here "religion" is a good thing, to an extent. But it is not "faith" or "God" or the essence of the gospel. If anything, "true religion" may be something like a handmaiden helping, in its desperation, to lead to the need for faith and the gospel. Note also Barth's implied attack, as so often in his book, on the optimism and faith in "progress" of liberal theology.

As the church seems to be for Barth "religion at its best," so Abraham for him represents man at its best. If man could be saved by his own efforts or achievements, surely Abraham would have been justified (118–23). But he was not by his works. And by "works" Barth means (as would just about all Protestant interpreters of his time) not just works of the Jewish law but any human deeds: "*Works* are the behavior of men, when they do not apprehend the judgement regulating the whole relationship of God and man" (367, commenting on Rom 9:32). "Abraham . . . stands under the krisis of everything human" (120). "Like all other men, Abraham stands under negation. That he awoke to his position and was aware of the krisis, that in this

---

as individuals, but all human beings are, in the system of salvation, the same: "for men are one" (51).

25. Ibid., 111.

krisis he feared God, that he heard the 'No' of God and understood it as His 'Yes'—this is Abraham's faith" (123).

The only way out of the predicament is by faith in Jesus Christ. But faith shows us we trust a God about whose real nature we can know nothing.[26] Faith, however, is not just confession of creeds or agreeing to propositions. "Faith is conversion: it is the radically new disposition of the man who stands naked before God and has been wholly impoverished that he may procure the one pearl of great price; it is the attitude of the man who for the sake of Jesus has lost his own soul. Faith is the faithfulness of God, ever secreted in and beyond all human ideas and affirmations about Him, and beyond every positive religious achievement" (98). "Faith" is "conversion" but to a completely apophatic notion of God. "Faith means motionlessness, silence, worship—it means not-knowing" (202). But that is the way to freedom. There is nothing more to do than "to go forth into the fresh air and to love the undiscoverable God" (76).

I have quoted so much of Barth because it is important to hear how he expounds his theology. The question now is, was this Paul's theology? Is Barth's problem the same problem for which Paul attempted an answer, the narrative his teachings assumed, and the solution proposed by Romans as read by historical criticism? I do believe Barth's theology is good theology, at least for the middle of the twentieth century and his political location.[27] But is it good history? To answer that question, I have to describe recent developments in scholarship on Paul and Romans and sketch out my own interpretation of the letter to the Romans.

The "center" of attention for the Letter to the Romans has, over the past several decades, shifted for scholars. Previously, especially in Protestant interpretation, the first half of the letter, say, Rom 1–5 or 1–8, has been taken as the theologically significant part of the letter. Today, on the contrary, many scholars believe we get to the true goal of Paul's writing only in chapters 9–11, for the theology, and chapters 12–15, for the practical matters.[28] Paul is writ-

26. See ibid., 46–47. The unknowability of God is a theme repeated throughout the book; contrary to his reputation as a "dogmatic" theologian in the popular sense of that term, Barth's theology is apophatic and much dependent on traditional negative theologians.

27. I could offer, though I will not here, criticisms of Barth's theology, at least as it appears in his commentary. For starters, I would fault it for its individualism and relative lack of interest in the social and political. I would criticize its universalism in its assumptions about "man," society, and "religion." But that is for another day.

28. There is so much published scholarship on the "new perspective" on both Paul and Romans that it is impossible to give even a representative list, but I would name as among

ing to a predominantly gentile church to explain to them his understanding of God's inscrutable will and his vision of what is yet to come. Paul's understanding of his call and apostleship (he would not have considered himself "converted" in any sense) is that he has been appointed by God as a special messenger to take the gospel of Jesus as Israel's Messiah to the nations outside Israel. This is because Paul reads certain Old Testament prophets as predicting that before the very end—when the Messiah will arrive, defeat the forces of evil, and establish God's reign in heaven and earth—all the nations will flock to Israel. All "the nations," the gentiles, non-Israelites will come to believe that they also must go to Jerusalem, worship the God of Israel, and await the arrival of his son, the Messiah. Before the final end, according to Paul, the nations must be evangelized and added to the body of Israel.

It is unclear just how Paul did it, but for whatever reason he came to believe it was not God's will that the believing gentiles follow the Law of Moses. God had never intended to bring the gentiles into Israel through circumcision and law observance. Paul's argument in Romans is that it was God's will all along to justify all human beings by faith, not by works of the Mosaic Law. This is proven for Paul by the fact that Abraham, the father of the Jews, was himself justified by his faith before he was circumcised and before Moses had given the law.

Note that in Paul's mind it was perfectly fine that the Jews keep their ancestral laws, but it was not required for gentiles. In fact, as Paul had argued in his more radical letter to the Galatians, if gentiles even attempt to keep the Law of Moses, they will be "cut off" from Christ; they will "fall from grace" (Gal 5:4). There are not, in Paul's preaching, two ways to salvation, one for the Jews by law observance and another for gentiles by faith alone. All, Jews and gentiles alike, are justified by grace through faith. But that need not mean that Jews should cease observing the law. In fact, it seems certain that Paul himself was a law-abiding Jew when he found himself in a Jewish context (see 1 Cor 9:20).

But Paul had said some radical things about the law in the Letter to the Galatians, so that he has developed a reputation for antinomianism by the time he writes his letter to the Romans. Paul is also planning a trip to Jerusalem, mainly to deliver money to the Judean church, money he has collected from all his churches, which are all gentile. In Paul's mind, the collection will

some of the most influential works Stendahl, "Apostle Paul"; Sanders, *Paul and Palestinian Judaism;* Stowers, *Rereading of Romans;* Gager, *Reinventing Paul;* Dunn, *The New Perspective on Paul.* For a fuller treatment of my own interpretation, see Martin, *New Testament,* 231–46.

cement the unity of his gentile churches with the Jewish church in Judea. So one of the main reasons he writes to the Roman church is to explain how he is not against the law but supports it, when its role is correctly understood. He does this also because he wants the support of the Roman church, which seems to comprise both gentiles and Jews, for his upcoming trip to Jerusalem.

Paul writes to explain with more nuance his views on the law. But he also writes to insist that although there may be an increasing number of gentiles in churches around the Mediterranean, the Jews still have priority in God's plan, and that although most Jews are currently unbelievers, that was God's will all along to allow for the bringing in of the nations. God's ultimate plan is to save "all Israel," granted, in some yet unknown manner (Rom 11:26).

The problem with Paul's plan is that he knows that the Judean disciples may not accept his and the gentiles' gift of money. Accepting the gift, after all, would imply that they approved of Paul's ministry and even of his theology. And they may not actually approve of either. If the Jewish disciples reject Paul's gift, that would be a serious blow to the unity of the Jewish–gentile church that is the goal of Paul's entire ministry.

At least for a significant consensus of scholars today, the Letter to the Romans is not about individual salvation of universal Man in any kind of abstract sense. It is not about universal human experience of guilt. It is not about some abstract doctrine of "justification by grace through faith alone" rather than "justification by human works and achievement." It is about ethnicity, politics, money, status, and the joining of gentiles into an eventually saved and united Israel in an eschatological kingdom. This may not be the "correct" theory of the original writing of Romans, but it is at least much more sensitive to the social, cultural, political, and ethnic situation of Paul's writing than is Barth's.

Barth makes of Romans something like a theological allegory for a twentieth-century rejection of liberalism, idealism, and optimism and the advocacy of a theology of crisis and existential decision in the face of the *absence* of knowledge of the nature of God. Barth takes Paul's reference to "the Jew" to refer to "religious or ecclesiological man" and "the Greek" to be a stand-in for "man of the world" (40, 63). But for Paul's rhetoric to work in his own context, his naming of "the Jews" must refer to actual Jews (though I think "Greek" for Paul is a stand-in for gentiles in general). Paul refers to "those under the law," and he seems obviously enough to *have* to be referring to law-abiding Jews (Rom 3:19–20). But Barth takes the reference to be "the idealists, the especially favored, those who have an experience of God or, at least, a remembrance of such experience" (87; see 87–91). I take it that Barth is thinking of "liberals" or perhaps of all humanity. But that would make no sense in Paul's historical context. Paul's references to Jews and gentiles must remain concretely ethnic. Barth turns it all to modern theological allegory.

For several entire chapters Barth reads any reference to "Jews" or "Israel" to be a reference not to actual Jews but to "the church" and Christians. Barth takes Paul's lament over his own people (Rom 9:1–5) to be about "the church," which is the best human "possibility" but not the gospel and not the "existential krisis" and paradox of faith. "Who can teach us to speak existentially and not ecclesiastically? No one except God. And even should we be taught of God, His incognito remains" (334; see 330–39). This is true of Barth's treatment of all of Rom 9–11. References to "Israel" or "my people" are taken by Barth to refer to the church. "Gentiles" are often taken by Barth to be people outside the church (see 400–405, for example). The "casting away" of unbelieving Israel, for Paul, is taken by Barth to be the "casting away" of "the church" (405). "And so all Israel will be saved" (Rom 11:26, NRSV), which in current scholarship is central for reading Romans as being about actual Jews, is interpreted by Barth to mean that *even the church* will need saving by God's grace and mercy (416).

Barth makes many other interpretive moves that cannot be supported by modern historical criticism. In interpreting Rom 1:19–21, where Paul is actually insisting that the gentiles *did* "know" enough about God to be culpable for forsaking the worship of the one God and inventing idols, Barth rather makes it all about *our not* "knowing" anything about God: "And what does this mean but that we can know nothing of God, that we are not God, that the Lord is to be feared?" (46–47). Again, I agree with the theology. As will become clear in this book, I am as committed as Barth to "negative" or apophatic theology. But for Paul's context in Rom 1, he must get his readers to accept that the gentiles *did* "know" enough about the God of Israel to be worthy of the punishment God meted out to them described in Rom 1:18–32.

There are many other instances where Barth's interpretations make fine theology but bad historiography.[29] In any case, Barth's interpretation

---

29. It is not clear, for example, what Barth means by "history" or "historical" when he insists that Abraham's "uncircumcision" has "a real status in history" (128).

of Romans is not historical criticism at all. It is acceptable theology based on bad history.[30] This will be a theme of my book: modern theologies of the New Testament were failures from a Christian point of view precisely because what they ended up offering was bad history, bad theology, or both. My task now is to demonstrate my thesis by analysis of two influential New Testament scholars of the twentieth century: Rudolf Bultmann as representing a more liberal approach, though he also rejected the liberalism of early German theology, and George Eldon Ladd, who was one of the most influential evangelical scholars of the New Testament in the last half of the twentieth century. I choose them not because they are especially guilty of the problems I am highlighting but precisely because they were both exceptional and famous scholars of their times. If they couldn't pull the genre off, perhaps it can't be done.

Rudolf Bultmann

I can spend fewer pages on Rudolf Bultmann's *Theology of the New Testament* because in many ways my criticisms of it are similar to those I have already leveled against Barth's Romans commentary.[31] In the middle of the twentieth century, people tended to read Barth and Bultmann as two opposite poles of German language theology: Barth often caricatured as the conservative and Bultmann the liberal. Indeed, in his *Introduction to the Theology of the New Testament,* published in 1958, Alan Richardson calls Bultmann's theology

---

30. I emphasize that this criticism of Barth's method applies to his insistence in *Der Römerbrief* that he is practicing a simple literal exegesis of Paul's intended message. In his later theology Barth admits that a historical, literal reading of the Bible will not necessarily produce adequately robust orthodox dogma, but that should not be seen as a problem. See his discussion of the doctrine of the trinity and the Bible in *Church Dogmatics,* I/1, pp. 301–12. I believe Barth was much less careful in his *Römerbrief* to distinguish legitimate *theological* interpretation from *historical* interpretation. And what Barth means by "historical" also becomes much clearer and more sophisticated in his later work. For example, in terms clearly influenced by Kähler's earlier differentiation between *historisch* and *geschichtlich,* Barth explains in *Church Dogmatics* I/1, p. 325, "Historical does not mean historically demonstrable or historically demonstrated. . . . What we mean by this is rather that the Bible always understands what it calls revelation as a concrete relation to concrete men. God in His incomprehensibility and God in the act of His revelation is not the formula of an abstract metaphysics of God, the world, or religion which is supposed to obtain at all times and in all places. It is rather the record of an event that has taken place once and for all, i.e., in a more or less exact and specific time and place." Barth was not so clear in his *Römerbrief.*

31. Bultmann. The German was published in 1948 and 1953.

heretical, a judgment most biblical scholars or theologians would reject.[32] From our perspective, at least if we are comparing Bultmann's theology to Barth's commentary on Romans, the two look much alike. They both give little attention to the doctrinal concerns of systematic theology, they reject the previous "liberalism" of earlier German theology, they claim that biblical theology is not concerned with political reform or challenge of political structures but is instead, at its best, about the existential decision individuals are called upon by the gospel to make in a situation of "krisis," or crisis. Much of my criticism of Bultmann's theology, therefore, and especially his treatment of Paul, will echo my critique of Barth above, both in terms of their theologies and their exegesis.

Famously, Bultmann argued that the message *of* Jesus of Nazareth and the "historical Jesus" itself are not New Testament theology but the "presupposition" of New Testament theology, which is not the message *of* Jesus but the preached message (the "kerygma") *about* Jesus Christ. Bultmann does proceed, however, to expound on the message preached and enacted by Jesus. As Barth had done, Bultmann projects the stereotypes of Judaism from his own German Protestant assumptions onto the Judaism of the time of Jesus and Paul. Jesus's message "is a great *protest against Jewish Legalism*— i.e. against a form of piety which regards the will of God as expressed in the written Law and in the Tradition which interprets it, a piety which endeavors to win God's favor by the toil of minutely fulfilling the Law's stipulations."[33] The Jewish emphasis on ritual and cultic laws ends up "vitiating" the "motivation to ethical conduct." "That is the result not only in the wide extent to which the idea of reward and punishment becomes the motivation, but also—and this is the characteristic thing for Judaism—that the obedience man owes to God and to His demand for good is understood as a purely formal one; i.e. as an obedience which fulfills the letter of the law, obeying a law simply because it is commended without asking the reason, the meaning, of its demand" (1.11–12). Moreover, according to Bultmann, "the error of Jewish legalism" leads necessarily to "works of supererogation" (1.12). In this quotation we see the common practice of the time to conflate a stereotype of Judaism with a matching stereotype of Roman Catholicism, here in typical Protestant condemnation of "supererogation," familiar since the time of Luther.

---

32. Richardson, *Theology of the New Testament*.
33. Bultmann, *Theology*, 1:11.

Bultmann insists, "Polemic against the temple cult is completely absent from the words of Jesus" (1.17). He explains that Jesus showed little concern for the temple cult because the temple and its cult had, by the time of Jesus, lost its centrality and meaning for Jews, "for Judaism was no longer a cultic religion, but had become a religion of observance" (1.17). This is a completely unhistorical retrojection into Jesus's day of the way Judaism was perceived in mid twentieth-century Germany: having no temple or sacrificial cult any longer, the Jews had turned to legalism and raised the significance of the Law to its highest and most ridiculous level.

Jesus was also not at all concerned with "an ethic of world-reform." Jesus's message is not about any kind of politics but concerns only the "individual": "It is an ethic that, by demanding more than the law that regulates human society does and requiring of the individual the waiver of his own rights, makes the individual immediately responsible to God." The "Reign of God" has nothing to do with "the molding of human society" (1.19). Here Bultmann introduces a term absolutely central to his program, but one he must completely redefine from its ancient (and certainly more accurate) meaning: "eschatological." Whereas "eschatological," when used by most scholars, necessarily has something to do with the "end of the world as we know it"—after all, *eschaton* means "end" in Greek—to Bultmann, good New Testament theology must not be about anything that will occur in the future. "Eschatological" rather refers to "Now," and an eschatological event is the proper response demanded of individuals by the preached message of the gospel *in the now-time.* What Bultmann means by "eschatological" is not political or social, in spite of the fact that any historically accurate interpretation of the "kingdom of God" in the ancient context must necessarily include reference to a heavenly–earthly establishment of God's social and political reign, and almost always *on earth.* What Bultmann means by "eschatological" is the relationship of the individual to God in a decisive, existential change of life in response to the preached message in the now-time.

There is nothing, therefore, "apocalyptic" about Bultmann's "eschatological." Thus he can say, "Judgment and salvation are eschatological events in the strict sense; i.e. events in which the present world and all history cease to be." Jesus "'de-historicized' God and man" (1.25). Therefore, "eschatology" for Bultmann, in the teaching of Jesus, has nothing to do with the actual end of this world or creation of a new heaven and earth. It is all about the individual face to face with the demand for a "decision" about God and his fate: "Jesus' idea of God does not essentially differ from that of the Old Testament and of Judaism, though it is true that in the common piety of Judaism faith in God the Creator had weakened even while it was strictly preserved in its official theology and confession" (1.23). As had many Protestant theologians before him, Bultmann here combines a connection of Jesus to the great Old Testament prophets with a *disconnection* of Jesus from his contemporary fellow Jews. What could have counted as the "official teaching" of Judaism in Jesus's day could only be a product of German Protestant fantasy.

Bultmann's "Judaism" is an anachronistic and dangerous stereotype.[34] Jesus's message is somehow eschatological without having anything to do with history, an actual end, or politics. Jesus's message has nothing to do with the temple or society, only with the individual. Jesus's message does not demand particular ethical actions, only a decision. This is all midcentury German, Protestant, dialectical theology, not the historical Jesus or even the Jesus of the Gospels. It isn't a decent construction of prerabbinic Judaism or even of twentieth-century Judaism taken without prejudice. It is modern ideology.

In any case, the climax of Bultmann's first volume comes not with Jesus or the "Hellenistic Church Aside from Paul" but with Paul, for Bultmann the "founder of Christian theology" (1.187). Paul's "conversion," Bultmann insists, "was not a conversion of repentance," which in Bultmann's system would place it too much within "Judaism" and the more "Jewish" forms of early Christianity. But Bultmann is not done: "Neither, of course, was it one of emancipating enlightenment." By these terms, Bultmann refers to ancient philosophy, the various kinds of "religion" he lumps under the terms "hermetic" and "Gnostic," and to modern liberalism, all in one. "Rather," Bultmann concludes, Paul's "conversion" "was obedient submission to the judgment of God, made known in the cross of Christ, upon all human accomplishment and boasting" (1.187).

As he had done for Jesus, Bultmann must also do for Paul: separate him as much as possible from "Judaism": "The immediate contrast is that what for the Jews is a *matter of hope* is for Paul a *present reality*—or, better is also a present reality" (1.279). Again, however, the word "decisive" characterizes Paul's gospel. "The contrast between Paul and Judaism consists not merely in his assertion of the present reality of righteousness, but also in a much more decisive thesis—the one which concerns the condition to which

---

34. I hasten to add that Bultmann cannot be accused of the *racial* anti-Semitism of the Third Reich. He was adamantly opposed to that. But he was influenced by the *religious* and *cultural* "anti-Judaism" of his time; and that is at least dangerously close to anti-Semitism. For the complexities of Bultmann's life and views on these topics, see Hammann, *Rudolf Bultmann*.

God's acquitting decision is tied. The Jew takes it for granted that this condition is keeping the Law, the accomplishing of 'works' prescribed by the Law.
In direct contrast to this view Paul's thesis runs—to consider its negative
aspect first: *'without works of the Law'*" (1.279). According to Bultmann, Paul
was no more interested in the historical Jesus than Bultmann was. What is
central is the *kerygma* of the significance of the Christ-event: "In the word
of proclamation Christ's death-and-resurrection becomes a possibility of
existence in regard to which a decision must be made, and in the fact that
faith seizes this possibility and appropriates it as the power that determines
the existence of the man of faith" (1.302).

Moreover, just as the message of Jesus had no concerns about cosmology, so Paul begins his letter to the Romans, his great attempt to explain
his theology to a church he did not found, not with cosmology but with
the "plight of mankind." This again differentiates Paul's message and theology from "the Hermetic tractates," by which Bultmann means all kinds of
theology or philosophy he considers to fall under the influence of "Gnosticism." Instead, Paul begins Romans "by exposing the plight of mankind,
so that then the proclamation of God's salvation-deed becomes a decision-
question" (1.301). The "man-under-the-Law" is made to see his situation as
the "'miserable wretch' groaning for deliverance from the 'body of death.'"

All of this may be good-enough theology, hyper-Protestant though it
is. But from the point of view of historical criticism, all the criticisms leveled
against Barth's presentation of the theology of Romans must be made also
against Bultmann's, as well as Bultmann's presentation of Paul entire. It may
be good theology. (I think it was, given the limitations of its historical, political, and ideological context.) It may be a stellar version of dialectical "crisis"
theology. But it is not good history. It is not a defensible historical-critical
construction of Paul or his letters.

Things do not get any better when Bultmann turns to the other of his
favorite New Testament "theologians," the author of the Fourth Gospel. As
he had for Paul, Bultmann takes his demythologizing program *into* the Gospel of John (not just as a secondary interpretation of John): "Is the devil
a reality for John in the mythical sense? That is very doubtful, to say the
least" (2.17). And as he had for Paul, Bultmann begins with the "plight" of
human beings, in this case, when they are *trying* to be religious. Without
reproducing the detailed critique I offer above about Bultmann's treatment
of Paul when he turns to John, I may simply summarize that Bultmann reads
the Fourth Gospel to be not about the relation of the author's community
to the Jewish synagogue, as would be taught by most scholars of our time.

Nor is the author of the Gospel concerned about conflicts between believers and nonbelieving Jews over the proper understanding of the divinity of Jesus, again as would be assumed by most scholars today. Rather, Bultmann takes the Fourth Gospel to be about the inadequacies of religion (see 2.27, for example) and the need for an existential decision by the individual in a situation of crisis (see 2.18). Again, this may be good theology, at least in the middle of the twentieth century and in reaction both to older forms of theological liberalism, on one side, and the German theology and ideology of the Third Reich, on the other. But it is not good historical criticism.

Along with many other scholars I have argued that the main message of the Fourth Gospel is about the correct acceptance of Jesus's true identity, as "divine" in a very "high" sense. It is also about communities of Jews fracturing and separating from other communities.[35] The message of the Fourth Gospel is both theological and social. Making the Gospel be about an individual's "decision" to arrive at a "self-understanding" changes the meaning of the Gospel to be about twentieth-century individualism and existentialism. Again, what *may* be good theology is here bad history.

George Eldon Ladd

George Eldon Ladd was one of the most respected scholars of the New Testament among conservative or evangelical Christians in the twentieth century. He spent a long career teaching at Fuller Theological Seminary. His *Theology of the New Testament* was written for and used as a textbook by seminary students, especially those at evangelical institutions. And Ladd saw his book as a major answer to what he viewed as more liberal treatments of New Testament theology, that of Bultmann especially: there are many references throughout Ladd's *Theology* to Bultmann's book, which had been published around twenty years earlier. I select Ladd's *Theology* because it is self-consciously and openly conservative and evangelical, yet he explicitly intends to follow the methods of modern historical criticism, and he fashions his book to fit squarely within the modern genre of Theology of the New Testament. I view it as perhaps the best of the genre from an evangelical scholar in the twentieth century. Thus I will use it also to advance my thesis

---

35. See Martin, *New Testament,* 152–67. Especially important for reading the Gospel and letters of John as reflecting the history of a particular community are the works of Raymond E. Brown and J. Louis Martyn. See Brown, *Gospel According to John;* Brown, *Epistles of John;* Martyn, *History and Theology;* see also Martin, *New Testament,* 168–78.

that modern "theologies of the New Testament" render either bad history, bad theology, or both. In the case of Ladd's *Theology*, I believe it is both.

Ladd agrees with Krister Stendahl and most other scholars contemporary to himself about what defines biblical theology in the modern world: "Biblical theology is that discipline which sets forth the message of the books of the Bible in their historical setting. Biblical theology is primarily a descriptive discipline."[36] That is, biblical theology should not be "constructive, systematic" theology offered as "normative" for a Christian or church. Its sole purpose, in this understanding, is to describe the theology of the different biblical books or authors as they would have been understood in their ancient context, as reflecting the "intentions" of the authors or the likely understandings of the texts by their original readers and hearers. Modern scholars must not read into the biblical texts the theologies they themselves happen to hold.

Ladd recognizes that this task necessitates the use of modern historiography, and Ladd understands "history" to be "the modern historian's reconstruction of the events of the past by the critical use of ancient documents. In such a reconstruction, there must be accepted critical procedures, 'ground-rules'" (29). At least when it comes to the stories and claims of non-Christian ancient texts, "history" will not admit the historicity of "mythology": "When one reads in Greek literature of the alleged activities of the gods among men, he does not consider this to be history but mythology" (29). Yet Ladd does not allow this differentiation between history and myth to affect his (therefore "uncritical") acceptance of all stories in the New Testament that critical scholars *do* take to be "mythology" (such as Bultmann, as Ladd laments). Ladd pushes all texts in the New Testament so that they may be counted as "historical" and also in agreement with what Ladd takes to be proper Christian doctrine.

Examples occur throughout the book. Recognizing that Paul's words in Rom 11:25–27, "All Israel shall be saved," *could* be read as a prediction by Paul that indeed "all Jews" will eventually "be saved," Ladd, who as a conservative Christian was scarcely going to accept some kind of "universal salvation" for Jews, insists that Paul need not mean "all Jews" but only "the people as a whole," though he doesn't explain what he means by that (562). Admitting that the list of the twelve tribes found in Revelation 7 "are not the twelve tribes of the Old Testament Israel" and moreover do not match any other list in the Bible, Ladd simply insists that this was a "deliberate irregular listing of

---

36. Ladd, *Theology*, 25. Ladd cites Stendahl's essay "Biblical Theology" mentioned above.

the twelve tribes" by John in order to indicate that it is to be read symbolically (627). Ladd accepts all sorts of stories of the New Testament as historical with no question. He quotes Paul's words in Acts 22:3 as the actual words
of Paul (360), in spite of much scholarship that has shown that the author
of Acts almost certainly composed the speeches himself. Ladd doesn't even
bring up the possibility of whether the Damascus road conversion narratives
of Paul are historical. He simply takes it for granted that they are (366).

Ladd briefly entertains the opinions of critical scholars that many
of the documents of the New Testament were not written by the persons
whose names they bear. But he ends up insisting that they all are authentic:
James, the brother of Jesus, wrote James; Peter wrote both 1 and 2 Peter; 1, 2,
and 3 John were written by the same person who wrote the Fourth Gospel,
and though Ladd refrains from insisting that he was John, son of Zebedee,
one of the twelve disciples, in the end he implies that it was: Ladd says that
the Gospel was written by one of the "intimate" disciples of Jesus (222). Ladd
does not explicitly say that Jude was written by Judah / Judas (the Hebrew
and Greek forms of the name), brother of James and therefore also a brother
of Jesus, but he implies as much since he never raises the question of the
pseudepigraphy of Jude and calls the author Jude throughout (607–8). Ladd
does not explicitly discuss the problems of taking all thirteen "Pauline" letters to be actually by Paul; he assumes they all are.

Throughout his book Ladd too often appropriates a certain rhetorical strategy popular especially among conservative Christian scholars. He
will admit that "a previous generation" may have held to a particular critical
view or that a more skeptical consensus may have existed in the past, but
in order to counter that previous view or consensus, Ladd merely points to
some more recent (conservative) scholarship that has made a case for the
opposite opinion. So, for example, though noting that "a generation ago" it
was customary to emphasize the radical diversity of teachings and assumptions in the New Testament, Ladd simply mentions other scholarship that
more recently has emphasized the unity of the New Testament documents
(33).[37] But pointing to conservative scholars who simply insist on a more
conservative interpretation is not the practice of historiography; it is just

---

37. A related problem, brought in also at places where Ladd wants to emphasize the
"unity" of the New Testament or the Bible, is Ladd's tendency to attribute a "view" or
"intention" to the text itself, even to the point of insisting that the entire New Testament
or the entire Bible *has* a "view" or "intention" (e.g., see 25, 29). Besides papering over the
differences within the entire Bible, this makes the added mistake of false ascription of
agency to an inanimate text. A "text" can't have a "view" or "intention," much less can
one demonstrate that the entire Bible does. For demonstration of the speciousness—and

claiming that because "someone else" has given conservatives permission to dismiss the more skeptical arguments of their colleagues, those more skeptical interpretations need not bother anyone. This is special pleading, not critical historiography.

That Ladd is not really a practitioner of modern, critical historiography is obvious in what he insists must be accepted as "historical." To remind ourselves: what should be accepted, at least in principle, as historical is an account that could and most likely would be accepted as historical by modern, professional historians—say, those holding professorships in the best universities and colleges *regardless of their religious inclinations or lack thereof.* If an account is put forward by a conservative Christian as historical and yet it is quite unlikely that anyone but a Christian would find the argument persuasive, that account is not granted the status of history. History is what is made by historians. Ladd seems not to understand that.

For example, Ladd insists that "Israel's history is different from all other history" (27). But to claim that the history of Israel is unique simply because Israel has been especially chosen and used by God is not to make a historical case at all. It is common knowledge among real historians that either (1) nothing in history—no human being, no nation, no people—is truly "unique," or (2) everything is. A historical biography will not present a George Washington that is *completely unlike* every other human being in history, or is *completely like* every other human being. Uniqueness is not really a historical category. Either nothing is or everything is—according to how one understands the term "unique."

Moreover, real historians do not include the actions of God in their histories. One may believe that God caused Washington to be the first president of the United States of America, but any historian of the American presidency who offers that as a historical thesis will be laughed out of court. So when Ladd simply insists that "biblical theology" *must* be allowed to describe "what God has done" in history, he has departed from historiography entirely (see 25). When Ladd claims, "History also reveals God in wrath and judgment" (27), he simply shows he does not recognize the difference between stories, which may or may not be historical, and history, which, in the modern world, does not claim to observe the actions of God.

Ladd insists on the historicity of the resurrection of Jesus and the empty tomb narratives (319). He says that the only reason people do not accept these

---

moral danger—of attributing agency to texts, see Martin, *Sex and the Single Savior,* 1–16; *Pedagogy,* 29–45; and discussion below in the chapter "Scripture."

as historical is because of their prejudice and adherence to a rigid, modern assumption that such things are not possible. But that is not at all the reason to reject the accounts as historical. Many scholars, including some Christian scholars, do not accept these as history because (as I demonstrate below in chapter 4 in my treatment of the historicity of the empty tomb narratives) there are contradictions among *all* the accounts. The stories contradict one another, and none of them even claims to represent eyewitness testimony to the actual resurrection. Not only is Ladd's treatment of the resurrection accounts bad historiography—actually not historiography at all by modern critical standards—it is also bad exegesis because he ignores the differences in the accounts about place, time, people, details, and more. Whereas Ladd often practices bad historiography, this is also bad attention to the details of the text, that is, bad exegesis.

One criterion we may use for deciding whether a scholar's account is one by a "critical scholar of the Bible" is the following: If one can predict the conclusion a scholar will arrive at with regard to authorship, historicity, or doctrinal "correctness" by knowing the author's confessional position, that author is not a critical scholar. If one can point to no specific issue in which an author *denies* the historicity, authenticity, or orthodoxy of a detail from the text, that author is not a critical scholar. A critical scholar of the Bible is one who is willing to offer an interpretation of a text of the Bible that does not necessarily uphold that scholar's own theological opinions.

Before leaving Ladd, however, I need to demonstrate my other claim about his book: that it is not merely bad history but also inadequate theology. This can be demonstrated in Ladd's treatment of the Holy Spirit and his lack of any discussion of the trinity. To his credit, he does not attempt to mount an argument for reading the trinity "in" or "out of" the New Testament. He seems to recognize that there is no doctrine of the trinity "in" the New Testament when read through the rigors and requirements of historical criticism.[38] But that just leaves him in a theological conundrum precisely because the trinity is one of the most central, significant, and indispensable doctrines of Christian orthodoxy.

Ladd does mention the Holy Spirit several times in his study, noting the many places where Paul's language about the "spirit," for example, may be taken as a reference to "the" Holy Spirit. But his most concentrated

---

38. "The dogma itself [of the Holy Spirit understood in trinitarian terms], then, is not in Scripture; it is exegesis of Scripture." Barth, *Church Dogmatics* I/1, p. 467; see, for the same admission about the doctrine of the trinity, 375–76, 381, 415, 467.

treatment of the Holy Spirit comes in one chapter devoted mainly to the spirit in the Gospel of John (286–97). Ladd takes "spirit" in John 4:23 to refer "to the Holy Spirit and not to inner 'spiritual' worship as opposed to outward forms" (292). The Holy Spirit is a person or at least "a separate personality" from Christ and the Father. John uses neuter pronouns for the "Paraclete," or Holy Spirit, when demanded by the grammar of the context (*pneuma* is neuter, so it takes a neuter pronoun: 295). But then John will switch and use male terms for the Spirit ("he"; 14:26; 15:26; 16:13). To Ladd, this demonstrates that the Holy Spirit is a person in the Gospel of John. Throughout this section Ladd is working with an *assumption* of trinitarian doctrine: the three persons of the trinity are all divine and all God but without being the same person; they are distinct but nonetheless One God. But Ladd never says any of this explicitly.

And that leaves Ladd with his insufficient theology. If Jesus is divine, is he divine as fully as God the Father is? If so, how? Is the Holy Spirit divine as Jesus is divine as the Father is divine? May we worship Jesus? May we worship the Holy Spirit? If we do, are we not practicing idolatry and polytheism? Without the doctrine of the trinity or something much like it, how does Ladd's theology avoid polytheism and idolatry, on the one side, or lack of recognition of the deity of Christ and the Spirit, on the other? Ladd, in spite of all his efforts to read the New Testament in line with Christian orthodoxy—even to the extent of practicing faulty historical criticism to get there—leaves his readers with insufficiently orthodox theology. The modernist theology of the New Testament project has ended up with bad history, bad theology, or both.

The Problem Is the Genre

My survey of the work of Barth, Bultmann, and Ladd is not meant to demonstrate that their proposals were especially bad. Indeed, I chose them because I consider them to be some of the best representatives of New Testament theology from the twentieth century. My point is that the genre itself is the problem. As long as Christian scholars insist that they are simply "describing" the theology that is really "in" the text itself, and they arrive at their conclusions using historical criticism, as long as the "meaning" they claim to "find" in the text is supposed to be also what the ancient author "intended" or the ancient audience would have understood, they cannot produce robust, sufficient, orthodox Christian theology.

Orthodoxy took several centuries to be developed. That is totally understandable. Disciples of Jesus apparently began "worshipping" him fairly soon after his death, after some of them had come to believe he had been seen alive after his death. They prayed to him; they took him to be a special mediator between themselves and God. They took Jesus to be the Jewish Messiah, but in a special way: as a messiah who was "divine," at least in some sense. Likewise, as their liturgies and prayers developed, they began speaking of a "spirit" that was more than simply God's spirit or Jesus's spirit but was itself a being with whom they could be in some kind of relationship. And eventually they also began thinking of that Spirit as having some kind of personality. As we will see throughout this book, doctrine and theology follow practice.[39] Making sense of one's beliefs is a felt need only once practices have become the first realities. Once early disciples recognized that they were worshipping Jesus and the Spirit alongside "God" and began realizing they wanted to remain believers in "the one God" and not become polytheists, they *had* to come up with rational ways to explain that to themselves. Thus the development, over a long period of time, of doctrines about the divinity of Jesus and the Spirit, their relation to "God," eventually termed "the Father" rather than simply "the only God alongside Jesus and the Spirit." Moreover, they had to explain to themselves—and to other Christians who disagreed with their understanding—the precise relationship between Jesus and the Father, the Spirit and the Father, the Spirit and Jesus. Christology, as it was to become more fully developed in the fourth century, and the doctrine of the trinity were not developed sufficiently by the authors of the New Testament to meet the needs of later Christians for making sense of their practices and liturgies. So expecting to find orthodox Christian doctrine "in" the texts of the New Testament read in their original historical context is unrealistic and anachronistic. The modern genre of biblical theology was flawed from the beginning, if the goal was to arrive at sufficient, robust, orthodox Christian doctrine and theology by a simple reading of the New Testament texts in their historical contexts.[40]

Thus we may survey many other examples of such attempts, organized and written in a variety of ways. Many of them make the assumption—the

---

39. The idea that doctrine follows practice is sometimes expressed by the Latin phrase *lex orandi lex est credendi*, or, even more briefly expressed (as is easy to do in Latin), *lex orandi, lex credendi*. See Basil, *On the Holy Spirit*, 11. This is from the introduction by Anderson. See also p. 90; §25.59, for an instance where Basil uses liturgy to guide doctrine. See also *Catechism of the Catholic Church*, 2d ed., paragraph 1124. John Zizioulas makes the point that Eastern Orthodox tradition "lives and teaches its theology liturgically": *Being as Communion*, 19.

40. For a few scholars who have come to the same conclusion, see Paddison, *Scripture*, 74–75; Adam, *Making Sense*; Meeks, "Why Study the New Testament?," 167–68.

modernist assumption—that to get the "best" or "purest" form of Christianity we must go to "the source," the "earliest" kind of Christianity. Walter F. Adehey, in his 1894 work, expresses this notion perfectly: "The literary and historical study of Biblical Theology should precede the more metaphysical speculations of Systematic Theology, because no just conception either of Judaism or of Christianity can be obtained before we have come to perceive the thoughts of the inspired writers in their original purity. Here we have the stream at its fountain-head."[41] Perhaps more recent scholars have come to be suspicious of the idea that Christianity is "purest" the closer we can get to "the fountainhead," but the overriding interest in "the original" meaning of biblical texts still rules much work, at least on New Testament theology.

Different attempts at New Testament theology may take different tacks or shapes and vary from conservative to less so. Whereas some scholars arrange their studies by chronology, treating books of the New Testament in order of their probable dates of composition, others organize theirs by theological topics.[42] In all cases, however, New Testament theology is a genre of historical studies that ascertains the primary meaning of the text as foundational in order then to be used or applied by modern theologians or everyday Christians. That is the problem with the genre and why it has been a failure, at least from an orthodox Christian point of view.

What This Book Is and What It Is Not

First, what it is not. Obviously, this book is not a theology *of* the New Testament. As I discuss various theological topics and particular Christian doctrines, I feel free to draw from the New Testament, to offer different kinds of readings, and to be creative in interpretations and applications of the text. I do at times use historical criticism, that is, the various tools and methods developed in modernity to construct the ancient meanings of these texts in their likely historical contexts.[43] But I often offer readings of biblical texts

41. Adeney, *Theology of the New Testament*, 2.

42. There are too many examples to cite, but to select a few: for chronological organizations, see Stevens, *Theology of the New Testament*; Morris, *New Testament Theology*. For topical: Richardson, *Theology of the New Testament*; Guthrie, *New Testament Theology*; see also Guthrie's discussion of these different options: 72. For a "mixed" organization: Bonsirven, *Theology of the New Testament*; Schnelle, *Theology of the New Testament*.

43. This chapter has already provided indications of what I mean by historical criticism, including word studies, comparison of the different documents of the Bible with one another but without interpreting one author simply by recourse to other biblical documents or authors, avoiding anachronism, etc. I have explained the historical critical

to convey theological truths though I know that the "meaning" I am taking from the text would not have been even understandable to the original author or readers. I practice creative anachronism. I read into the text all kinds of views I would not say are simply in the text. This is creative, Christian interpretation that *uses* the text of the Bible as something with which I "think theologically."

I should, though, address the issue of why just "theology with the New Testament" and not with the whole Bible? Scripture for Christians is the entire Bible, Old and New Testaments. Why do I focus in this book on the New Testament? First, I want to be very clear that I agree that Christian scripture is the entire Bible. I do not believe Christians should especially privilege the New Testament over the Old. I am no Marcionite who believes we can ignore, dismiss, or denigrate the Old Testament. Though I will occasionally focus on passages from the Old Testament (and I explain in the chapter titled "Scripture" below why I am content to use that term rather than "Hebrew Bible" or other recent suggestions), I concentrate on the New Testament merely because that is the area of my expertise. My choice to concentrate on the New Testament says nothing theologically but is simply an example of my own limitations as a scholar.

Further on what this book is not: it is not an apology for or defense of Christianity, orthodoxy, or theology. I happen to believe that God needs no defense from me or from anyone else. If readers want to dismiss a particular argument of mine or a particular doctrine or theological idea I am seeking to explain, that is fine with me. I am not offering an apology of anything for anyone. I am merely attempting to explain why and how I continue to find traditional Christian doctrines and confessions "true," why I'm willing to confess the creeds, even though I am a critical scholar who knows much of the Bible is *not* "true" when taken as history or science. This is not an apology but an attempt at explanation and illustration.

Finally, the book is also not evangelism. I am not particularly concerned to convert anyone to Christianity. I don't believe anyone should come to faith out of fear. I do not, could not, trust a God who created and maintained an elaborate structure to torture human beings for eternity. I will say below why there may be some ways I could understand "hell" as a reality, but not at all in the traditional sense of a place where sinners are left to roast and suffer forever at the will of God. Given my faith and theology, that is simply

---

method more fully elsewhere, so I am brief here: see Martin, *Pedagogy*, 3–9; Martin, *New Testament*, 322–29.

an impossibility. So I have no reason to run about attempting to evangelize or convert anyone. I offer my attempts at theology because I find theology meaningful and comforting (though also sometimes disturbing, as all good theology must at times be), and if that helps anyone else, fine. But my goal again is explanation and illustration, not proselytism.

Now for what the book is. In this book I attempt to offer a nonfoundationalist, postmodern, Marxist, orthodox, ecumenical, and provisional theological interpretation of the New Testament. First is that it is theology. I am attempting here not just an interpretation of the theological assumptions or views of the biblical authors. I am instead actually offering my own theology, the theological understandings I have held over many years that help me make sense of what I confess in church.

I do not believe theology is "talk about God," though I recognize that to be a common way theologians have sometimes defined "theology."[44] I believe God is so radically unavailable to us in God's very self that we should refrain from thinking that our theological musings or declarations are actually "about God," as if God is "comprehensible" rather than, as I argue below, ultimately "incomprehensible."

Moreover, if theology must be understood as talk about God, that would mean, it seems to me, that atheists or agnostics could not "do" theology. Or that Jews could not practice Christian theology. But I have known Jews who seemed to me to be good theologians even of *Christian* propositions and beliefs. Theology is second-order reflection on first-order language about God and faith. Theology is not faith, nor does it require faith. It may sometimes be, in that traditional phrase, "faith seeking understanding" (*fides quaerens intellectum*). But for me theology is simply showing how statements of faith and belief can be seen as rational, sensible, and coherent. Theology, in this book, is to be understood not as talk directly "about God" but as "talk about talk about God."[45]

I emphasize, however, that this is not to imply some kind of epistemological hierarchy between "talk about God" and "talk about talk about God," as if one is higher than the other or as if one provides the foundation for the other. It is merely to admit that many Christians may not need, in their own lives, lots of reflective theology. They may worship, believe, pray, and follow traditional liturgy with no felt need for elaborate reflection about the why of it all. My approach is just to admit that Christian theology, when done right,

---

44. See, for example, Volf, "Theology for a Way of Life."

45. Theology, in the words of Frei (and I add that he is talking about Christianity, not just any and all "religion"), is "a second-order discipline dependent on the first-order language" of Christianity: *Theology and Narrative*, 96.

proceeds from Christian practice and belief rather than *preceding* or *prescribing* Christian practice.

"Foundationalism" is the term I have used in several publications to describe a certain modernist understanding about the relation of "fact" to "evidence." In science the idea was that the job of scientists was just to "observe nature," to put aside all bias and prejudice and simply "describe" the "world" they "discover." But as many studies have demonstrated over the past few decades, that has never been the way scientists actually work. Rather they begin with ideas, they invent experiments, and they create facts. Scientific "facts" are made, not "found."[46] (I like the philological "fact" that the English word derives from the Latin *factum*, literally meaning "something made.") Foundationalism is the idea that we, scientists with nature or readers with texts, can find some place that will provide a dependable "basis" of firm, secure, incontrovertible "knowledge" on which we can then build systems of secondary values, beliefs, systems of thought or belief. Nonfoundationalists argue that no such place exists in the universe, either for science or history or textual interpretation. It is interpretation "all the way down."

Foundationalism in textual interpretation is what I've been illustrating in this chapter: the idea that we will be on more secure ground in our interpretations of scripture for ourselves if we first "find" the ancient, historical "meaning" of the text. On that "foundation" we can then build our (admittedly more speculative) modern theologies or ethics. Nonfoundationalists such as myself argue that there is no "meaning" "back there" in history or "in the text" to be uncovered *before* "interpretation" can then take off. It is all interpretation. The difference between "knowledge" and "belief" is simply one of degree of certainty—more or less—but knowledge is never completely and indisputably certain beyond all doubt and interpretation.[47] This book is based on a nonfoundationalist theory of reality, including texts and their meanings.

And that dispute of modernist foundationalism is one of the things I mean by "postmodern." I can illustrate something of what I mean by "postmodern" with a citation of Carl Braaten from his introduction to Martin

---

46. I have discussed foundationalism and antifoundationalism elsewhere, so my discussion here is limited. See Martin, *Sex and the Single Savior*, 1–5. For just a few studies of scientific methodology and philosophy: Van Fraassen, *Laws and Symmetry*; Van Fraassen, *Empirical Stance*; Latour and Woolgar, *Laboratory Life*; Latour, *Pasteurization*; Latour, *We Have Never Been Modern*; Herrnstein Smith, *Belief and Resistance*.

47. As Johannes Hoff points out, in a book on the epistemology of Nicholas of Cusa, our lack of *certain* knowledge relates not only to God but to everything we attempt to "know." Hoff, *Analogical Turn*, 71.

Kähler's *So-Called Historical Jesus and the Historic Biblical Christ.* Braaten commented that Kähler's career pursued more a theological than philosophical direction, but, he adds, Kähler "always retained the philosopher's love for ultimate reality, universal validity, and absolute certainty."[48] I would say that trio provides a good portrait, not of all "philosophy" but of modernism. The modernism of the nineteenth and twentieth centuries searched for ways to discern and describe "ultimate reality" free from bias, prejudice, or even interpretation. For any truth to be ultimately true, moreover, it had to be universally valid. And modern science was the search not for half truths, interpretations, or beliefs but absolute certainty. What makes a position or theory or theology postmodern is that it has given up on those quests. It still has the hangovers from modernism; for example, it uses modern inventions such as science and historiography, but it has lost the confidence that we human beings have any place in the universe we could find so as to arrive at ultimate, universal truths that will provide us with absolute certainty.

Postmodern is not premodern. Postmodern thinkers such as myself have no nostalgia to return to the premodern or medieval or ancient. We recognize that we are ourselves to a great extent products of modernism. We just no longer have confidence in the results of modernism, and we no longer believe even in the questions of modernism. We believe that true statements will be true in some context and not true in other contexts or when interpreted in different systems of meaning-making. Thus throughout this book I make the case that no doctrine or theological proposition is always and universally true. If it is true at all, it is true only "in a sense," perhaps in a historical sense, or a theological sense, or a Christian sense, or a mythological sense. I also argue that any Christian statement, even if true in some sense, will necessarily also be false when interpreted in a different sense. I take it that I think this way because my thinking is postmodern. I have gone "through" modernism but have for the most part left its epistemologies behind.

By using the term "Marxist" to describe my approach, I simply mean I have been convinced by Marx and Marxist scholarship that the most important phenomenon to be critically studied and debated in our time is capitalism. Instead of taking capitalism to be "natural," the "end of history," "human nature," or "just the way things are," Marxists, in my usage, believe our lives are shaped, influenced, and even oppressed by the social, cultural, and economic system of capitalism more than by any other comparable force,

---

48. Braaten, in Kähler, *The So-Called Historical Jesus,* 4.

whether culture, family, psychology, nature, or whatever other thing anyone may suggest. By citing Marxism, I mean that whatever I want to study, I need to keep its material manifestations and activities and realities in the forefront of my mind. I mean that historical materialism—the analysis of material, social, cultural realities—must never be left out of our methodologies.

By calling my approach Marxist, I am not advocating any kind of communist prescription for society or government. What I call postmodern Marxism is the acceptance of the diagnosis of capitalism by Marx, but without entertaining any of the "prescriptions" offered by him or any other theorists about "what we should replace capitalism with." I don't know what should or will replace capitalism. But Marxism has taught me to think of capitalism not as simply natural or necessarily "the way things are and the way we human beings act and will always act." Marxism teaches us to realize constantly that capitalism—its modes of production, its social and political structures, its ideology—is historical. There was a time when it was not, so there will certainly be a time when it will be no longer. Our job now is to think about capitalism, to avoid being sucked into its ideology and self-defense and "naturalness," and to realize that human beings do not *have* to be oppressed by capitalist exploitation and ideology forever. By focusing, even when doing theology, on bodies, class structure and class conflict, gender, economy, and politics, my theology is materialist, or Marxist.

But why am I so concerned about orthodoxy? It is certainly not because I am afraid that if I don't remain faithful to traditional Christian doctrine I will "go to hell" as a "heretic" or "heathen." As I said, that kind of notion of hell is nowhere part of my theology or worldview. I am concerned with orthodoxy simply because that is my starting point. I find myself remaining in churches, saying the creeds, reciting the prayers of the Book of Common Prayer or other prayer books, even though I may interpret those statements, confessions, or doctrines in less than traditional ways. My attempt to remain orthodox is simply because that is where I find myself.[49] Indeed, though many of my readers may assume that orthodoxy is the possession only of Christians who are conservative or reactionary in their theology or politics or both, a main goal of my writing is to take orthodoxy out of the hands of conservative Christians and to show both scholars and laypeople how to read the Bible beyond historical criticism.

---

49. "A theologian must always start with what is already there." Volf, *After Our Likeness*, 5.

But what I mean by "orthodox" is nothing very exact. I simply mean the kind of Christian statements and claims made by classical Christian thinkers, such as the "Rule of Faith" of Irenaeus, along with the great ecumenical creeds, such as the Nicene Creed, the Creed of St. Athanasius (*Quicunque Vult*), and the Apostles Creed, along with the "Definition" of Chalcedon.[50]

It may be noticed that I cite what I take to be the great ecumenical creeds from before the splits among Roman Catholics, Eastern Orthodox, and Protestants. Those great creeds are called ecumenical because, at least as the church has traditionally claimed, they were formed by councils that included Christians from "the whole inhabited world," or, the *oikoumene,* to transliterate the Greek. Though I was raised in a fundamentalist church in small-town Texas, I have for decades attended Episcopal churches, and I am an active member in a high church, Anglo-Catholic Episcopal parish. One aspiration of our parish is to be "catholic" in the sense of representing the commonly held doctrines associated with the three main branches of Christianity: Roman Catholic, Eastern Orthodox, and Protestant, all in the broad senses of those terms. Thus I have avoided including discussion of what I take to be Roman Catholic doctrines special to the Council of Trent or later decisions and proclamations, such as the immaculate conception, transubstantiation, or papal infallibility. I do discuss in the chapter titled "Spirit" below the Filioque Controversy that so unfortunately divides Eastern from Western churches, but I avoid taking a firm stand on one or the other side of that issue.

Though I admit that some of my views are doubtless influenced by my past and present affiliations, my theology has been heavily influenced also by central and famous figures of theology, such as Augustine and Thomas Aquinas. In fact, Thomas has come into my thoughts mainly through four contemporary theologians who all interpret Thomas through their leftist political views and through Wittgensteinian "ordinary language philosophy." I am here referring to the Roman Catholic Irish or British theologians Herbert McCabe, Fergus Kerr, Nicholas Lash, and to my Yale colleague Denys Turner. Thus, though I admit influences from Protestantism and particularly the Anglican tradition, I intend the theology here explained to be recognizable as orthodox, "basic Christianity" also by Roman Catholics and Eastern Orthodox Christians, at least for the most part.

---

50. For the "Rule of Faith," see Irenaeus, *Demonstration of Apostolic Preaching,* 6, and *Against Heresies* 1.10.1.

Finally comes merely my admission that this theology is, as all theology must be, incomplete and provisional. Much better theologians than I have insisted that all Christian theology is provisional.[51] The doing of theology is never ending. We must be constant in reform, revision, experiment, if for no other reason than we must remain open to all new and unexpected movements of the holy spirit.[52] I especially sense my own inadequacies, as someone trained more as a historian and biblical exegete than as a constructive theologian. But I take heart in the knowledge that good theologians before me have insisted that all Christian theology is and must be provisional. This one certainly is.

51. See Frei, *Types of Christian Theology*, 146. "Truth" in science is also "always provisional": Potter, *You Are Here*, 87.

52. I more often speak of the "holy spirit" in this book rather than of the "Holy Spirit" for a few reasons. Mainly, I want to keep front and center that "Holy Spirit" is not a name for the third person of the trinity. And as I explain in the chapter titled "Spirit" below, the holy spirit is much less "personal" in our minds, for most of us, and in Christian tradition than is God the Father or Jesus. Sometimes I also avoid capitalizing "father" and "son." That is to remind us that these are also not names but titles. I think sometimes using "Father" and sometimes "father," and sometimes "Son" and sometimes "son" keeps before us the fact that these are words that work in various ways, sometimes admittedly like names, sometimes like titles, sometimes simply as terms that denote relations. The variation is intentional and, I believe, theologically heuristic.

CHAPTER 1
Knowledge

It is ironic that Paul has suffered a reputation as a dogmatist, often considered the first doctrinaire, authoritarian, know-it-all theologian of Christianity. Admittedly, Paul can come across as authoritarian at times: "Shall I come to you with a rod?" (1 Cor 4:21); "I consider myself not at all inferior to these 'superapostles'" (2 Cor 11:5); "If I come again, I will not hold back" (2 Cor 13:2).

But this is the same author who otherwise demurs about what he claims he knows, what any person can know, about God. Paul quotes Isa 40:13, "Who has known the mind of God?" (Rom 11:34). At least in this context, we are doubtless to assume that Paul's implied answer would be, "No one!" Paul insists that we mere human beings, even apostles, must accept the inscrutability of God's will, even to the point of not understanding whom God chooses to save or not (Rom 11:33). Elsewhere, Paul quotes the same passage from Isaiah but follows it up by saying that believers, because of the spirit, actually do "have the mind of Christ" (1 Cor 2:16). The context, however, indicates that what Paul means is that we have enough of the guidance of the spirit to recognize that what is "foolishness to the world"—in particular, the crucifixion of the son of God—actually constitutes the "wisdom and power of God." But that does not detract from Paul's insistence that our knowledge, especially about God, is limited.

In other contexts Paul first makes some positive statement about knowing God but then remarkably retracts it and seems to correct himself. To the Galatians, Paul first writes, "Now that you have come to know God" but then reverses himself from the active to the passive voice, "or rather *to be known by God . . .*" (Gal 4:9; my emphasis). Paul makes a similar move in 1 Corinthians: "Anyone claiming to know does not yet know; but whoever loves God *is known by him*" (8:2–3; my emphasis). In fact, this is a foreshadowing in the letter of the much more famous passage that perhaps should be studied less for what it says about weddings and romantic love than about the much less romantic notion of Christian *agape* and its relationship to knowledge: I mean chapter 13.

The chapter begins with the relationship between love and speaking in tongues, or glossolalia: "Even if I speak in human or angelic languages, but do not have love, I am merely a loud gong or clanging cymbal" (13:1). But Paul quickly brings in the much more important relationship of love to knowledge: "Even if I have [the gift of] prophecy and I know all mysteries and all knowledge . . . " (13:2). After his justifiably famous and moving description of love—and in our sentimentally obsessed culture we must constantly remind ourselves that Paul is speaking not of romantic love but of ethical concern and action for others—Paul returns to knowledge: "Love never fails. Though there are now prophecies, they will end; though there are tongues, they will cease; though there is knowledge, it will come to an end. For we [now] know in fragments and we prophesy in fragments" (13:8–9). And then the climax: "For we see now as if in an enigmatic mirror, but then we will see face to face. Now I know in fragments, but then I will know just as I have been known. For now, faith, hope, and love remain, these three. And the greatest of them is love" (12–13).

Note how Paul concludes the section with an echo of the theme of "being known" we have seen him use elsewhere—precisely in order to emphasize the *lack* of certain knowledge we human beings can expect to experience in this life. Paul admits that he was known, and here the implication is "by God." And in the eschaton, at the end of time, he will finally know as he has been known. Note also that of all the attributes and virtues Paul ascribes to love—it bears all things, believes all things, hopes all things, endures all things—Paul never says that love "knows all things." Love, like us, also must wait in order to know. We as Christians don't know; we believe.

Paul's reticence about what we currently know is not matched by those New Testament letters later written in his name by his followers and imitators. The author of Colossians, a later follower and imitator of Paul, expects full knowledge, even for his readers. He prays for them, "in order that you might be filled with the knowledge of his will in all wisdom and spiritual understanding, that you may live worthily of the Lord in all sufficiency, in every good work bearing fruit and growing in the knowledge of God" (Col 1:9–10). This writer may have good reasons to claim that he and his readers already possess all knowledge they need for salvation. Apparently, he was writing to refute claims by other Christians that they possessed extra or special "knowledge" or "salvation" needed by the Colossians. So he writes to insist that the Colossians already have sufficient knowledge for salvation.

Later still, the author of Ephesians imitates the author of Colossians (who was attempting to imitate Paul, we remember, though in these points he departed from Paul's own theology) in claiming full possession even of "the heavenlies." His readers, he insists, have already been filled with "all wisdom and knowledge," or φρόνησις (Eph 1:8). God has already "made known" to them "the mystery of his will" (1:9). These sentiments may well be understandable if these authors were defending "Paul's gospel" against teachers who were offering something "more"—a "more" they were claiming was essential for salvation, but the assurances of Colossians and Ephesians show the extent to which later disciples of Paul would go beyond Paul's much more eschatologically reserved epistemology.

In fact, Paul's radically reserved epistemology allows us to rethink a modernist assumption that we no longer need or can afford: the assumption that there is a difference in kind, a foundationalist difference between belief and knowledge. As critical theorists have argued and demonstrated in the past few decades, the actual difference that can be demonstrated between what we normally distinguish as knowledge as opposed to belief is simply a difference in degree of assurance about things we believe are true.

In many of her writings but perhaps best argued in her book *Belief and Resistance: Dynamics of Contemporary Intellectual Controversy,* Barbara Herrnstein Smith shows that a firm distinction between knowledge, that is, facts based on a firm foundation of empiricism or logic, and belief, say, notions about reality that are contingent and changeable, unlike knowledge, cannot be sustained. I would make the point by showing that what we call knowledge consists of beliefs we hold especially firmly and experience as common sense or ultimately provable by something like science or history. I would attempt to make the point by insisting that knowledge and belief are simply different locations along an epistemological spectrum of certainty to uncertainty.

What I call epistemological foundationalism is the modern notion that we *can* know something, anything, in a way that can never be disconfirmed, and we can do so simply by looking at "just the facts" or observing "nature" or any other supposed source for "certain knowledge." On the contrary, there is no knowledge that is arrived at without recourse to persuasion. All knowledge is, in the end, simply belief held very confidently—confidently enough that we feel completely safe acting on that knowledge. As I have shown elsewhere, much modern thinking about the "meaning" of texts shares a similar foundationalism: some people seem to believe that if we just read the text more carefully or with completely open minds or play by the proper rules of interpretation, we will see or hear or discover the "true meaning" of the text.[1] Few instances of this kind of "textual foundationalism" have caused more harm than the modern interpretation of the Bible. If we give up this kind of modernist epistemological foundationalism, we may find better, more fruitful, indeed, more Christian ways to read scripture. If we, along with Paul, give up the idea that we *can* "know," we may end up with a more feasible notion of knowledge itself.

Other parts of scripture may come into play for this topic. The Gospels are often taken, at least by modern, conservative Christians, to be all about "making known" truths—about Jesus, God, ethics, the world, and life. That is far from the case in many instances in the Gospels. Mark is especially frustrating for a reader who wants "just the facts." People often, for instance, expect the parables to be morality lessons or plain indicators of an obvious or perhaps a hidden truth. But in Mark the opposite seems to be the case. Jesus teaches in parables *so that people will not see or understand.* Jesus ends the parable of the sower with the enigmatic, "Let whoever has ears to hear, hear" (Mark 4:9). This has never received, to my mind, a sufficient interpretation. It could mean, "You want to listen? Listen, for all I care. Or not."

The Gospel of Mark continues by noting that only when Jesus was alone with his closest followers, including but not only "the twelve," does he say, "To you the mystery of the kingdom of God has been given; but to those on the outside, it happens only in parables, in order that 'Those seeing will see and not understand, and those hearing will hear and not comprehend, lest they repent and be forgiven'" (Mark 4:11–12, quoting Isa 6:9–10). After an interpretation of the parable of the sower, one that strikes most scholars as perhaps more confusing than the parable, and after a few other parables, the author claims that Jesus spoke to the crowds *only* in parables, "but privately he explained everything to his disciples" (4:34). As many scholars have pointed out, however, the "explanation" referred to does not really make sense of the puzzles, confusions, and misunderstandings experienced by the disciples themselves in Mark—or countless generations of readers

1. Martin, *Sex and the Single Savior,* 1–16.

since. The Gospel of Mark is the Gospel of the "messianic secret," the Gospel in which Jesus's closest disciples continually seem to "get it wrong," and the Gospel whose abrupt ending—an empty tomb but no sight of a risen Jesus; a promise of an appearance to the disciples "in Galilee" but no narration of one; a Gospel with a risen but absent Lord—inspires unending, differing interpretations by scholars and lay readers alike. Knowledge in Mark is more mystery than certainty.

This is clearly what Matthew, who used Mark as a source, made of the story, even emphasizing it beyond Mark. After quoting Mark 4:11, Matthew adds, "For whoever has, it will be given to him and he will overflow; but whoever does not have, even what he has will be snatched from him. That's why I speak in parables to them, because seeing they will not see, and hearing they will not hear and not understand" (Matt 13:12–13). Matthew then expands Mark's quotation of Isaiah, as if to emphasize the fact that it is God who keeps knowledge from the people and gives it only to a select few.

One would think that with the Gospel of John we would find at least some security in knowledge. After all, the Fourth Gospel emphasizes "knowing" and "knowledge" and revelation constantly, like the ringing over and over again of Johannine thematic bells so characteristic of his style.[2] John's favorite word for "know," οἶδα, occurs almost eighty times in the Gospel, far more than in any other Gospel. The word "see," ὁράω, occurs some thirty times, again more than in any other Gospel. Another word for "see," βλέπω, occurs sixteen times in John, which is comparable to the frequency of its use in the other Gospels. βλέπω seems to have a bit less theological or epistemological connotation in John, often referring simply to someone seeing something happening. But some form of βλέπω is the word used for the coming "to see" of the man born blind in John 9, a story that can be read practically as an allegory for how believers come to "see" the truth that Jesus is the Messiah (John 9:7, 11, 15, 18, 19, 21, 25, 39, 41). In spite of all this emphasis in John on knowing and seeing, the Gospel turns out to be no less of a puzzle than any other canonical Gospel. Moreover, Jesus is there more a "riddler" than in any other Gospel.

As is well known, Jesus is presented as "the revealer" par excellence in the Fourth Gospel: "No one has seen God at any time. It is the only begotten God, the one in the embrace of the father, that one has made him known" (John 1:18) The Greek ἐξηγήσατο, translated here as "made known," might be rendered with the barbarism "he has exegeted him," that is, *interpreted*

---

2. For fuller discussion and examples, see Martin, *New Testament*, 159–65.

God, made the meaning of "God" clear: "The one who sent me is true, and what I heard from him, these things I say to the cosmos. . . . Just as the father taught me, these things I speak" (8:26, 28). These are only a few instances of the many in John where Jesus is presented as the revealer, the purveyor of true knowledge. The trope is everywhere.

But the Fourth Gospel itself works against these claims of lucidity. Even in the chapter just quoted, chapter 8, we find a pattern that is repeated throughout the Gospel: a dialogue is begun with people believing in Jesus, accepting his claims, only to end with their rejection of Jesus and hostility toward him—and the apparent hostility is usually provoked first by Jesus. The encounters begin well only to end in confusion and confrontation. We are told, for instance, at 8:31, that many of those listening to Jesus at that point believed in him. As if to emphasize the point, the next verse reminds us that what Jesus is about to say, he is saying "to those Judeans *who had believed in him*" (8:32; my emphasis).

But the dialogue goes downhill from there. When they ask why Jesus says they will be made free, since they are not after all slaves, Jesus ends up accusing them of plotting to murder him (8:37). When they claim that Abraham is their father, Jesus again insists that they are trying to kill him (8:40). When they react by insisting that they are not bastards but children of God, Jesus retorts that they are children of the devil (8:41–44). By this time Jesus has successfully turned those who began by believing in him into his enemies, so they end up convinced he is possessed by a demon (48). At the end of the (non-) dialogue Jesus makes the astounding claim (astounding at the time, at least) that he himself is the "I am" revealed originally to Moses and as a person who existed *before* Abraham. This finally provokes his hearers to fulfill Jesus's (self-fulfilling) prophecy: they do take up stones to kill him, though for the time being he escapes (8:58–59).

The pattern recurs many times in the Gospel of John. Nicodemus begins as an inquirer and learner, but by statement after inscrutable statement Jesus seems to rebuff him (3:1–10). In chapter 6 Jesus again engineers events so that he seems to go from success to failure. In reaction to those who had followed him, even sought him out, Jesus first accuses them of wanting only the bread he had provided. When they ask instead for the "true bread from heaven" (6:34), Jesus first claims that he is that bread and ends up with what certainly would have been heard as demands for cannibalism (6:52–59). And when the people understandably balk, Jesus finally insists that only those to whom "it is granted by the father" will believe in him anyway (6:65). So why bother?

Even apart from this repeated plot structure, in which claims to clarity end up repeatedly in fact with opacity, the Fourth Gospel leaves us with riddles, puzzles, and questions. How should we translate the terms in 3:3, when Jesus tells Nicodemus that one must "be born ἄνωθεν"? As "born again" or "born from above"? The Greek means both. In spite of an entire "born again" industry among conservative American Christians, mostly based on this very verse, we have no idea whether the author meant one or the other—or both. Nicodemus initially takes it as meaning "again." But with Jesus's subsequent comments about "spirit" and "wind," we might just as easily take it as meaning "from above." After all, the themes of "above/below" and Jesus being "from above" are much more dominant in John than any theme of "rebirth."[3] But that still can't completely settle the exegetical question. We just don't "know" what the Greek "meant" to the author.

What is signified in John 19:34 by the statement that "blood and water" gushed out of Jesus's side when he was pierced? Is this a reference to baptism and the eucharist? Is it supposed to be an indication that Jesus is really by this time dead? The text doesn't give us adequate hints to know. When Jesus refers to eating his body and drinking his blood in John 6:51–58, is this a reference to the eucharist—the establishing of which John omits from his Gospel at the Last Supper, apparently supplying in its place the foot washing (John 13:1–12)? Scholars disagree, but there is no way to be certain simply on the basis of the text as we have it.

When the disciples see the resurrected Jesus, why don't they recognize him? Is his body in a form so different that they just don't recognize him until he does something "special," such as saying their name or showing them where to fish or making them breakfast (20:14, 17; 21:4, 12)? What does Jesus mean in his prediction to Simon Peter, "When you grow old you will stretch out your hands, and someone else will put a belt around you and take you where you do not want to go"? (21:18). The author then explains, "He said this to indicate by what sort of death he would glorify God" (21:18). But what sort of death is that? By legend Peter was crucified upside down. But this text cannot very well be made to mean specifically that. What does it mean?

And finally, who after all is "the beloved disciple"? By tradition, again, it is John, son of Zebedee, who is depicted throughout history in art as a young man, beautiful and often girlish. But there is no reason from the Fourth Gospel itself to identify the beloved disciple with John. Yet there are

3. See, for example, John 3:13, 31; 6:38, 41–42, 50–51, 58; 20:17. Said of the spirit: 1:32–33.

no other good candidates indicated by the text either.[4] It must remain, in spite of popular opinion and the confident assurances of misguided scholars, a riddle, a puzzle, a mystery. But that fact becomes another, this time huge, indication that knowledge is not, after all, such a certain thing in the Fourth Gospel. Knowledge is not a ready commodity in John.

But what *can* we say about knowledge in John? First, I have hinted that the Gospel teaches that only those people God chooses may actually receive true knowledge (see also 6:44). And in fact John 12:40 echoes Matthew and Mark in teaching that God has "blinded the eyes" and "hardened the hearts" of many human beings so that they are unable to turn to God for healing. It is a common early Christian explanation of why so many people don't accept the gospel: God has not elected them, and therefore they cannot truly hear the good news.

John also suggests, moreover, than when people come to belief it is usually as a result of being led to knowledge by other people. Faith is social. The message of much of the Gospel is "Come and see!" (1:39). "Signs" are given, even enumerated, in the Gospel, and these are for the most part presented as perfectly acceptable means of coming to faith, though there are, again, some comments that seem to denigrate "faith" that has depended on "signs" (for example, 4:48; 20:29)—another puzzle. The author, in the end, admits he wrote his Gospel as something like a sign meant to produce belief (20:30–31). The idea that faith is socially produced is indicated in other New Testament passages: "How are they to call on one in whom they have not believed? And how are they to believe in one of whom they have not heard? And how will they hear without someone proclaiming?" (Rom 10:14). The entire book of Acts is a story of people coming to faith mostly as social events. Even Paul, who receives his own special revelation, must have Ananias explain its significance and consequences (Acts 9:5, 15–18), and Peter's private revelation must be interpreted through the events at Cornelius's house and the meeting of the church in Jerusalem (10:44–48; 11:18). We all must depend to some extent on others for knowledge of God and Christ. Knowledge is social—as are we.

Finally, the Fourth Gospel suggests even that some kind of belief, faith of some sort, must precede knowledge. If we take "darkness" in the Gospel to

4. One might guess that the puzzle about who the "beloved disciple" is can be settled by citing John 11:3, where Martha and Mary mention to Jesus their brother, by saying "he whom you love." I think this to be a possible but unlikely interpretation. I provide a few reasons in chapter 5 below.

symbolize lack of knowledge and "light" to symbolize its possession, Jesus's statement in 12:46 is suggestive: "I, as light, have come into the cosmos in order that everyone who believes in me will no longer remain in darkness." We all make a move toward knowledge only when we begin with a willingness and hopefulness to learn. Some sort of faith is necessary before knowledge is possible.

Traditional Ways of Debating Knowing

Christians have often debated how they should conceive of how they know. Traditional terms, topics, and concepts tend to recur and in fact tend to be opposed sometimes in misleading dualisms or dichotomies. Is there some kind of knowledge of God that exists in human minds by nature? Is "natural theology" possible or commendable? Or are all human beings completely dependent on "revelation," even the "special revelation" of the Word in Jesus Christ, for having any proper knowledge about things divine at all?

The New Testament has most often been hauled into this court on the side of revelation, which is not surprising since so much of the New Testament suggests that the gospel is itself a revelation, sometimes the only revelation, of the truth about God. But there are resources in the Bible and even a few in the New Testament for thinking that at least some kind of knowledge of God has always been available to human beings. Most biblical indications of "innate" knowledge of God come from Old Testament documents. In his book on theological anthropology, for example, David Kelsey focuses his exegetical attention mostly on the Old Testament "Wisdom" literature, especially Proverbs, Ecclesiastes, and Job, which, he claims, works with a more pragmatic notion of knowledge and wisdom: wisdom of the world, human nature, and even God derived more from the everyday than from some special revelation. He calls it "epistemologically anthropocentric." Knowledge in Wisdom literature is "human-centered in its way of knowing the quotidian."[5] As Kelsey notes, much of Wisdom literature talks little about revelation, except what we can learn with our brains and our eyes: "Go look at the ant! Observe its ways and be wise" (Prov 6:6).

Though mine is a book on using the New Testament for theology, we cannot neglect the Old Testament completely. In the interests of orthodoxy we reject the Marcionite objection to the scriptures of Israel, even if we may

---

5. Kelsey, *Eccentric Existence,* 200 (the book is in two volumes, but pages are numbered throughout sequentially, so I cite merely the page number).

allow ourselves to interpret them through Christian lenses (as I will argue more fully in the next chapter). The dominant emphasis on revelation over "natural theology" in the New Testament documents is understandable given the fact that those New Testament texts were so often written from a distinctly minority position, even from a sectarian social position and ideology. They therefore tend to stress the "special" knowledge available only from their own sources. We might do well to balance that emphasis by returning regularly to these Old Testament sources that allow for an admission of universal and innate knowledge of (at least the existence of) the divine.

In fact, in the ancient world it was important to many Jews that gentiles were "without excuse" in their idolatry because all humanity had once upon a time been monotheistic and worshipped the true God, that is, the God of Israel. The idea becomes popular especially in certain second temple Jewish circles reflected in noncanonical writings, such as *1 Enoch* and *Jubilees*. They assume that humanity originally all worshipped the God of Israel, but that human beings had been deceived, perhaps by the "Watchers," those superhuman, angelic beings who mated with human women and caused the birth of giants or monsters. This reading of the story of the "sons of god" mating with the "daughters of men" from Genesis 6 was taken to mean that polytheism and idolatry (and warfare, cosmetics, magic, and many other evils) entered human and cosmic history at precisely that time in the deep past. Originally, "all the nations" had known the true God. So they are "without excuse" in their rejection of God and in the creation, by their own hands, of "gods."[6]

This is precisely the assumption lying behind Paul's condemnations of idolatry in Rom 1, and so, not accidentally, this is where Paul comes closest in his writings to something that might be called an "innate knowledge of God," at least theoretically and originally available to all human beings. In Rom 1:18–32 Paul is not talking about all humanity, including the Jews. Rather, he is talking about the gentiles: "For what is knowable about God is obvious to them. For God made it obvious. For God's invisible attributes, his eternal power and divinity, have been discernible and knowable since the creation of the cosmos by means of those things he has made, in order that they may be without excuse. For although they knew God, they did not give him the proper glory or thanks. Rather, they gave way to worthless speculation in their thoughts, and their senseless minds became dark. Claiming to be wise, they became fools, and they exchanged the glory of the invisible

---

6. See my discussion and references cited in Martin, *Sex and the Single Savior*, 52–54.

God for likenesses of images of a mortal human being and birds and beasts and reptiles" (1:19–23). This is as strong a statement as one can find in the New Testament of the universal knowability of at least the existence of God along with some of God's attributes. Not all theologians have been willing to accept it as really teaching some kind of "natural theology." But I believe it is certainly patient of just such a reading.

Indeed, another New Testament passage that approaches this sentiment is the speech put in the mouth of Paul in Athens by the author of Acts. Speaking to Greek philosophers, who had their own ideas about innate knowledge of divine things, Paul insists that all human beings descended from one original ancestor, with God intentionally fixing the "times" and "boundaries" of human existence to encourage all people to search for God, to grope for him, and perhaps even to "find" him, "though in fact he is not far from each of us" (Acts 17:27). This is not the point in his speech where Paul "loses" his audience. That happens when he mentions Jesus and the resurrection. At this point most of the Greek philosophers would have agreed with much of what Paul was saying, with the exception of his rather rude, presumptuous rejection of all "other" gods. But they would have had no problem admitting there was some kind of natural knowledge of the divine in all of humanity.[7]

In spite of the long debate and sometimes fierce arguments against any kind of "natural theology," there are ways we may make use of the notion.[8] We may, without denying a doctrine of special revelation, even as necessary for Christian faith, think about how "natural" some knowledge of God is. Even agnostic and atheistic philosophers and scientists have been offering theories of why we human beings may be "naturally" inclined to "religion."

---

7. If Romans 7:14–21 is taken to be a reference to the human being before coming to faith and Christ, the "I" who claims to "know" what is good even when unable to "do" it could be taken as an admission by Paul that there is some knowledge of "good," and therefore in some way of "god," even in the unregenerated human being in a sinful and "natural" state. But there is much debate nowadays about what kind of speaker is being constructed here by Paul. It seems not to be strictly autobiographical and may be an instance of "speech-in-character" (προσωποποιία or ἠθοποιία), in which Paul is taking on a "character" of a generic human being outside the grace of faith. For Romans 7 as an instance of Paul using "speech-in-character," see Stowers, *Rereading*, 266–72; but see also "speech-in-character" in Stower's "Subject Index." For discussion of the different possibilities, see Sanday and Headlam, *Epistle to the Romans*, 184–86; Jewett, *Romans*, 455–66.

8. One of the most famous being the attacks by Karl Barth against Emil Brunner, in what came to be called the Barth–Brunner debate of 1934. For the two main pamphlets conveniently included in one volume in English, see Brunner, *Natural Theology*.

From the point of view of experts in religious studies, what many of these scientists are taking as "religion" is perhaps simplistic. They tend to assume, showing an enduring modernist Protestant assumption that colors popular views of what counts as "religion" even among those who are not religious, that "religion" is mainly some kind of cognitive belief in a supreme being or many supreme beings.[9] Cognitive scientists working in biology and psychology have argued that the brains of human beings seem to be hardwired for religious beliefs.[10] Some evolutionary biologists believe they have "solved the problem" of "religion," that is, why human beings everywhere seem to have religion of some sort, by suggesting that coming up with meaningful systems related to higher beings or making sense of reality in "religious" ways, like the "supernatural" or some such notion, made evolutionary sense for the development and survival of the human species.[11] If scientists can see a rationality in proposing some kind of "innate" religious impulse in human beings, why can't theologians make some kind of sense of the idea? One could see that the older theological notion of an inherent, innate "knowledge of God" is a theological version of a scientific proposal that human beings are, by nature, a religion-making or a god-making species.

After all, even apart from Christianity or any other "revealed religion," it does seem that most human societies throughout history and the world (not to say all) have "made sense" of their world by imagining that they themselves were not the most intelligent or powerful beings occupying the universe. People looked at the universe around them and assumed or came to believe that there were beings superior to human beings in power and intelligence, if not in morality, somewhere in the universe, sometimes visible, sometimes not. Since we human beings tend to relate all our universe to ourselves, an admittedly self-centered trait, it surely can't come as a surprise that we imagine that there may exist other beings who are of higher intelligence and who are otherwise superior to us. Why should humans have believed that there existed in the universe no being superior to us in

9. For one of the best arguments that it is anachronism to retroject the modern category of "religion" back into the ancient Mediterranean, see Nongbri, *Before Religion*.

10. See a popular account of these ideas presented by Paul Bloom, "Is God an Accident?" In my opinion, one problem with Bloom's account, a problem that besets many scientists who write about "religion" without having studied different things that might count as "religion" in a theoretically or philosophically informed way, is his very assumption about what "religion" and "the supernatural" are supposed to be. See the critique of these assumptions in Nongbri, *Before Religion*.

11. For example, Wilson, *Darwin's Cathedral*. See also evolution.binghampton.edu/religion/ (accessed September 6, 2014).

intellectual power and sophistication? A belief in God or something like gods must surely be one of the most natural things about us as a human species. Some kind of theological version of "natural theology" is the "making sense" of that observation via the doctrines of Christianity.

There is much more about knowledge coming by revelation in the New Testament, so much so that explicit demonstration by examples is doubtless unnecessary: they are in just about every book. What may merit a bit more attention is the great variety of ways in which knowledge is revealed to people in the Bible. It comes most centrally through the revelation of the divine in the person of Jesus Christ himself (prime examples may be John 1:14–18; Mark 9:2–8 and par.; 1 Cor 1:3–7; but there are many others). But knowledge from God comes also through angels (Luke 1:26–38), through dreams (Matt 1:20–23), through visions seen while in the body (Acts 10:9–16), through visions seen while out of the body (2 Cor 12:1–4), through live prophecies (Acts 21:10–11), through glossolalia once it is "interpreted" (1 Cor 14:27), through the *pneuma,* or spirit or breathing, of God (1 Cor 2:10–16), and through the written text itself, both that of the Jewish scriptures and the evolving New Testament texts (2 Pet 1:20–21; 3:14–16), to provide only one incomplete list.

I will return to the topic of revelation especially in the chapters on scripture and the holy spirit below. For now I wish to comment further on the traditional pairing of knowledge of God from nature, or innate in human beings, and from revelation. For much of Christianity it was believed that Christians could accept both as sources of knowledge of God. In certain forms of Protestantism "natural theology" was treated with suspicion or rejected entirely. But the pair has done something of a dance throughout theological history.

And it is not difficult to see how that pair, innate knowledge of God combined with revealed knowledge of God, can be correlated with other traditionally paired oppositions. Much philosophy has concerned itself with the opposition of "rationalism," or deductive reasoning, with "empiricism," Descartes being a classic example of the former and John Locke, George Berkeley, and David Hume of the latter.[12] And here again we may look to the New Testament to consider the role of empiricism in the doing of Christian theology.

12. I am here collapsing much larger debates into this simple opposition. I do not intend to enter debates about intuition, deduction, induction, or many other topics. But the simplicity is merited by the limited work I am here asking this opposition to do theologically.

The New Testament is full of self-aware proclamation of truths: "If I had not come and spoken to them, they would not have sin; but now they have no excuse for their sin" (John 15:22). For the Gospel of John, knowledge of God, Jesus, and sin is not inherent in people naturally. They get knowledge of sin from the teachings of Jesus. And after Jesus leaves his disciples and returns to the Father, the Paraclete is the "spirit of truth" who provides knowledge in the absence of Jesus (15:26; 16:7, 13). Paul's proclamations include his speech and letters but also his body. He uses his imprisoned body as proclamation of truths: "What does it matter? Just this, that whether through false motives or true, Christ is proclaimed, and in this I rejoice" (Phil 1:18). Paul even uses the empirical fact that the gospel is being proclaimed to demonstrate the truth of his gospel.

But we see instances of the importance of empiricism in theologizing also in the practices of the church itself as portrayed in the New Testament. The church in Jerusalem is caused to "change its mind" about whether gentiles can be fully members of the church without being circumcised or keeping kosher. The initial impetus had been a revelation given to Peter. But the other members of the church seem to become fully convinced only by the *fact* that, even before their baptism in water, the gentiles had received the outpouring of the Spirit, demonstrated by their speaking in tongues as the first Christians had done on Pentecost. As Peter reasons, "If then God gave them the same gift he gave to us when we believed in the Lord Jesus Christ, who was I to hold God back?" The people's response is just as important: "Upon hearing this, they were silenced and gave glory to God, 'Then also to the gentiles has God given the repentance that leads to life'" (Acts 11:17–18). Recently, scholars have urged that our own contemporary churches should take a lesson from the story: since it seems obvious that gay and lesbian Christians have been given the holy spirit by God and manifest its inspiration by their lives in the church, the churches should also accept them fully as they are, without requiring them to reject their homosexuality.[13] Though others have rejected the analogy, it seems to me a perfectly good example of scriptural reasoning. In any case, this is certainly an example of the church in the Bible doing theology by empirical observation.

Paul tries the same, though we can't know in this case if he succeeded. Paul asks the Galatians, "Did you receive the spirit through works of the law or through the hearing of faith?" (Gal 3:2). The empirical fact that these

13. See, for example, Siker, "Homosexual Christians"; Fowl, *Engaging Scripture,* 97–127; Martin, *Sex and the Single Savior,* 159–60.

gentiles received the spirit at their baptism (it is, at any rate, an empirical fact for Paul and presumably for them) is used by Paul in an argument to make a theological point. Another point to be learned from the example of Acts 11 as well as Paul's arguments in Galatians is that knowing, in a Christian epistemological context, is a communal affair. We do not learn the truth simply as individuals but in communion with the saints—all the saints, that is, all other members of the body of Christ now and forever, even those now dead. Paul appeals to the church to recognize correct knowledge about the law and faith and justification. Peter and James appeal to the gathered church for true knowledge about inclusion of previous "outsiders" within its bounds. For Christians, knowledge is communal.

Yet empiricism is not a completely dependable foundation for knowledge. I argue in this book that there are no completely indisputable epistemological foundations available to human beings, at least not in this world. But our experiences can be used—I argue *must* be used—along with the experiences of others for theological reasoning. What we see of the world around us is to be used, in fact will be used whether we realize it or not, when we think theologically.

The fact that our seeing may not be reliable is also addressed in the New Testament: "The lamp of the body is the eye. If therefore your eye is ἁπλοῦς [a word that can mean simple, single, sound, healthy, generous, or different combinations of those], your whole body is illuminated; but if your eye is πονηρός [painful, bad, evil, ill], your whole body will be dark. If therefore the light in you is darkness, how great is that darkness!" (Matt 6:22–23; par. Luke 11:33–34). These verses are about the importance of perception; we may say even attitude. If my faculty of observation, whether of the world, of other things, of other people, of one's own situation, is bad or unhealthy, I will myself be in a bad, unhealthy state. Having good perception is necessary for having good internal health. This is not, therefore, just a statement of fact, though it is that; it is given as a moral lesson: we ourselves are morally responsible for how we perceive things. Jesus is telling us to train our eyes to see well, not badly, not in an evil way.

But this also means we are not destined to only one way of seeing. We can learn to see properly. We can train our eyes to see in a godly and loving manner. And in fact, we have to. Seeing properly—godly perception, correct seeing—is a learned and practiced skill. Through much of my life one of my favorite sayings has been, "Everyone is responsible for his or her own happiness." That would be cruel to say to someone who is truly grieving, clinically depressed, in terrible pain, or in a truly dire situation. But it is something most of us would do well to tell ourselves regularly. Seeing the world around us in a positive, accurate way is a moral, personal, and social responsibility (naïve optimism that denies the facts is no virtue either). Thus, though empiricism cannot be an absolutely reliable means to correct knowledge, we must learn to use it and use it well, even when doing theology.

Thus I am heartened when Pavel Florensky calls theology "an *empirical* science."[14] In the context, he is making the point that "formulas" attempting to depict certain activities of the holy spirit are unsatisfying because people tend to want to derive those formulas from *exceptional* personal experiences of the spirit. But it is not possible to derive such formulas that way, "for the formulas grow in the soil of a common, everyday Church life, in a field of common, constant phenomena, and not in connection with singular points of spiritual life." He is making the point that, special "revelations" aside, theology should be derived from common Christian experience. That makes theology "an empirical science."[15]

In the end, we should embrace notions of both empiricism and innate knowledge. We need not believe that the human mind is a "blank slate."[16] Neither need we deny the cultural construction of all specific content of "knowledge." We are both natural and cultural animals. The problem with much Christian debate, in my view, has been an uncritical assumption of a dichotomy between the two and the fact that they have so often been overlaid with other dichotomies: innate knowledge versus revelation; rationalism versus empiricism; nature versus nurture. Even the opposition between "Christ" and "Culture" has done much theologically misleading damage. For example, some Christians insist that "nature" and "Christ" go together: homosexuality is "against nature." Only a mistaken "culture" could say otherwise. Other Christians claim that "nature" is opposed to "Christ,"

14. I quote from the excerpt anthologized in Rogers, Jr., *Holy Spirit*, 217–36, at 224; for the full text: "The Comforter," in Florensky, *The Pillar and Ground of the Truth*.

15. See also the essay by Stephen Fowl excerpted in Rogers, Jr., *Holy Spirit*, at 304. Though she does not use the term "empirical" to describe her method, that is precisely what Mary McClintock Fulkerson did when she based her study of theology on her observation of the ways a specific church went about both interpreting scripture and doing theology publicly over several years: *Places of Redemption*, see esp. chapter 6. Something like what I mean by "theology done empirically" seems to be similar to recent developments in German language scholarship using the concept of *gelebte Religion* ("lived religion"). See, for example, the various essays collected in Grözinger and Pfleiderer, eds., "*Gelebte Religion*."

16. Famously criticized by Steven Pinker, *Blank Slate*.

and only "revealed" knowledge of God is "true." Does this kind of confused thinking then make "revelation" something "cultural"?

The problem with these pairings is that they can lead to false conceptions or disjunctions or dichotomy. As noted above, many sciences are debunking older notions that people's minds are completely clean slates whose every way of thinking is formed by culture. Indeed, the idea that our selves are completely constructed *by culture* was a *progressive* reaction to older beliefs that gender and sexuality are, at least in all "normal" persons, "naturally" constituted and *not* a matter of choice, cultural relativism, or historical construction. In that political moment, it was a good strategy to demonstrate how gender, for example, is to a great extent culturally variable and constructed. One is not "naturally" a man but must learn to be a man by the terms of a particular culture.[17]

Several years ago many gay people were alarmed when some scientists, or popular writers trying to use science, wondered if they could find "the gay gene." Other gay advocates, though, were eager to do so. Some people believed that if science could find "the gay gene" they could then demonstrate scientifically that being gay is, for some people, completely "natural." Others worried, though, that finding a "gay gene" might just cause heterosexist persons or institutions to urge genetic engineering to "ungay" people or fetuses. The problem here (besides the fact that some people and institutions, it seems, will always try to use science for evil and unjust ends) lies in the dichotomy itself. It really does not matter, from an ethical point of view, whether people are gay "by nature" or "by culture." The fact is, many people simply *are* gay, cannot imagine themselves otherwise, and are quite happy about it.

The facts we must keep in mind here are that, for one thing, any piece of "knowledge" or technology can be turned to either positive or negative uses. Knowledge about "nature" does not prescribe the ethical ends to which that knowledge will be put. That issue requires ethics and politics. Second, all such dichotomous thinking is probably wrong. Even if we gay people experience ourselves as "always homosexually oriented in a natural, hardwired way," we must also recognize that we can conceive of and act out our sexuality only in learned ways. We may have been "born gay" in some way, but any way in which we "are gay," even in ways we "experience" our sexuality,

17. Perhaps the most famous study is the philosophical one by Judith Butler, *Gender Trouble;* see also Butler, *Bodies That Matter.* Another study of the cultural construction of gender and sexuality, published the same year as Butler's *Gender Trouble,* is Eve Kosofsky Sedgwick, *Epistemology.* Both scholars were influenced by the multivolume *History of Sexuality* by Michel Foucault.

is cultural and learned. This is also true, and also for many people, whether or not they are Christian or even religious at all. For the person who is such, it likely doesn't matter, from a purely intellectual point of view, how it came about. Dichotomies between nature and nurture or nature and culture need to be deconstructed and avoided.[18] Likewise, we may properly give up all older arguments about whether knowledge is innate or learned, whether theological truths are internally and naturally "known" or can be had only via revelation. The proper Christian answer must be "both."

Traditional Theological Proposals for "Knowing"

Different Christian communities and institutions have sometimes attempted to bring order and clarity to theological-epistemological debates by offering schemata or labels for the diverse "sources" or "resources" for Christian knowing. For Roman Catholics, traditionally, sources such as scripture and tradition as well as reason and empiricism are cited, but as a final recourse most Roman Catholics point to the church's *magisterium,* the teaching office of the Vatican, including the pope. How one is to interpret scripture, for instance, must bow to the instructions of the church's actual institutional hierarchy. Anglican churches have traditionally pointed to reason, tradition, and scripture, sometimes called the three-legged stool. Methodists broadened that model to speak of a quadrilateral, which adds to the Anglican three experience, usually thought of as the specifically religious or spiritual experience each individual and the collected church can attest to and recall.

Such models need do no harm and may even be helpful *if* they are taken as heuristic examples or tropes. But they must not be taken in a foundationalist manner that denies or hides the necessity and vagaries of actual human interpretation. None of these "sources" serves simply as an innocent source of information outside human interpretation. Thus an avoidance of epistemological foundationalism can permit the use of these tropes for thinking about knowledge without getting caught in the uncritical beliefs that these sources or authorities can somehow save us from the uncertainties of human interpretation.

And each religious community must recognize dangers with its citation of particularly delineated "sources" for divine knowledge. Since for the Roman Catholic Church, as a particular human physical institution, the magisterium is composed of and controlled by particular human beings—in fact *old men of limited worldly experience,* not to mention limited experience

18. See Tanner, *Theories of Culture.*

of women and sex (let's hope)—simpleminded obeisance to those particular men, even though they may claim to disappear into the spiritual institution, gives authority to specific, historical, embodied *men* in a way that may justifiably be seen as idolatrous. The structure, in actual practice thus far, is certainly antidemocratic and perpetuates the past injustices of hierarchy, monarchy, and patriarchy.

The problem with "tradition" is that the word refers not to something one can point to in nature or observe as it stands still. Rather, tradition is the flow, the changing current, we, as Christians, *live in*. It cannot be separated from scripture because scripture is the early Christian tradition (or at least a few strands of it that survive in texts). And we never interpret scripture except within tradition. Tradition is simply the church in its memory and presence. Scripture also should not be separated from the rest of our lives but should provide the textual context in which we live our lives. All our theologizing and living should be informed by scripture, as I will argue further in the next chapter, which means that it doesn't actually function as one source among several others. In a similar way, "experience" does not refer to one source separated out from the rest of our lives. Everything we do, say, think, and believe is experience.

These different sources overlap and flow into one another. Moreover, there is no reason not to add other sources, named and differentiated. We could, for example, separate modern science from "reason" and consider it a special source. "Reason" then would refer to general human rationality, but we could recognize modern science as a special source alongside simple, general rationality. We could separate, as some theologians have, a privileged "hermeneutic of the oppressed" as a special source of authority. The systems proposing these different sources of Christian knowledge at various times by theologians may have been useful in previous debates among groups with dissimilar priorities, for example, Protestants versus Catholics, Anglicans versus Roman Catholics, Methodists versus Anglicans, but they have also caused problems by mistakenly convincing at least many Christians that more security than is actually possible in interpretation may be had and that theology could be rightly constructed by appeal to a particular "method."

The Necessity of Interpretation

Any statement may be true or false. In fact, all statements may be both true and false. This is a central supposition and technique of my analysis here. And for this book, as I will demonstrate much more in the chapter about the nature of God, it is an important aspect of religious statements. I argue that people should learn how to recognize that any statement about God must be seen to be potentially false in any context but may also be true in some contexts. My proposal about statements always being potentially both true and false, however, is not just a proposal about God or religious propositions: it is an observation about language in general.

We must recognize at the start that language is not simply a matter of propositional statements about fact or simply proposals that are either true or false according to whether they correspond to reality or not. We human beings do many things with language, as I will repeat on occasion. Saying "I love you" may indeed be a proposition about a fact, but it does much more than that. As philosophers of language have taught us, language is about performance as much as about propositions having to do with reality.[19] If we didn't all already assume that, we would be in a state of constant confusion and muddle. Imagine a person coming out of a theater after watching a play in which one of the actors had said, "It is raining," and the person complains to another that the man in the theater had been lying because it wasn't raining at all. If the audience member took the statement within the play actually to be a statement about current reality outside the theater, she or he was just not understanding how the language was working.

Even if we limit our analysis, however, to linguistic constructions that claim to be propositional statements about reality, we must remind ourselves how they can be true *and* false. This is so because statements don't tell us how to interpret them or in what context they are taken to be working. The naked statement doesn't bring its context or correct interpretation with it—when it is, that is, a naked statement. So the simple statement, "This man is my father" cannot even be evaluated as true or false or even as meaningful until we assume a context. It may be true if I am pointing to my biological father or to my adoptive father, but those are not the exact same "meanings" or "propositions." It may be true if I am pointing to my spiritual director or to my academic *Doktorvater*. The statement must be interpreted by someone, who must either be supplied a context or assume one. If even the *meaning* of the statement may change given different circumstances, so also will its *truth*.

Some people think that arithmetic or mathematical propositions must always be true universally if they are true at all. In all cultures and times $2 + 2 = 4$, they will say. But that should be accepted only if we are taking

19. The classic study along these lines is J. L. Austin, *How to Do Things with Words*.

those mathematical statements *as* "mathematical" statements. If someone tells me 2 + 2 = 4 always and in every imaginable circumstance, I may respond, "I don't believe you. If I put two male cats and two female cats in a room with plenty of food and water and then open up the room again in six months, I'm unlikely to find four cats. I may find fewer, though I'll probably find more. So two plus two doesn't always make four." Someone may well note that I'm being intentionally contrary or even loopy, but that still doesn't prove that the statement "two plus two equals four," *as a bare statement,* is always true. Even that statement has to be interpreted within a context.

Mathematicians know that even if taken as a mathematical statement, 2 + 2 = 4 may still not be true. It is true if we are assuming a system of ten integers, in which the first number is 1 and the numbers "turn around" at 10. It would also be true if we were assuming only four numbers, in which case 2 + 2 would in fact equal 4, but 2 + 3 would equal not 5 but 1 since after the 4 the next available number would return to 1. This is often explained by pointing to a clock with twelve numbers. Nine o'clock plus five hours will not equal 14 o'clock because there are no numbers after 12 on a 12-hour clock. In this system, 9 + 5 = 2, two o'clock, that is. Even statements that many people believe are necessarily and universally "true" are true only if they are interpreted correctly within the appropriate system and in the appropriate way.

The truth of statements becomes even more complicated, it seems, in the realm of religion. Christians who accuse only "liberals" of "interpreting away" the "truths" of Christian scripture are by that very accusation being hypocritical because there are no Christians who believe literally in everything one can find in the Bible. Even to get into the discussion we must assume how we establish the meaning of statements in scripture. For the moment let us assume that when conservative Christians talk about accepting the truth of a biblical account or statement, they mean accepting what the original author is likely to have intended or the meaning of the text as understood by an imagined original audience. If that is what they take to be "the meaning of the text," which is, in fact, what most conservative Christians mean, they themselves certainly do not adhere to their own standards.

There are many things ancient texts relate and ancient Jews and Christians believed that almost no modern people believe any longer, no matter how theologically conservative they are. Almost no one believes God tells world leaders to attack and annihilate entire populations, including children and infants (1 Sam 15:1–3 is just one such example). If taken literally and historically, the Bible describes a world in which the sky is an actual, physical, firm dome, like bronze or glass, and stars are literal lights affixed to that ceiling, and behind that dome was water (Gen 1:6–8; Job 37:18; Ps 148:4).[20] Almost no one in our modern world believes that hell is a literal, physical space one may visit if one could burrow down far enough underground, but that is certainly what was being described for ancient persons when Jesus was said to have "descended into hell" to preach to the dead (1 Pet 3:19). Very few Christians today, even when they confess to believe in "the resurrection of the flesh," insist that the resurrected body will necessarily be composed of the exact same physical flesh—the same molecules, we might say, to use a modern term—though that is what seems to be described by the Gospel of Luke, and it is certainly what was considered the "orthodox" view eventually of the ancient church.

Modern Christians, as all Christians have always done, are constantly interpreting scriptural or doctrinal statements so that they can believe them.[21] In the twentieth century many people criticized Rudolf Bultmann because he insisted that modern Christians needed to "demythologize" Christian language and concepts for modern belief to continue at all. There are quite legitimate ways to critique Bultmann and his particular brand of modernism.[22] But if one takes "demythologization" to refer to all modern interpretations that take an ancient literal, historical statement that is obviously not acceptable to us and reinterpret it to have a less literal or less historical meaning, just about all Christians do that all the time if they use the Bible for their own lives and faith.

This raises the question, though: how is a statement of scripture or doctrine true or not? I will argue that for a scriptural account to be "historically true" it must pass muster by meeting criteria commonly used by modern historians to establish an account as "historically true."[23] But I argue that a statement that may not be "historically true" may indeed be true in a different sense, that something may be "Christianly true," that is, theologically

20. See the discussion in Dudley, *Broken Words,* 134.

21. An excellent ancient example is the long discussion of biblical passages that Origen insists *cannot* be taken literally but must be interpreted "spiritually." See his *On First Principles,* book 4, chapters 2 and 3.

22. See, for example, some of my own criticisms of Bultmann in the introduction above.

23. This is similar to a principle delineated by Kelsey: when theological arguments are mounted from other disciplines (e.g., history, literary criticism, philology, and metaphysics—he doesn't mention sciences, but I would), those kinds of arguments must meet the "formal standard of excellence" of that discipline. So an argument from "history" used even in theology must nonetheless meet the standards of normal, modern, academic historiography. See *Eccentric Existence,* 23.

true for Christians, even if it is not "historically true." It is almost certain, if one "plays by the rules" of modern historiography, that Jesus of Nazareth was not born in Bethlehem. But I find nothing wrong with taking it as true in the discourse of scripture and Christian tradition. The two accounts of Jesus's birth in Bethlehem in Matthew and Luke (and we should note that the two accounts have almost nothing in common except *that* Jesus was born in Bethlehem and born of a virgin named Mary who was betrothed to a man named Joseph) may be interpreted to express theological truths acceptable to modern Christians. Since statements may be true or false according to how they are interpreted, I argue that "historical" interpretations are simply not the same kinds of things as "theological" interpretations. A historical account of the likely birth of Jesus may be good and true history but not theology. And a theological account of the birth of Jesus may be good and true theology but not history. Sometimes in this book, therefore, I contrast the truth of an interpretation of scripture when it is interpreted theologically, "Christianly," or even "mythologically" with the falseness of the account if it is taken as a piece of historiography, and vice versa.[24]

If we take the word "myth" to refer to a narrative account that is not "true" literally or historically—that is, it describes something that cannot be constructed and accepted by modern historiography—but that we may take as expressing "something true" about our world or experience in our world, there is nothing wrong with talking about "true myths" of the Bible or Christianity. Accounts that I as a historian would insist cannot be accepted as "historical" but also that I, as a Christian theologian of a sort, would accept as "myths that are true" would include the myth of Adam and Eve; the tower of Babel; the story of the "fall" and later doctrine of original sin; the origin of

---

24. My entire project assumes the conclusions of what broadly may be called discourse theory and associated with the theories of language, textuality, and meaning making of the work of, especially, Michel Foucault and Mikhail Bakhtin. Modern historiography is a "discourse" in which only some kinds of statements even make sense, much less can be judged to be "true" or not. Theology and even "mythology" function as different "discourses," in which the "rules" for judging the sensibility or "truth" of a statement are different from those within "history." The question, for example, "Will you close for me?" will make sense only within some particular discourse. If said in an operating room, in the discourse of medicine, it might mean one surgeon is asking another to suture up an incision. In a court of law, on the other hand, within the discourse of jurisprudence, it might mean one lawyer is asking another on the same team to "close" an argument. Or it could signify a storekeeper asking his clerk to close up shop. Thus, modern historiography is one "discourse" that plays by one set of rules. I take both theology and mythology to be other "discourses" that play by different rules.

the rainbow; the story of Jonah, the great fish, and Nineveh; the story of Job; Jesus's exorcism of Legion; the desert temptation of Jesus. It seems obvious to me that to take any of these stories as historically "true" is to show a complete lack of understanding of the standards of modern historiography. But since I do believe that with proper interpretation each of these stories can be seen to express larger truths about the world and human nature and God's grace, I must be able to differentiate "historical" truths from "mythological" or "theological" truths.

Then there is another category that perhaps is even more controversial. There are myths or stories in the Bible I believe we ought to doubt even on purely theological grounds. In other words, I would argue that these are not historical truths, but I would also provide arguments (and will at different points in this book) as to why I reject them even as "true myths." In that case I must provide theological as opposed to historical arguments and reasons. Included in this category for me would be the existence of hell as a place of eternal suffering and punishment engineered and operated by God. There may be other ways I could use *some* notion of "hell" theologically, but it wouldn't be that particular myth with God's agency so construed. I also believe we must argue against any myth depicting God as causing disease and suffering. These myths, I would argue, are not only "historically" false but also "theologically" false or at least not true in any way I can now imagine.

Much of this book, therefore, will be dedicated to illustrating how religious beliefs, doctrines, and stories *may* be analyzed through the lens of modern history but *must* be analyzed through the lens of Christian theological reasoning. Illustrating how those two different kinds of analysis and evaluation may be done is the main purpose of the book. But we must begin by acknowledging that (1) statements may be both true and false, (2) their truth and falsity depend on how they are interpreted, and (3) a theological evaluation of truth is different from a historical evaluation of truth, though the former may indeed at times use the latter.

What Is Faith?

According to quite dominant popular assumptions, especially modern assumptions, "faith" refers to mental assent to some proposition about reality. There are certainly places in scripture to support this notion. The most famous is James 2:19, where the author is arguing against the more "Pauline" teaching that faith apart from works is what justifies: "You believe God is one. Fine. Also the demons believe—and shudder." Here the author is obviously taking "faith" to mean basic mental agreement with the proposition of monotheism.

But in so many other scriptural passages we can see that faith has a much broader and deeper meaning. The Greek word πιστεύειν may also often be translated as "to trust." The author of 1 Pet 2:6 quotes Isa 28:16: "Behold I am placing in Zion a stone, a cornerstone elect and honorable, and everyone who trusts [πιστεύων] in it will not be put to shame" (NRSV). "Having faith" in Christ is not merely believing that he exists or even believing certain propositions about his nature; rather it is more than anything trusting him with one's life.[25] This meaning comes out also when πιστεύω, but in the passive voice, is used to refer to someone "entrusting" a thing or task to someone else. Paul regularly speaks of himself as having been "entrusted" with the gospel of his ministry (1 Cor 9:17; Gal 2:7; 1 Thess 2:4; see also 1 Tim 1:11; Titus 1:3). God "trusted" Paul to carry out his assigned task; God "depended on" Paul.

The Letter to the Hebrews brings out this meaning by a long string of examples. "Faith is the assurance of things hoped for, the conviction of things not seen" (11:1, NRSV). Noah proceeded in building the ark by faith (11:7). This reference to Noah's boat reminds one of a statement by Alister McGrath: "Faith is not simply about believing that a ship exists; it is about stepping into it, and entrusting ourselves to it."[26] Abraham's faith is demonstrated by his stepping into an unknown future on the basis of promise and acceptance of that promise (11:8–12). His faith is an openness to an unseen future: that the future will bring good. Note that Hebrews does not dismiss a notion that "faith" may include an aspect of "believing that," as in an assent to a proposition: "Without faith it is impossible to find favor; for it is necessary that those who will approach God believe that he exists and that reward will come to those who seek him" (11:6). But the overwhelming meaning of "faith" in Hebrews is one of a willingness to depend on something, a willingness to begin a journey without fully knowing the end. Indeed, this is precisely the Christian notion of faith Martin Luther King, Jr., was invoking when he made his famous statement, "Faith is taking the first step even when you don't see the whole staircase."

We see this aspect of faith also when we notice how often in scripture it is linked to "hope." Again, the classic case is provided by 1 Cor 13, where

---

25. The "cornerstone" quotations, also from Isa 8:14 and Ps 118:22, must have been quite popular in early Christianity, probably because they helped explain the "rejection" of Jesus by "the Jews." See also 1 Pet 2:7; Rom 9:33; Matt 21:42; Mark 12:10; Luke 20:17; Acts 4:11.

26. McGrath, *Theology*, 11.

faith, hope, and love are strung together. Love comes out as superior but faith and hope are close behind: "Now remain faith, hope, and love, these three. But the greatest of these is love" (13:13). The connection occurs elsewhere. In Rom 4:18, Abraham believed παρ᾽ἐλπίδα ἐπ᾽ἐλπίδι, usually translated as "hoping against hope." But it can also be translated, at least from the point of view of pure grammar, as "by hope upon hope."[27] Abraham believed through hope that he would become the "father of many nations" when there was as yet no firm evidence of that beyond the promise of God. In Rom 15:13, Paul writes, "May the God of hope fill you with all joy and peace in believing, to the end that you abound in hope in the power of the holy spirit." Note that joy, peace, and hope come with believing. Believing is an attitude, a way of living in joy, peace, and hope.

In fact, theologians have been saying for a long time that we should conceive of Christian faith more as a way of life than as assent to a list of propositional assertions. As Herbert McCabe puts it, "So far as God is concerned what we are offered in the Church and its scriptures is not further *information* but a share in his *life*."[28] And one need not be a theologian or even a believer to recognize the fact. The philosopher Simon Critchley, speaking about Paul but making a point that would apply to much Christian theology, explains, "Paul's conception of faith is not, then, the abstraction of a metaphysical belief in God. Nor is Christ some Hegelian mediation to the divine or a conduit to a transcendent beyond. Faith is rather a lived subjective commitment to what I have called elsewhere an infinite demand."[29] Terry Eagleton, professionally a literary critic though no stranger to theology, makes the point: "Faith . . . is not primarily a belief that something or someone exists, but a commitment and allegiance—faith *in* something which might make a difference to the frightful situation you find yourself in, as is the case, say, with faith in feminism or anticolonialism."[30] With his characteristic wit, Eagleton complains that many people commit "the blunder of believing that religion is a botched attempt to explain the world, which is like seeing ballet as a botched attempt to run for a bus" (50).

These statements are much in line with the portraits of faith in Paul and Hebrews but also elsewhere. Faith may sometimes refer to belief "that"

27. Some commentators note that the more literal translation of the phrase would be "hope beyond hope" or "beyond hope in hope." See, for example, Jewett, *Romans;* Cranfield, *Epistle to the Romans,* 1:245–46.

28. McCabe, *God Matters,* 19.

29. Critchley, "You Are Not Your Own," 226.

30. Eagleton, *Reason,* 37.

something is true, but in its most profound Christian sense it is a way of life, a commitment. We may also evoke the notion, often linked with the names of Aristotle and Pierre Bourdieu, of *habitus,* which may include a notion of "habit" in the English, meaning an action that comes so naturally to us from having done it so often that we don't even think about how to do it. Like playing a piano: if I think too much about what my fingers are doing I likely won't be able to do it. Or, as both Bourdieu and Ludwig Wittgenstein put it, playing a game the rules of which we usually follow automatically and with no need for self-reflection. To Bourdieu, habitus is much more than that; it is a complex notion used to analyze how societies organize themselves and people learn socially how to behave.[31] But it is a useful theological notion as well, as Michel de Certeau has demonstrated.[32] To evoke another image, faith is a "stance" we take toward the world.[33] It may be a decision or it may be just the way we find ourselves standing as we face reality and the future. At any rate, all these ways of thinking of the nature of faith deliver us from the mistaken, and especially modernist, idea that Christian faith is mainly assenting to intellectual propositions about nature and God.

To address a related issue, many people either lose their faith or criticize Christianity because they mistakenly take it to be a philosophy or something very like a philosophy, by which I mean they expect Christianity to be an intellectual system that is responsible for providing satisfactory answers to just about every conceivable intellectual question or problem. True, Christianity can bear some of the blame for this in that Christians themselves have too often presented Christianity to be just that. So if evolutionary biology is true, then Genesis is wrong because it is now just outdated, bad science. Many people, through, I believe, inadequate theological education, have assumed a "God of the gaps" kind of theology, that is, "God" is just the causal force or fill-in for things we cannot yet "explain" with science or philosophy. Or since people ask about the problem of evil or suffering in the world—"Why, if God is both good and created the world, do we have such evil and suffering in it?"—and they are, wisely, not satisfied with any of the answers different

---

31. Bourdieu, *Logic of Practice,* 9–12 *et passim.* Sedmak, taking his lead from Duns Scotus's teachings that "faith is a practical habitus" ("Der Glaube ist . . . ein praktischer Habitus, ein praktischer Akt"; "theologia est practica"), pursues how we may think of "orthodoxy" and "heresy" as related less to pure statements than to lived life or "form of life." "Der Glaube ist praktisch."

32. De Certeau, *Practice.*

33. I first used this term "stance" to describe faith in my essay "Promise of Teleology." I borrowed the image from Van Fraassen, *Empirical Stance.*

Christians have historically given, that just proves for them that Christianity is not "true." But the better idea is that Christianity was never "supposed" to be a philosophy in the first place.[34] Christianity, understood correctly, should not *claim* to offer intellectually satisfying answers to all intellectual questions, even legitimate intellectual questions.

Christianity does offer some answers to the problems of evil and suffering, but they are answers of this kind: "In spite of suffering and evil, God is still love and healing." Or recall the answer given by God to Julian of Norwich, "All shall be well, and all shall be well, and all manner of things shall be well."[35] That is not an intellectual, propositional answer to the philosophical question of evil. But it may well be an existentially, emotionally, or psychologically helpful "answer." The mistake is to take Christianity to be a philosophy responsible for answering all our questions. Christianity offers a gospel and faith, not answers to all our questions, even our very good questions. Christianity is not a philosophy.[36]

Another common mistake is to think that faith need always be a choice. Protestant emphasis on individualism, again especially in the modern world, has so influenced popular ideas about religion that many people conceive of religious commitment as fundamentally a choice, even to the extent of exaggerating the presence or need of "conversion" in all religious experience. But many Christians who have grown up in the church will not have experienced it that way. It is, for them, just natural. Just "the way I feel." As Eagleton puts it, "Faith—any kind of faith—is not in the first place a matter of choice. It is more common to find oneself believing something than to make a conscious decision to do so—or at least to make such a conscious decision because you find yourself leaning that way already."[37]

Eagleton goes on to make another valid point about faith and choice or at least a Christian idea of faith: "The Christian way of indicating that faith is not in the end a question of choice is the notion of grace. Like the world itself from a Christian viewpoint, faith is a gift."[38] Recall Rom 15:13 from above and

---

34. "There never has actually been a *philosophia christiana*, for if it was *philosophia* it was not *christiana*, and if it was *christiana* it was not *philosophia*." Barth, *Church Dogmatics*, I/1, p. 6.

35. See, for example, Frykholm, *Julian of Norwich*, 55.

36. As Chesterton would insist, the book of Job does not constitute a "theodicy." It is rather the refusal to give one. See Ker, *G. K. Chesterton*, 615, citing J. P. de Fonseka, ed., *G. K. C. as M. C.*, 37–39, 45–49, 51.

37. Eagleton, *Reason*, 137.

38. Ibid., 138.

note that, according to that passage, faith is not produced by the believer but is a gift from God. To the Philippians, Paul writes, "Because of Christ, [God] has given to you not only to believe in him but also to suffer for him" (1:29). The Greek verb for "given" here, ἐχαρίσθη, may also be translated as "granted" or even "graced." The Greek is a verb form of the noun we also translate "grace." To the disciples in Rome, Paul says, "Thanks be to God, because you were slaves of sin, but you obeyed from the heart the form of teaching to which you were entrusted [that is, "handed over": παρεδόθητε]" (Rom 6:17). Note that the believers did have something to do: they "obeyed." But what they obeyed was the gospel to which they "were entrusted." The passive indicates that the initial action was done by God. God "handed over" these people to the gospel. God is the source of their faith.[39]

The logical extension of this line of thinking, an extension adamantly rejected by most modern people, including perhaps most Christians, is the doctrine of predestination. I treat the themes of election and predestination more fully in the chapter titled "Human" below, where I address more fully issues of salvation, but I do wish to bring the topic up briefly here for what it may tell us about Christian knowledge. If Christians think of themselves as "preordained" to believe (see Rom 8:29–30), that God is the one who brings about "the obedience of faith" (Rom 16:26), that God "elected us before the foundation of the cosmos (Eph 1:4–5), that we are saved not "from ourselves" but "as the gift of God" (Eph 2:8), then we certainly can take no credit for our faith or our knowledge. We didn't produce it, we can't be proud of it, and we shouldn't worry about it. Our faith springs so little from our own effort that we may imagine God having decided to give it to us, as a gift, before we ever existed. Predestination is a radical way of saying not only that we cannot

---

39. The rest of Rom 6 goes back and forth between the actions of the believers and the actions of God upon them. And the treatment culminates in Rom 6:23: "For the wages of sin is death, but the free gift of God is eternal life in Christ Jesus our Lord." The entire section is built on the metaphor that the believers are "slaves" of God. The people can respond to their deliverance to righteousness, but they are "slaves" in the entire process, beginning to end. They are, at least in a sense within Paul's rhetoric, deprived of "free will" to exercise what will lead to their righteousness. It is God's action from beginning to end, though they can "obey" it—that is, accept the free gift willingly rather than unwillingly. One is reminded (though it is not completely the same) of the older Stoic notion that a person is to fate like a dog tied to a cart. The cart (fate) goes where the divine providence of the universe destines it to go. The dog can go along willingly or unwillingly; but it will go along. Though Paul does not talk so rigidly, this passage goes some way in that direction. At any rate, it surely indicates that people may take no credit for their righteousness and therefore no credit for their faith.

save ourselves by works; we can't even save ourselves by our faith, since it is only by God's grace that we even have it.

As we have already seen to some extent, however, there are stories and passages in the New Testament that imply that faith *is* the responsibility of individual people and that if they don't have it they'd better conjure some up. One can get the idea from some biblical texts that faith is something like a virtue one gets credit for or can attain on one's own. Or elsewhere faith seems to be something like a tool people can use to get what they want. "And seeing their faith, Jesus said to the paralytic, 'Child, your sins are forgiven'" (Matt 9:2). "Your faith has healed you" (Matt 9:22). To his disciples who could not heal a boy with a demon, Jesus says that it was because of their "little faith." "If you have faith even the size of a mustard seed, you will say to this mountain, 'Move from here to there!' And it will move; and nothing will be impossible for you" (Matt 17:20). I take these examples from Matthew, but they are often paralleled in the other Gospels.

We may interpret such passages as teaching us to encourage ourselves and others to believe, to buck up at times. We can indeed help one another's faith: "So we may be mutually encouraged by one another's faith, yours and mine" (Rom 1:12). People can learn to be more faithful, filled with hope, and less cynical. So there is some place for these lessons that we, at least to some extent, are responsible even for our hopes and fears and so in some way for our faith. In other words there's no reason to let Paul win the day and reject James. Both views—that faith is a way of life and a gift from God (Paul) and that faith includes believing some truths and must be supplemented by our effort (James)—may be true when interpreted truly.

But passages such as these have been used to great harm also. When people who want to believe are berated by others when they cannot, no good is done. And the terrible evils of modern "gospels of prosperity," by which people are urged by "superpastors" to "name it and claim it"—even when the "it" is not love, peace, or hope but a new Cadillac or a huge house—that is the gospel perverted until it *is* no gospel, much less a gospel of prosperity. To twist the promises of Jesus about what faith can do into simply an underwriting of capitalism or consumerism is immoral.

And so it is that we must continually remind ourselves that the higher Christian doctrine teaches that faith itself is a gift from God. This is one of the many places where we see that something in scripture may be true when taken one way and false when taken another. And two apparently contradictory theological teachings may both be true when interpreted rightly.

Faith, Knowledge, and Grace

The relationship between faith and knowledge is complicated in philosophy. It is perhaps even more complicated in theology when it is good theology. But my argument has been that no firm dichotomy may be made between the two and that both must be continually placed in the context of grace. Since faith is a gift from God given through divine grace and not attained by our efforts or merit, we Christians need not be very concerned when someone asks us, either sincerely or sneeringly, "Why do you still believe? With so little absolutely firm evidence and some heavy counterevidence, why do you have faith?" If faith is a gift from God, we need not explain it.

But we are reminded of 1 Pet 3:15: "Always be prepared to give an answer [a "defense," an apologia] to anyone asking for an account concerning the hope within you." So let me attempt two. In keeping with the methodology I sketched out above, these will be two quite different accounts, one sociological, the other theological. I want to insist that although they are very different "explanations" of "why I believe" and although they may be taken to be contradictory, I believe they are both true accounts. They explain, however, by using two separate discourses.

I have been asked many times, actually, why I still believe, almost always from people who have come across writings or lectures of mine that seem to challenge the historical veracity of the Bible or that expose much of the tawdry history of Christianity. My first answer is, "I don't know." But then I offer my sociological-psychological answer.

It may well be that I have faith just because I was raised that way. Having grown up in a religious family, itself the product of generations of Christian people, I may be psychologically inclined or habituated to assume some ultimate meaningfulness of the universe and the centrality of faith for life. Moreover, my family, though attending a very conservative church, was generally liberal and progressive. We weren't particularly bothered if others did not go to church or went to a different church. We tended not to worry if other people weren't as "religious" as we were. One could say that we didn't have a chip on our shoulder—a "faith chip." But just because we didn't have a "faith chip" on our shoulder, we perhaps did have a "faith chip" in our brains, something like a computer chip that inclined us to be religious. That is to say, whether from socialization, familiarization, nature, or culture, we were, so to say, hardwired to believe. And because I grew up and imbibed Christianity in such a social situation and always found it meaningful, I have been socially structured to have faith. This seems to me a completely good sociohistorical answer to questions about my faith. And I think it is certainly true.

But now for the theological answer. As should be obvious from this chapter thus far, my favorite answer to people who wonder why I have faith is, "Because God allows me to. For some reason beyond me, God gave me the gift of faith. You'll have to ask God why." For some reason, I and many other Christians—fully cognizant of all the historical problems about Christianity, of the checkered history of Christian institutions, of the hypocrisy and intolerance of so many Christians, and of the paucity of evidence that love will prevail in the end—find ourselves still willing to take the great myths of traditional Christianity as saying something we find to be true. We can hear scripture read, recognize where it is no doubt problematic and dangerous, and yet perceive something in it that sounds like the word of God. We participate in the liturgy and, even when wary of its residual notes of violence and patriarchy, nonetheless experience within it the beauty and glory we believe must be signs of God. We find faith a comfort in affliction and sickness, and we find our joy increased in its celebrations. We don't know why. We just do. And scripture allows us to take that as it is: an inscrutable and inexplicable gift from God. We need no other reasons or explanations.

As we have seen in this chapter, there are at least two reasons for epistemological humility for Christians, reasons for us to force ourselves to be content with not knowing in a full, final, or foundationalist sense. We might call one the mythological reason and the other an empirical or philosophical reason. As shown by writings of Paul analyzed above, we don't know now because the end has not yet come. This is the eschatological reservation of Christian epistemology. Christianity should make no attempt to answer all questions, and even the answers it does give must always be seen as provisional. We don't yet know as we will know. Though Paul is the clearest advocate of eschatological reservation in the New Testament, he is not the only one. "Nothing is hidden that will not be revealed, or secret that will not be made known" (Matt 10:26; par. Luke 12:2). In thinking theologically, Christians must remind themselves of the temporary, incomplete state of all our knowledge.

Then there is the empirical or philosophical reason. We know by our own experience that our knowledge is precarious and our experience not completely reliable. We and all others have been wrong many times. We cannot actually trust our own eyesight. Though we can think theologically only by depending on our experiences (which, remember, include reading scripture, hearing tradition, and listening to one another, among all other ways we experience God's word), we must remember that our experiences are never infallible, are always possibly misleading, and are always subject to human interpretation, as undependable as that may be. Our very experiences teach us to be wary of experience, even when we have no other way to think, indeed even to think theologically.

Thus we are in what could be felt to be a sad state. But it may also be interpreted as a state of grace. As human beings we can never claim certainty for our knowledge or credit for our faith. But that is not a bad place to be. It simply reiterates that we must be content to trust God. We must remember that we are nonetheless responsible for how we use our knowledge and our faith. We have been given gifts by God, but we are responsible for how we use them. "From everyone to whom much has been given, much will be required, and to whom much has been entrusted, much more will be asked" (Luke 12:48). Our goal is to rest in the knowledge that we cannot now know fully but to determine that we will exercise our brief and partial knowledge as ethically and lovingly as we can.

I have made the point before: we can probably do no better than to follow Augustine's advice that any doctrine—and here he is specifically discussing different interpretations of scripture—cannot be "true" in the Christian sense unless it promotes the double commandment that we love God and our neighbor.[40] Any interpretation of scripture that does not work for the good of ourselves and our fellow human beings to the glory of God cannot be the "literal" and true meaning of that passage of scripture. The rule is applicable to all Christian epistemology. The beginning and end of Christian knowing must be the rule of love.

---

40. See Augustine, *De doctrina christiana* 3.33–34, 35 (10.14); 3.55 (16–24). See also Martin, *Sex and the Single Savior,* 12 *et passim* (see "love" in the index); Martin, *Pedagogy,* 83–85. Johannes Hoff, in discussion of Nicholas of Cusa, also comments on love as the ultimate guide in epistemology: *Analogical Turn,* 199–200.

CHAPTER 2

Scripture

"Scripture," for Christians, is the text of the Bible when read in faith and by the leading of the holy spirit in the community of the body of Christ. It is important to begin a theological account of scripture, moreover, by making explicit what scripture is *not*. Scripture is not simply "the text" itself in its physical form. That is, scripture is not any one manuscript or recension or version or edition of the Bible. Also, scripture is not to be equated with "the canon," though "canon" may have a valid theological role to play in Christian thought and practice. Third, scripture is not the same as "the gospel." Before getting into an account of what scripture *is*, I will explain why I believe it is important to understand why scripture is *not* to be equated with any of these three other theological terms.

The Text

A huge confusion settled over many Christians in modernity, one caused mainly by the invention of the printing press and modern modes of publishing the Bible. With the rise of the modern discipline of textual criticism of the Bible, people were dismayed at the realization that there were thousands upon thousands of disparities among various manuscripts even of just the New Testament, not to mention the text-critical problems related to the Hebrew Bible. In spite of conservative claims to the contrary, some of these differences were important, even theologically, and since Protestants had based so much of their faith on the idea that they could get reliable doctrine and ethics from a straightforward, literal reading of the Bible alone, the fact that the very text of that Bible by necessity was a product of human scholarship and decision proved for many a stumbling block. If the "original text" of the Greek New Testament was supposed to be the infallible word of God, the fact that no one could really claim access to that "original text" caused problems for faith and theology.[1]

The anxiety, however, was founded on a bad theology of scripture to begin with. Scripture should not be equated with any particular physical document, even the imagined "original text" of the autograph, say, of Paul's Letter to the Romans. Christians throughout history had read scripture in many forms. The textual source of Christian faith, among other "sources," such as preaching, spoken word, and all other ways Christians come into contact with the gospel as the word of God, is scripture, that is, the Bible in whatever form Christians encounter it. And the scripture that elicits the congregational responses "The Word of God" and "Thanks be to God" is the text that is read out, in whatever language, version, or edition. This is no less a matter of having faith that God is trustworthy and that the holy spirit will not mislead us than is any other aspect of trusting God and the holy spirit. It is perfectly legitimate that scholars practice textual criticism, and perhaps even fine if they do so using some kind of imagined entity such as "the original text" of the New Testament, but it is not necessary for the existence of Christian faith.

This theological fact should have been obvious even by analysis of uses of "scripture" by authors of New Testament documents themselves. At the beginning of the Gospel of Mark, the author says that he is quoting Isaiah:

> Look, I am sending my messenger before your face,
> He will prepare your way;
> A voice crying in the wilderness,
> "Prepare the way of the Lord,
> Make straight his paths." (Mark 1:2–3)

But only the last three lines of the quotation are from Isaiah (40:3), and even then Mark has himself taken "his" to refer to Jesus, whereas the reference

---

1. Perhaps the most famous expression of this anxiety about the "original text" can be found in Ehrman, *Misquoting Jesus*. For example: "What good is it to say that the autographs (i.e., the originals) were inspired? We don't *have* the originals! We have only error-ridden copies, and the vast majority of these are centuries removed from the originals and different from them, evidently, in thousands of ways" (7).

in the Hebrew Bible is to God. The author also seems to have added "your" to the first two lines. The quotation is actually a conflation of three different texts. From Exod 23:20–21 we get the words "ahead of you" or "in front of you," according to how one chooses to translate the Greek: "I am going to send an angel [the Greek may be translated as "messenger" or "angel"] in front of you, to guard you on the way and to bring you to the place that I have prepared. Be attentive to him and listen to his voice; do not rebel against him, for he will not pardon your transgression; for my name is in him" (NRSV). In its full quotation it hardly fits the role Mark assigns John the Baptist, so the author understandably used only part of it. From Mal 3:1 we get the words "prepare the way": "See, I am sending my messenger to prepare the way before me, and the Lord whom you seek will suddenly come to his temple" (NRSV).

This is a good example of the "free" interpretation of scripture practiced by authors of the New Testament; it is also a good example of their often free *quotation* of scripture. We have no way of knowing whether the author intentionally picked and chose and combined these three texts to create a "new" piece of scripture. He may have been using some kind of handbook of prophetic texts Christians had already begun collecting, or he may be attempting to quote from memory. But the church has never considered this a particularly disturbing passage, in spite of the fact that Mark is "quoting" a "passage of scripture" that does not actually occur in our Old Testament.

True, later Christian authors attempted to "correct" Mark here. One of his first correctors was the author of the Gospel of Matthew, who used Mark as one of his sources, but discriminately. Matthew leaves out the material from Exodus and Malachi and thus correctly quotes the passage from Isaiah, though also adding "his" to refer to Jesus (Matt 3:3). Luke also makes the correction, though he adds more of the passage from Isaiah to expand the quotation for his own theological purposes (Luke 3:4–6).[2] Later scribes also recognized the misattribution, so some of them changed the wording in Mark to read simply "in the prophets" or "in Isaiah and in the prophets."[3] There is no reason, however, for Christians to be concerned about what exactly is "scripture" here. We don't need to "correct" Mark so that he "correctly"

2. Luke's theme that the lowly will be raised and the high and mighty brought low is reflected in the lines "Every valley shall be filled, and every mountain and hill shall be made low" (Luke 3:5; NRSV). And his theme of salvation being taken to the entire "world" is captured in the last line he quotes from Isaiah: "And all flesh shall see the salvation of God" (Luke 3:6; NRSV).

3. See the textual apparatus in any good edition of the Greek text.

quotes Isaiah or "correctly" names his sources. And if we encountered a manuscript that contained a later scribal "correction" of Mark's wording, we need not worry that we there are not reading scripture. Scripture is the text brought to Christians by the holy spirit in whatever form we encounter it.

Another fact that helps illustrate this issue is that ancient Christians almost all used a Greek translation of the Hebrew Bible whereas almost all modern Christians use some modern translation not of the Greek Old Testament but of the Hebrew Bible. The very "text" of scripture used by ancient Christians, including all the writers of New Testament documents, was different from the text in use by most modern Christians. This is not simply an instance of a difference in the *language* of the text, such as the fact that Spanish speakers use a different text of the Bible from English speakers. The ancient Greek versions of the Hebrew scriptures sometimes offer significantly different readings from any literal translation of the Hebrew. The ancient translators may have had a different Hebrew text in front of them from ours today, but it also seems that they simply translated the Hebrew so that it made better sense to them or better fit their theology or needs. The ancient translators sometimes "hellenized" the very content of the text so that it fit their own cultural situation better. Anthropomorphic depictions of God, for instance, were changed or even deleted in order better to fit Greek philosophical notions that insisted the divine cannot be embodied. Hebrew words that referred to earlier ancient Near Eastern concepts or things no longer relevant or understood are translated into Greek that reflects a later Egyptian cultural context, Egypt being where many of the Greek translations were made.[4]

These changes are not necessarily negligible. In Mark 7:6–7, the author has Jesus say, "This people honors me with their lips, but their hearts are far from me; in vain do they worship me, teaching human precepts as doctrines," supposedly a quotation of Isa 29:13 (NRSV). Mark then adds the words of Jesus: "You abandon the commandment of God and hold to human tradition." But the NRSV more accurately translates the Hebrew of Isa 29:13 as, "Because these people draw near with their mouths and honor me with their lips, while their hearts are far from me, and their worship of me is a human commandment learned by rote." The point in Isaiah seems to be that the people are giving only lip service to God while their hearts are not in it.

---

4. See Reventlow, *History of Biblical Interpretation*, 22–23; an excellent recent study emphasizing both the extent of changes from Hebrew to Greek in the LXX and their theological significances is Law, *When God Spoke Greek*, esp. 170.

The Markan point, rather, is that the people are substituting human teachings for God's. Jesus makes a different point by citing a Greek translation of Isa 29:13 that probably did not match the Hebrew version. (I mean the Jesus of the narrative of the Gospel of Mark; the historical Jesus probably spoke Aramaic, may have quoted a Hebrew version of the scriptures, and probably did not speak Greek.) The quotation in Mark, at any rate, does not match our Bibles.

To cite just one more example (there are many), the author of Acts wants to take Ps 69:25 as a prophecy about Judas: "Let his homestead become desolate, and let there be no one to live in it" (Acts 1:20, NRSV). But the Hebrew, at least the versions we have, has a plural subject: "May their camp be a desolation; let no one live in their tents." It may be that the author of Acts made the change so that the prophecy better referred to the fate of Judas. Or perhaps he was looking at a Greek version that had already made the change or reflected a different Hebrew source. (The LXX also has the plural forms.) Either way, he was using a significantly different "text" of scripture from the one we modern Christians use, that is, in the West.

None of this is a great cause for theological concern. It simply demonstrates, as many different examples and issues could, that what counts as scripture for Christians cannot be identified with any particular text of scripture in any one physical form. As I said earlier, scripture is any text of the Bible brought to Christians by the holy spirit and read by Christians in faith and by the leading of the holy spirit. Trusting scripture to convey the word of God to us is just as much a matter of faith as is any other article of faith.

Canon

We also should not confuse the theological category of scripture with that of canon, though both may have perfectly legitimate roles to play in our theology. "Canon" originally meant any kind of rule, measuring rod, or list. So the term "canon" refers not to the Bible or to scripture but to a list of what books different Christian churches take as having particularly high status, perhaps even a unique status as authoritative for revealing the word of God. But Christians throughout time and all over the world have never come to unanimous agreement about what that list should include.[5] Thus

---

5. For good discussions of the meaning of "canon" in general as well as the development of the various Christian canons, see the several essays in Thomassen, ed., *Canon*.

Roman Catholics and Anglicans include books that survive in Hebrew (as does the Hebrew Bible accepted by Jews and most Protestants and published in modern editions) but also some that survive in Greek but not fully in Hebrew. The ancient church accepted those books, nowadays called the Apocrypha. The argument by early Protestant Reformers to leave those books out of the Bible was an innovation. Different Eastern churches also have diverse canons. Besides the Apocryphal books accepted by the Roman Catholic and Anglican churches, Greek Orthodox and Slavonic Bibles also include 1 Esdras, the Prayer of Manasseh, Psalm 151, and 3 Maccabees. The Greek canon also includes 4 Maccabees. Almost all churches have the usual twenty-seven books of the NT, except that the book of Revelation is excluded from the liturgy of Eastern Orthodox churches.[6] And there are still other Christian canons besides these mentioned. Just about all Christian communities accept the notion of scripture, but they do not agree on the extent of the canon.

Modern Christians also tend to reject as noncanonical ancient texts that even our New Testament authors accepted as scripture. The author of Jude relates a story in which the archangel Michael refuses to rebuke the Devil, leaving it to God to do so (Jude 9). The author is apparently taking as scripture a text not accepted as canonical by Christians today.[7] A bit later Jude quotes a passage from the ancient collection of texts scholars group together as *1 Enoch*, again a noncanonical source for most Christian churches.[8] If one of our canonical sources itself quotes, apparently as "scripture," a text we do not take as canon, that should make us wary of a too heavy theological dependence on the category of canon. We need not insist too much on the precise boundaries of the canon or on the necessity of using only the canon for divine guidance. If our canon was not the controlling rule for interpreta-

---

6. For a discussion of different books accepted by different Christian communities, see Ward, "Tradition and Traditions," 254 and nn. 8–11; for the Eastern Orthodox churches' position on Revelation, see Francis, "'Blessed.'"

7. The actual source of the story is not certain. Many scholars take it as a reference derived from the *Assumption of Moses* or the *Testament of Moses*. Indeed, there is some possibility that those are two titles referring to basically the same work, or two different versions of the same work. At any rate, scholars are agreed that the author takes it from a noncanonical source. For a thorough investigation of possible sources, see Bauckham, *Jude, 2 Peter*, 65–76.

8. Jude 14–15 includes a quotation from *1 Enoch* 1:9. The Enochic literature is considered noncanonical by most churches but is counted among the eighty-one books of the Ethiopian Bible: Haile, "Ethiopian Church," 5:2859.

tion for the "brother of the Lord," as the author of Jude at least wants us to believe about his identity, why should it be for us?[9]

Another example of the flexible nature of the category of canon is the inclusion in almost all modern Bibles of John 7:53–8:11, the story of the woman taken in adultery. It is almost universally agreed by historical critics of the Bible that the story was not part of the "original publication" of the Fourth Gospel, however we imagine that "publication" taking place, which is a complicated historical question in itself. The passage is famous and much loved by Christians, and justifiably so. It teaches a welcome message about withholding judgment of others. But it is not in our oldest and best manuscripts of John, and it seems to have been added later, probably in the second century, many decades after the writing of the Gospel. Almost all modern, critical versions of the Greek text and English translations indicate the textual conundrum by putting the passage in brackets or double brackets, usually explaining in a note that the passage is not in the best manuscripts and was likely added later.[10]

People who believe that scripture is what was most likely originally written by the texts' first authors may object to including the passage in modern Bibles at all. After all, the modern assumption has been that the published version of the Bible should be as close as possible to the "original autographs." If just about all critical scholars believe that John 7:53–8:11 was not in the form of the Fourth Gospel that was written, edited, and copied for sending around—what counted in the ancient world as "publication"—in the first century, or the early second century if that is the preferred date of the writing of the Fourth Gospel, then why include the passage in our Bibles at all?

But one could make an argument, I believe, that the story has been taken to be scripture by the vast majority of Christians for much of the history of the use of the Gospel in the church at least since the Middle Ages. The story has been taken as teaching an important, indeed divine, lesson about love, grace, and forgiveness and about the universality of human sin. The passage is scripture because the church has taken it to be scripture. But if we accept that proposal and stop worrying too much about whether a passage from, probably, the second century or later should be included in our canonical versions of the Gospel of John, that should also demonstrate

---

9. For recent scholarship on Jude and its relation to 2 Peter, see Jeremy Hultin, *Jude and 2 Peter: A Commentary.* See also Hultin, "Literary Relationship," 27–45.

10. For an account of the history of the passage, see Knust with Wasserman, *Jesus, an Adultress.*

that the boundaries of the canon should not pose as significant a theological problem as it often has been taken to do. It demonstrates that the theological category of scripture is not the same as the category of canon and that the very category of "canon" need not be nearly as theologically important as is often claimed, even if we do affirm, along with different churches through history, that "canon" is a proper theological issue. In other words, we may (I prefer *should*) take the theological issue of canon seriously without attributing to it too much theological weight with regard to the interpretation of scripture.[11]

Gospel

The third theological category I wish to distinguish from scripture is *gospel*. I take "gospel" to refer to whatever linguistic entity is taken to encapsulate the good news that God provides for human beings through the actions, faith, and faithfulness of Jesus Christ. In my usage, "gospel" corresponds to what theologians, especially those influenced by modern German scholarship, have called the kerygma: the preached message that promises salvation and converts human beings to faith in God through Jesus Christ. The specific wording of these "kernel" messages can never be finalized into an invariable formula. It is the "saving message" of what God has wrought for us through Jesus Christ, and the holy spirit uses that message to inspire faith in us.

I will point to several passages of the New Testament as providing examples of the basic gospel message. The theologian James Alison cites three credal-like statements from three New Testament sources that I will mention as brief examples of the gospel or kerygma (he does not use these terms in his context).[12] One is the famous John 3:16: "For God so loved the world that he gave his only Son, that whoever believes in him should not perish but have eternal life" (I follow Alison in quoting the RSV). But he also lists

11. This is clearly in part my answer to the entire agenda of "canonical criticism" in biblical and theological studies, the most important representative of which is Brevard S. Childs, *Old Testament as Scripture;* and Childs, *New Testament as Canon.* My answer to such proponents of canonical criticism is that the very category of canon is too insecure and too historically contingent to provide any kind of "foundation" for Christians. Moreover, I do not believe the advocates of canonical criticism have delivered the kinds of substantial *theological* supports for the method. I also don't believe that the canon, contrary to the usual claims of these authors, *can* or *does* provide the kinds of "controls" over interpretation claimed for the method. What "canonical critics" get out of the Bible is due not to "the canon" but to their own theological and ideological tendencies.

12. Alison, *Joy,* 118.

Rom 3:22–25: "For there is no distinction; since all have sinned and fall short of the glory of God, they are justified by his grace as a gift, through the redemption which is in Christ Jesus, whom God put forward as an expiation by his blood, to be received by faith. This was to show God's righteousness." And 1 John 4:9–10: "In this the love of God was made manifest among us, that God sent his only Son into the world, so that we might live through him. In this is love, not that we loved God but that he loved us and sent his Son to be the expiation for our sins." I might add the even briefer statement in 2 Cor 5:19: "God was in Christ, reconciling the world to himself." One might take each and all of these as very brief expressions of the gospel. In order to get the "whole story," one needs the Gospels themselves and, moreover, read within the context of the entire "narrative" of scripture as a whole. The gospel is, in any case, a narrative of what God has done in Jesus Christ with the salvific results communicated continuously to the church by the holy spirit.[13] The precise wording of the gospel can never be delineated. It is the story of Jesus Christ, and it can only be told over and over again in different forms and for different occasions.

Scripture is not the same as the gospel. Scripture consists of all those texts through which we may hear the gospel. Scripture is not our only source for the gospel. We may learn the gospel through oral preaching, through teaching from our parents or others in youth, through the liturgies of the church, through music, even through the stained-glass windows, art, and architecture of churches. The holy spirit may use many media, including those we may not now know or recognize, to bring to human beings the saving message of God. As Christians, we may believe that scripture is the most important source of the gospel. We may privilege scripture over other written sources for knowledge of God. But we must never believe it is the only source. To deny that the holy spirit may use resources other than scripture in particular to bring the gospel to human beings is to deny the freedom of the holy spirit and to deny our own experiences of hearing the grace of God communicated through many different channels of our lives and world.

This is one reason I believe it is misleading to describe Christianity as a "religion of the book." It is true that we may group Judaism, Islam, and Christianity together as members of a family, each of which takes as central to its faith and action revered texts and, to some extent, shared texts. But I believe that both Judaism and Islam give an even more central role to their

---

13. The theologically knowledgeable reader will hear the influence here of one of my teachers, Hans Frei, especially from his *Eclipse*.

revered texts—the Mishnah and Talmuds, along with the Hebrew Bible, for Jews; the Quran for Muslims—than Christianity should. I believe, for instance, that it would be theologically a mistake for Christians to give the kind of pious respect to the Bible that Muslims tend to give to the Quran. Moreover, the church must not become captive to the "bible-olatry" of some forms of modern, especially American, Christianity. Christians may revere the Bible, but we should also feel free to treat that text critically and freely.[14] The saving message for Christians is the gospel, in whatever form it comes to us, not scripture. Scripture is the tool used by the holy spirit—or rather *one* of the tools—to deliver the gospel. But Christians are not converted by scripture. We are converted by the gospel. Both the gospel and scripture are useful theological categories, but they should not be confused.

Old and New Testaments

From very early in the history of Christianity, from the mid-second century at the latest, Christians sometimes struggled with what to do with the Jewish scriptures. Famously, Marcion in the second century taught that Christians should reject the scripture of the Jews, that the god depicted there was not the Father of Jesus Christ and that Christians should have their own sacred writings that should displace Jewish scripture in the church. Marcion's views about the creator god being different from the Father of Jesus Christ have been mostly rejected through the centuries, but his unease about Jewish scripture has come up time and again in Christianity. For many reasons, however, the majority of the church and its leaders have insisted that Christians must retain the Jewish scriptures as holy and authoritative, an Old Testament alongside a New Testament.

Since it is my goal in this book to advocate Christian theology that remains connected to traditional Christian orthodoxy, and since both traditional usage and some credal statements have taught that the church retains essential scripture in the Old Testament, I would urge the same position even if only for the sake of continuity with the history of the church and orthodoxy. But there are also important theological arguments that can be made for doing so. For our world, one of the most important is that the church must maintain its connection to, indeed *dependence on,* Judaism and the God of Israel. It is imperative that Christians acknowledge our histori-

---

14. "But the Reformers also propose that even though the text is 'sufficient,' we ought not to worship it." Frei, *Theology and Narrative,* 163.

cal connection to Israel and to Jews themselves. This dependence must be regularly reiterated with humility and tenacity.

Many Christians unfortunately have been taught to read the Old Testament in anti-Jewish or anti-Semitic ways, differentiating the God of the Old Testament as one of "justice" or "punishment" or "legalism" from the God of the New Testament, who is the loving, merciful father of Jesus Christ. Some Christians, therefore, tend to denigrate or ignore the Old Testament, unhappy with some of the stories they read there and having little access to more sophisticated means of interpreting "hard texts." Those Christians, though, should be taught that the answer to difficult passages in the Bible (for they are in the New Testament as well, though too many Christians don't recognize that fact) is not to get rid of the passages or the Old Testament but to learn proper ways to interpret the Bible in theologically and ethically fruitful ways.

These attitudes toward the Old Testament reflect an ideology of Christian supersessionism: the notion that Judaism has been superseded by the advent of Christianity. Christianity "replaced" Judaism as the "true religion." Fortunately, in recent years much work has been done to challenge Christian supersessionism, especially in scholarship but also sometimes in churches.[15] Supersessionism must also be avoided in Christian use of the Old Testament.

Some scholars have pointed precisely to the problem of supersessionism in the very terms "Old Testament" and "New Testament." They have advocated that Christians should not use the former term at all but replace it with, say, "Hebrew Bible." Others have suggested that the traditional terminology should be replaced by the terms "First Testament" and "Second Testament." I believe such suggestions about terminological revision on this matter are mistaken. We must avoid supersessionist ideologies and theologies, but the alternate terms have their own problems, and they ignore some theological arguments for retaining the traditional titles.

The first thing to note is, indeed, simply that calling the two Testaments Old and New is itself ancient and traditional. Indeed, some have taken them to go back to the Apostle Paul himself, who spoke of a "new covenant" in 2 Cor 3:6. On closer reading, Paul was not there talking at all about what we mean by the Old and New Testaments. The New Testament hadn't been composed yet. By "new covenant" Paul meant the covenant God made with all humanity through Jesus Christ and marked not by "outward"

---

15. I treat this subject at greater length in the chapter titled "Church" below.

circumcision but by the "circumcision of the heart." And by the "old covenant" in 2 Cor 3:14, Paul probably meant the Mosaic Law, the Torah, not the entire Old Testament as we understand it.[16] The earliest use of the terms "Old" and "New Testament" to refer to the collections of books may be in the writings of Tertullian around 200 CE.[17] But that is still ancient enough to merit hesitance in pushing for innovative terminology for scripture.

The traditional terms also correctly reflect the chronological fact that the early Christian writers themselves used the then-existing Jewish scriptures as their own scripture and that the church later took certain early Christian writings as supplementing, but not replacing, older Jewish scripture. The two testaments were seen as two different bodies of texts, the latter springing from, appropriating, and supplementing the older without replacing it. The very fact that the church has resisted allowing the New Testament documents to replace those of the Old Testament indicates that supersession does not necessarily follow from the use of the terms "Old" and "New."

There are also good reasons to reject the suggested alternatives. The term "Hebrew Bible" is a perfectly good one in certain contexts. In a non-Christian or ecumenical setting, with Christians in dialogue with Jews or others, it may be preferable to avoid referring to these texts as the Old Testament. To insist on using the term "Old Testament" to refer basically to the Hebrew Bible of modern editions or to the scriptures of ancient Israel in a context where Jews and others are talking about simply the Bible or the Hebrew Bible or the Tanakh may convey ignorance, arrogance, or supersessionism.

But even in these contexts, "Hebrew Bible" may be misleading or not quite accurate. As noted above, the texts used by ancient Christians—indeed, almost all Christians up until the Reformation—was not the *Hebrew* text but some Greek version or, later and in some cases, a Latin version sometimes based on a Greek version rather than the Hebrew.[18] To use "Hebrew Bible"

16. Heb 9:15 speaks of "the first covenant" as different from the "new covenant" or "better covenant" he takes to be guaranteed by Jesus (Heb 7:22; 8:8). Though references to a "new covenant" occur in the New Testament, specific language about an "old covenant" is rare: see also Luke 22:20; 1 Cor 11:25; Heb 12:24.

17. Tertullian, *Against Praxeas* 15; *Against Marcion* 4.6. In *Against Marcion* 3.14, Tertullian calls them "two testaments of the law and the gospel," but he doubtless means by that the Old and New Testaments in their entirety, as least as he knew them. Trans. Peter Holmes, *The Ante-Nicene Fathers*, vol. 3.

18. For the importance of the Greek translation even for the later Latin versions, see Law, *When God Spoke Greek*. The Greek was important in regard to the later Latin versions because of the dependence of the Old Latin versions on some version of the LXX.

to refer to the scripture read by Paul or other ancient Christians would introduce an error of anachronism, implying that they were reading some Hebrew text similar to modern Hebrew Bibles based on the Masoretic Text or a modern critical edition. Thus in contexts in which I want to avoid any implication of Christian hegemony and avoid the term "Old Testament," but in which I do want to refer to the scriptural texts of Israel appropriated by ancient Christians, I have preferred to use the term "Jewish scripture." Or, if I am referring to the church's appropriation of Jewish scripture as its own, say "the Christian Old Testament." But to insist on using the term "Hebrew Bible" is often misleading even in secular, scholarly contexts or ecumenical situations.

There is also the issue of canon here. "Hebrew Bible" implies the "canon" of the Masoretic Text used by many Jews and modern scholarly editions. But the canon for most Christians before the modern era, as discussed above, was larger than the modern Hebrew Bible. Using a more neutral term such as "Jewish scripture" acknowledges that ancient Christians were dependent on a collection of Jewish scripture transmitted to them in some language besides Hebrew, a collection whose boundaries were larger than the Hebrew Bible, and a collection the boundaries of which were not firmly set until much later; in fact, those boundaries, as I have noted, have never been agreed upon by all Christians everywhere. For these reasons, related both to language and boundaries of the canon, the term "Hebrew Bible" can be misleading and less accurate than a term such as "Jewish scripture."

The issue of the different language versions of Jewish scripture invites theological consideration for Christians. Some differences between the Hebrew and Greek versions read by ancient Christians were not insignificant but carried theological consequences. Perhaps the most famous is the Greek of Isa 7:14. According to the Hebrew, the prophet spoke of a "young woman" bearing a son. Early Christians, depending on a Greek translation, took the prophecy to speak of a "virgin" bearing a son, causing them to take it as a reference to the virgin birth of Jesus by Mary. The different versions led to different exegetical, and even theological, consequences. In this case, Christians may want to take both the Hebrew Bible and the ancient Greek versions to be "scripture" for themselves. Christians should be able to reflect critically on *what* counts as "the text of the Christian Old Testament" and

---

The importance of the LXX in the East is even more obvious, since the LXX or translations of it (not of the Hebrew) provided and still provide the Old Testament text for many Orthodox churches and Christians.

how it should therefore be interpreted. But calling it the Hebrew Bible may be as theologically misleading as it is historically confusing.

Calling the two testaments First and Second is problematic again both for secular as well as theological reasons. It is true chronologically (though if one took the entire Apocrypha as included in the "First Testament" there may be some overlap between the writing of some New Testament documents and some Old Testament documents),[19] but it can give the impression that the Old Testament is more important for Christians than the New, conceding priority to it not only chronologically but also in value or usage. That would be wrong. We may think of the two testaments as being of equal value to the church. We may even consider the New Testament to be in some sense more central for Christians because without the teachings of the New Testament we would not be Christians in the first place and therefore have no connection to the Hebrew Bible at all. We Christians, it could be said, "come to" the Hebrew Bible *via* the gospel conveyed to us, at least in part, in the New Testament. Moreover, as I've argued and will argue, it is incumbent on Christians to interpret the Hebrew Bible *through* or *by means of* the message of Christ. Therefore, if there is to be any "priority of value" between the two testaments, it should be recognized as residing (empirically speaking!) in the New Testament rather than the Old Testament.[20] To Christians, the New Testament is their "first testament" in some important senses.

Christians, I suggest, should retain the use of the term "Old Testament" to signal that we Christians interpret these texts in ways different from interpretive methods used by Jews and by those using exclusively historical-critical criteria. The idea that Christians should interpret Israel's scriptures in particularly Christian ways—a perfectly legitimate claim—means that Christians, while respecting that the Tanakh is the Bible of the Jews and respecting their ways of interpreting it, will not be limited to the "historical" meaning of these texts but will take them as referring, in a Christian context and at least in part, to Christ and the life of the church in Christ.

19. Third Maccabees may have been written in the first century CE; 4 Maccabees could have been written in the first century CE; the writings that now make up 2 Esdras (5 Ezra; 4 Ezra; and 6 Ezra) were written from around 100 CE to the third century. I take these datings from the introductions to these books in *NOAB*.

20. My oblique reference here to "empiricism" is meant simply to signal that if one *observes* the actual ways most Christians use the New Testament compared with the Old Testament, the New has important status and function not equally manifested by Christian use of the Old Testament.

This statement is similar to my argument that Christians should not limit their interpretations to those approved by modern historical criticism or give priority to historical-critical interpretations. If Christians interpret the Hebrew Bible with purely historical-critical methods, they will not find Christ or the Christian God there, that is, a triune God. If Christians interpret the New Testament using only modern historical criticism (if they do it rigorously and properly, that is), they will not find orthodoxy there, an argument this entire book is attempting to make. For Christians to find Christian orthodox meanings in the Bible, we must read the Old Testament and the New Testament through Christ. Which means we may use modern historical criticism but will not allow those methods to *rule* our ultimate interpretations of scripture.

There are potential problems in the Christian retention of the Old Testament as well as that term for it. But the proposed alternatives have problems of their own, both from the point of view of secular scholarly accuracy and from Christian theology. The alternatives also have the drawback of being unnecessarily innovative and disconnected from Christian history and tradition. In the end, the recent worries about the "Old Testament" are one more example of the unavoidable impurity of language and the problems generated when people are motivated by an unrealistic desire for "pure" language. There is no such thing as purity in language. All terms are tainted. The way to avoid their misuse is through ethical diligence, not searching for some term that is pure or untainted.

The "Authority" of Scripture

The author of 2 Timothy famously says, "All scripture is inspired by God and useful for teaching, for refutation, for correction, for training in righteousness, in order that the person of God will be qualified, equipped for every good work" (3:16). The word here translated as "inspired by God" is θεόπνευστος, literally "God-breathed," as the word we often translate "spirit" (πνεῦμα) may also refer to breath, wind, and even more refined substances of the cosmos and the human body.[21] The author of 2 Timothy is clearly referring to Jewish scripture, though we don't know for sure what exactly counted as scripture for him at that time. The church has traditionally taken the text, eventually, to include in its reference also the documents of the New

---

21. More on this topic in the chapter titled "Spirit" below.

Testament. Thus the basic doctrine of the inspiration of scripture has never in itself been much of a controversial subject in the church.

Though that is the only place in the New Testament where we find the actual term θεόπνευστος, we do find a similar statement about scripture in 2 Pet 1:20–21. Here, the translation and interpretation of the passage may be debated, so I will quote it from the NRSV rather than supplying my own translation: "First of all you must understand this, that no prophecy of scripture is a matter of one's own interpretation, because no prophecy ever came by human will, but men and women moved by the holy spirit spoke from God."[22] Though the author is speaking particularly of "prophecies," he probably took this aspect of prophecy to be true for all scripture. New Testament authors, for instance, took the Psalms also to be "prophecy" and Moses to be a "prophet" (see, e.g., Matt 11:13; Acts 2:25–31; 7:37).

The meaning of the passage, however, may be debated. It may also be translated, less elegantly than in the NRSV, but still literally, "Knowing this first, that every prophecy of scripture is not [a matter] of private [ἰδίας] interpretation [ἐπίλυσις], for no prophecy was brought [ἠνέχθη, "was carried"] by the will of a human being, but being carried [the same Greek word in a different form: φερόμενοι] by the holy spirit, human beings spoke from God." As this translation implies, there are ambiguities. First, is the author talking about prophecies we find in scripture? Or is scripture itself the "prophet"? It seems that either is possible—or both.

Second, it is not clear whether the author is focusing merely on the means by which prophecy occurred, that is, God speaking through prophets by means of the holy spirit, though that seems certainly part of the message.[23] But he may also be speaking about how prophecies should be *interpreted*: that Christians should avoid "private interpretation" of scripture. After all, the word ἰδίας, which means "of one's own" or even "private," modifies "interpretation," sounding as if the author is urging that interpretation of scripture should not be left up to individuals but should be done in concert, certainly with God but also perhaps with the Christian community.

22. For "men and women" the Greek has ἄνθρωποι, "human beings" in grammatically masculine form, which the NRSV takes, no doubt correctly, to be gender inclusive. After all, the author knows there are female prophets in scripture also.

23. I am not sure the author is referring to what we would think of as the third person of the trinity (I'm fairly sure he is not, at least in actually the trinitarian sense) or simply to God's own spirit. For complications when to read the Greek to refer to "the" holy spirit or simply a form of *pneuma* that happens to be "holy," see the chapter "Spirit" below.

This was the position advocated by Ignatius, who may have been a contemporary of the author of 2 Peter (Ignatius's letters are dated around 110; 2 Peter was probably written in the first half of the second century). Ignatius has had disagreements with other Christians over interpretation of scripture. They insisted on their own, private interpretation. When Ignatius responded, "It is written," they answered, "That is just the question." The main strategy Ignatius uses to attempt unity, as he does through all seven of his letters, is to insist that no Christian should do anything "apart from the bishop" and if possible the presbyters. Neither baptism nor the eucharist nor even congregational gatherings are truly Christian if done without the bishop. Thus Ignatius attempts unity also when interpreting scripture by invoking the community of faith and especially the bishop as its head.[24]

To return to 2 Pet 1:20–21, if we go simply by the Greek, these two verses may be interpreted in different ways. But instead of doing the "normal" practice of most historical critics and assuming that we must choose which of these interpretations is the "correct" one, we may play with the multiplicity to bring out the multivalences of scripture. The prophecies of scripture—and all of scripture itself heard as a "prophet"—may have a human author, but the ultimate author is God, speaking through the holy spirit.[25] And rather than thinking that each of us is sufficient "on our own" to interpret scripture, we must do so in community, a community that includes the holy spirit and the other two persons of the trinity. This is what "inspiration of scripture" means.

The "inspiration" of scripture does *not* mean, however, what many modern Christians have taken it to mean. For many modern Christians, the inspiration of scripture has meant that the Bible is inerrant or infallible, even when read literally as a history book, a rule book, a source of scientific knowledge, or a blueprint for human action or church organization. The inspiration of scripture has been mistakenly taken in the modern world to slight or misuse critical theories about *the way* scripture *ought* to be interpreted. Thus people believed that one could read scripture as one would read a newspaper, literally and woodenly looking for information about history

---

24. See Ignatius, *Philadelphians* 7–8 *et passim* through the other letters.

25. Even if it is unlikely that the author of 2 Peter worked with a trinitarian understanding of the *person* of the holy spirit (he probably considered the "spirit" to be simply the *pneuma* of God, without the complications of actual trinitarian doctrine), we, as trinitarian Christians, may legitimately *interpret* the text as a reference, for us, of the role of the holy spirit in revelation and interpretation of scripture.

or nature, not to mention doctrine and ethics. That this sort of simplistic notion of scriptural interpretation is not really Christian interpretation may be
demonstrated, among other means, by noting how New Testament authors
and characters themselves, including Jesus, interpret scripture. If the very
New Testament authors do not interpret scripture in that way—and if Jesus
as depicted in the Gospels did not do so—why should modern Christians
think that the only legitimate way to interpret scripture is by some kind of
literal interpretation that can be defended by modern methods of "staying
true to the human author's intention"?

And examples are all over the Bible. When Jesus is asked by the Sadducees about the resurrection, an idea they rejected, he rebukes them by saying
they know "neither the scriptures nor the power of God" (Mark 12:18–27;
see also Matt 22:23–33; Luke 20:27–40). But Jesus's own answer can be found
nowhere in Jewish scripture read historically or literally: "When the dead
rise they will neither marry nor be married, but they will be as the angels in
heaven" (12:25). And then, the passage Jesus quotes to prove this teaching is
what God said to Moses at the burning bush: "I am the God of Abraham,
and the God of Isaac, and the God of Jacob" (Ex 3:6, 15, 16). On the face of it,
there would seem to be nothing about that quotation to do with the resurrection at all. So then Jesus adds, "God is not the God of the dead, but of the
living. You are much deceived."

Now, the Sadducees may have been "much deceived," but if judged by
modern standards of a "literal" reading of a text, they actually had a much
better case than Jesus did. In the first place, it is quite a stretch to take that
quotation from Exodus to say *anything* about the resurrection. And Jesus's
explanation would seem also to be at least problematic. After all, God *is*
the God of the dead as well as of the living. And the Sadducees apparently
did not accept more "recent" beliefs in the resurrection precisely because
such notions were *not* taught in the Torah and the prophets, unless one finds
them there through innovative interpretation.[26] So, *judged by modern standards of literal and historical interpretation,* the Sadducees were the better
interpreters of the text.

Jesus fares no better, by modern standards, that is, when arguing with
the Pharisees about divorce (Mark 10:1–12; see also Matt 19:1–12). Jesus first
asks the Pharisees (according to Mark's version) what Moses commanded.

---

26. Two passages that might be taken to refer to some kind of resurrection are Ezek
37:1–14 (the valley of the dry bones); and Dan 12:2–3, but both passages could be read as
referring to only a partial restoring of a people, not to the general resurrection of all dead.

Knowing their scriptures, they quote Deut 24:1 and 3, where "Moses" does indeed allow men to divorce their wives and marry another woman. What is forbidden is taking the wife back later if she has been with another man. This would seem to be an open-and-shut case of a scriptural "rule" about divorce and remarriage. But Jesus ignores that passage, which is actually about divorce, and insists that all divorce is forbidden (there is no "exception clause" in Mark, unlike Matthew) and that if a divorced man marries another woman or if any other man marries a divorced woman they have thereby committed adultery.[27]

The texts Jesus quotes to back up his own teaching are two from Genesis: "Male and female he made them" (Gen 1:27; 5:2); and "because of this, the man shall leave his father and mother and be joined together with his wife; the two shall be one flesh" (Gen 2:24). But neither of these texts is about divorce at all, again from a modern methodological point of view. One could argue that the passages are not even about *ethics* at all but are simply etiologies of marriage. Jesus here is breaking a cardinal rule of interpretation, one that was taught in the ancient world as well as the modern: interpret the more obscure passage by means of the clearer passage; do not use a passage whose interpretation is questionable to interpret a passage whose meaning seems clear.[28] The passage from Deuteronomy quoted by the Pharisees provides a fairly clear teaching about when divorce and remarriage are permitted according to Mosaic law. Jesus rejects that passage and instead quotes two that, on the face of it, say nothing at all about divorce. Jesus's methods of interpreting scripture do not match those that have been urged for many years by most modern, Western Christians.

Paul's interpretation of the Genesis stories of Sarah and Hagar in Gal 4:21–5:1 is another example of "biblical" interpretations of scripture that do not live up to "modern" standards. It is, in fact, an allegorical interpretation, not a literal one—and one that may well strike us as counterintuitive. Paul takes the two women to represent two "covenants," one of freedom and one of slavery. But whereas one would surely assume that Sarah was the mother of the Jews, and Hagar the mother of non-Jews, Paul reverses them. Hagar, representing slavery, corresponds to "the Jerusalem of now," that is, those who are not part of the faith community of Paul. And Sarah is "our mother,"

---

27. For an argument that even Matthew, in spite of his "exception clause," also has Jesus forbid divorce outright, see Martin, *Sex and the Single Savior*, 134–37.

28. See, for example, Augustine, *De doctrina christiana* 3.83 (26.37); Ferguson, *Biblical Hermeneutics*, 161.

that is, the mother of Paul and these uncircumcised gentiles. Those Jews who do not believe in Jesus have been deprived of their mother, Sarah.

Examples of biblical authors not "playing by the rules" of modern, literal interpretation of scripture are everywhere. Paul insists that the passage in Deut 25:4 forbidding people from muzzling an ox while it is threshing grain must not be interpreted as if God were concerned about oxen. Its meaning is that preachers should be supported by congregations (1 Cor 9:8–10). The entire Epistle to the Hebrews is one typological or allegorical interpretation of the Old Testament after another. Paul and the author of Hebrews may have believed that scripture was "inspired," but that did not mean they read it in what any modern person would consider a straightforward, simple, literal way as a source for anything we would recognize as history, science, or even ethical rules or doctrinal propositions. The way the authors of the New Testament treated their own scripture, and doubtless the way the historical Jesus did so, demonstrate that whatever they meant by the "inspiration" of scripture, it was nothing like what that has meant for fundamentalist or evangelical Christians in the modern world.

Thus, like every other proposition or confession, theological or otherwise, the claim that "scripture is infallible" is both true and false. It is false if taken to mean that the Bible, read just like an instruction manual, a history book, a biology textbook, or even a book of dogma and doctrine, will provide straightforward answers in propositions that correspond to reality. It is false if it is taken to mean that the narratives of Genesis provide a correct "history" of the beginnings of the universe and human beings. It is false if it is taken to mean that the accounts of Jesus's words and actions can be accepted as "what really happened" according to modern historiographical methods. It is false if it is taken to mean that Paul's statements about behavior should be followed by modern Christians the way we would follow Robert's Rules of Order or some "owner's manual" for our bodies and lives. In other words, the statement "scripture is infallible" is false if it is taken the way it has been by the great majority of modern Christians in the past two hundred years.

But like almost all the theological propositions or confessions addressed in this book, it is true if it is interpreted correctly. It is true if it means that Christians may justly trust that scripture, as long as it is read in faith by the leading of the holy spirit, will not lead us to fatal error. We may trust scripture to provide what we need for our salvation. We may trust that we can read scripture in prayerful hope that God will speak to us through our reading that text. But ultimately this belief—or, perhaps better put, this stance, attitude, or *habitus*—is actually an expression of our faith not in a text but in God and the holy spirit. We "leave it up to the holy spirit" to protect us from damnable error in our readings of scripture. We depend on God to keep us with God in our readings of scripture. Properly understood, the doctrine of the infallibility of scripture is a statement less about a text and more about God.

One of the traditional ways of talking about this sort of relationship—among us, the text, God, and the holy spirit in particular—has been to speak of the perspicuity of scripture. Scripture is said to be "perspicuous." This is not a claim that the text of scripture will never be puzzling to us, or that we may not experience frustration about interpreting the text, or the feeling that it may be hiding something from us. The doctrine of the perspicuity of scripture says that scripture is clear *enough* to provide us with salvation and correct doctrine. As Hans Frei put it, "The text is more nearly perspicuous than not. . . . For the Protestant Reformers, governance by the *sensus literalis* in the reading of Scripture as well as its perspicuity entailed that in principle there is no interpretive outsider. Calvin has it that our hearts and minds may need illumination, the text does not. It is plain for all to read."[29] But I reiterate that this is a doctrine we accept by faith; it is not strictly provable empirically, as can be seen in the fact that so many Christians, whether laypeople or fully trained scholars, "find" such different "meanings" in the same texts.

As with the "infallibility" and "perspicuity" of scripture, I believe there are dangers and possibilities also in the Protestant slogan *sola scriptura*. It may be confessed as long as it is taken as a statement of faith about the perspicuity and sufficiency of scripture. But it is dangerous and false if taken the way it has too often been done. "The Bible" has not been (this is an argument from the empiricism of Christian experience through the ages) and cannot be the only source of knowledge of God if that is taken to mean that we learn nothing of God from one another, from preaching, from tradition, or from the institution of the church—even "the church" empirically and historically understood. Christian experience teaches us that we learn about truth, God, and ourselves from many places and persons in our lives together.

If sola scriptura is taken to mean *our* "Bibles," the insistence on "scripture only" would cut us off from the earliest Christians, offending the doctrine of the communion of saints. Christians did not have "the Bible" in any sense we have it until a few centuries after the beginning of the church. Those Christians who lived in the first generations of Christianity, therefore,

---

29. Frei, *Theology and Narrative*, 108; see also DeHart, *Trial of Witnesses*, 203.

would have been living in a different theological-epistemological reality from ours if we insist that Christians get their knowledge of God only through "the Bible."

As I argued in the previous chapter on epistemology, the absolute rejection of any kind of "natural theology" is an exaggeration, and a dangerous one. We may well agree that "revelation" is necessary for sufficient knowledge of Christ, but we may also believe that God, in God's boundless mercy, has allowed some kind of "revelation" also in the objects and persons we encounter in the world even outside the church. As I demonstrated more fully in the previous chapter, this point of view seems to be a fair reading of much of the Bible, including the vast "Wisdom Literature" of the Old Testament, Paul's statements in Romans 1, and "Paul's" sermon in Acts 17. Sola scriptura is unacceptable if it denies the freedom of the holy spirit to bring knowledge of God to us from any possible source, including "nature," "reason," the church, and tradition.

Yet there are ways in which sola scriptura can indeed be taken as true. The slogan may be interpreted to mean that all possible true knowledge of God we get from any other source we will ultimately find in scripture if the text is properly interpreted. Sola scriptura may constitute the belief that scripture is the *princeps inter pares* of all possible sources of knowledge of God. It can be itself a stance of faith that scripture, *if properly interpreted,* contains as full a revelation of God as we human beings can tolerate or comprehend and that all other sources for knowledge of the divine must "take a back seat" in some way to scripture. Or, better put, we will confirm all true knowledge of God from wherever we initially received it if we interpret scripture rightly.

My continued insistence on the centrality and necessity of interpretation for all these formulations should be obvious. "Infallibility," "perspicuity," sola scriptura, all will be true when interpreted properly and false when interpreted wrongly. This is not a new suggestion. Indeed, it was precisely the position of those early Anglican divines who were attempting to navigate between the claims of authority by the pope and hierarchy of the Roman Catholic Church on the one hand and the claims for sola scriptura and the infallibility of scripture by more radical Reformers on the other. They ended up agreeing with the Reformers on the centrality of scripture, that people should read it in their own vernacular, that it should be the basis of preaching, and they were even willing to agree that scripture was infallible. But they also knew that scripture could be made to say anything and that certain ways of using the Bible were leading to radical individualism and the proliferation of sects. So they argued that scripture was indeed infallible but that all human *interpretation* was quite fallible. Scripture itself could be considered as infallible as long as no one claimed infallibility for his or her particular interpretation of scripture. These men weren't stupid. They knew what they were doing. By admitting the infallibility of scripture but the fallibility of human interpretation and realizing that there *are* no "meanings" of scripture available to human beings apart from those produced by human beings, the Anglican divines and theologians rendered infallibility an article of faith rather than a weapon that could be used by any one side to bludgeon the other side in a doctrinal dispute.[30]

The issue of the Bible as a weapon in human debates prompts consideration of talk about the "authority" of scripture. In my opinion the term has been entirely overused and abused in modern religious discourse. We can agree that scripture exercises a special "authority" in the church. We privilege these texts over others in liturgy and preaching. We look to the Bible to discern the voice of God in ways we do not look to any other text. And we may even venerate scripture in a way we do not even other texts we respect and honor.

But surely the dangers of language about "authority" should not be lost on any Christian of our world. Authoritarian posturing by abusive fathers, bishops, popes, dictators, and presidents are constant presences in our world. The submission of women to the authority of their husbands, fathers, pastors, priests, and popes is still constantly being enforced. Riot police are called out to kill, beat, and imprison their fellow citizens, all in the name of "maintaining order and authority." There is no way language about authority can be used without provoking overtones of hierarchy, inequality, patriarchy, and injustice, at least to those people attuned to injustice and yearning for equality and mutuality.

Again, to admit the other side of things, "hierarchies" are not all bad. Hierarchies are in fact necessary in order for our societies and even our computer systems to work. We arrange our forms of knowledge in hierarchies, without implying by that any violence or injustice. So the *word* "authority," like "hierarchy," does not carry within itself its injustices. But images of the "authority" of scripture, of "submitting" to scripture, even of "obeying" scripture—at least in our societies and for people attuned to inequality and

---

30. See Greer, *Anglican Approaches,* especially the quotation from John Locke at 78: "Scripture," said Locke, may be "infallible," but "the reader may be, nay cannot choose but to be, very fallible in the understanding of it."

hoping for a more just and egalitarian society—all such language is dangerous and potentially harmful.

For those reasons I tend to avoid using language about the "authority of scripture." That language also does not correctly reflect my own experiences of scripture or those I discern among the fellow believers of my
church. I believe in nurturing better images of what scripture is and how it is
important for us, how we listen to it and respect it. For me, scripture is better
imagined as the context in which we live our Christian lives. Scripture is the
environment for the church. Scripture is the space we inhabit, the sanctuary
where we meet God and Jesus by the guidance of the holy spirit. Scripture is
not something "over" us bearing down on us or ordering us around. It is the
air we breathe, the water we Christian fish swim in. If we nurture more adequate, helpful, theologically defensible notions and images of "what scripture is," we can dispense quite safely with the problematic, dangerous, potentially violent and abusive—but unfortunately almost ubiquitous—metaphor
of scripture as our authority.

Another problem with speaking of scripture as authority is that it may
personify scripture in ways that are theologically problematic. It is quite true
that biblical writers themselves speak in ways that personify scripture. In
John, the scripture "speaks" (7:42; 19:37). In Acts, it "foretold" (1:16). Paul
especially personifies scripture. Paul regularly depicts scripture (ἡ γραφή;
"the writing") as "saying" something (Rom 4:3; 10:11; 11:2; see also 1 Tim 5:18).
It was even scripture, rather than God or Moses, who spoke to Pharaoh in
Ex 9:16 (Rom 9:17). But Paul goes even further in his personification of scripture. Scripture "foreknew" (προϊδοῦσα) that God would justify the gentiles
from faith (Gal 3:8). Scripture is even the agent who "imprisoned together
[συνέκλεισεν] everything under sin" (Gal 3:22).

It may be that Paul even thought of "Scripture" as an actual cosmic
agent or person, something like an angel, as Jews seem to have done sometimes for "Wisdom." It is a live debate among scholars, after all, whether Paul
used the terms "Sin" or "Death" to refer to actual beings and agents in the
cosmos—he *does* attribute actions and intentions to them—though some
scholars insist this is mere personification of abstract entities.[31] I would argue that at least in his use of the terms "principalities and powers" Paul was
probably referring *both* to abstractions *as well as* to evil angelic beings *and*
to the Roman rulers. There is no way, by means of historical criticism, to
establish firmly one way or another what was going on in Paul's own mind.

---

31. I discuss the various possibilities in the chapter "Human" below.

But certainly Paul was capable of resorting to lively personification, and he repeatedly did so with "scripture," speaking of it as of a person.

The dangers of doing so for modern Christians, though, are evident. For one thing, it has risked "bible-olatry" for many Christians (as mentioned above), who revere the Bible to the extent that they speak of it as one would a person of the trinity. Some Christians venerate the Bible so much that they believe it to be a sin, for example, to deface one or put one in the trash, believing that one must dispose of a Bible only by a respectful and ritual burning—as if the Bible were supposed to be treated like the American flag, with all the exaggerated, sacrosanct, indeed, idolatrous honor given to that object of American religious devotion. On the contrary, Christians must not worship the Bible or give it anywhere near the kind of respect with which we approach God the Father, Jesus, or the holy spirit. Scripture may be venerated as the prime means used by the holy spirit to teach us about God and our world. It must not be taken as an actual agent whom we worship.

Another problem in speaking of scripture as an agent is that people are again lulled into actually believing the (false) myth that the Bible speaks, and our job is merely to listen. Indeed, the people who talk most about the Bible "speaking" are often those most guilty of ignoring or masking their own agency in biblical interpretation. The Bible becomes the speaking "agent" who is supposed to supply its own meaning or control people's interpretation of itself. But in our postmodern environment, in which we must be diligent to our own and others' likely ideological misuse of scripture, we cannot allow the personification of scripture to lead to the masking of human interpretive practices that are the actual agents that produce those "meanings" of the Bible so many people point to in their attempts to oppress other people. In spite of the fact that Paul and other writers in the New Testament talk about scripture speaking and perhaps even assuming that scripture is an actual being of the cosmos, we Christians of today must be wary of attributing agency to the text itself. We must not avoid acknowledging our own responsibility as very human and therefore fallible interpreters of scripture.

Christians may indeed express their "faith in scripture" if that is meant to signal the proper Christian respect for this text over others, but we should be wary of such language and attitudes. Properly speaking, we have faith in God the Father, Jesus Christ, and the holy spirit. We do not trust scripture to save us. We trust God to save us through Christ's activities, the knowledge of which is mediated to us by the holy spirit using scripture as the main, though not the only, medium. Any other "faith in scripture" risks an idolatry of the text.

Proper Interpretation: Where Is "Meaning"?

As is no doubt already clear, one of the fundamental principles of this book is the observation that the "meaning" of a text is not some property inherent in the text itself but is generated by the interpretive activities of readers. Texts do not "mean"; people "mean" with texts. This is not a proposal for how people *ought* to interpret texts. This is not a suggestion for an interpretive agenda. It is first and foremost an empirical observation of how human beings actually do read texts and "get meaning" from them. This is also not meant as any kind of foundationalist claim for empiricism as a philosophical position. I am not suggesting that we can arrive at "true" knowledge simply by "observing" our world. Observation is just as fallible as any other human activity. The claim, instead, is a rather low-level one: if we pay attention to how we and others read texts and interpret them, we can see, even through everyday examples, that the texts themselves don't control or constrain our interpretations of them. Texts do not in fact speak to us or impart their contents. We have to read them, and our reading of them is a product of our human agency and activity. Readers make meaning when they read texts. The texts—in the most literal sense of that word, that is, as physical objects displaying letters and words—are inanimate objects that have no power to compel or constrain interpretations of themselves.[32]

I have defended this observation many times, mostly by providing examples of how human beings, in many different contexts, actually use language and derive meaning from linguistic events, including jokes, spoken mistakes, general texts, and the Bible.[33] I will not repeat those arguments and examples here. But because it seems common sense to so many people that meaning must reside in the text itself or, even more common, that the meaning of a text is equivalent to the intentions of the author, I will provide one more example to demonstrate that, in our everyday uses of texts, we actually do *not* equate the meaning of a text with authorial intention, even if

---

32. Miroslav Volf objects to my and others' more radical "reader's response" theory of texts and "meaning," my insistence, for example, that "texts" really are just inanimate and meaningless "things" until interpreted by someone. Volf insists that "texts" are not "mere things" but are "social relations" among different persons. *Captive,* 28–32. I answer with what I take to be a supremely simple empirical observation: a text hiding away in the bowels of a library for decades or centuries is obviously *not* a "social relation." Texts (the actual physical objects) cannot have anything to do with "social relations" until some actual human being reads and uses them. Volf wrongly anthropomorphizes physical objects such as books and texts.

33. See in particular Martin, *Sex and the Single Savior,* esp. 1–35; *Pedagogy,* 29–45.

we sometimes assume that we do. Remember that this example is meant as an empirical description of how we read texts to arrive at meanings and that it demonstrates that the meaning of a text is not the same thing, even in our regular usage, as the author's intentions.

Let's say Mr. Smith and I need a contract so he can lend me money in exchange for my writing up and filing his tax return. I agree to the general principles and allow Smith to draw up a contract we both sign. The contract looks like this:

1. I, Smith, hereby lend you, Martin, $500.
2. If you, Martin, provide me, Smith, the service of filing my taxes, you need not repay the loan.
3. If you, Martin, do not provide said service, I, Smith, will not expect to get back the amount lent.

If we imagine "meaning" as something that "resides" in a "location" (a conception of "meaning" I would eventually dispute), where does the meaning of the language of this text reside?

It is certainly not simply in "the text itself" apart from some interpretation of it. Before these spots on a page can have any meaning, one must be able to read them. One must know English, the common meanings of these English words, which one had to learn through socialization, and how to read, which one had to learn through much socialization, for most of us in school. More than that, one probably must know something about the genre of contracts, again, a knowledge that is socially mediated and learned. So understanding this text cannot be a matter of simply "listening" to the text, as if the text could speak out loud so that a child who could speak and understand English but who could not read would be able to understand it. No, one must be able to accomplish all the complicated skills, learned through socialization, necessary for interpreting the text. One must *interpret*. The "one" here is the reader, who is therefore the one rendering the "meaning" though obviously constrained to some extent by socialization and context.

But the "meaning" is also not in the "intention of the author," at least not in any empirical sense of that term. This is demonstrated if I, having received this written contract from Smith, realize that he probably just made a mistake, perhaps even an unconscious typographical error. Read literally, that is, using the normal, everyday methods of reading one would normally use for reading contracts rather than, say, poems, Smith is cheating himself: I don't have to pay him back if I file his taxes; but according to a "normal" reading of the last sentence, I also will not have to pay him back even if I do *not* file his taxes.

Let's say I am an honest person (for the sake of argument) working with Smith's interests as well as my own in mind. I may go to Smith and say, "You made a mistake. The last sentence doesn't say what you *meant to say*." Smith looks the text over again, or reads it, which is to say, interprets it again. He notices that he meant to write "I will expect" rather than "I will not expect." He thinks, "Perhaps I got confused by the presence of so many negatives." He says, "You're right: the text does not *say* what I *meant*." So he changes the text to read, "I will expect to get back the amount lent." Now, one could just then insist that this proves that we use authorial intention to settle the meanings of texts, and that may be correct: we often use *our constructions of what we think must be the author's intention* when we interpret texts. But that does not at all prove that *the meaning of the text* is equivalent to *the author's intention.* This is proved by the very fact that I, as a reader, noticed that what the text "said" (that is, how a contract normally would be read) was not what Smith probably *intended* to say.

The problems with authorial intentions as providing the meaning of the text can be illustrated with further thinking about my contract with Smith. Let's imagine that Smith is actually a rather sly person, and he has a soft spot in his heart for me, knowing I'm going through some financial difficulties. Once I point out to him his "mistake" in the contract, he shrugs and says, "Just sign it and let's be done with it." He has *intentionally* written the contract so that legally I will never have to repay him. And he has done so because he does not want me to have to repay him. This could be a way to give me the money outright but make it seem like a loan.

This turn in our thought experiment is just to illustrate that Smith's intention may be one or the other. We have no way of *truly* knowing his intention unless we ask him, and even then he could lie to us or be mistaken himself. We have no way of knowing, by reading the text, whether Smith *intended* to write, "I will not expect" because he wanted to make the loan a grant or whether he intended to write "I will expect" and just made a mistake. Either way, the illustration demonstrates that the meaning of the text is not the same thing as the intentions of the author. The "normal" meaning of the text, in "normal" situations, is the likely interpretation of the text by competent speakers of the language using "normal" practices of textual interpretation. The meaning of the text is created in its interpretation.

Some people seem to feel that a firm "reader response" explanation of the reading of texts and the "location" of their meaning in the reading activity offensively exalts the human reader above the authors of the text and the text itself. It seems to fly in the face of those Christians who want to claim themselves "to stand under the text of scripture rather than over it." It seems arrogant.[34] "How can this person be so arrogant, to think he has the right and power to 'make' the text mean something?" To argue that readers create meaning when they interpret texts and that texts can themselves have no actual agency in the production or control of meaning appears to many people to be not only counterintuitive but even hubristic.

I argue that the situation is just the opposite. To admit that we make meaning when we read texts is an admission that we never do merely "see" things innocently and without interpretive agency. It is to admit our own activity and responsibility for what we "see" in texts. In fact, the actual position of arrogance belongs to those who believe that what they "see" in the text is simply what is objectively "there" after all and that if others do not take the text to "say" what they believe it says, those others are simply disingenuous or deluded. Those persons who think they are passively "hearing" the text or its message, believing that they "refuse" to push their own beliefs "onto" the text, are actually by that stance taking a more hegemonic epistemological position. They are attempting to mask their own interpretive agency—often even from themselves in a practice of self-deception—by insisting that the interpretation of the text they are advocating is not their own but comes from the "authoritative" agent of the text itself. That is the position of self-delusion and arrogance. It is much more humble to admit that we human beings are constantly seeing the world in our own ways, reading texts through our own eyes, and generating meanings by our practices of reading and interpretation. The explanation of reading and textuality provided by reader response theories is better supported by actual observations of how human beings read texts, and it provides a less authoritative, less hegemonic account of our interpretations of texts.

Proper Interpretation: What Is Scripture "About"?

In order to analyze better and worse ways of interpreting scripture, we need to return to the issue of "what scripture is" or, to put it a bit differently now, "what is scripture about?" Earlier in the chapter I argued that we should

---

34. Miroslav Volf succumbs to this misunderstanding, following Terry Eagleton: Volf, *Captive*, 28–29. See Eagleton, *Meaning*, 116: "troublingly narcissistic." I insist, on the contrary, that being blind to one's own necessary interpretive activities—not just "listening to the text"—is where narcissism resides.

not confuse the theological category of scripture with any particular, physical "text," whether imagined original manuscripts, editions of the Greek, or any particular versions, or with the categories of "canon" or "gospel." Those are all important and valuable theological terms, but none of them is the same thing as "scripture." The related question "what is scripture about?" also stimulates theological reflection and important distinctions.

Reading most modern biblical scholarship, one may come away with the impression that scholars study scripture with the goal of finding something "behind" or "beyond" the text of scripture itself that provides the "subject matter" of scripture. Christians regularly ask what scripture says "about" different issues, such as politics, sexuality, or any number of other ethical topics. Theologians sometimes seem to be mining scripture to see what it says "about" some particular doctrinal topic: creation, the trinity, the deity of Christ, salvation or justification, or the end of the world.

A case in point is the rhetoric used by James Dunn in his *New Testament Theology: An Introduction.* Several times Dunn insists that any scholar or any New Testament theology "must" do something or other in order properly to read the New Testament theologically. New Testament theologies must take into account that the Jewish scriptures we take as the Old Testament were still in a state of flux when our New Testament writers used them (20–24). Dunn insists that we should experience the various texts that later came to make up our Old Testament, along with others that did not but were known to our New Testament authors, *the way they experienced them.* But why is that a Christian theological interpretation of scripture? It seems to me to be using the New Testament as a source for historical narrative about canonical development. Dunn also insists that the New Testament texts be understood *in their own historical contexts* rather than being read through the lens of later orthodoxy (see, e.g., 5–6). Though without getting explicit Dunn is insisting that the historical critical method is therefore not only indispensable to theological interpretation of the Bible but also foundational to it. Dunn insists, as any good historical critic would, that New Testament theology *must* take into account the wide diversity of theologies represented by the different books and authors of the New Testament. That may well be true as a point of history, and it may even be good advice for theology, but Dunn gives no *theological* reasons for observing that diversity: he just insists that since that historical point is valid, it must also rule a theological reading of New Testament scripture. But isn't that, again, doing "history" rather than "theology"? Dunn argues that New Testament theologians must take into account the historical Jesus and pre-Easter "traditions" that derive from faith and beliefs of and about Jesus even while he was still alive (26–32). I will argue below, in the chapter titled "Christ," that although we *may* pay attention to modern constructions of the historical Jesus (for that is all they are: constructions), Christian theology *need not* do so because Christian theology is about interpreting *scripture* theologically, not about looking to the text as a "window" into "history."[35]

In other words, *why* "must" a reader "play by the rules" Dunn here lays out? What, in the end, is the reader "after"? What is the Christian reader of the New Testament looking *for* behind or beyond the immediate text of the New Testament? The answer in the case of Dunn's analysis seems to be that the text of the New Testament is the starting point for the search for scripture's subject matter, which seems to be located in the ancient author's intentions, or in the history one can construct using the text as a resource, or in the ancient practices and beliefs of the early church. The text of the New Testament is here important for Dunn's project because it provides the source or resource for some other thing outside or behind or beyond the text that is supposed to provide the subject matter of the text. Scripture is here important not for what it "says" on its surface or in that it provides an environment for theological reflection and imagination, but because somehow scripture "points to" or "refers to" some "truth" that exists apart from the mere reading of the text itself.

I believe a better theology of scripture can be had by insisting on the nonreferentiality of scripture. We may indeed look to the text of the New Testament as a historical resource for our own construction of the history of early Christianity, the historical Jesus, or aspects of ancient society and culture. We may with good reason read the New Testament in an attempt to construct the possible intentions of the human authors of its different texts. We may use source and redaction criticism and even textual criticism to "mine" the New Testament to trace its literary and textual history. All these are fine scholarly endeavors. But I argue that they are not the first or ultimate goal of Christian theological reading of scripture. Rather, once we see scripture not as a way station on the way to some other "truth" but as the site of Christian life, thought, and worship, we will come to see that the "subject matter" of scripture is not some proposition of doctrine or ethics or some

35. Dunn, *New Testament Theology.* I choose Dunn as an example here not because he is a particularly egregious example of "historicism" from modern biblical scholarship but because he is a well-respected New Testament scholar known to advocate balanced views of both biblical scholarship as well as theology. He is a distinguished scholar who just happens to provide here an example of a practice that is pervasive in the discipline.

historical account of the beginnings of Christianity. Rather, the subject matter of scripture is scripture itself.

Admittedly, we will as Christians say that scripture is "about" God, Christ, the holy spirit, the gospel, even the world and ourselves. But this is true not in the sense that we search scripture merely to find some kind of propositional answer to our questions about those as subjects for speculation or "knowledge." We may indeed believe that scripture is about God, for example, without making the mistake of believing that the meaning of scripture is to propose some kind of philosophical or theological proposal about the precise nature of God—that the meaning of scripture, for example, is to affirm the doctrinal statement that "God is father." Scripture is "about" God, but it is not to be taken to be a book of theological propositions that may be accepted as true or rejected as false. Rather, we should think of scripture as the environment in which we live and through which the holy spirit leads us to knowledge of the reality of God and Jesus Christ. We should not look to scripture just to see what it says about history or merely to provide some straightforward answer to a question about doctrine or ethics. We should look to scripture to provide the context for our life with God.

We may take some lessons from noting how New Testament authors themselves read scripture. Above, I commented on how Paul and some other authors of the New Testament take scripture to be an agent who "speaks," among other activities. In the previous context, I was concerned to point to potential problems in ascribing agency to scripture, since it may lead to the masking of the agency of human interpreters of scripture. Here, on the other hand, I wish to point to their language to show how they cite scripture simply "on its surface," as it were, without thinking that they must go "behind" it to some history to which it points or to some authorial intention by which it asserts its authority. To cite only one example from the many possible, when Paul says in Rom 4:3, "So what does scripture say?" he feels no need to establish that the author of Genesis was any certain person or that the author *meant* to make a point about works, faith, and justification when he wrote, "Abraham believed God, and it was counted toward him as justification" (Gen 15:6). The simple surface level of the Genesis text—not the history lying behind Genesis or the author's intention—supplies the information needed. And Paul *may* have believed himself that the text was really supposed to be "about" circumcision, but from our distance we must admit that *if* that was Paul's conviction, he doesn't seem to have been correct. We need not affirm, that is, that Gen 15:6 was, in its historical context or even, as we would understand it, its "literary" context, "about" circumcision in order to accept Paul's interpretation of the scripture. Paul sees the gospel message in the text of scripture without feeling the need to go someplace outside scripture to prove that his reading is actually "the meaning" of the text. This is a practice from which we may learn: we read scripture for the meanings that reading generates in faith, not to find some kind of information to which scripture points.

So scripture, for Christians, is not about the history lying behind the text, though it is perfectly acceptable to use the texts of the New Testament to construct such a historical account. Scripture is not about the intentions of the human author, though we may, again, legitimately guess what those may have been. Scripture, for Christians, is not about the ancient meaning of these texts, as if once we settle on how ancient readers likely would have understood these texts, we have "the meaning" of the texts. And, in spite of the implications of some of those theologians writing in the past few decades about narrative theology, we should not look to scripture simply to discern some kind of narrative or "narrative shape" contained in, pointed to, or supplied by scripture. We may indeed, with good cause, read scripture or even the entire Bible to derive from it a "narrative" of the "acts of God" or whatever other subject matter we assign to that narrative. But the central purpose of scripture is not to convey a narrative. Or, put differently, we should not read scripture to find a narrative that gives meaning to scripture; rather, we read scripture to find the meaning of the narrative—if, that is, we are using a narrative as a heuristic tool for theologizing, which, in my opinion, we need not always do. At any rate, the narrative does not provide the meaning of scripture; our reading of scripture provides the meaning of any possible Christian narrative. Scripture is not about a narrative. Scripture is about itself. We don't read scripture looking for something else to supply its meaning. We read scripture to experience meaning itself.

Interpreting the Bible in the Bible

As I have indicated, we can learn a lot from paying careful attention to how New Testament authors themselves interpreted scripture. Since their interpretive practices are not at all beholden to modern historical criticism, we may try to imagine ourselves out of the "monology" of the modern historical method, which limits readers in what may be considered "proper" readings of the texts. It is not that we *must* interpret scripture as the ancient authors did, only that we may use their interpretations to spark our postmodern interpretive imagination.

Take, for example, a text I have already mentioned: the interpretation of Gen 15:6 by Paul, on the one hand, and James, on the other. In its "original context," though what that would mean is itself highly debatable and speculative, the statement is already ambiguous in the Hebrew.[36] According to the NRSV, it reads, "And he believed the Lord; and the Lord reckoned it to him as righteousness" (Gen 15:6). But the second "Lord" is actually not in the Hebrew, which has simply "he." Scholars have thus pointed out that the subject of the clause may be Abraham: on the basis of God's sign to Abraham in the stars and God's promise, Abraham reckoned trustworthiness to God. Abraham decided at that point that *God* was "righteous," that is, trustworthy.[37] But the text may also be interpreted that God took Abraham's belief in God as indicating Abraham's trustworthiness. Either interpretation—or both—is possible. In fact, the more capacious interpretation may be that through their dialogue and stargazing together in the night, God and Abraham nurtured a relationship of mutual trust and faithfulness.

Paul takes the text in a very different direction, and in two different letters. For Paul, the passage is a proof-text that true faith, faith after the model of Abraham, has always been faith that does not depend on works of the Law. Abraham, Paul insists, was not yet circumcised when God "reckoned righteousness" to him. Thus the righteousness was dependent not on circumcision but simply on faith. And Paul interprets circumcision here to stand for the entire Law. Whether Paul intended "works" here to refer to all human endeavors, as was the interpretation of Luther, or merely in this context and Galatians to refer to works of Torah is debatable. But in Paul's exegesis, Abraham is a type for all believers: all believers, including all the "nations," that is, the gentiles, are justified by faith, not by works of the Law/law, so gentiles, as children of Abraham through faith, need not obey the Law.

In Gal 3:6, written, I believe, before Romans and representing a bit more "radical" sounding Paul than Romans, Paul brings other texts from

---

36. What precisely would count as the "original context" of Gen 15:6 is unclear. Would it be the "final" redacted version of the Torah—at whatever date we imagine that to have taken place? Or do we imagine that the book of Genesis circulated prior to its incorporation into the Pentateuch? Or do we take the "original context" to be some Ur-text or tradition containing stories about Abraham the patriarch? "Original context" is always an uncertain and imagined thing but even more so for ancient texts and even more so still for especially ancient parts of the Hebrew Bible. "Original context," therefore, is an imagined, constructed mental phenomenon made for heuristic interpretive purposes.

37. David M. Carr offers this interpretation in his annotations at the bottom of the page in the *NOAB*.

Genesis into the account and expands his treatment to make the more radical point that anyone who attempts to rely on works of law is "cursed" (3:10). Here, Christ, which includes Abraham and the Galatian believers, is opposed to "the curse of the law" (3:13). From Romans one would get the impression that it was simply not necessary for gentiles to observe Jewish law. In Galatians, though, Paul had made the more radical argument that the Galatians who even *attempt* to keep the law will by that action find themselves "cut off from Christ" (5:2–4). If the Galatians allow themselves to be circumcised, they will end up themselves as the severed foreskin of the Lord, cut off from his body. It is no wonder that Paul, in Romans, probably had to back off these more radical statements he had made to the Galatians. It is also a powerful, though strange, way to read Genesis.

As is well known, James takes exactly the same text to have almost the opposite meaning. James quotes Gen 15:6 after citing the willingness of Abraham to sacrifice Isaac (James 2:21–24). Like a good modern exegete, James insists on putting the text in its broader literary context. He notes first that Abraham *did* righteous works of obedience to God. It is only then that he says, "Abraham believed God, and it was reckoned to him as righteousness." Why should someone like Paul take that statement completely out of the context of Genesis, which goes out of its way to portray the righteous *actions* of Abraham and his radical *obedience* to God? For James, it is only in the fuller context of the Genesis stories of Abraham that his faith can be seen correctly. His faith "was brought to completion by the works" (2:22, NRSV). The conclusion: "You see that a person is justified from works and not from faith alone" (2:24), and "faith without works is dead" (2:26).

Modern scholars are certainly right in pointing out that the "disagreement" here between "James" and "Paul"—for we are dealing with characters literarily created by the author of the Letter of James, not with the historical James or Paul—seems not really to fit right. The author of James seems to be setting up an opponent who on the surface looks a bit like Paul but doesn't actually match Paul's own position. To Paul, faith was never simply mental assent to the existence of God. James thinks he can dismiss his "opponent's" position by pointing out that "even demons believe" in the existence of "the one God" (2:19), yet demons are certainly not righteous or justified. Paul took faith to be a much more robust concept: it was the willingness to throw one's lot completely in with God as manifest in Jesus Christ; it was not belief "that" God exists, but faith "in" God to justify and save. Faith, for Paul, as is widely recognized and acknowledged, was the giving up of oneself to God and entrance into the body of Christ through trust and baptism. The demons could never have that kind of faith. So what James means by "faith" is simply not what Paul means by the same word.

Moreover, what James means by "works" is probably not what Paul meant. As I have mentioned, some scholars take Paul to use "works" to refer to "works of the [Jewish] law," not to any behavior whatsoever. One may also take "works" in Paul to refer to any human action undertaken in an attempt to "earn" one's salvation. But Paul never would have suggested that believers had no ethical or moral responsibilities. He may indeed have balked at saying that any "good deeds" could be considered works that would in any way earn God's approval. But he certainly was not advocating, as James seems to imply, that followers of Jesus could lead immoral lives with impunity. Many scholars, therefore, noting the quite different things *meant* by "works" and "faith" in Paul and James, downplay any difference and insist that there was no actual disagreement.

That, however, goes too far in attempting to smooth over differences among early Christian sources. Whether or not "James" was actually targeting Paul (recall that James the Lord's brother was certainly not the actual author of the letter; it is pseudonymous and written much later than the life of James the son of Joseph and brother of Jesus), he is probably targeting some kind of "Paulinism" known to him within the early Christian movement. I believe that the author *did think* he was writing a corrective to Paul's own letters and their influence in early Christian communities. At any rate, we have the fascinating opportunity to observe two New Testament writers interpreting the same passage of scripture to opposite ends. Even in the New Testament itself scriptures can be taken to mean very different things, even opposite things.

Another remarkable interpretive strategy of New Testament authors is the way they read Jewish scriptures to be ultimately not concerned with the original author or the ancient past but to refer directly to their own time, to Jesus and the early community of faith. Scripture is constantly being "fulfilled" in their present. Matthew's Gospel provides one of the thickest examples of "fulfillment" meanings of scripture. The virginal conception of Jesus was a fulfillment of Isaiah's prediction (in the Greek version) that a virgin would soon bear a son (Matt 1:23; Isa 7:14). The birth in Bethlehem (Matt 2: 5–6) fulfills Mic 5:2. The holy family's flight to Egypt (Matt 2:15) fulfills Hosea 11:1. The slaughter of the infants (Matt 2:16–18) fulfills Jeremiah 31:15. The family's move to Nazareth fulfills some scripture either known to Matthew but not to us or imagined by him (Matt 2:23). And we've come only to the end of the second chapter of the Gospel.

There are other cases in which an author claims a fulfillment of scripture when we cannot find a passage in our Bibles that corresponds to the "prophecy." One of the most famous I've already mentioned: Paul's claim that Jesus was raised from the dead "in accordance with the scriptures" (1 Cor 15:4). The sense among the New Testament authors that they were living out the scriptures is so prevalent that we have become overly accustomed to it and don't always notice just how remarkable it is. It is not that Matthew denies that the texts he cites had something to do with Moses or Isaiah or Jeremiah in the past. But it is clear that the more important referent of the text is to the history of Jesus and his church not to the ancient context. The ultimate reference is to "us" and "our time."

We sometimes do not notice, because of our familiarity with the theme, that this prophecy and fulfillment interpretation causes scripture to live through time. Scripture is not anchored somewhere in the past. Its true meaning for the early disciples is not to be found in the distant past but in the recent past of Jesus and the current present of the church. Scripture in this way travels through time, knotting the church and its experiences with the long story of Israel and the God of Israel also portrayed in the texts. Scripture connects Moses and ancient Israel to Jesus and the disciples of Matthew's church. Even the command by Moses to avoid muzzling the ox was not meant for ancient oxen but as a lesson on how "we" should treat "our" apostles (1 Cor 9:8–11). Or as Paul elsewhere says, "Whatever is prewritten was written for *our* instruction" (Rom 15:4; my emphasis). By interpreting the ancient text through the sieve of all time that has passed since its first writing up to our time and insisting that scripture is directed first and foremost to our own time and experience, the biblical authors unite themselves with the past conveyed through the scripture. Scripture travels through time. Scripture ties the community through time, making the people of faith and their beliefs transhistorical.

This is the reason writers in the New Testament need not refer to "tradition" as an epistemological source separable from the text of scripture. These writers are certainly capable of using language evoking the passing of knowledge through what we call tradition. Paul uses such language when he cites a list of witnesses of the resurrection, a list he no doubt learned from disciples before him and which he passed along, in turn, to the Corinthians (1 Cor 15:1). He uses the language of oral tradition when he says that he "handed on" to the Corinthians the words of institution of the Lord's Supper, which he claims to have "received from the Lord" (1 Cor 11:23). Sometimes, as he seems to be doing here, Paul exaggerates his independence from other disciples before him, nowhere more than in Galatians, where he insists that he learned practically nothing from the apostles preceding him (Gal 1:12). We can tell these are exaggerations because Paul's language does sometimes betray the process of tradition, and his formulations of sayings of "the Lord" closely resemble similar sayings we find in the Gospels. Besides the example of the institution of the Lord's Supper, which has much in common with the same event as narrated in the Synoptic Gospels, Paul's citation of Jesus's teaching on divorce sounds much like what we see in the Gospels (1 Cor 7:10). Paul cannot be quoting the Gospels since they had not yet been written, and contrary to some minority opinion there is no good reason to think the Gospel writers are getting their versions from Paul. Again, in spite of Paul's exaggerations to the contrary, he obviously did learn much from the oral traditions about Jesus passed along in the earliest communities, and he in turn passes along those traditions to his followers.

But even though New Testament writers actually do *use* traditions and pass them along, they never feel the need to appeal to tradition as a particular "source" of knowledge or teaching existing somehow apart from or alongside scripture. And I suggest the reason they do not is because their interpretive methods *make scripture present* for themselves. They *interpret* scripture so that it *incorporates* the developments through history we would call tradition. Thus Matthew need not say that the text *originally* referred to Moses but now, *because of the later teachings and discoveries of the church,* it refers to Jesus and his own community. He does not posit first scripture as an authority which is then supplemented by tradition, as developments made by the faith that may build upon but are different from scripture. Scripture itself moves through time and therefore *embodies* subsequent developments. The way scripture is interpreted renders any appeal to tradition unnecessary.

And I urge that we may move beyond the modernism of the previous centuries, when it was felt imperative to speak about scripture as one epistemological source of divine knowledge, but whose meaning had to be first located in the past, and "tradition" as an other, perhaps secondary or supplemental epistemological source. In a postmodern church we don't really need a category of "tradition" separate from scripture as long as scripture is interpreted to reflect the sedimentation of Christian experience of the past. We interpret scripture in the context of the church, including the church as it has lived for the past two thousand years. We interpret scripture *through* our experiences as members of the body of Christ, including members of that body now long dead. Therefore, what we may have called tradition is not separable from our interpretations of scripture but is part of it. What Christians have often called tradition should be understood simply as the combined experiences of the church, and we should interpret scripture within the context of those experiences, just as we interpret scripture within our current contexts. Tradition as a separable epistemological source is unnecessary—indeed, it is not even comprehensible—once we learn how contextually rich our own interpretive practices can be—or rather *should* be. If we see scripture and ourselves as closely united to the church and its long history, we will find less need for tradition as an epistemological source separate from the interpretation of scripture.

This is therefore one of the useful things we may learn from observing how Jesus and the authors of the New Testament themselves interpret scripture: scripture relates to us, not only or even primarily to its original historical location or its human author. Scripture is *ours*. Scripture is about us. We don't even need to divide our interpretive practices into two different events or stages. We don't need first to ascertain "what it meant" and only then build upon that knowledge to say "what it means."[38] Scripture, if we follow the examples of the New Testament writers themselves, is *on its surface, all the time, already about us*. Scripture speaks directly to us, given that we interpreted it correctly and by the leading of the holy spirit. We have also seen that we may use scripture to correct scripture. Jesus and Paul countered some readings of scripture by citation of other scripture. We should feel no modernist twangs of guilt if we also do so.

Some scholars have argued we do not have the right to interpret scripture the way Jesus, Paul, and other New Testament authors do.[39] That objection seems perverse to me. We expect ourselves to use Jesus and the apostles as models for imitation in many things. The "imitation of Christ" (*imitatio Christi*) is a difficult goal, one posing dangers in our knowing precisely what we *should* attempt to imitate of Jesus's life and what not. I see nothing valuable, for instance, in self-flagellation in an attempt to imitate the sufferings of Jesus, but then I am a Protestant and perhaps cannot understand a certain kind of Roman Catholic piety that prompts at least some believers to inflict pain on themselves. We certainly may not imitate Christ in his claim to be equal to God, and we may not imitate his soteriological activity by claiming that it is completely within our power to save other human beings. But saying that we may not imitate the interpretive methods of Jesus or early

---

38. See the discussion in the introduction above.

39. See discussion of the issue, along with reference to scholars making such an argument and his own refutation of it, in Hayes, *Echoes*, 178–92.

Christians seems to me an exaggeration of the difference between us and them. I believe, rather, that their premodernist interpretive practices and habits can helpfully inform our postmodern ones. We can ignite our interpretive imaginations by following their examples in reading scripture for ourselves and our circumstances. To do less cuts us off from the premodern church and ends with us back in the monology of modernist historicism and moralism.

CHAPTER 3

God

It seems a bit ironic to have a chapter titled "God" in a book that is itself theology. After all, every chapter of this book is in some sense about God. This chapter, however, is necessary in order to focus on central issues of the existence and nature of God, including a few classical theological problems and debates. When we read the New Testament not looking in the first place for what it says about Jesus, the Spirit, human beings, the church, and other legitimate topics but for what it says just about "God," what might we learn?

Given that question, I must immediately confess, however, that the chapter is not so much about God as about what it means to say, "I believe in God." In fact, one of my main themes will be that Christians can say nothing ultimately and perfectly "true" about God in God's very self. As I argue below, I believe we are limited in the end to identifying what we *cannot* know about God rather than demonstrating what we *do* know. My concentration, in any case, is on the nature of Christian faith: What am I doing when I confess, "I believe in God"?

I have no interest in offering reasons to believe in God. I do not argue for the existence of God. The existence in my life and in the lives of others of some kind of faith in God is taken as the starting point. I examine the meaning, the function, what we are doing (or should be doing) when we confess to believe in God. This is to a great extent, as I forewarned in the chapter on epistemology, an empirical account: I examine myself (and to some extent others, insofar as I can make out) in order to discern what I am "doing," indeed, what I "mean," when I say, whether to others or to myself, that I believe in God. The New Testament cannot "on its own" answer that question. It can, though, help us create answers.

Portraits of God in the Bible

As anyone having the least familiarity with the Bible knows, there are all sorts of names for God and depictions of God's emotions and activities that strike just about any modern human being as problematic at best and offensive and horrifying at worst. But this has always been so. Even within the pages of the New Testament we find characters and authors providing interpretations of other scriptural texts that explain how a "first reading" or a "literal reading" of a text about God must not be right and how the truth of the text must be seen through more elaborate interpretation or by reference to some alternative scriptural passage.

Jesus does it. When Jesus, as demonstrated in the chapter on scripture above, ignores or rejects the Pharisees' citation of Deut 24:1 as indicating that God allows divorce and remarriage (Matt 19:3–9; Mark 10:2–9), he is rejecting what most people would see as "the literal" reading of the passage. Jesus's hermeneutical activity, as portrayed in the Gospels, is itself an interpretation of a text with the purpose of substituting one vision of God for another. Paul does the same. When Paul questions a literal reading of Deut 25:4 (1 Cor 9:9), he is implying that his God *must* not be very concerned about oxen. "Is God concerned with oxen?" The particle that begins the sentence, μή, implies a negative answer. We may feel Paul is being a bit too anthropocentric here. We may prefer to imagine that God does very much care for the well-being of oxen. But that just demonstrates that we and Paul have different conceptions about the nature of God. Even within the scriptures themselves, therefore, we see people practicing theological interpretation in order to correct what they take to be incorrect or offensive notions about God, even those they find in scripture.

Perhaps the most radical of such cases is supplied in the second century by Marcion. As just about any Christian has done through history, Marcion noticed that the God depicted in the Old Testament says and does things no good God should do. Marcion's way of solving that problem was by insisting that the "god" of Jewish scripture was not the same God who was the father of Jesus Christ but a bungling and even evil god. Marcion took Jewish scripture as historically accurate, in that it truly depicted the actions of a god, but it was not the same god as proclaimed by Jesus and the Apostle Paul.[1] Another second-century Christian, named Ptolemy, an advocate of what scholars call Valentinian forms of Christian thinking, taught something similar. Ptolemy also thought that the "god" who gave the Law of Moses and was depicted in most Jewish scripture was not actually "evil," but simply "just." That god was an intermediate god, neither the perfect God nor the devil but merely the "craftsman" god who created the universe.[2]

Again, this is one early Christian, though we might say heretical, attempt to read scripture, to confront portrayals of God that seem obviously unacceptable for moral and theological reasons and to deal with that apparent contradiction. Neither Marcion nor Ptolemy provides a solution for those of us wanting to affirm later creeds and Christian orthodoxy, but it is one way Christians interpreted scriptural depictions of God so that they did not impugn or hinder a more theologically acceptable understanding of God.

Those church fathers we label orthodox recognized the need for such interpretation, especially when dealing with popular notions of God or even scripture. Many of them believed that at least some scripture could not be acceptable unless interpreted figuratively or allegorically. Origen, for example, recognized that the Marcionites were correctly reading the text "literally" when they questioned the justice of a god who would punish children, grandchildren, and great-grandchildren for the sins of their ancestors, so he insisted that the literal reading of the text must be inadequate.[3]

As Rowan Greer has noted, Origen was always on the watch for even the most innocent statements about God that could lead a Christian astray if taken too literally. Even the prayer "our Father in heaven" "should not be understood to confine God to a place and so imply that He is corporeal."[4] The Lord's Prayer must be interpreted so as not mislead to false notions of God's true nature. But Origen's strategy for dealing with objectionable depictions

1. There is confusion in our sources about whether Marcion taught that the creator god was merely "just" or perhaps bungling or whether he was actually evil. I am convinced by Sebastian Moll that the earliest and best sources depict Marcion's Demiurge as actually evil, not simply "just." See Moll, *Arch-Heretic Marcion;* and "Marcion." For other recent scholarship on Marcion, see Foster, "Marcion," and the various essays collected in May et al., *Marcion,* especially the essay by Löhr, "Did Marcion?" 131–46.

2. See *Ptolemy's Epistle,* in Layton, *Gnostic Scriptures.*

3. See Origen, *De principiis* 2.5.2, and discussion in Moll, *Arch-Heretic,* 18, 57.

4. Greer, introduction to Origen, *Origen,* 7; Origen, *On Prayer* 23.3, p. 127, in Greer, *Origen.*

of God—indeed, "impossible" depictions—in the scriptures is not to reject the scriptures or to take those as depictions of some "heretical" god, as did Marcion, but to interpret them properly, which may mean "not literally."[5] This is not just the practice of biblical interpretation; it is the practice of Christian theology: interpreting an inadequate notion of the nature of God by proposing an alternative.

From the beginning of Christianity (and for Jews, before that), Christians have recognized the inadequacy, even offensiveness, of some biblical representations of God when read "literally," "commonsensically," or "naively." Christians often think first of the Old Testament when wondering about problems of biblical depictions of God. Was God really "walking in the garden" of Eden enjoying the evening breeze when he called out for Adam (Gen 3:8)? Was the Almighty sincerely asking a real question when he asked Adam where he was (3:9)? Even Christian children have balked when they read that God said, "Let *us* make man in *our* image" (Gen 1:26, my emphasis; "But who could be there with God?!"), at least until their well-meaning Sunday school teachers assured them that God was there talking to Jesus and the Holy Spirit, an interpretation that also satisfied many ancient Christian readers. Should we really agree with the psalmist who thought God would bless those who bashed infants' heads on rocks (Ps 137:9)? It is not at all surprising that Christians through the centuries have offered various interpretations to deal with such texts.

But we too often don't recognize that such issues arise also within the New Testament. We may be more familiar with passages from the Old Testament, for example, that portray God as having a body.[6] According to Gen 32:22–32, God even uses his body in a wrestling match with Jacob, in the end knocking Jacob's hip out of joint in order to escape before daylight, something like a modern vampire. It is less noticed that the New Testament also speaks of God's body. In Rev 4:2–3, John says he "saw" God sitting on his throne up in the sky somewhere, in what must be described as a very "physical" appearance indeed. Later in the narrative John notes that God held out a scroll in his "right hand" (5:1). Christians refrain from taking such descriptions of God as "literal," and it would probably be rather heretical to do so.[7]

---

5. See *De principiis* 4.2–3.

6. For studies of the embodiment of God in the Hebrew Bible, see Kamionkowski and Kim, eds., *Bodies;* for discussion of God's body in ancient Jewish and Christian sources, including the Bible, see Moore, *God's Gym.*

7. Thomas Aquinas got around the problem of Old Testament depictions of the embodiment of God by pointing to the statement in John 4:24 that "God is spirit" and

Our scriptures also depict God in ways we probably should see as morally offensive. When Paul speaks of the wrath of God that is coming to destroy all nonbelievers (1 Thess 1:10), are we to imagine that the almighty, ineffable, loving God suffers from anger and jealousy and has trouble controlling his temper? In parables the Gospel of Matthew depicts God as a moneylender who has a debtor tortured until his entire debt is repaid (Matt 18:34); and as a king who consigns a guest to eternal darkness and punishment for failing to wear the right outfit to a wedding (Matt 22:11–14). In the New Testament we come across passages that seem to compare God to a slave owner (Luke 16:13, and often in parables), an unjust judge who is won over only by importunity (Luke 18:2–8), a rich man who rewards a dishonest accountant (Luke 16:1–12), a businessman who exploits other people (Matt 25:14–30), a nobleman who kills subjects disloyal to him (Luke 10:21).

We can hardly take all these scriptural portraits of God as "true" representations in any kind of straightforward or literal way of the God we worship. We could, like Marcion, attempt to cut them out of our Bibles. Or we could, like Ptolemy, attribute them to a secondary god different from the God of love whom we worship. I suggest, though, that we follow those early Christians we call orthodox. The solution is not rejection of the text or a multiplication of gods but *interpretation*. We *interpret* these texts, as we must interpret *all* texts, so that they render more adequate, edifying truths that reflect what we truly want to affirm about the God of our faith and confessions.

Even depictions of God we might not initially find so offensive turn out to be nonetheless potentially false and dangerous, which is to say that if they are not *taken* in a "true" manner, they can also lead us into theological error. One of the most common portraits of God is as a king, indeed as *the* king of "all nations" (Rev 15:3). The popularity of the term "kingdom of God" in the Gospels is itself a constant reminder that God is a monarch.[8] Ancient

---

admitting that the other portrayals were, in a phrase of Fergus Kerr, "unavoidable anthropomorphisms." See Kerr, *After Aquinas*, 77; Thomas Aquinas, *Summa Theologiae* 1.1.9.
This assumes that the Greek πνεῦμα referred to something not "physical," an assumption that may not have been shared by the author of the Fourth Gospel. For my argument that πνεῦμα in the ancient world was almost always considered what *we* would think of as a "physical substance," see Martin, *Corinthian Body*, 21–25; and chapter 5 below.

8. The term occurs many times in Mark, Luke, and Acts, with fewer appearances in John (3:3, 5), in the "Pauline" corpus (Rom 14:17; 1 Cor 4:20; 6:9, 10; 15:50; Gal 5:21; Eph 5:5; Col 4:11; 2 Thess 1:5), and in Revelation (12:10). This list does not include many other references to God's or Jesus's "kingdom" in slightly different wording or when the term is a verbal form designating their "reign" as kings. Matthew's preferred terminology is "kingdom

persons, whose world was literally ruled by several "kings" of various levels of competence and morality, may well have had no problem thinking of God as a king. In fact, they probably would have been incapable of *avoiding* the concept, since all "gods" known to them in antiquity existed in political structures just like human beings did. Zeus and Jupiter, therefore, were not just "kings"; they were something like "kings squared," "hyper" monarchs. Naturally, in the minds of ancient people, if there was only one god, he would have to be a supreme king.

And we can imagine how the image may have functioned for ancient Christians and for most Christians throughout the centuries in a positive manner. Kingship denoted power, sovereignty, superiority. If one wants help from one's god, it would be natural to hope that such a god was powerful enough to deliver. Our dependence on God and our confidence that God has the ability to help us may be strengthened by reflecting that our God is the most powerful being of the universe.[9] Perhaps that use of "king" could be helpful.

Or maybe not. Is God the kind of king we have already seen in the New Testament, the kind who punishes a slave for not rendering a suitable return on his investment and then slaughters his subjects who had objected to his coronation (Luke 19:14)? Modern readers are often unaware that in the Greek-speaking eastern half of the Roman Empire, the word often used to designate the emperor was βασιλεύς, "king." Julius Caesar and his son Augustus had been careful to avoid the title *rex,* "king," for themselves in Latin, knowing the political danger that came with claims of monarchy within Rome. But their subjects in the East never bought into the subterfuge. They constantly referred to the emperors by calling them kings. We can see this in modern translations of 1 Pet 2:13 and 17, where the author instructs his readers to accept and honor "the king." The translators of the RSV and NRSV are no doubt correct when they translate *basileus* here as "emperor." That's the "king" his readers thought of with this reference, I'm sure.[10] The

---

of heaven," probably a pious circumlocution, but the reader would no doubt have known that the "king" of that kingdom was God or Jesus or both.

9. As I will explain below, from a Christian point of view it is not true to take God to be an entity "of the universe," but I am here describing what I take to be the dominant beliefs of people in the ancient world, almost all of whom assumed that their gods *were* part of the cosmos. Perhaps a few philosophers of the late ancient world might have disagreed, but their notions of divine "transcendence" never trickled down to the vast majority of the populace.

10. See also John 19:15 for a reference to the emperor as "king."

author of Revelation, in his depiction of God as a king, himself uses a term commonly connected to the emperor when he calls "The Lord our God" a παντοκράτωρ, the "ruler of all" (Rev 19:6). God and Jesus in Revelation are the reverse image of the evil, beastly emperor of Rome: they are instead righteous emperors. They are, nonetheless, emperors. It probably did not occur to ancient Christians to find it worrisome to think of God as a king or even an emperor, even though they were quite aware that many emperors they knew about were untrustworthy, incompetent, even evil and dangerous—precisely because they were "all-powerful." But should we ignore the potential problems with the title?

I don't believe we modern Christians should always be comfortable with thinking of our God as an absolute monarch. It goes against important values I insist we should still cherish, *even if* those values have been given to us more by modern liberalism than by traditional religion, values such as equality, freedom, and democracy. Thinking of God as a male, superior, all-powerful, and arbitrary monarch is precisely what has driven many people away from Christianity.

We may, in fact, use the New Testament itself to critique the ancient image of God as king, and kings themselves, not to mention emperors. According to Luke, Jesus taught his disciples, "The kings of the nations lord it over them, and those who are in authority over them are called benefactors. You must not do the same, but the greatest among you must become like the youngest, the leader as a servant. . . . I am among you as one who serves" (22:25–27). Jesus (or Luke) knows that kings are expected to "lord it over" their subjects, and he explicitly rejects that model of leadership. We may imagine Jesus modeling the only kind of "kingship" of which he approved in the way he staged his entry into Jerusalem. He chooses to enter the city not on a charger or even an average horse but on a young donkey (John 12:13–15) or, in the terms of Zech 9:9, "the foal of an ass." Jesus rejects the image of the superior and overbearing king and comes as a humble king who submits even to his subjects. In other words, critiques of "kingship" as a model for God's nature can be found even in the New Testament.

Another popular image for God can be seen as just as much of a problem —when finally analyzed critically, that is. From the beginnings of Christianity both God and Jesus have been portrayed as a shepherd. In John 10:1–16, Jesus says he is "the good shepherd" who lays down his life for his sheep. Matthew and Luke relate a parable of the shepherd who leaves ninety-nine sheep that are safe to search out one that is lost (Matt 18:12–14; Luke 15:4–7). Luke relates the touching detail of the shepherd lifting the sheep he has found to his shoulders to take it home (Luke 15:5). It is no wonder that such texts, especially reinforced by Ps 23 (see also Ez 34:11–16), have been a central representation of God and Jesus in song, literature, and art.

But, and again I say this is true of every image or notion of God we human beings can entertain, the nice image can mask potentially harmful meanings, as ideology always does. It may make us forget that shepherds eat lots of mutton and lamb chops. Shepherds eat their sheep and turn their skins to many uses. How differently would we interpret the parable from the Gospels if it ended with the man slaughtering the recovered sheep to provide a festal dinner for his friends and neighbors?[11]

Many Christians believe that "Father" must be an indispensable name for God. And as long as we are able to interpret this title to represent only a good, loving, gentle, forgiving, self-controlled father, it may well work for most people theologically. But it is demonstrable that people who have been abused by their father often have difficulty thinking of God as their father. I will argue below that even if we are careful to exclude any possible negative connotations of "father," it is still a dangerous notion of God if it is taken, as it is by many people, including some theologians, to mean that God is more appropriately considered male than female or to have masculine traits rather than feminine. That, I will argue, is also idolatry. But it is idolatry to *equate* God with *any* name, role, or notion we humans can conceive.

The late ancient writer called by history Dionysius or Pseudo-Dionysius made what I consider to be an indispensable point about humans' use of divine attributes. He insisted that the most dangerous qualities or characteristics we attribute to God are precisely those that at first seem the most fitting, words such as power, might, goodness, even love. Dionysius (the text is obviously pseudepigraphical, but I will sometimes call him Dionysius for convenience) explains that scripture uses both "similar" and "dissimilar" "sacred images" for God.[12] We may realize the inadequacies of thinking of God as truly having an arm or hand or suffering passions as human beings

---

11. As Kenneth Burke argued many years ago, we must be ready to analyze the ideological uses of all kinds of literature, which he illustrated by reminding us that shepherds protect sheep—and then sell them for slaughter: *Rhetoric,* 27. See also the discussion meant to show how "shepherd" is an analogy that may in some ways work for "God" but certainly in other ways does not: McGrath, *Theology,* 24.

12. The works were written under the name of Dionysius, meant to refer to "Dionysius the Areopagite" mentioned as being with Paul in Athens in Acts 17:34. No one knows who the actual author was or exactly when he wrote, but scholars date the writing to sometime in the late fifth or early sixth centuries.

do, which demonstrates that we recognize that these scriptural images of God are dissimilar in important ways to God's true nature. But Dionysius insists that even those images we may take as more similar to God's nature, such as "Word," "Mind," or "Being," must be seen as still inadequate: "Now these sacred shapes certainly show more reverence and seem vastly superior to the making of images drawn from the world. Yet they are actually no less defective than this latter, for the Deity is far beyond every manifestation of being and of life; no reference to light can characterize it; every reason or intelligence falls short of similarity to it."[13] Every word or image for God is defective because God must be beyond them all in ultimate reality.

So Dionysius explains how "similar" images may be even more dangerous than "dissimilar" ones: we may be tempted to think the word "Love" or "Good" captures the true nature of God, but that would be wrong. Later in the same treatise Dionysius discusses common images for "heavenly beings," in this context meaning more specifically angels, but he would certainly make the same point for God. He speaks of biblical images for angels: "High-flown shapes could well mislead someone into thinking that the heavenly beings are golden or gleaming men, glamorous, wearing lustrous clothing, giving off flames which cause no harm, or that they have other similar beauties with which the word of God has fashioned heavenly minds." In that case we would be better off to use more earthy or even crass terms for divine entities: "Indeed the sheer crassness of the signs is a goad so that even the materially inclined cannot accept that it could be permitted or true that the celestial and divine sights could be conveyed by such shameful things" (2 141A-B). To help us avoid idolatry or misleading thoughts about God, we might prefer the dissimilar or crass images or terms over the apparently similar or holy.[14] Biblical writers, therefore, "honor the dissimilar shape so that the divine things remain inaccessible to the profane and so that all those with a real wish to see the sacred imagery may not dwell on the types as true. So true negations and the unlike comparisons with their last echoes offer due homage to the divine things" (2 145A). *Negative* terms for God like "invisible," "unbounded," "immortal," "inaccessible" and obviously dissimilar images are often better because they stop short of claiming to posit God's

---

13. Pseudo-Dionysius, *Celestial Hierarchy* 2 140C. I use the translation by Luibheid, *Pseudo-Dionysius*. Reference numbers are to the chapter of the work (thus, here chapter 2 of *Celestial Hierarchy*) followed by the column numbers and letters of the Corderius edition of Migne. For the Greek, see Suchla, ed., *Corpus Dionysiacum*, which uses the same means of reference.

14. So also Thomas Aquinas, *Summa Theologiae* 1.1.9, citing Dionysius.

true nature. They therefore are less likely to mislead us into idolatry or the idea that we have finally captured God's true reality.[15]

Negative (Apophatic) Theology

Dionysius is a central figure within the long tradition of apophatic theology, theology that insists that whereas many things we say about God may be true *in a sense,* they are ultimately not true because no human speech can express or capture the essence of the ineffable and undefinable God. A literal meaning of "define" is "to set limits or boundaries," something Christian theology has insisted cannot be done for God. Apophatic theology insists that though some of our thoughts about God may *approach* the reality of God or may help us establish some kind of *relation* to God, nothing we can say or think will fully and completely correspond to God's essence or true nature precisely because of the limitations of our human nature and the infinity of God's.

It is easy to see by rather simple thought experiments how negative theology works, moving from the ridiculous to the sublime, which is precisely the way the process is described by some church fathers: an ascent through denials.[16] Though we as children may have begun with a conception of God as a very old man with a white beard sitting in the sky behind a cloud and compulsively controlling every detail of earthly activity, we tend to give up such images as our faith matures. But how much do we give up and still remain Christian believers? If we do away with the beard do we still have "God"? May we also dispense with the "old man"? or the sky? or the cloud? or the control? or the details? Perhaps we come to believe that ultimately God is in control of the universe, but we no longer require ourselves to believe that God is actively and personally engineering all the details, such as whether or not I find a parking space. Is that still "God"? Which of the many traditional

15. See Louth, *Denys the Areopagite,* 45; McCabe, *God Still Matters,* 27.

16. Speaking of the biblical authors, Dionysius says, "But they prefer the ascent through negations. This way draws the soul out of what is connatural to it, and leads it through all divine conceptions which are transcended by the One that is beyond every name and all reason and knowledge, and brings it into contact with Him beyond the uttermost boundaries of the universe, insofar as such contact is possible to us" (*Divine Names* 13 981B). This translation from Louth, *Denys the Areopagite,* 96. For translation of the full texts, see Luibheid and Rorem cited above. See also the description Gregory of Nyssa gives of Basil's "ascent" toward the unknowable God in *Against Eunomius* II: 89 (*GNO* II, 252:24–253:17), quoted and discussed in Ludlow, *Gregory of Nyssa,* 231.

notions of God can one dispense with—*ought* one dispense with—and still honestly claim to believe "in God"? Apophatic theology would answer: In some sense, all of them.

Though there are certainly biblical passages that promise knowledge of God, there are those that can be cited for negative theology. The Gospel of John begins by admitting that "no one has seen God" (1:18; see also 1 John 4:12), and though the NRSV translates the rest of the verse as, "It is God the only Son, who is close to the Father's heart, who has made him known," that may not be the best translation. The word here translated as "made known" is ἐξηγήσατο, from which we derive the English "exegesis." It can mean anything from "lead out" to "relate" or "narrate." In this context I would prefer to translate it as something like "interpret": Jesus "interprets" the Father for us. But that is a long way from clear, definite, firm "knowledge" of the very nature of God. And anyone who has read the Fourth Gospel carefully will recognize how full it is of puzzles and paradoxes. It seems to pose as many questions about God as answers.[17]

According to Colossians, Jesus is the "image of the invisible God" (1:15). The author of 1 Timothy calls God "immortal" and "invisible" (1:17). Hebrews also speaks of God as "invisible" (11:27). Paul uses the words "unsearchable" and "inscrutable" for God's activities and deeds (Rom 11:33), and Paul's personal experience confirmed it for him. What Paul heard when he was himself "snatched up" into "paradise" were "unspeakable words," perhaps better translated here as "wordless words" to capture the Greek paradoxical term (ἄρρητα ῥήματα; 2 Cor 12:4). What Paul saw and heard was "ineffable," which might more strongly be interpreted to signify not merely a prohibition against but the impossibility of its expression.

Even in those rare cases in the New Testament when someone claims to see God, the vision is not really so clear or obvious. As I mentioned above, in Revelation John claims to have entered the heavenly throne room of God. He says he saw the "one seated on the throne" (Rev 4:2), but his description defies clear picturing: "The one seated there looks like jasper and carnelian, and around the throne is a rainbow that looks like an emerald. . . . Coming from the throne are flashes of lightning, and rumblings and peals of

---

17. See the discussion in McCabe, *The Good Life*, 73–74. McCabe notes that the Latin Vulgate has *enarravit* and concludes, "Anyway for John, what we have in the Word becoming flesh is a narrative and not a vision. Not a seeing but a listening to and sharing in a story. In becoming flesh the Word becomes a character in a story, a persona" (74). For reading John as full of puzzles and riddles, see Martin, *New Testament*, 152–67.

thunder" (4:3, 5; NRSV). Finally, John claims to see a body part that is more familiar: he saw a scroll held "in the right hand of the one seated on the throne" (5:1). But that's all we're offered. If we're looking for realism, this is not a very satisfying picture of God's body.

John's vision is an appropriation of the very similar one reported centuries earlier by the prophets Isaiah and, to a lesser extent, Ezekiel. There also, though, the visions are coy about what God actually looks like. Though Isaiah worries that he is "lost" because he has "seen the King, the Lord of hosts" (Isa 6:5), he doesn't seem to have seen much at all, except the "hem" of God's robe that fills the temple (6:1). This is more like "seeing" an "unseeable" God.[18] It is therefore significant what the Gospel of Mark takes from the passage of Isaiah. Mark quotes Isa 6:9–10, "They may indeed look, but not perceive, and may indeed listen, but not understand; so that they may not turn again and be forgiven" (Mark 4:12; compare Matt 13:14–15; Luke 8:10). Parables in Mark, like any possible vision of God, hide more of the essence of divinity than they reveal. God's body is unseeable, even in a vision. God's essence is unknowable.

Church fathers may have been influenced by ancient philosophy, especially the Platonism that was becoming more and more influential from the second century CE onward, but they believed they were following scriptural teaching when they emphasized that we cannot know God's essence. Clement of Alexandria taught that we should meditate on how all our notions of God must be lacking, and by means of that meditation "we would draw near somehow to knowing the Almighty, not knowing what he is, but what he is not."[19] Gregory of Nyssa wanted to modify more radical negative theology in order to admit that we may approach some kind of knowledge of God, but he nonetheless insisted that any kind of full comprehension of the divine is humanly impossible. Speaking of the "name" of "God," he says, "For this name, which indicates the substance, does not tell us what it is (which is obvious since what the divine substance is is inconceivable and incomprehensible)."[20] Augustine famously said, "If you can grasp it, it's not God."[21]

---

18. See the analysis of the Isaiah passage in Landy, "I and Eye in Isaiah." And compare Ezek 1.

19. *Stromata* 5.11.71; trans. Radde-Gallwitz, *Basil of Caesarea*, 57.

20. *To the Greeks from Common Notions* (*Gregorii Nysseni opera* 3.1:21.20–22.3), trans. Radde-Gallwitz, *Basil*, 200. See Radde-Gallwitz in general for the relationship of the moderate negative theology of the Cappadocians to that of others.

21. *Sermo* 52.16 (*Patrologia Latina* 38.360). See McGrath, *Theology*, 104.

Some of the best quotations and arguments in this vein come from Pseudo-Dionysius: "We offer worship to that which lies hidden beyond thought and beyond being."[22]

> Therefore God is known in all things and apart from all things; and God is known by knowledge and by unknowing. From him there is understanding, reason, knowledge, touch, perception, opinion, imagination, name and many other things, but he is not understood, nothing can be said of him, he cannot be named. He is not one of the things that are, nor is he known in any of the things that are; he is all things in everything and nothing in anything; he is known to all from all things and to no-one from anything. For we rightly say these things of God, and he is celebrated by all beings according to the analogy that all things bear to him as their Cause. But the most divine knowledge of God, that in which he is known through unknowing, according to the union that transcends the mind, happens when the mind, turning away from all things, including itself, is united with the dazzling rays, and there and then illuminated in the unsearchable depth of wisdom.[23]

Everything good we can imagine, and the ability to imagine itself, we have as a gift from God, but we must never claim that God is any of those things in any way we can imagine. As John of Damascus would later put it, here quoted by Thomas later still, "We cannot know what God is, but only what he is not."[24]

In the last few decades many theologians have worked to reclaim the use of this kind of apophatic theology to speak about the nature of Christian faith in a postmodern age, and they have done so often by returning to Thomas Aquinas.[25] Paraphrasing Thomas, who is himself echoing John

22. *Divine Names* 1 589B.

23. Ibid., 7 872A-B. I take this translation, only slightly modified, from Louth, *Denys the Areopagite*, 88. I have altered Louth's "Of him there is . . . " to "From him there is . . . ," which I believe more clearly reflects the meaning of the Greek.

24. From John of Damascus, *On the Orthodox Faith*, book 1, chapter 4; Thomas, *Summa* 1.2.2; trans. Bauerschmidt, *Holy Teaching*, 48.

25. For some recent discussions of the return to apophatic theology made easier by postmodernism, see Hoff, "Dekonstruktive Metaphysik"; Hoff and Hampson, "Cusa"; Hoff, *Spiritualität*.

of Damascus, Dionysius, and others, Fergus Kerr says, "We cannot know of God what he is but only what he is not; so we begin by denying of God the marks of the creaturely condition."[26] As Herbert McCabe puts it, "So for St. Thomas, when we speak of God we do not know what we are talking about. We are simply taking language from the familiar context in which we understand it and using it to point beyond what we understand into the mystery that surrounds and sustains the world we do partially understand."[27] This all perhaps seems counterintuitive to many people, believers and un-believers alike, who think that what it means to be a Christian is to "know God." As McCabe elsewhere notes, "Readers of Aquinas, however, including some of those who see themselves as his disciples, have the utmost difficulty in taking him seriously when he says that we simply know nothing of the nature of God."[28] "God," to Thomas, is merely a label we place at the spot where we wonder, "Why is there something rather than nothing? What does it all mean? Why anything rather than nothing?" Aquinas knew he could not provide a fully satisfying answer. "God" is the label Christians use for the human question of "meaning." As McCabe concludes, "We do not and can-not in this life know the answer but we label it 'God'—*et hoc omnes dicunt Deum.*"[29]

Many contemporary theologians reclaim these ancient Christian ideas. As Denys Turner writes, "In showing God to exist reason shows that we no longer know what 'exists' means."[30] Discussing Karl Barth and Jacques Der-rida, Graham Ward insists, "Although we cannot talk about God, and have no direct knowledge of Him, neither can we cease talking about God, and having the promise of knowledge about Him."[31] And in the words of Kath-ryn Tanner, "God is incomprehensible, beyond human powers of positive explication through concepts and speech, because God is without limits or bounds."[32]

---

26. Kerr, *After Aquinas,* 185, drawing mainly from *Summa Theologiae* 1.2–11.

27. McCabe, *God Still Matters,* 27; see also McCabe, *God Matters,* 40.

28. *God Matters,* 40.

29. Ibid., 41, quoting Thomas but without reference. See also Bauerschmidt, *Holy Teaching.*

30. "On Denying the Right God: Aquinas on Atheism and Idolatry," 158. Elsewhere Denys Turner speaks of "the land of unknowing that is God." *Thomas Aquinas,* 143–44.

31. *Barth,* 232. Barth's theology is replete with such statements. See, for example, *Church Dogmatics* I/2, p. 750: "Of God it is impossible to speak, because He is neither a natural nor a spiritual object."

32. Tanner, *Christ the Key,* 53.

There are people, many of them, who think Christians are people who think they have God figured out. They "have the goods" on God. They claim to know what God is like, what God likes, what God really is. Unfortunately, people who think there are such Christians are too often right: there are Christians like that. But that is Christianity at its worst. At its best, Christianity, all the way from ancient times to today, admits it knows nothing of what God truly is. There are and have been Christians who came to realize, through sometimes wonderful, sometimes painful meditation, learning, and prayer, that we end up with a radical unknowing when it comes to the true reality of God. We may believe; we may hope; we may try. But we end up realizing that when we say "God is," we don't really know what we're talking about. We have come to realize that we no longer know what we mean by "God" or "is." What we know when we, at our best, look into the mystery of the existence of the universe—a mystery we label with the incomprehensible term "god"—is that we don't know what we're talking about when we talk about God.

Transcendence

It is just about impossible for human beings to resist the temptation to think of God as being like a human being, just infinitely bigger, more powerful, and immortal. God is thought to be just the most important and superior item in the universe. McCabe describes the situation as follows:

> Very frequently the man who sees himself as an atheist is not denying the existence of some answer to the mystery of how come there is anything instead of nothing, he is denying what he thinks or had been told is a *religious* answer to this question. He thinks or has been told that religious people, and especially Christians, claim to have discovered what the answer is, that there is some grand architect of the universe who designed it, just like Basil Spence only bigger and less visible, that there is a Top Person in the universe who issues arbitrary decrees for the rest of the persons and enforces them because he is the most powerful being around. Now if denying this claim makes you an atheist, then I and Thomas Aquinas and a whole Christian tradition are atheistic too.[33]

33. McCabe, *God Matters*, 7.

The doctrine of transcendence works to refute such ideas and to convince us that nothing we can imagine God to be will actually *be* what God truly is, precisely because God is completely different from, completely other than, the universe. God is not identical with the universe. God is not even "outside" the universe. God is not another thing in addition to the universe. God is utterly different from and other than the universe. The "being" of God must be something completely alien from anything we, who are very much in and part of the universe, can imagine as "being."

It would be anachronistic, to judge by the standards of modern historical criticism, to claim that the writers of the documents of the New Testament entertained a doctrine of divine transcendence. I don't believe the theology of Paul or any other New Testament author was sophisticated enough or influenced enough by philosophy to work with a category like divine transcendence in the sense important for later Christian theology. I have argued elsewhere that for the classical Greek and Roman worlds and thus for the earliest Christians there was no such thing, for example, as "the supernatural" as a realm of reality apart from or alongside the realm of "nature."[34] Perhaps in the more complex theologies of Christians influenced by later Neoplatonism," such as Dionysius, we can see the beginnings of some kind of notion of supernatural that may correspond tenuously to what has counted for the supernatural in modern thought.[35] But for authors of the first two centuries—and I would argue this to be true for Greeks and Romans as well as Christians—whatever gods or beings exist at all must exist "in nature" or as part of nature, which word is usually taken to mean "all that is." So when I read the New Testament looking for doctrines of divine transcendence, I do so not believing that I am simply "recovering" the intention of the original human authors.

A nonfoundationalist reading of scripture, however, makes such concerns about anachronism irrelevant. We are perfectly within our rights as (postmodern?) Christians to read biblical texts as teaching the transcen-

---

34. Martin, *Corinthian Body,* 4–6; *Inventing Superstition,* 13–16.

35. I have no interest in figuring out when and where the category of "the supernatural" was invented. There are no terms in the classical Greek or Roman worlds that could be translated that way, in spite of misleading modern English translations. But with Pseudo-Dionysius, we do at least find an author (writing in the fifth or sixth century) who speaks of things that are not "contrary to nature" (παρὰ φύσιν) but "above nature" (ὑπὲρ φύσιν). See, for example, *Divine Names* 6 856D–857A. The same author uses also an adverb for knowledge derived "supernaturally" (ὑπερφυῶς; *Divine Names* 2 649D). Much later, Thomas Aquinas uses the Latin adjective *supernaturalis* and shares notions of transcendence with Dionysius. See the impressive listing of references in Murray, "Spiritual and the Supernatural."

dence of God. When we read in John 13:1 that Jesus is about to go "out of the cosmos" and "to the father," we may take that to indicate that God is not part of the cosmos but something completely "other" than it, transcending the universe. The author of Ephesians insists that God "elected us in him before the foundation of the cosmos" (1:4–5). God is here not part of the cosmos, not part, that is, of the universe at all.

One of the ways the Gospels teach divine transcendence is by emphasizing the radical difference between God and human beings: "What God has yoked together, let no human being separate" (Mark 10:9; see also Matt 19:6). A camel passing through a needle's eye or a rich man entering the kingdom of God is impossible for mortal human beings, but not for God (Mark 10:27). Indeed, the tenth chapter of Mark seems to have as one of its themes the emphasis on the radical difference of God, even to the point of approaching what would later be considered heresy. Jesus says, for instance, that he doesn't have the authority or power to assign seating on his right or left in the kingdom, implying that only God, but not he, Jesus, can do that (Mark 10:40).

Modern Christians may wonder about the passage in the same chapter where Jesus seems to deny any divine status for himself. When a man asks Jesus what he must do to gain eternal life and calls him "good teacher," Jesus says, "Why do you call me good? No one is good but God" (10:18; Luke 18:19; the wording is changed a bit in Matt 19:17). Perhaps we could figure out a way to interpret this strange saying in a way that could sustain the orthodoxy of Jesus's divinity, yet insofar as these passages are taken to represent Jesus's humanity, they also indicate the radical difference of God from us and the entire universe.

Dionysius insists that God's transcendence relates to how we should think of God's "eternity." Most people imagine that God is a being who existed "before" the world and will exist "after" it, and that is one permissible way to talk about God. But there is no before or after when it comes to God's reality. In other words, God's existence is not just a very long version of ours, as if his infinity meant that he exists in some kind of infinite extension of time. On the contrary, there is no such thing as time in God's being except the eternal point of now. The eternity of God is not like a line that goes on forever. It is more like a point of presence. As Dionysius puts it, "He is nothing. He is no thing. The categories of eternity and time do not apply to him, since he transcends both and transcends whatever lies within them."[36]

---

36. *Divine Names* 5 825B. So Boethius: "Eternity is the complete and total possession of unending life all at once" (*Consolatio Philosophiae*, book V, prose 6; English: Rand ed.,

McCabe has put this in a nice, pithy way. Instead of thinking of God as existing outside or along with the universe in any kind of manner like the universe but just as a different thing, McCabe says, "It is not possible that God and the universe should add up to make two."[37] It makes a nice equation: $G + U \neq 2$.[38] The transcendence of God means not just that God is another being bigger than the universe, but that the beingness of God is something we can never understand in relation to any existing thing we know about in the universe or any existing aspect of the universe. Utterly different.

Keeping this transcendence in mind may help people avoid problems that come with slipping into thinking that God is just a "super" person but basically with the same tendencies we know all people to possess, people with whom we find ourselves in competition, people from whom we may be wary of receiving gifts, people from whom we may need protection. As Tanner notes, "God is not a kind of thing among other kinds of things; only if God is transcendent in that way does it make sense to think that God can be the giver of all kinds of things and matters of existence; and only on that basis—God as the giver of all gifts—does it make sense to think of a non-competitive relation between God and creatures."[39] God is so unlike the universe—not another thing within any genre of things—that every name we give to God, every concept we have of God, will ultimately mislead us from God's true nature. The doctrine of divine transcendence helps us remember that.

Immanence

When they first encounter it, many Christians are wary of the doctrine of divine transcendence. How can we take comfort from or "relate" at all to a god who is utterly different from anything we can imagine from our experiences in the universe? If God is really so separate and different from us,

---

Stewart, et al., eds., *Boethius*. I cite the quotation from Coll, *Christ in Eternity*, 14, who proceeds (same page) to paraphrase Thomas Aquinas similarly: "God is eternal in the sense of being distinct from time." According to Brian Davies, the idea that "eternity" and "time" are completely distinct not only is important for Thomas but also is "a virtually constant tradition" from late ancient Neoplatonism through medieval theology. "Eternity is the life of the intelligible world without successiveness." Davies, *Thought of Thomas Aquinas*, 103; see also 103–9.

37. McCabe, *God Matters*, 6; see also Eagleton, *Reason*.
38. "God is not a determinate object in the world." Williams, *Resurrection*, 84.
39. Tanner, *Jesus, Humanity, and the Trinity*, 4.

how do we worship him—or it? What use is it to believe in a completely transcendent divine entity? These are legitimate questions, and traditionally their concerns are answered by insisting that the doctrine of transcendence must always be accompanied by the contradictory-sounding doctrine of divine immanence: the teaching that God is fully "in" the world even without being "part" of it.

And again, as was the case with the doctrine of transcendence, I would say that the New Testament provides resources for thinking about divine immanence, even though I would admit that probably none of the authors of New Testament documents would have been philosophically educated enough to recognize it as a theological doctrine. They do, however, use language that connects God very closely to the universe and ourselves.

The most common New Testament lessons about God's immanence in the world are taught by stressing Jesus's role as "God with us" or the representation of God in the world, embodied even as a human being. The Gospels especially can be mined to teach divine immanence by focusing on the incarnation. That is a function of immanence to be taken up better in the chapter below on Jesus. Moreover, many New Testament texts stress the nearness of God by emphasizing that Christians possess, within us, God's very spirit (see, for example, Romans 8 and 1 Cor 2:12). God's *pneuma* pervades the very bodies of Christians. I will take up that indication of immanence in the chapter on the spirit.

But there are other indications in the New Testament of God's immanence in the world and in us. Ephesians says that God is "above everything and through everything and in everything" (Eph 4:6). God pervades the universe and everything in it. The New Testament uses significant prepositions to describe God's relation with us. God is "with" us (Phil 4:9). God "works in" us (Phil 2:13). Our lives are "hidden within God" (Col 3:3). This last phrase brings up a point made by theologians: if we are uncomfortable thinking about God being "in" the universe, as if that would imply that God is "part of" the universe, an idea contradicted by the doctrine of transcendence, we may alternatively imagine that the universe is "in" God: God contains the universe in God's self. The world cannot "contain" God; rather, as Tanner puts it, "God contains the world."[40] Or, in the words of Richard Norris, "God is not 'in' the world (or for that matter 'outside' it). On the contrary, the world is 'in' God, who is the 'place' in which the finite order is set, and is therefore non-mediately present to it; and that, oddly enough, explains why

40. Ibid., 43.

'no one has seen God at any time' (John 1:18)."[41] In other words, the radical immanence of God can be expressed as saying that the entire universe, including ourselves, lives "in" God.

Yet, according to Ephesians, God is also "in" us. We are "full" of God (Eph 3:19). The first letter of John puts it both ways. When we love, it says, we are by that action living "in" God, and God is also living "in" us (1 John 4:16). Paul's sermon in Athens as narrated by the Acts of the Apostles makes Paul sound even philosophical, quoting Greek philosophers to make the same point. Paul says that all human beings "live and move and exist" in God (Acts 17:28). Paul is here probably citing Greek philosophers who probably meant such a phrase to express their own pantheistic theology: the teaching, that is, that God is not just "immanent within" the universe but *is* the universe.[42] The universe, for such non-Christian philosophers, is God's body. In order to avoid equating God with the universe, Christian orthodoxy teaches the immanence of God in the universe without God being a part of the universe or even the universe itself entire. Acts quotes even pantheistic Greek philosophy, at any rate, to support the closeness of God to the world and all human beings.

We may be more creative, however, in reading some narratives and sayings in the Gospels to teach divine immanence. According to Mark, Jesus makes a statement the radical nature of which is usually missed by most readers. Challenged about his disciples rubbing and eating grain on the sabbath, Jesus says, "The sabbath was made for human beings, not human beings for the sabbath" (2:27). This is a radical statement. Its implication would be that all laws and rules may be ignored or broken when people feel that it is in their and others' interests to do so. We human beings are perfectly within our rights to make up our rules as we go along or ignore rules if we judge them to be against our interests. What if all of us went around obeying only those laws we had decided were "for" us? The saying is so radical that both Matthew and Luke omitted it (assuming they were using Mark, as I believe they were), leaving in place only the accompanying saying, "The son of man is lord of the sabbath" (Mark 2:28; Matt 12:8; Luke 6:5), not such a radical saying in itself for Christians. Matthew and Luke no doubt avoided

---

41. Richard Norris, "Trinity," in Rogers, ed., *Holy Spirit,* 26.

42. The saying has been variously attributed to Epimenides and Posidonius. For discussion, see Conzelmann, *Acts of the Apostles,* 144–45; Barrett, *Acts of the Apostles,* 2:847–48. I believe Fitzmyer's rejection of a Greek philosophical source for the saying is overly skeptical: see *Acts of the Apostles,* 610.

Mark's more radical statement precisely because it seemed so offensive or nonsensical.

But we may take Mark's radical saying as speaking to human nature in its relation to divine nature. If we accept that the law was given by God, but that God gives us the authority to abrogate it, that puts us practically in the place of God, or, put another way, it makes no distinction between God and us. It puts us in God's role. God gives us divine rights and role. Such a reading does emphasize the nearness of human beings to the divine in a surprising way.

A scene earlier in the same chapter in Mark may be read similarly to speak of divine immanence. When Jesus announces that the paralytic's sins are forgiven, the scribes mumble that only God can forgive sins (Mark 2:1–7). Jesus divines their thoughts and asks which is more difficult: to forgive sins or to heal the paralytic? The point in Mark, read as it would be by a decent historical critic, is that "the son of man has authority [ἐξουσία] to forgive sins" (2:10). The point in Mark, on the most "historical" reading, is to demonstrate something about *Jesus's identity,* not about whether or not God does actually reserve to himself alone the authority to forgive sins.

But there are other ways we could read the passage. For one thing we might take a lesson from it that would be wrong rather than right: that people who suffer do so because of some sin they have committed. They deserve their disease. Jesus's words certainly seem to assume that. We could reject that interpretation on theological grounds derived from elsewhere, perhaps even elsewhere in Mark; but see especially John 9:3.

But we could also read the text to reject any idea that God alone can forgive sins and that Jesus, precisely in his role as "the son of *man*" here rather than the "son of God," demonstrates that all human beings can forgive sins and in fact that we do so all the time when we forgive others, even when we need to forgive those who have sinned not only against us but also against others. There may be a time when we say we have no right to forgive people for harm they have done to others; in that case forgiveness is not ours to offer but belongs only to those harmed. But that may be only one side of a two-sided lesson, the other side being that sometimes we need to be able to forgive others as God forgives, completely and freely. Here again the text would be taken as emphasizing our nearness to God rather than emphasizing God's sovereignty. It thus, read this way, emphasizes God's immanence rather than transcendence.

A related doctrine that ends up emphasizing divine immanence is *creatio ex nihilo,* God's creation of everything out of nothing. Many people mistakenly think about creation as simply the beginning of the universe. It is something they think about as happening in time, just at a very early time. But creation is not something that happened in time. It was the creation of time itself. And God's activity of creating the universe is not something God did long ago and then was done with, as if he dusted off his hands and stopped creating at the end of the sixth day. That is the mistaken "clockmaker" notion of God's role in creation: God just got the clock started and then sat back and watched it run.[43] Creation, rather, is a constant divine activity.[44] God is constantly upholding the reality of the universe, giving it whatever energy it has, giving it whatever life it has, giving it whatever reality it has. Creatio ex nihilo is not just about the beginning of the universe. It is about the ongoing, constant radical necessity of the world to depend on God for its existence. That in turn highlights God's immanent relation with the universe.

So yes, the New Testament notes that God "created all things" (Eph 3:9). God is the one "for whom and through whom everything exists" (Heb 2:10). God is the "builder of everything" (Heb 3:4). Even if there are other "worlds," all possible "worlds" were made by God (Heb 11:2). But the New Testament also notes the ongoing activity of God in creating: God *gives* (present tense) life to "all things" (1 Tim 6:13). God "provides us everything richly for our pleasure" (ἀπόλαυσις; 1 Tim 6:17). As Ian Markham explains, the creation stories in the Bible are not scientific accounts of the beginning of the universe. They are not even mainly about the beginning of the universe. Markham interprets the creation account as "poetic" and as "myth": "It describes in a metaphorical way the dependence of the world upon the creator."[45]

The New Testament contains many texts that are highly eschatological and even apocalyptic.[46] Thus is it not surprising that they sometimes

43. See Nicholas Lash's criticism of this model in his *Holiness*, 80–81.

44. In a wonderful piece of "creative" exegesis—that is, one not bound by the strictures of modernist historical criticism—James Alison takes Jesus's use of mud to heal the blind man (John 9:6) to link back to the use by God of clay or earth (Hebrew: *adamah*) to create "man" (Adam): "So, here, what Jesus is doing is the act of finishing creation." *Faith Beyond Resentment*, 6. The pun doesn't work in Greek, and it is quite unlikely, I think, that the author of the Fourth Gospel knew Hebrew. But this is just the kind of creative interpretation I'm advocating in this book. We need not satisfy the modern philologian or historical critic in our interpretations. Alison cites John 5:17, "My Father is working up until the present, and I also work" (16), as indicating the ongoing creation by God, in work of both the Father and Jesus. See also 17: "The Sabbath is the symbol of creation not yet complete."

45. Markham, *Understanding*, 111.

46. I use "eschatological" to refer to any emphasis on "the end" or any expectation of future fulfillment of current promises, whereas "apocalyptic" refers to more specific elements taken from ancient apocalyptic literature, such as the expected Parousia of a mes-

foretell a time in the future when we and the universe will be taken up into God or combined with God in a way not possible until then. Though we have already seen texts from Ephesians suggesting that Christians are already united with God, it also predicts a time in the future when the entire universe will be gathered "in" God (1:10). According to Paul, Christ works so that in the end "God may be all in all" (1 Cor 15:28). God promises to human beings that God will "live in them and walk among them" (2 Cor 6:16; a loose quotation by Paul of Lev 26:12). According to some New Testament texts, therefore, there is something like a "reserved" unity with God we now can only anticipate. That reservation and expectation have always had some place in most Christian theology: we enjoy God's presence around and in us now, but we also await the full blessing of the "beatific vision" of God's self.

McCabe makes some helpful points here: "I think it is true and very, very importantly true that the point of human living lies *beyond* itself but not *outside* itself. This is because I think that in the end the point of human living lies in God, who is beyond us but not outside us. God, unlike the birds or any other creatures, cannot lie outside us because he creates us and sustains us all the time, making us to be and keeping us as ourselves. So to say that the point of our lives is in God is not to point to something outside us but to a greater depth within us."[47]

This is one way of making sense of the catechetical teaching that the purpose or goal of human existence is "to glorify God."[48] Modern people especially are likely to be put off by such language because they think of God as another person "other" than and "outside" us. God is such an egotistical person that he created us solely for the purpose of his enjoying our admiration of him? The teaching can be properly understood only if we do *not* think of God as a different *person from* us but more as the underwriting of our very selves. When we allow ourselves to sink into the beauty and glory of God, we are at the same time sinking into what we as human beings truly are at our best. We are embracing our own creation by being grateful to the creator.

The Sermon on the Mount contains a beautiful passage that combines observing creation with the goodness and care given by God and ends by

---

siah or other deliverer, a battle between good and evil, a final judgment, and final reward or punishment.

47. McCabe, *On Aquinas*, 53–54.

48. The Westminster Shorter Catechism, for example: "Man's chief end is to glorify God and to enjoy Him forever."

forbidding worry or anxiety. After insisting that no one can serve both God and money, Jesus continues,

> Because of this I say to you, do not be concerned with your life, what you will eat or what you will drink, nor with your body, what you will wear. Isn't life more than food and the body more than clothing? Study the birds of the sky: they don't sow or reap or gather into storehouses, and your heavenly father feeds them. Aren't you more than they? Which of you by worrying can add one inch to your height or one day to your life? Why are you concerned about clothes? Learn from the flowers of the field, how they grow. They don't work or spin. And I tell you that even Solomon in all his splendor was not decked out like even one of these. But if God so dresses the grass of the field, which is here today and thrown into a furnace tomorrow, how much more will he do for you, you little-faiths? Therefore do not worry, saying, "What will we eat?" or "What will we drink?" or "What will we wear?" For all these things the gentiles pursue. For your heavenly father knows that you need all those things. But look first for the kingdom [of God] and his justice, and all these things will be given to you also. Therefore, do not worry about tomorrow, for tomorrow will worry for itself. Sufficient for a day are its own troubles.[49]

"Each day's worries are good enough for that day" might be another way to put that last sentence. It is as if Jesus is teaching us that, at least for Christians, worrying is not only unnecessary and stress-making. It is also a sin. Observing God's creation should convince us of God's presence and care for us. God's ongoing creation of the universe is proof of God's goodness and immanence within it.[50]

---

49. Matt 6:25–34. As always in this book, the translations from the New Testament are mine unless otherwise noted. "Of God" is in brackets in my translation because it is in brackets in the Greek New Testament I use here (United Bible Society, 4th rev. ed., 1983). Since Matthew's preferred wording is "kingdom of heaven" rather than "kingdom of God," it seems odd for "of God" to be his wording here. That observation, accompanied by the fact that some ancient manuscripts leave out "of God" or have other wording here, prompts the editors of the Greek to put the words in brackets.

50. "And when man is placed under the Word and under the command of the Word, he is really free. Free from worry about himself. But also free from worry about others. And free from worry about the whole development of human affairs in the Church and

To make the point with empiricism: this is actually what faith means for many people, Christian and non-Christian alike. Observation of the world is what makes many people believe in an unknown deity. For many people, to look at the world—a sunset or, better yet, thousands of sunsets; a forest; an ocean; the sky; a waterfall; the miracles of animals of all kinds; of human beings of all types—and then to say we do not believe in God would be saying that we, we human beings, are the best designers in our universe.

In a way that could be considered true. We human beings *may be* the most intelligent beings of the universe, but only because, as I have insisted, God is not part of the universe. But when we look at the absolutely stunning beauty and complexity of the universe we actually can see and then say there is no God, that does seem to mean we are saying that we human beings, as far as we now know, are the supreme intelligences of any possible existence. We are the best artists and architects that can exist. Better than any imagined artist or architect who could have fashioned the clouds at sunset, the waves on a beach, the trees of a forest, the insects of all known continents. We are thereby saying that we are the highest level of designer possible in our imaginations.

The thing that makes many people say they believe in God is the wonder of the world.[51] This is not a "proof." It is merely to say that the wonder expresses itself in some of us as faith in God. Faith is merely the expression of the wonder that we live in a world wonderfully made. And "made" by some being supremely superior to us. We couldn't make any of this. That is what some people mean by faith in God.

While there are problems with the doctrines both of transcendence (if it implied God's indifference to the universe) and of immanence (if it implied that the universe *is* God or that God is one item among others in the universe), theological errors can be avoided if the two doctrines are held together. (I explain below why theological errors *ought* to be avoided; it is not simply out of fear of being labeled a heretic.) Christian doctrine avoids the idolatry of equating God with the universe precisely because of the Christian doctrine of transcendence: God can be immanent in our universe because

---

the world. . . . But the very prayer, Thy will be done, is in fact an admission that I need not worry about it, because that is not my business." Barth, *Church Dogmatics* I/1, p. 275.

51. Johannes Hoff and Peter Hampson point to Nicholas of Cusa as especially depending on the idea that we see God in the beauty of the cosmos: "The idea that the cosmos is theophanic or 'God showing' and so praise worthy is thus at the heart of Cusa's worldview." They cite here especially *De Venatione Sapientiae* 18.51; 19.54. See Hoff and Hampson, "Cusa," 122.

God is radically other than the universe. God is not another thing alongside
the universe. Precisely because God is transcendent God can contain the
universe but not be contained by or exhausted by the universe.

This combination is noted by many theologians. As Henk J. M. Schoot
puts it, discussing the theology of Thomas Aquinas,

> God is not transcendent in the sense that he needs a difference to
> be the unique one he is. God is not different within a certain ge-
> nus, on the basis of a common similarity. . . . God is "outside" of
> any genus, and thus God is not different from creatures the way
> in which creatures mutually differ. God differs differently. . . .
> Such an account undermines the opposition between transcen-
> dence and immanence, because God is not transcendent in such
> a way that he is simply "outside of" or "above" the world, and
> thus not transcendent in such a way that it would exclude his "de-
> scent" into the world. . . . All of our language about God should
> be analyzed in such a way, as the analysis of words and proposi-
> tions used analogously in fact does, to account for this unique
> uniqueness of God.[52]

Or as Rowan Greer notes, commenting here on early Christian texts such as
the second-century *Shepherd* of Hermas and combining emphasis on creation with transcendence and immanence: God is "one, who made everything from nothing, and who is uncontained while containing all."[53]

Hans Küng argued that we should not pine after beliefs about God that
many of us can no longer accept, ideas, for example, that God is a "miracle-
working helper in distress and ready to fill in the gaps; the God—that is—
who is to be invoked in nature and history only at the point at which we
can get no farther with our human science and technology."[54] But Küng insists there are other ways to believe in God available to thoroughly modern,
thinking people:

> What is by no means obsolete, however, is the question about the
> God of the new world picture, who is to be understood as the
> transcendent-immanent, all-embracing, all-permeating, most

52. Schoot, *Christ the "Name,"* 144.
53. Greer, introduction to *Origen,* 8.
54. Küng, *Does God Exist?,* 333. Most of the text is in italics in Küng's original.

real reality in man and in the world: the God—that is—who can be the answer to the questions of ultimate and primary interpretations, objectives, values, ideals, norms, decisions, attitudes, to the questions of the ultimate or primary why and wherefore, whither and whence, of man and the world; the God—that is—who as the Unconditioned involves us unconditionally, quite personally in the midst of and through all the relativities in the world, who sustains us, supports and embraces us (infinitely distant and yet closer than we are to ourselves) as ultimate and primary ground, support, and goal of all reality.[55]

The combination of divine transcendence and immanence is not a modern invention, as we've seen. It goes back at least to Christian theologians of late antiquity. But ironically, as Küng here points out, it also has reemerged as central to the theology of many modern and postmodern Christians, who find ourselves, against the odds, continuing to "believe in God" but in ways we may have trouble explaining. It is a complicated and complex faith and may not look like the faith of our childhood. But it is nonetheless faith.

Marilynne Robinson's award-winning novel *Gilead* struck me as a fine literary example of the coming together of divine transcendence and divine immanence. Sometimes in history transcendence has been linked more to some forms of Protestantism, especially the Calvinist emphasis on God's "sovereignty." And immanence has appeared more "Catholic," with its emphasis on the incarnation, ritual, the everyday, the saints—all as the "embodiment" or "revelation" of God.[56] Robinson's novel brings these two traditions together. The first-person narrator of the story is himself an aging Calvinist preacher who is writing the story as a message held in trust for his very young son, the product of a late-in-life marriage to a younger woman. The birth and play of the boy seem to cause the old preacher to wake up to the bits and pieces of God seen in youth, life, and all the world around him. His Calvinist theology had rightly taught him to respect the "otherness" of God. But he is now discovering, to his and our delight, that God may truly be encountered in nature, the ordinary, the everyday, his neighbors, his wife, and in his beautiful boy. The novel, written by an author well steeped in Calvinist theology, is a wonderful fictional illustration, though not by any

---

55. Ibid., 333–44; here again, most of the text is italicized in the original.

56. My posing of this difference in emphases is really only an appearance or impression. In reality, Protestants have always embraced the incarnation and immanence, and Roman Catholics have always acknowledged transcendence.

means an allegory, of the mature Christian combination of the doctrines of transcendence and immanence.

Divine Simplicity

In classical theology, exemplified by Augustine, Pseudo-Dionysius, and Thomas Aquinas, to name only the obvious suspects, the doctrines of divine transcendence and immanence were combined with divine simplicity. As Dionysius says, speaking of God's nature, "In fact he is nothing less than the archetypal God, the supra-divine transcendentally one God who dwells indivisibly in every individual and who is in himself undifferentiated unity with no commixture and no multiplication arising out of his presence among the many."[57] Unfortunately, the doctrine of divine simplicity is not at all intuitive to most people. Divine simplicity is not so simple after all.[58]

The theological idea was inspired by ancient Greek philosophy, Plato especially. According to much ancient philosophy (though there are always exceptions and several different philosophies had their own ideas), the most perfect supreme god, which was often taken to be the source of all other divinities, was an immaterial being. Since it is the nature of matter to change, and since change was understood necessarily to be from better to worse or from worse to better, god could not change and could not therefore be material. Matter is complex and alterable, and therefore god must be simple and unalterable. Many ancient philosophers took a sphere to be the most perfect form imaginable, so that the sun, moon, and stars, understood as perfect spheres, were higher divinities than any of those of mythology that took other forms, such as human or animal. The sphere was considered a superior form precisely because of its unity and simplicity. So the most supreme god must also be a unity and simple.

I have shown elsewhere that much of this philosophical preference for unity over diversity, oneness over dichotomy or plurality, and simplicity over complexity was taken over by philosophy and medical theory from earlier Greek political theory.[59] And the emphasis on singleness, unity, and simplic-

---

57. Luibheid, *Pseudo-Dionysius*, 67 (2 649C).

58. But see the excellent explanation by Turner, *Thomas Aquinas*, 119–21, 226.

59. See Martin, *Sex and the Single Savior*, 85, and references there cited. Much of my *Inventing Superstition* is an attempt to argue for and illustrate the derivation of fundamental philosophical and medical ideas from earlier political theories and ideologies of the Greek democracy and its opponents.

ity was often emphasized more by conservative, *antidemocratic* ideology. The Greek democracies were founded on the assumption of difference between the few rich and the many poor, two classes expected to be in constant opposition and conflict. The democratic constitutions were designed to control those oppositions and balance them without getting rid of them. The response from conservatives was often to deplore difference and conflict and to urge unity, though admittedly a unity in which the poor and the rich stay in their respective places and thus retain difference between the two classes. The emphasis on singleness, unity, and even sameness characterized more the political ideology of conservatives than the assumptions of the democrats.[60]

Applying these ideas to theology and developing them further, some philosophers insisted that the supreme deity, being completely simple, one, and unified, should not be thought of as a being (an essence) who also has certain characteristics ("accidents" or "ways of existing"). That would divide the divinity into "essence" and "existence." It would imply that god was a being, like we are beings, who also "happens" to be "good," say, as we imagine for all human beings. Ancient philosophers insisted that such notions destroy the unity and simplicity of god. So they insisted that god's nature could not be divided into his being and other characteristics or virtues in which he "participates." If god is completely transcendent in relation to the universe, god cannot participate in anything outside god. So rather than say, "God is good," they would say, "God is goodness itself." This was taken to maintain the simplicity and unity of God with God's self necessary for the transcendent and immanent deity.

Adopted in late antiquity by Christian theologians, these notions were taken to add more ammunition to the claim that God is not a being who also happens to exist, in the sense that I am a human being who happens to exist. I, at this time, do exist, but there was a time when I did not exist and there will likely be a time when I no longer exist. The universe is a being that came into existence and may end its existence. (I leave it to theoretical physicists and cosmologists to settle that question.) But God does not "have" existence. God is being itself. God cannot *not* "be" because God is being itself. The (eventually) Aristotelian-Thomist way of saying this is that there is no distinction between God's *essence* and God's *existence*.

60. See, for example, my analysis of the ideology of "concord" (*homonoia*) speeches in ancient rhetoric: *Corinthian Body,* esp. 38–47; summarized to some extent in chapter 7 below.

That may seem like a picky, philosophical differentiation of words with no real difference, but it has theological uses. For example, we should not think, as most of us usually do, of God as a huge, cosmic being who also happens to be good—but may, if we are unlucky, be bad. God is not good in the same way that I, as a human being, may be good. Rather, God is goodness itself. There is no "accident" of goodness that *may be* attached, as a separate quality, to the "essence" of God, to use the Aristotelian-inspired language. The only reality that is goodness itself must find its fundamental identity in God. Put another way, God is not a person who may or may not love. God is not a person who happens to be loving. God is love itself. "Loving" is not a quality that expresses something about God. Love gets its very nature from God. As Henry Chadwick explains about Augustine, "Augustine accepts that God is one 'substance,' as long as no one imagines goodness to be an accidental quality of divine being. Unlike in man, in God it is not one thing to be, another to be good. God's attributes are not other than himself."[61]

One way of putting this is to say that "God" is not a noun, a word that functions by naming something, but a verb. The meaning of "God" is "to be." "My name is I am" (see Ex 3:14; John 8:58). God is "to love." God is not a loving person but the reason that love can "be" at all. God is not a person who created the universe to "exist" alongside God's self. God is the reason the universe can exist at all because God is the "is" behind or underneath all "existences" (ways of existing) at all.

Some people object that the notion of divine simplicity is not worthy of Christian theology because it is "not biblical" and "comes from" Greek philosophy. Such an objection is rather naïve and philosophically unsophisticated itself. In the first place, as I have insisted, whether or not some idea is "biblical" or not depends on how someone *interprets* the Bible not on whether the "text itself" somehow "contains" that property "within" it. Nor does it depend on whether the ancient biblical author "intended" to place divine simplicity "into" his text. I argue that we Christians are well within our rights to read the New Testament as teaching divine simplicity, even if the ancient human authors had no notion of this admittedly philosophical idea.

The objection also suffers from ideological self-deception or dishonesty. It implies that we can use some kind of language to talk about God and our faith that is "pure" and "untainted" by "foreign" influences. That notion is false. We have no language that is applicable *only* to Christian topics. All

---

61. Chadwick, *Augustine*, 120.

our language comes to us from elsewhere. And if we are at all philosophically educated or inclined, we will automatically use ideas and language we
learned from some kind of philosophy to talk about our faith. The search for
"purity" (in the sense, often, of whether or not something is "biblical") in
language is misguided and ideologically loaded in harmful, deceptive ways.
The crucial question about the doctrine of divine simplicity is not whether it
is "biblical" but whether it is useful. Whether it *helps* or *hurts* Christian faith
and our understanding of it.

We need not take on all the different aspects of ancient philosophical (usually Platonic) notions of divine simplicity in order to find it useful.
For example, the ancient philosophical author Alcinous argued that God
could be neither bad nor good since that would mean God "participated in
something, to wit, goodness."[62] I have admitted that this can serve to make
a good point, precisely by forcing us to be careful about *every* attribute we
claim for God. I have no problem, however, thinking of God as complex or
participating in something or even as changing. I just don't share the ancient
philosophical assumption that all change must be from better to worse or
vice versa. Neither do I assume that change would destroy God's infinity or
necessarily place God in time. I simply assume that when I say something
about a change for God (when I read about God "repenting" in the Bible, for
instance) I am saying something that may be true about God *in a sense* but
that must not imply time for God or change between better and worse. But
I also recognize that when I say God does *not* change, that is also true *only
in a sense*.

Divine simplicity, though, may be useful if it guards us from moving
toward idolatry, that is, looking at any attribute *as we know it* and assuming
that God is "that" or "like that" in a human way.[63] We may think of God as

---

62. Alcinous, *Handbook of Platonism* 10.4, trans. and with introduction by John Dillon,
18. (I have altered the translation slightly to fit the syntax of my sentence.) See discussion
in Radde-Gallwitz, *Basil of Caesarea*, 50. We should note that Alcinous was apparently not
a Christian. The point about "participation" is well explained by Kathryn Tanner, though
she is speaking here generally about divine simplicity, not about Alcinous in particular:
"One can say God does not participate in being but *is* it: to be *God* just is to *be*. In God
there is no distinction between what God is—God's essence—and God's existence. To
participate in being is, by definition, not to be it, if participation means participating in
what one is not; and therefore with participation arises a distinction between essence and
existence, the very composite character that constitutes created things." Tanner, *Christ the
Key*, 8–9.
63. As Hauerwas puts it, "Aquinas was right that only God is pure act. Only in God are
existence and essence one. Accordingly, our language about God is necessarily analogical,

"father" only by continually knowing that only the very truth of "father-hood" in its most unimaginably pure and good nature is God's nature, not that God might be like any "fathers" we know, who may be overbearing, authoritative, domineering, or cruel—and male! I may not be particularly concerned, as ancient philosophers certainly were, to save God from having "accidental properties." But it does help to remind me that when I say, "God is good," no notion we have of "good" can correctly represent God's good-ness. God is goodness itself in a perfection we cannot even imagine.

And that is the fundamental aspect of divine simplicity stressed by Thomas Aquinas and many Christian theologians. As McCabe explains Thomas's position: "The predicates we attach to the word 'God' have, indeed, different meanings in that their meaning is derived from our understanding of these things as properties in our world, but what they refer to in God is a single mystery which is quite unknown to us. We have some understanding of the wisdom that God creates in us, but when we say that God is wise we mean neither that he is the creator of wisdom in us, nor simply that he is not foolish; we mean that the quality we call wisdom in us exists in God in some higher and utterly mysterious way (cf. *Summa Theologiae,* Ia, 13, 5)."[64] As is true of so many Christian doctrines, divine simplicity is best used to keep us from false or dangerous notions about God, not for saying anything ultimately positive about God's true nature, as if, for example, being "simple" were inherently superior to being "complex."[65]

And there are certainly clues from the New Testament with which we may think about the oneness and simplicity of God. The *shema* from the Old Testament but cited as central by Jesus in the New begins by declaring God's oneness: "Hear, O Israel: the Lord our God, the Lord is one" (Mark 12:29; see also Zech 14:9: God's "name" is "one"). We may correctly imagine that in its original contexts the saying functioned to differentiate the "one God" of Israel and the church from the "many gods" of other peoples. The point was

---

which means that theology has the task of helping the church not say more about God than needs to be said." *Hannah's Child,* 52.

64. McCabe, *God Still Matters,* 26.

65. Note the way Fergus Kerr similarly explains the doctrine in Thomas: "Denying that God is a being with qualities, as created beings are, leads to a conclusion some readers find bizarre. In particular, since God is not a being with properties, we cannot say that God is, for example, wise or just, as if wisdom, justice, and so on, are qualities that God might or might not have. On the contrary: 'God must be his own godhead, his own life, and whatever else is predicated of him' ([*Summa Theologiae*] 1.3.3). No doubt, we may go on picturing God as a being with virtues; but that remains an anthropomorphic conception." *After Aquinas,* 77.

God's singularity, not God's simplicity. But as I have regularly argued in this book, we need not limit ourselves to the ancient meaning.

Likewise for many other references to God's oneness. "I and the father are one" (John 10:30). "God is one" (Rom 3:30 and Gal 3:20). "There is no other God but one" (1 Cor 8:4). "There is but one God" (1 Cor 8:6). "One God and father of all" (Eph 4:6). "For there is one God, and one mediator between God and men, the man Jesus Christ" (1 Tim 2:5). The New Testament is sprinkled with the theme.

We find even more to think about if we realize that a Greek word often translated in the New Testament as "sound" or "healthy" has as its more basic, fundamental meaning "single" or "simple." Jesus says, "The light of the body is the eye. If therefore your eye is ἁπλοῦς, your whole body will be full of light" (Matt 6:22; see also Luke 11:34, which is almost identical in wording). The basic meaning of the word is "single," "one," and by extension "simple," as opposed to "double," "two-fold," or "compound" (διπλοῦς). In fact, the LSJ (1968), in spite of listing several similar meanings of the word, has no listing as "healthy," demonstrating simply that the other translations are much more common, certainly for classical Greek but probably also for ancient Greek more generally. In other words, the meanings of the word as "healthy" or "sound" derive from the older, more basic meaning of one, single, or simple.[66]

Modern translators, I believe, are perfectly within their rights to translate the word to reflect health rather than unity. As I noted above, much ancient medical theory took unity, singleness, and simplicity to be attributes of the healthy body, individual or political. And I take it that Jesus, in the quotation, should be taken as talking about the eye when it is working in its proper manner, as a whole, healthy, sound eye. But we may also take the saying as Jesus praising the quality of singleness and simplicity—innocence, we could also say. And as those virtues Jesus urges are possible only because they are given us as expressions of God's own nature, Jesus also here teaches and praises the simplicity of God.

These different theological concepts or themes—we could also call them tools, practices, handles—I have been treating in this chapter—negative theology, transcendence, immanence, divine simplicity—all work together to help us talk about our faith while knowing we cannot really know God,

66. A form of the word (as a noun rather than an adjective) occurs in Eph 6:5 and Col 3:22 to urge slaves to "singleness of heart." In Rom 12:8 it is used to encourage people to give in "simplicity" (in the KJV; translated as "generosity" in the NRSV).

at least not like we can know anything or anyone else. We Christians have learned through much experience—for some of us the experiences of our own lifetimes, but for all of us the accumulated experience of theology and life contained in Christian history and tradition—that all words for God are inadequate. Every word for God may mislead, be untrue. If we think we can replace the unspeakable, unknowable, true God with any word or combination of words, we have at that moment descended into idolatry. No human word is adequate for God, even those words we believe have been given to us by God in revelation. Thus much of the best Christian theology provides word pictures of what God may be like that it knows are true, if they are true at all, only partially and "in a sense." We can never look straight at God, at least not in this life. When we try to look at God, it is as if she is over somewhere else, just outside our direct line of sight, as if we see God only fuzzily on the very periphery of our vision, as someone we know must be there but on whom we cannot "get a bead."

That's why the best attempts to speak of the God of our faith are sometimes with poetic or literary metaphors. We may use our imaginations to think of pictures or things to which we may compare God while their inadequacy is obvious to us. Or, as when we attempt to wrap our minds around the seeming impossibilities of modern physics, we may pose definitions that we know we cannot really understand. So one such definition cited by the novelist, essayist, and I would say theologian whom I've already mentioned, Marilynne Robinson, is apropos: "God is a sphere whose center is everywhere and whose circumference is nowhere."[67]

Idolatry

As I have briefly noted, these various doctrines—apophatic theology, transcendence, immanence, and divine simplicity—are useful not because they

---

67. Robinson says she learned the quotation from her brother but didn't know where he got it. The saying may have originated with a book attributed to a legendary figure of scholastic mythology, Hermes Trismegistus, *Liber XXIV philosophorum*, II: "Deus est sphera infinita cuius centrum est ubique, circumferentia vero nusquam." See Hudry, ed., *Le Livre des XXIV Philosophes*. The author and date of the composition of this philosophical compendium are unknown, but it is probably medieval. The saying seems to have been known by Alain de Lille (c. 1128–1202/1203), Nicholas of Cusa (1401–64), Blaise Pascal (1623–62), and even several Puritan theologians. The idea, or something like it, is referred to or quoted from ancient times to modern. Robinson, *When I Was a Child I Read Books*, 86.

are self-evidently true, or because they point to some kind of fundamental knowledge we have of the universe or God, or because they have been "proven" by philosophy. They are useful only because they help us avoid idolatry. But theologians do not often enough point out *why* idolatry is wrong. I agree that idolatry is dangerous, but I believe we need to be more explicit about what is wrong with idolatry. What makes idolatry so dangerous?

That idolatry is dangerous may be taken from the abhorrence of idols ("images" of gods that are not truly god) and idolatry (the "care and feeding" of those images and those gods; service to and worship of those images and gods) so apparent in the New Testament. What is probably our earliest extant document of the New Testament, Paul's first letter to the Thessalonians, begins with his reminder that his original preaching to them had involved mainly an attempt to turn them away from their native gods, from what Paul calls idols (1 Thess 1:9). Greeks would not usually have used that term for their gods and images since the word itself implies that the images and statues are in some way "false," in classical Greek meaning something like "phantom." As we can see from 1 Thess 4–5, Paul seems to have failed to inform the Thessalonians, in all his initial teaching among them, about the resurrection or indeed any afterlife hope at all, but he did make a condemnation of idolatry a key element of his first instructions.[68] The most basic element of Paul's gospel must have been the necessity for gentiles to reject their traditional gods and turn to the God of Israel and his representative, Jesus.

In 1 Cor 10:14, Paul says, "Flee idolatry!" In Gal 5:20, he lists it among the most serious vices. For Paul, as probably for most Jews at the time, idolatry was a "gentile" sin par excellence (see Rom 1; 1 Pet 4:3). So Paul insists that the Corinthians should not even eat with any fellow believers who have not completely cut themselves off from idolatry (1 Cor 5:11). We must remember how socially disruptive this must have been for many of his converts. So much of ancient life of the Mediterranean revolved around social events and even eating itself that were deeply implicated in acknowledging the gods of one's people, family, and city. It would have been very hard to avoid mingling in one way or another with what Paul calls idolatry. Recognizing this, Paul does not tell the Corinthians they cannot eat or associate with idolaters themselves, only with any fellow believer who is tainted in some way by idolatrous behavior.

---

68. For discussion of the strange absence of such instruction about afterlife in Paul's initial instruction to the Thessalonians, see my *New Testament*, 210–12, summarized briefly in chapter 6 below.

We can see the fear of idolatry in the fact that so many early Christians went out of their way to avoid eating any food and probably drinking any wine that had been implicated in the worship of other gods. According to the Acts of the Apostles, the early church forbade gentile converts from eating anything that had been part of a sacrifice to an idol, which would have included probably most meat sold in marketplaces (Acts 15:20; 15:29; 21:25). This strict avoidance of "idol meat" is also demanded by the author of Revelation (2:14, 20). Paul's position is a bit more moderate. He said that believers could share in eating such food as long as they were not involved in the worship of the idol or the actual sacrificial cult itself and only if they had superior knowledge that could protect them from any potential harm threatened by such eating (1 Cor 8:8; 10:19). But Paul's "solution," which takes up all of 1 Cor 8–10, is none too clear and has led to an entire history of exegetical debate about what precisely he meant.[69] And Paul may well have been an exception: most evidence suggests that the vast majority of early Christians believed they should avoid any contact with materials that had been part of a sacrifice or offering to an idol—evidence again of their utter fear of idolatry and of idols themselves.

But we have evidence that early Christians were able to expand the definition of "idolatry" to include behaviors beyond the worship of or service to actual images of gods. They broadened the meaning to include allowing the desire for anything whatsoever to rise to the desire for or honor of God we should nurture. Thus Colossians and Ephesians teach that love of money, greed, is also "idolatry" (Col 3:5; Eph 5:5). The Greek word translated here as "greed" (πλεονεξία) is broader than simply a desire for more and more money, though it certainly includes that. It means any kind of "grasping" behavior, wanting "more than one's fair share." That would make almost all of us idolaters at least much of the time.

So already within the pages of the New Testament, Christianity recognized the dangers of idolatry and broadened the traditional definition to include putting anything at all in the place we should reserve for God alone. What idolatry is putting in the place of the hidden being and the mystery we designate by the label God is any other thing at all, anything we can see or even imagine, anything at all of the cosmos, the universe. If anything of the universe *can* be made into an idol, that means God must be radically *other* than and different from the universe and everything in it. As Nicholas Lash puts it, "If Christian discourse is not to become idolatrous, it must be

---

69. For my own take on the topic, see *Corinthian Body,* 179–89.

permanently iconoclastic."[70] The doctrines of transcendence and divine simplicity and the practice of apophatic theology spring from, we may imagine, the Christian abhorrence of idolatry.

But, again, why is idolatry so dangerous? The idea in much traditional or popular religion is that idolatry is wrong because God is offended when we turn our attentions away from him to someone else or if we make another of our lovers equal to him. This is a rather mythological understanding of why idolatry is wrong—mythological because it provides a narrative that seeks to show something about God but does so by making God too much like us human beings. God is not Othello. Idolatry is wrong but not because it hurts God. And God is not some jilted boyfriend or cuckolded husband who may beat us up for dating someone else. That myth needs rigorous critique.

When we encounter in the Bible such images of God as jealous and forbidding idolatry because he is just the kind of selfish god who wants us "all to himself," we must carefully interpret them, even "demythologize" them. We may indeed read biblical descriptions of God's jealousy or wrath, but then such passages must be subjected to interpretation so that we see how they may be in some sense true but in other senses false. If we imagine that God is sad when we forsake him for some other god, that probably won't harm our theology or faith too much. We can then imagine that God grieves when we commit idolatry because God knows we will end up hurting ourselves in the end. God grieves because God knows we are going to come to grief. That could be an acceptable way to interpret biblical images of the jealous God. But we must remind ourselves that ultimately we do not hurt God by our idolatry, we hurt ourselves. God, in forbidding us from substituting anything in the universe in God's place, attempts to protect us from *being harmed,* not from harming God.

Thus we may indeed use biblical images of God to help us think of why God wants us to avoid idols. The prodigal son (Luke 15:11–23) thought he could replace his father by means of his inheritance and self-reliance. His father, though grieved and certain it would all end in sorrow, let his son go. The father, though, was not offended at his son's behavior nor did he punish the son when he later realized his mistake and wanted to return. If God is pained by our turning to substitutes for the true God, it is the pain of the father of the prodigal, not the anger and passion of a spurned lover.

A mother may attempt to persuade her daughter that someone with whom the daughter has fallen in love is not a suitable partner for her. If the

---

70. Lash, *Matter of Hope,* 132.

mother does so only because she is jealous of her daughter's affections and wants to keep her daughter "for herself" alone, she is acting out of selfishness and spite, not true love. But she may indeed sincerely believe that the object of her daughter's affections will end up bringing only pain to her daughter, and she may experience her daughter's pain with her. That is the only kind of "jealousy" God feels for us. That is the only reason the scriptures warn us so much against idolatry. We will end up just hurting ourselves.

Idolatry is bad, therefore, not because it offends God, as if God is a person who becomes upset at being neglected or mistreated. Idolatry is bad because it is dangerous. The danger it poses is that it so often leads to a loss of faith. What makes idols dangerous is that we eventually discover that they aren't, after all, very good gods. Money lets us down. Lovers and friends cannot be everything. Success and pride end up disappointing. Even values and goods that seem ultimately good eventually let us down. Even "love" in and of itself may disappoint or fall short. That's why "love," at least in any of the ways we may imagine it in our limited human imaginations, can't be substituted for "God."

Negative theology teaches that even good images become idols if we imagine "that image" is truly and fully "God." If we take "father" to be a necessary or sufficient "image" for God, we may stop believing in God when we find that "father" can fail. Many people have ended up losing their faith because they came to distrust their previous, insufficient images of God. They allowed their beliefs *about* God to take the place of the ineffable and unknowable God. When they decided that the grandfatherly, authoritative god of their childhood was not worth their respect, they lost their faith entirely. But the Christian teaching about the danger of idolatry should have taught them that their older god wasn't God after all. Their idol led to their loss of faith. Once we really confront our idols or seek to depend on them for what we really need from God, those false gods prove that they are lousy gods. Idols are gods that ultimately fail us. That failure often leads to atheism. Idolatry is dangerous because it so often leads to atheism or at least to a loss of faith.

"God" Is Not God's Name

Much of what I have been advocating regarding the ineffable nature of God's being can be illustrated by disputing a practice of some Christians who avoid pronouncing "God" or even writing it out, substituting instead "G-d" or "G*d." Some, no doubt, do so in imitation of Jewish avoidance of speaking the name of God as found in the Hebrew Bible, the Tetragrammaton: Hebrew letters usually transliterated YHWH. The word has no vocalization in Hebrew script, no vowels, we might say. Though it was translated as "Jehovah" in early English translations, most modern English versions use LORD, with small caps, to indicate where in the Hebrew text the Tetragrammaton occurs. Many Jews traditionally substitute the Hebrew word for "lord," *adonai,* or some other title for God instead of reading out YHWH. This practice is reflected also in the New Testament, where the Greek usually has κύριος, "lord," when quoting the Old Testament, which it always does in Greek translation.

The rationale given by some Christians for using "G-d" or "G*d" is that such substitutions, in the words of Elisabeth Schüssler Fiorenza, "indicate the brokenness and inadequacy of human language for naming the Divine."[71] But such an explanation at least elides the fact that the practice came from imitating conservative Jewish avoidance of pronouncing what is a "name" for God in the Hebrew Bible, YHWH. In doing so, such Christians are, in my view, turning the common noun "god" *into* a "proper name" in Christianity, an alteration that never should happen in the first place. "God" is not the name of the Christian god.

I believe substituting "G-d" or "G*d" for "God" actually compounds the theological errors it attempts to correct. For one thing, the practice too often springs, I believe, from a desire to find "pure" and "right" language about God, words that will avoid potential problems of the traditional word "God." But this desire for purity in language is misguided and misleading. We have no pure words. Especially when speaking of God, but actually when speaking of anything, human language can never be pure. It can never avoid potential error. It is a fact of human language that all our words are tainted and may lead us or others astray. That is why we need to learn proper interpretation, interpretation that shows how Christian language may be appropriate but how it is also fallible.

---

71. Schüssler Fiorenza, *Democratizing,* 3n9. Schüssler Fiorenza first began using the spelling "G-d" in *But She Said* and *Discipleship of Equals.* By the time she wrote *Jesus: Miriam's Child, Sophia's Prophet,* Jewish feminists had objected to that spelling, mainly because it "suggests a very conservative, if not reactionary, theological frame of reference" (191n3), so she shifted again to "G*d." I find both spellings actually do the opposite of what Schüssler Fiorenza wants to do: they tend to *highlight* the "naming" function of the letters, precisely because such substitutions look like an imitation of a Jewish attempt to avoid saying the Hebrew "proper name" of the deity.

The substitution of these different spellings and symbols for "God" is even more seriously misleading, as I hinted above, because it actually implies that "God" is God's proper name, in the same way that YHWH functions as the name of the God of Israel in the Hebrew Bible. The New Testament, on the contrary, never attempts to transliterate or translate "YHWH" into Greek. This may reflect no more theological sophistication than that the writers are themselves using Greek translations, which had already made the substitutions for them. But I prefer to take the New Testament as offering no proper name for god the father, the god of Israel, as a lesson that the Christian god has no name.

Instead of substituting "G-d" or "G*d" for "God" we should instead emphasize the theological truth that the Christian God in its fullness, that is, as the full godhead or trinity, has no name. We may certainly assume that God's "proper name" could be "Jesus," but we then would need to remind ourselves that "Jesus" is the proper name for only one person of the trinity, not the entire godhead. Or Christianity, out of respect for the Hebrew Bible, could revert to using YHWH for the name of its god. But as I argued above in the chapter on scripture, we should not assume that the Hebrew Bible, in any of its later editions or instantiations, whether as the Masoretic Text or some modern edition, is *the* Old Testament for Christians. And reverting to YHWH as the name of God for Christianity would be a significant departure from Christian liturgical practice and tradition, not to mention the practices of the New Testament writers. Unless we want to say that God's personal name is Jesus or YHWH, neither of which option I believe to be commendable, we should get used to the idea, the very ancient, orthodox idea, that the Christian god has no name.

People—even scholars—tend too quickly to forget that "god" in ancient Greek was not a proper name. This is easier to remember when we read the texts in Greek because they so often use the word θεός ("god") with the definite article ὁ ("the"). When reading Greek, it is easier to read ὁ θεός as "the god" rather than "God." Unfortunately, using God without the article makes it easier to take it mistakenly in English as a name, a tendency made even more tempting by the fact that it is almost always capitalized when referring to the god of Christianity. It would actually be better for an orthodox understanding of the nature of the Christian deity to leave it uncapitalized and with the article. Perhaps we should say "the god" when speaking of the Christian deity, just as we speak of "the" holy spirit. It would remind us that "God" is not God's personal name, and that for Christianity God has no name.

McCabe makes the salient point, moreover, that the term "god" is one Christianity took over from Greek polytheism. It is, he notes, a borrowed word. To Greeks the word denoted simply a god in general. They knew it wasn't a proper name for any god. In fact, that is precisely why many non-Christian Greeks thought followers of Jesus must be atheists: they worshipped something that didn't even have a name![72] But McCabe insists we turn this to orthodox advantage. God, he says, "is always dressed verbally in second-hand clothes that don't fit him very well. We always have to be on our guard against taking these clothes as revealing who and what he is."[73] Reminding ourselves that "god" is a generic term for any god in Greek might keep us from slipping into the mistake of assuming our god has a name, and it is "God."

I noted that this is an ancient Christian position. As Andrew Radde-Gallwitz notes, in the opinion of Clement of Alexandria, "We have no proper name for God."[74] Lash explains why this is important: "Common names are names proper to individual members of a class: 'tree' names all the things that count as trees. Proper names are names proper to individual members of a class: all the readers of this text are human beings, but I am, I think, the only Nicholas Langrishe Alleyne Lash. But the incomprehensible and holy mystery we worship is not, I have been urging, a member of *any* class."[75]

Reminding ourselves that the Christian god has no name speaks to the ultimately ineffable nature of the divine in orthodox Christianity. It reminds us of the necessary unnameable nature of the god of our faith.

Faith and Despair

But what is faith? If faith is not simply believing "God exists" or "God is this or that," if faith is not simply intellectual assent to some proposition about God, what is it? If I don't have to believe that God is a grandfather in the sky, what do I believe that still constitutes faith?

As I have already implied, for many Christians, especially those familiar with the long Christian tradition of apophatic theology, faith sometimes

---

72. See, for example, the *Martyrs of Lyon* 52, found in Eusebius, *Ecclesiastical History* 5.1.52.

73. *God Still Matters*, 3.

74. Clement, *Strommata* 5.11.82. See also Radde-Gallwitz, *Basil of Caesarea*, 53. Clement gets the point from Plato. See *Parmenides* 142a; and commentary in Clement of Alexander, *Les Stromates: Stromate V*, 2:265–66.

75. Lash, *Holiness*, 14.

boils down to a way of being in the world in which one lives as if the universe is meaningful and the ultimate meaning has to do with goodness and love. For some people, this can even be a decision. They know that the stories about God's actions as we read them in the Bible may be "myths," which is simply to say they are narratives that attempt to teach some truth about God's nature by means of portraying God as if God were like a human person or an animal, when we know that God is not a human person or an animal. God is not really a physical person who walks in a garden. But the story may allow us to imagine God as our friend who seeks us out. "Myths" in this sense are stories about God that may be true on some kind of deep level but cannot be true in a simplistic literal or historical understanding. So some Christians, even if not believing such stories "literally" or "historically," still decide to accept the idea that God is what supplies meaning to our universe, and that is a good and loving meaning. They decide to live their lives *as if* love is the ultimate, most important value of our world and our lives. For some Christians, that is, faith is a decision to live their lives under the influence of Christian teachings and values, including the assumption that the universe is meaningful, even when it seems not to be.

Other Christians don't experience their faith so much as a decision, something they once upon a time chose or they choose continually. They rather experience their faith as something that chose them. They find they simply discover themselves comfortable in the belief that their world and lives are meaningful, and they attribute that meaning to the grace of a god who allowed them to rest in an indescribable and ultimately unprovable faith. Many of us, even having gone through periods of doubt and questioning, find that we still are content to recite the Apostles Creed and the Nicene Creed and to read and believe the scriptures, even when we know that those texts must still be interpreted in a never-ending, ongoing attempt to "find" the proper meaning in them. Yet we experience this more as a discovery we already believe and are content to live in a faith in God rather than something we must continually "stoke up" or decide to do. But this also is faith.

A classical word that designates this sense of a "way of being" or way of life is *habitus,* as I mentioned in chapter 1, "Knowledge." The concept is Aristotelian and taken over by Christian theology. It is not the same thing as "habit," which usually has negative connotations for us and is taken to refer to actions we regret but have trouble escaping. "Habits," we usually think, are things we want to break. In examples suggested by Frederick Christian Bauerschmidt, here referring more specifically to the theology of Thomas Aquinas, chewing one's fingernails is a habit; speaking French is a habitus:

"A *habitus* is an acquired quality or disposition that makes it possible to act in a particular way—even inclines one to act in that way."[76] For most of us, driving a car is a habitus: we had to learn how to do it and to practice it for a time, but now we do it automatically and without thinking much about it.

As habitus, faith is a learned and regularly reinforced manner of living, living *as if* the universe and our lives within it are meaningful and *as if* that meaning is good rather than evil, love rather than hate. (Paul knew about living "as if": see 1 Cor 7:29–31.) We have no proof the gospel is true. That's what makes it faith rather than knowledge. We find we have developed a habit of believing, a habitus of faith.

This understanding of faith is itself empirical, however. I derive the idea of what faith is not from wishing it were so but from actually observing how I and other Christians I know "believe," how we remain in the church willing to confess its creeds even when we know one may legitimately doubt, even when we know that other reasonable people do *not* believe. Whether we came to this faith and remain in it because of quite materialist socialization, whether we remain in the church out of habit, or however else one may wish to explain our experience apart from appeal to God, we choose to believe, or simply do believe, that we have faith because God gave us—and gives us—the miracle of faith. We have the habitus of faith by the grace of God. That is as good an explanation of faith's existence as any other.

For other people, both Christians and non-Christians, it may be unsatisfactory to say that my faith consists in the acceptance of the proposition that the universe has meaning, or that there may be a "reason" for the existence of the universe, or that I have come to believe that life is ultimately about love, even though I admit that whether love exists or not is something we will have to take on faith rather than find "proved." Skeptics of this account of faith may respond, "But that's not what I mean. I mean do you believe that God exists somewhere 'out there'?" To which the answer must be, "Of course not. That is ridiculous." The reason it is ridiculous is that there is no "there" "out there," either *inside* the universe or *outside* the universe, "where" God *could* "exist." As we have seen, the doctrine of divine simplicity teaches that God is the ultimate One, with no divisions or multiplications. God is not someplace out there. In any case, in the end it doesn't matter whether someone else accepts or rejects this somewhat minimalist account of what constitutes "faith" in its most basic sense. It is an empirical fact that this is what constitutes faith for many Christians, and that fact is proof enough that it is faith.

76. Bauerschmidt, *Holy Teaching*, 135n11.

But if faith is an assumption that the universe and our lives in it are meaningful, the opposite of faith is not simply some ascription to a proposition that "there exists no God." The opposite of faith is rather the horrible experience of coming to the conclusion that the universe and our lives are meaningless. For me, the true opposite of faith is not modern, and by now traditional, atheism or agnosticism. It is despair: the feeling deep down that our world and we are meaningless.[77] Loss of faith is despair, which shows finally why idolatry is so dangerous. Idolatry doesn't harm God. And apart from God's compassion for us, human despair doesn't harm God. Idolatry is wrong because it leads us to despair of our false gods and ultimately to the danger of despairing of life itself as meaningless.

A "Personal" God?

For many Christians, however, any faith that does not profess a "personal" God cannot be true Christian faith. Must one believe in a "personal" God in order to be faithful?

Unfortunately, most of the time it is not particularly clear what is meant by the term "personal God." Is this meant in the same way we might talk about a personal trainer or a personal assistant? There is an old joke about the Episcopalian lady who, when asked by her neighbor if she had "accepted Jesus as her personal Lord and Savior," replied, "But dear, that would be a bit selfish, wouldn't it?" I believe that the easy way people talk about their "personal God" should be examined more critically than is typically the case.[78]

There are, as a matter of fact, plenty of definitions of God in the New Testament that are rather *im*personal. God is said to be πνεῦμα, which though usually translated "spirit" meant something rather different in the ancient Greek world than it does in this modern English translation. As I have demonstrated elsewhere, and as I will explore more thoroughly in the chapter below titled "Spirit," pneuma was considered the "stuff" that energized the world, human bodies, and everything that was alive.[79] It was a stuff that enabled thinking, by working in the brain, feeling, by moving back and forth through the body, seeing, by traveling in light into the eyes and further

77. I hasten to add that I do not here mean psychological depression, which I take to be a medical—and often biological or physical—condition for which people ought to seek help and healing.

78. For some problems with the term "person" when applied to God or the "persons" of the trinity, see Barth, *Church Dogmatics* I/1, pp. 355–59.

79. See my *Corinthian Body,* 21–25, 123–29; see now the fuller exposition in Engberg-Pedersen, *Cosmology.*

into the brain, and hearing, by moving into the ears and then into the brain or the heart. Almost all ancient persons of the period of the New Testament documents would have assumed that pneuma was some kind of physical stuff, only of a very fine, invisible, rarified nature. But they would likely have heard the phrase "God is pneuma" as stating that God was the energizing stuff of the universe and the matter of intelligence and life. We may imagine they thought of pneuma the way many of us might think of oxygen or energy.

If we didn't "know" that energy is just matter in another form ($e=mc^2$), we also could consider that "god" is the energy that runs and sustains the universe. (I put "know" in quotation marks because for most of us what we "know" about physics and cosmology is just what scientists tell us to believe.)[80] To equate god with what scientists call energy, therefore, would be to misidentify god with the stuff of the universe itself, and I will shortly explain why that is a problem for orthodox Christianity. But we may certainly say of God that God is what makes the universe run, that God is the force that sustains the existence of the universe. Those are perfectly orthodox things to say about God and may be inspired by the New Testament teaching that God is pneuma.

The First Letter of John defines God as "light" (1 John 1:5). Here, too, ancient people may have identified divinity with what we would see as physical light, that is, what we call the waves or particles of light. Christians would demur again from the exact equation, but we could easily see the text as teaching that God is the subsistence of light, the thing or force that underlies the existence of light, the reason light is possible.

The same letter offers this other definition: "God is love" (4:8). Note that the text doesn't say God is a "loving person" or "God is someone who happens also to love." Given the discussion on divine simplicity above, we can now recognize the difference: God is not a person who happens to love. God is *love itself.* Though "love" is a wonderful thing, perhaps the best thing of all, the word is nonetheless something more like an "abstraction," a "force," or a "state of being" than a "person."

Though the first verse of the Gospel of John more exactly says, "The word became God" and "The word was God," it is certainly not a stretch to say that God *is logos.* The Greek λόγος does mean "word." But, as is well known, it also refers to speech more generally, to a conversation, a speech

---

80. For one author's attempt to explain what science "knows" or just accepts as "true" even without understanding, see the many examples provided by Potter, *You Are Here.* His discussion of $e=mc^2$ occurs at 150.

given on some occasion. It also means "rationality" or "reason" and can come to be "meaning." So we may take John 1:1 as offering the definition "God = rationality or meaning itself." As I've put it already in the chapter, God is the reason there is anything at all, the *logos* of the world, not to be identified with the world, but its reason. This may be somewhat like what the author of Colossians means when he says that Jesus, as the image of the invisible God, is the force that "holds together" all things (Col 1:17). God is like gravity, only different.

Another doctrine taught by the New Testament may, surprisingly, be relevant here. Some writers speak of God as working in the universe and toward human beings in "foreknowledge" or "preordination." God is the reason some people believe and others do not (Rom 9:11–22). God "destined" Christians for salvation (Eph 1:4–5). God is the one who knows what is coming but may not yet exist. 1 Pet 1:2 speaks of the "prognosis of God" as God's foreknowledge, implying that God is outside space-time; God is the meaning of the universe beyond time. All this is much like the way ancient Greeks thought the universe functioned: through "fate." In this way of thinking, God is the "mind" of the universe. For us, this might be like thinking of God as the software of the world. At least, that wouldn't be far from the ancient conceptions, including perhaps that implied by early Christian notions of predestination and election. We can live, if we live at all, only within the "will," the "mind," of God.

All these ideas, read off the pages of the New Testament even by the modern means of traditional historical criticism, at least give us postmodern Christians permission to think about God in what may feel like "impersonal" ways indeed. A Christian faith need not avoid imagining the God of our belief with images that are more "impersonal" than "personal."

For some people these have been the only ways they could "believe in God" at all. Baruch Spinoza (1632–77) rejected the dualism of his time, promoted to a great extent by the science and philosophy of René Descartes (1596–1650), that posited "nature" as one thing in existence alongside another realm in which existed God and whatever else was thought to be "supernatural," such as possibly souls, angels, demons, or whatever. Spinoza did not at all reject the existence of God; he just insisted that God *was* the unified, eternal, infinite intellect that sustains "Nature." God is "the universal, immanent, sustaining cause of all that exists."[81] God is the cause for the sustenance of mo-

---

81. An excellent introduction to both Spinoza's life and philosophy is Nadler, *Spinoza;* this quotation is Nadler's words (229), describing Spinoza's views.

tion in the universe. Spinoza could speak of "substance," but he didn't mean merely physical matter. There was also thought, which is substance but not physical matter. That nonphysical "substance"—call it "thinking substance" perhaps—which is absolutely necessary for the existence of all of nature, is, for Spinoza, God. In the end, for Spinoza God *is* the fullness of Nature.[82]

There was nothing particularly new in these ideas about God and nature. Spinoza's thought has a great deal in common with ancient Greek philosophy, especially Stoicism, though I think it would be a mistake to call Spinoza a Stoic.[83] Spinoza's notions have much in common with the second-century CE physician Galen, who could talk about "Nature" as if it were a "god" just as much as Zeus, or more so.[84] Albert Einstein was deeply influenced by Spinoza's theology. For Einstein, the order, beauty, and harmony of nature, the regularity of nature—one could even say its "laws"—was what Einstein called God.[85] Like Spinoza, Einstein rejected any idea of God as a person who intervened in "nature," judged and rewarded or punished human beings, or any such thing. Faith, to Einstein, was his firmly held belief, even in the face of new theories in physics that might suggest otherwise, that the objective world exists independently of our observations and is ruled by consistent laws. Einstein insisted he was neither an atheist nor an agnostic, and he was willing to call his beliefs religious. As he put it, "Try and penetrate with our limited means the secrets of nature and you will find that, behind all the discernible laws and connections, there remains something subtle, intangible and inexplicable. Veneration for this force beyond anything that we can comprehend is my religion."[86] Einstein could speak of "the infinitely superior spirit" or "a superior reasoning power" of nature.[87]

What Spinoza and Einstein were rejecting was not God, but the belief in a separate realm of existence alongside nature that could be dubbed the

---

82. For these several points, see Nadler, *Spinoza,* 187–88, 210, 231.

83. A major goal of much of ancient Stoicism was the complete extirpation of the passions, and there were Stoics who believed that the goal was attainable, not by many people, but by at least a very few great men (see Martin, "Paul Without Passion," in *Sex and the Single Savior,* 65–76). Spinoza believed that wise people would control their passions but that their extirpation was not possible.

84. See Martin, *Inventing Superstition,* 109–24.

85. Much of my description of Einstein's "theology" comes from Walter Isaacson's biography, *Einstein.*

86. Ibid., 384–85, quoting from Kessler, ed., *The Diaries of Count Harry Kessler,* 322 (entry for June 14, 1927).

87. See Isaacson, *Einstein,* 388, for these terms. For other points of this paragraph, see also 20, 84, 334, 384–93.

supernatural. What makes their beliefs unlike what I have been describing as "orthodox Christianity," however, is not their rejection of "the supernatural" but their willingness to identify God *with* nature. Orthodox Christian doctrine, I have been attempting to illustrate above, has always attempted to avoid identifying God with the universe or anything in the universe. But Christian doctrine has done so by teaching the radical transcendence of God apart from nature, and yet God's radical immanence throughout nature. God is not another thing beside nature, but also God is not to be simply equated with nature. God is the reason for the existence of everything that exists, whatever we may include in "nature." But that need not lead to a positing of a realm of *other* created things (angels, souls, whatever) that exist in a *different* realm we call the supernatural. As I have argued elsewhere, the "supernatural," in the way modern people have posed it since at least Descartes, did not exist for almost all ancient people either, who just assumed that nature included everything that is, at least up until the period of late antiquity, say, the fourth or fifth century CE.[88]

I am proposing that a viable postmodern Christian faith may appropriate forms of Christianity that existed before the split between "the natural" and "the supernatural." We need not have our reality split up into two separate realms of created things, "nature" and "supernature," in order to avoid identifying God with nature. That was the mistake of much modern Christian teaching since the Enlightenment. The mistake made by Spinoza and Einstein, however, was a different one, but from the point of view of orthodox Christianity a mistake still. That was the mistake of *identifying* God *with* nature. We avoid both mistakes by saying that the only uncreated being is God. Everything that exists exists because of God and exists, as far as we know, as part of the universe. Yet God is not the universe or anything in the universe. We don't need a realm of "the supernatural" to retain faith in God.

This avoids unnecessary and unfortunate thinking about "laws of nature" and "miracle." According to much modern thinking, "miracles" are events in which God "breaks into nature" from the outside and "overturns or goes against" the "laws of nature." That is, however, not what ancient Christians meant by "miracle."[89] For one thing, very few of them, if any, used any

---

88. See Martin, *Corinthian Body*, 4–6 *et passim*; Martin, *Inventing Superstition*, 13–16.

89. Note, for example, that for Augustine miracles cannot be "contrary to nature." As he says, "Nothing intrinsically impossible falls within divine omnipotence." *Contra Faustum Manichaeum* 26.3–5; quoted from Chadwick, *Augustine*, 79. So also Thomas Aquinas: "Grace does not destroy nature, but perfects it." *Summa Theologiae* 1.1.8.2; I quote Fergus

notion about "laws of nature." The Greek words from which we take the various words we use for miracles—"sign," "wonder," and "miracle" itself—all just meant something amazing, out of the ordinary, wonder producing, awe inspiring. It is only a modern idea that "miracle" by its very definition is an act of God or some other "supernatural" agent that is impossible according to the "laws of nature."[90]

As a prominent and brilliant (and Christian) philosopher of science, Bas C. van Fraassen, has demonstrated, we ourselves don't need, and scientists can't prove, the very existence of "laws of nature." Van Fraassen convincingly argues that the concept may have done service in some developments of modern science, but it was an invention we don't really need, one that does not actually matter for the real doing of science, cannot be proven, and is philosophically unlikely.[91] The belief that acts of God must be an intervention of the supernatural into the natural realm, breaking God's own constituted "laws" of nature, moreover, just seems to many of us theologically suspect and maybe offensive. As McCabe notes, even though Thomas Aquinas used a Latin term that could be considered a precursor to the modern "supernatural," "Aquinas didn't see miracles as God intervening to interfere with the world. God, thinks Aquinas, cannot literally intervene in the universe because he is always there—just as much in the normal, natural run of things as in the resurrection of Christ or in any other miraculous event."[92] Or, in a phrase I quite like, Paul J. DeHart says, "God's presence and revelation do not 'punch a hole' in the world; God meets humanity, both in Christ and in culture, not apart from but in the very historical contingency of the human act."[93]

None of this is to say we must deny the possibility of miracle. It is just to think about such events differently. Instead of thinking of them as "interventions" of "the supernatural" into nature or as events that "break the laws of nature," we consider them signs of the constant creation and sustaining of the universe by God. The actions of God are seen as part of our universe, God not being completely separable from our universe or, better put, the

Kerr's English here, preferring it over the Dominican (Blackfriars) version. See Kerr, *After Aquinas*, 138.

90. For a string of attempts to define "miracle," see the several citations furnished by Licona, *Resurrection*, 134–36n3.

91. Van Fraassen, *Laws and Symmetry*. For a further attack on scientific epistemological foundationalism, see his *Empirical Stance*.

92. McCabe, *Faith Within Reason*, 101–2.

93. DeHart, *Trial of Witnesses*, 274.

universe being impossible apart from God's presence. God does not "need" the universe, but the universe cannot exist without the immanent being of God "under" it or "containing" it.

The modern natural/supernatural dichotomy (and for the most part *as a dichotomy* it is "modern") has historical relevance. But its theological relevance should be to cause us, in a more "postmodern" age of Christianity, to abandon thinking of "miracle" or "the supernatural" in the modernist (scientific and fundamentalist!) Cartesian dichotomy and rather think of miracle as the marveling attribution to divine power of events in our world we cannot fathom. There is no need for "supernatural intervention" or "suspending the laws of nature" in a postmodern—scientific as well as theological—environment.

And, to get back to the question that prompted this section, there is nothing wrong with thinking of God as a "person," but the more sophisticated our theological thinking becomes, the more we should keep in mind that portraying God as a person is mythological thinking. There's nothing wrong with mythological thinking. As human beings, we can hardly avoid using stories or narratives with which to "think" God. We can hardly avoid attributing human characteristics to God if we participate in most worship or liturgy at all. But we should realize that just as calling God a "father" could be misleading and dangerous—and by attributing human and historical actions to the unknowable god of the universe is therefore "myth"—so calling god a "person" does constitute a "myth" and therefore may be misleading, as are all myths, even good ones.

God in the New Testament

I have spent much space in this chapter warning about how anything we can say about God will necessarily be false in some sense, so there is no reason to take uncritically any particular image, description, or doctrine of God from the text of scripture. But we may indeed read the New Testament to inform how we think of the nature and character of God.

Above, I spoke about scriptural portrayals of God as the creator of the world, making all that is from nothing: creatio ex nihilo. This is a doctrine about God I believe we may return to regularly with profit. As I pointed out above, however, we would do better to think of God's creation of the universe—and us in it—not in terms of a "once upon a time" past event. Rather, we should remind ourselves that God is constantly creating. And we need not see that as some kind of "supernatural" intervention in nature. The miracle of God's creation of our world lies not in God's "punching a hole" in the universe but in God's ongoing, gracious, loving supply of all that is good. We look at every child as a miracle and a fresh creation from God. We rejoice in the passion of a lover as a creation of God. We cherish the love of our family and are reminded all the time that God, as creator and miracle worker, rewards us with all good things—not for anything we have done or not done but because of God's unavoidable nature of giving us good things. It is impossible, against the very nature of God, for God *not* to give us good things. That is what it means to worship God and thank God for the ongoing and sustaining creation of the universe. We become grateful beings and learn to live our lives with the habit of gratitude and joy in the universe and in our lives in it. Even in smaller things, like the fun and comfort we take in a loyal dog or a playful cat and what they bring to our household, is a sign, a sacrament, of God's creative action in our world. The New Testament teaches us all this by teaching us that God is the creator. And by teaching us to look at the birds of the air and the lilies of the field.

The doctrine of creation is fairly straightforward, both in scripture and in our confessions and creeds. We might, though, use the New Testament a bit more creatively to learn about the nature of God. The Sermon on the Mount, for instance, is usually taken as a passage about ethics: how we should learn to live. But right in the middle of the sermon in Matthew's version, Jesus says, "Therefore, be perfect as your heavenly father is perfect" (Matt 5:48). In Luke, which presents much of the same material but in a "sermon on a plain," the saying is somewhat different: "Be compassionate just as your father is compassionate" (Luke 6:36). This is a sign that the sermons are not to be read merely as an ethic or a string of behaviors taught by Jesus to people, though they certainly are that. Here we are informed more explicitly what we may have picked up throughout the sermon: these behaviors are right because they reflect the nature of God.

We are to be peacemakers (Matt 5:9) because God makes peace—and *not* war! God is the one who mourns when we suffer (5:4). God is the one who suffers without retaliation (5:38–41). The point of the beatitudes is not that people should *seek* to be persecuted (5:11) or to grieve (5:4) or perhaps not even to be "poor in spirit" (5:3) if that is taken to mean "poor-hearted" or sad. In those cases, the beatitude is promising relief from current hardships and suffering, signifying if nothing else that God is not the one who causes the suffering but the one who will bring relief.

Many of the beatitudes do teach an ethic. People *should* hunger and thirst for justice, be merciful and compassionate, be pure in heart, and be peacemakers. But this is precisely because these are imitations of the nature of God. Peacemakers are particularly called "children of God" (5:9). And those who are pure in heart see God, no doubt, because that is God's nature also (5:8). The beatitudes, therefore, as we interpret in a bit more creative way, may be taken as teaching us the nature of God. God is one who relieves those who are "poor in spirit," who comforts the grieving, who raises up the lowly, who fills the hungry and dispenses justice, who is merciful, who makes peace, and who saves the persecuted. These activities and traits identify what God is.

Other passages may also be read more creatively to teach us what God is. Note, for example, how many of the salutations or closings of New Testament letters repeat some of the same benefits: "Grace to you and peace from God" (Rom 1:7; 1 Cor 1:3; 2 Cor 1:2; Gal 1:3; Eph 1:2; Phil 1:2; Col 1:2; 1 Thess 1:1; 2 Thess 1:2; Tit 1:4; Phlm 3; see also 1 Pet 1:2; 2 Pet 1:2). "Grace, mercy, and peace" (1 Tim 1:2; 2 Tim 2; 2 John 3). "May mercy, peace, and love be yours in abundance" (Jude 2). These are the things God provides because these are the things God is. The sense of well-being that many people express in their spiritual experiences of the divine are captured in these: the feeling of gratitude for gifts and the freeness of the gift; the experience of forgiveness and being a recipient of mercy; an inexplicable sense of peacefulness. On those occasions, and would that they were more frequent for more people, we are experiencing those sensations because we are experiencing the presence of God and coming to know God's true nature.

God's Gender

Some New Testament parables give us the opportunity to think about God's gender. Obviously, the most common way to talk about God's gender, both traditionally but most commonly today also, is by using male pronouns and terms. But there are parables that might be taken to suggest otherwise. According to Matt 13:13 and Luke 13:21, the kingdom is compared to yeast "that a woman took and mixed in with three measures of flour until all of it was leavened." The parable reads like an allegory: the yeast is the kingdom of heaven (Matthew) or God (Luke); the flour is the world; and thus the woman must be God.

In the twentieth century, biblical scholars often argued that the biblical parables were not allegories and that interpreting them as allegories, where each detail was supposed to "stand for" something else symbolically, was anachronistic and wrong.[94] Many of us were taught that such allegorical interpretation of parables was a mistake of premodern or medieval Christian interpretation. Parables, we were told, generally make one point, and to interpret them as elaborate allegories was "eisegesis." This is itself, though, a modernist prejudice. Even the biblical writers provided allegorical interpretations of their own parables, as the interpretations of the parable of the sower in the Gospels themselves show (see Mark 4:13–20, and par.). For those of us not limited by a concern to reproduce the exact meaning in the mind of the ancient author, or of Jesus for that matter, there should be nothing holding us back from offering allegorical interpretations of biblical texts. It just so happens that many of the parables supply great opportunities for allegorizing. And with this parable, we could therefore say that one teaching of the parable is that God is female.

I find this interpretation of the parable especially interesting because I am familiar with some cultures in which making bread or some other particular food tends to be always associated with women rather than men. In many Latin American cultures, for instance, men may indeed do quite a lot of cooking and other food preparation, but it has long been traditional for tortilla making to be strictly "women's work." Over years of traveling in Central America, for instance, I saw women preparing tortillas every day. I never saw a man doing so, though that need not mean it didn't happen. But in my experience in Latin America it has regularly been considered women's work to make the ever-present tortilla. Perhaps, therefore, the parable is playing on some ancient assumption that women would normally make the bread, and so it would be fitting for God here to be represented as a woman.

Luke provides another such parable. He tells of a woman who had ten coins but lost one (15:8–10). She lights all the lights, sweeps the entire house, and searches every inch until she finds it. But Luke doesn't leave the story there. He proceeds to add that she is so glad that she calls all her friends and neighbors and tells them to help her celebrate because she had found the one lost drachma. Then Jesus concludes, "I tell you, it is just like that.

94. The best-known advocate of this view was Joachim Jeremias, *Parables of Jesus* (I believe the first publication in German was 1947). The point had been made extensively at least as early as Adolf Jülicher, *Die Gleichnisreden Jesu* (1888–99), and repeated by C. H. Dodd in lectures at Yale in 1935, published as *The Parables of the Kingdom,* which Jeremias admits heavily influenced his own later work. At any rate, especially since the publication of Jeremias's work, the argument against "allegorizing" the parables has been nonstop in modernist historical criticism, repeated countless times by New Testament scholars.

There is celebration among the angels of God when one sinner repents."
And again, the parable lends itself to allegory: the friends and neighbors are
the angels of God, the coin is a sinner, and therefore obviously the woman
is God.

There are other hints in the Bible that God is female. In many ancient
Jewish texts, "Wisdom," which is from a feminine word in Hebrew and in
Greek is one that even we today use as a female name, Sophia, was taken
to be a female consort of God or sometimes to stand for God herself. And
there are other biblical images portraying God as a mother or caring nurse.
Though the Bible tends to refer to God with masculine language and imagery, there are opportunities enough to meditate on the femaleness of God.

Some conservative scholars argue against using anything but masculine pronouns for God. Elizabeth Achtemeier, for example, after some un-
convincing other arguments, ends up basing her case on a rather simplistic
proclamation: "The Bible uses masculine language for God because that is
the language with which God has revealed himself."[95] This is classic question begging. The very debate is whether *we should take* masculine language
about God *to be* such an obvious "revelation" of God's intentions. The entire discussion is about whether or not the Bible *should* be interpreted as a
revelation that God is male. And Achtemeier seems not to realize that she
is, after all, interpreting, as if God just spoke to her "his" intentions—as divine "revelation" about God's gender. Against the kind of rejoinder I would
make against Achtemeier—that God is so totally "other" than everything in
creation that we must be wary of claiming what we certainly "know" about
God—she just insists that we know him now because of his self-revelation,
as if revelation gets rid of the need to maintain our acknowledgment of our
ultimate ignorance of God's exact nature—for instance, that he is male rather
than female. In another essay in the same volume, Roland M. Frye goes so
far as to say that "God the Father" and "the Son of God" are not ways we
name God among other ways, but these particular terms "become transparent equivalents to the divine reality, words by which the divine persons are
called, addressed, recognized, or known."[96] Given what I've already written
so much in this chapter, one should understand why I find such talk about
"transparent equivalents to the divine reality" not only baffling but utterly
idolatrous. Those who claim so confidently that they *know* that "Father" is
God's proper name suffer two cases of arrogant idolatry: they insist they

95. Achtemeier, "Exchanging God," 5.
96. Frye, "Language for God," 42.

know God's one and noninterchangeable proper name, and they enshrine their own patriarchy and misogyny as gods.[97]

Robert W. Jenson, it seems to me, gets himself into theological and ideological difficulties because of his insistence that *only* masculine names can be used for God. He insists, though there is absolutely no way to prove any of this, that "monotheistic discourse cannot be conducted without personal pronouns for God, and within Judaism and Christianity these cannot be feminine or neuter."[98] I see no reason to accept either claim. Monotheism is possible without personal pronouns. And if the only proper representatives are thought to be particular ones and not others, the theologian has just again descended into idolatry. God cannot be *identified* with *any* particular word.

A corresponding theological mistake made by Jenson is his way of speaking about the church in its relation to God. If God is male, then for Jenson Israel or the church must be female, which leads his rhetoric into ways of speaking about females in relation to males that are misogynist. His language regularly contrasts the inferior, dependent female in contrast to the superior, dominant male: "When the church accepted that her Lord had deposited her in history, that the time between Resurrection and fulfillment would not be a historical instant but had occupied and therefore might yet occupy a succession of generations, she might have confessed her hope refuted."[99] The passivity of the female church and the activity of the masculine god pervade his rhetoric and therefore his theology and thus implicate it in the ideology of patriarchy.

Jenson believes he knows the precise and only proper "name" for the divine. He argues that the exact terms "Father, Son, and Holy Spirit" are *the* personal name of God. "The triune phrase offers itself as the unique name for the Christian God, and is then dogmatically mandated for that function by its constitutive place in the rite that establishes Christian identity. The church is the community and a Christian is someone who, when the

97. See, for instance, Torrence, "Christian Apprehension," 120–43, in *Speaking*, at 132. Many of the authors of this collection make the same or similar errors—errors of simple logic as well as of Christian theology. For cogent arguments against taking "Father" to be God's "name," see Thompson, *Promise*, esp. 175–78. I disagree with Thompson's views of scripture, at least as they seem to be in this book: she speaks as if "revelation" is something we simply get from scripture historically; she continues, that is, to mask somewhat her own interpretive agency.

98. Jenson, *Systematic Theology*, 5n4.

99. Ibid., 23–24.

identity of God is important, names him 'Father, Son, and Holy Spirit.' Those who do not or will not belong to some other community."[100] Jenson apparently knows God so well that he can tell which people God doesn't want in church just by hearing what "name" they use for God. And that "unique" (the *only* permissible name for God) must be the two-thirds masculine name of "Father, Son, and Holy Spirit" (Holy Spirit isn't "masculine" either in Greek or English). These statements strike me as the worst kind of false pride—and idolatry.

Kathryn Tanner has addressed the subject in a thoughtful essay on whether or not Christian liturgy should be altered to reflect better current beliefs about the fundamental equality of men and women, male and female, in broader Western culture but also in many churches. She does so by first surveying patristic discussions which show that many church fathers were uncomfortable with some possible interpretations about the fatherhood of the first person and the sonship of the second. For example, according to the "zero sum" understanding of procreation in ancient culture, fathers necessarily lost something of themselves when they gave up what they had to give up of their own bodies in order to produce offspring.[101] But it would be heretical, the church fathers thought, to say that the Father lost anything of himself in begetting the Son. This notion prompted these early church theologians, as Tanner illustrates, to insist that different terms and images should be used, as they are used in scripture, to talk about the relationship between the Father and Christ, such as light source and its radiance or fountain and the flow of water that comes from it, along with several others. These authors also know that scripture itself sometimes uses feminine images, such as "Wisdom," with which to speak about the first or second person of the trinity. The ancient theologians go even further, however: they think analogically about the Father's generation of the Son by comparing it to Mary's generation of Jesus, thus attributing a feminine "begetting" to God also.

The main point made by the patristic writers is that once we recognize the "gendering" of "father" and "son," we are better off if we do not limit ourselves to those terms but use others as well. As Gregory of Nyssa puts it, "There is no appropriate term to be found to mark the subject adequately, we are compelled by many and differing names, as there may be opportunity,

---

100. Ibid., 46.

101. Tanner, "Gender." For explanation of the "zero sum" ideology of antiquity, including its importance in medical theory, gynecology, and gender ideology, see Martin, "Contradictions of Masculinity."

to divulge our surmises as they arise within us with regard to the Deity."[102]
As Tanner summarizes, "Multiple terms are not a bad but a good thing; and
that, it is supposed, is why one finds so many in the Bible."[103] Given that the
exclusive use of masculine terminology for God or any of the trinity tends
to lead to female subordinationism and the oppression of women—as is well
proven simply by history and empirical observation—not only may we, but
we *must* use different ways of speaking about God and each person of the
trinity, including feminine images and terms. Love and justice simply demand it.[104]

God Is Love

My invocation of love provides a useful segue to the conclusion of this chapter. At the center of scripture and repeated several times in the New Testament is the insistence that love is the very nature of God and the most
important value and guide for both law and gospel. As is well known, when
asked what was the most important command of the Jewish Torah, Jesus
pointed to love of God and love of neighbor. Paul did the same, except he
went so far in a couple of places that he left off the command to love God and
said simply that "the whole law is summed up in a single commandment,
'You shall love your neighbor as yourself'" (Gal 5:14, NRSV). To see that this
was not a mere slip of the pen for Paul, we can point to his later letter to the
Romans, in which he repeats that every other commandment is "summed
up in this word, 'Love your neighbor as yourself'" (Rom 13:10, NRSV). Most
people assume that certainly the command to love God takes precedence
over the command to love other human beings, but Paul would have none
of it. Paul would not have rejected the commandment to love God. He assumes it. There is no possibility of love at all without the source of love, God.
So the love of God is simply assumed as the source of love itself. But anyone

102. Gregory of Nyssa, "Answer to Eunomius' Second Book," in *Nicene and Post-Nicene
Fathers*, 5:308.
103. Tanner, "Gender," 409.
104. Many other theologians these days advocate and practice gender variation in
naming God. Herbert McCabe does so in a way that is both playful and makes the point,
simply by alternating, as in this example: "So God's concept of Herself, if He had such a
thing, and God's enjoyment of Herself in this concept, if He had such enjoyment, would
not be things other than God but simply divine, simply God." *God Still Matters*, 60. I could
not have said it more "queerly."

who thinks love of God can be done without love of neighbor is deluded. We demonstrate that we love God *only* when we are loving others.[105]

Many other texts could be cited to emphasize the utter centrality of love in the gospel. Paul's famous chapter 13, on love, from 1 Corinthians is one of the most impressive. But even 1 Timothy, a text many of us think of as ideologically problematic in its hierarchy, support of slavery, and even legalism, makes the same point: the "goal" of all law and instruction "is love from a pure heart" (1 Tim 1:5). At the end of this long chapter on theology and the nature of God, the first, best, and final answer is, "God is love."

105. Note the point made by Sarah Beckwith, quoting Thomas Aquinas, that it is impossible to separate love of God from love of neighbor: "This would have been quite alien to Thomas Aquinas, for example, who said that love of God includes love of neighbor because 'it is specifically the same act whereby we love God, and whereby we love our neighbor.'" *Shakespeare*, 156; citing *Summa Theologiae* 2.2.25.1 and 2.2.58.1.ad6. Karl Barth also repeatedly makes the point that love is the most central point of the nature of God. See, for example, *Church Dogmatics* I/2, pp. 371–401. He considers but ultimately rejects equating loving God with loving neighbor: pp. 402–3. I think to make that reservation is to uncouple love of God from love of neighbor; it strikes me as a misguided attempt to emphasize the sovereignty of God over the love of neighbor. I insist the two loves simply cannot, in Christian doctrine or practice, be separated at all.

CHAPTER 4

Christ

There are few topics in Christian theology that better illustrate the inadequacies of historical criticism than Christology. Christian scholars have long attempted to interpret the New Testament—even through the ascetic methods of modern historical criticism—to render a fully orthodox account of Christ, but those attempts are at best strained. The truth is that if read by the normal rules of modern historical criticism, the documents of the New Testament do not contain fully orthodox doctrines of the nature of Christ. Only by moving beyond historical criticism can we arrive at orthodox Christology.[1]

By "orthodox" I mean doctrines about Jesus that affirm, at least, the declarations of Nicea and Chalcedon. The first of these is that of the trinity: the teaching that "God" is one being in three "persons": the father, the son, and the holy spirit. Kathryn Tanner formulates a good summation of the traditional understanding, which she rightly considers noncontroversial: "I assume, for example, that the persons of the trinity are distinct from one another not just in their actions with reference to the world but in and of themselves; that they are perfectly equal to one another in divinity, and that, for all their differences, they are perfectly one, utterly inseparable, for

---

1. "The dogma as such [i.e., the eternal deity of Christ] is not to be found in the biblical texts. The dogma is an interpretation. But we can convince ourselves that it is a good and relevant interpretation of these texts. We thus accept it." Barth, *Church Dogmatics* I/1, p. 415.

instance, in both their being and action."[2] The combination of the confession of the (1) "equal" divinity of (2) three distinct persons who are yet (3) united as "one God" constitutes orthodox trinitarian doctrine as normally understood.

Nowhere in the New Testament, judged by the criteria of historical criticism, do we find this combination. We do find many references to "God" and "Jesus" and "Christ," but the precise relationship among these terms—or "persons"—is often unclear. Scholars who confidently read the New Testament writings as teaching any kind of doctrine of the trinity as it came to be known in later Christian orthodoxy may have good theological reasons for doing so, but they are not, in that activity, practicing good historical criticism.

It is not just that the trinity is nowhere explicitly affirmed in the New Testament; there are texts that seem to contradict the doctrine, again, read through the lens of historical criticism. The Gospel of Mark, for example, certainly thinks of Jesus as the "Messiah" and the "son of man."[3] But it is unclear whether the author of the second Gospel considered Jesus to be "god." The Gospel does use the term "son of god" for Jesus.[4] The centurion at Jesus's crucifixion, noting how Jesus died, speaks of him as "God's son," but it is unclear what that would have meant to an ancient audience. The translation could be, "Surely this was *a* son of *a* god." But in the ancient world, even that need not mean the son was also "god" himself.[5] It certainly would not necessarily mean that the son was a divine being *in the full sense* the highest god was. In spite of modern apologists who make arguments such as, "Just as the son of an elephant is an elephant, so the son of god must also be god," ancient persons would not have seen things that way.[6] This is made clear even within the Bible itself. Several texts speak of human beings as "sons of God" without ascribing true divine status to them or at least without ascribing the kind of divine status Christians later attribute to Jesus Christ.[7] Moreover,

---

2. Tanner, *Christ the Key*, 148.

3. Notably in what may be taken as a climax of the Gospel at Mark 8:29. "Son of Man" occurs many times in Mark, as in the other Gospels.

4. See Mark 3:11; 5:7; see also 1:11; 9:7; 14:61; "son of god" occurs also in modern editions of Mark 1:1, but some ancient manuscripts lack the term in that verse, so its inclusion could be debated.

5. For a good, recent account of the various things "son of god" could have meant in the first century CE, see Peppard, *Son of God*.

6. I have been unable to find this statement in print. Perhaps it is in my head just from hearing the claim made by preachers and apologists in my fundamentalist youth.

7. See Matt 5:9, 45

in Mark 10:18, as we saw in the previous chapter, Jesus seems to be denying divine status for himself. It is quite possible to read the Gospel of Mark—if done without later Christian assumptions—and take Jesus in Mark to be a human but not divine figure.

Although Paul certainly believes Jesus is divine in some sense, he seems not to accord to Jesus complete divine equality with God the father. He can speak of "Christ" and "God" as two different persons in a hierarchical relationship. When Paul in 1 Cor 11:3 offers something of an equation—Christ is the head of man, man is the head of woman, God is the head of Christ—we must assume subordinate relations in each case. The parallelism doesn't work otherwise. Christ is no more "equal" to "God" than "man" is to "Christ." The same seems to be assumed later in 1 Cor 15:24–28: "God" temporarily put "all things" under subjection to Christ, who, after subjecting "all things" to himself, then puts everything again under subjection to God, including himself.

Some texts of the New Testament do accept the divinity of Jesus, but they seem not all to agree about *when* Jesus *became* divine. Some early Christians believed that Jesus was a mere human at his birth, but that he was "adopted" as God's son sometime later. According to what may be the "original reading" of Luke 3:22—"You are my son, the beloved; today I have begotten you"—Jesus is begotten by God at his baptism.[8] According to some other early Christians, apparently, Jesus became God's son only at his resurrection, as reflected in passages in Acts. In one sermon delivered by Peter in Acts, God "made" Jesus "Lord and Messiah" at some point (Acts 2:36). In a later sermon of Paul in Acts, one statement suggests that God adopted Jesus as his son at the resurrection (13:32–33). Paul himself seems to betray knowledge of such a Christology in one of his letters. In Rom 1:4, Paul says that God "designated" Jesus as son of God "by resurrection from the dead."[9] The most normal meaning of the Greek would be that God *made* Jesus his son by means of the resurrection, in the way a priest or pope or other authority "made" someone a king or queen—at the time of the declaration or coronation. That this terminology is recited by Paul is significant, since Paul himself seems to believe that Jesus was God's son already in some preexisting state (see Phil 2:5–11). I take it that Paul is here quoting a formula about

8. See my fuller treatment of these passages in Martin, *New Testament*, 261–65.

9. I believe the NRSV translation "declared" to be a misleading one for the Greek ὁρισθέντος. It means to "mark off," "ordain," "designate," whether speaking of a boundary or an office. It would be unusual to take it to mean simply to "declare" a state of affairs already long in existence.

Christ he has encountered elsewhere.[10] At any rate, one can cite New Testament texts that, on their face, do not teach a very orthodox Christology, and certainly not trinitarian.

It will be my contention in this chapter, however, that we need not become bad historians in order to be good theologians. Even if the New Testament authors were not familiar with the doctrine of the trinity as it became defined in the great councils and creeds, we may take the liberty of reading the New Testament *theologically* (rather than *historically*) as teaching trinitarian theology.

As is the case for most of us today, so also we can see from ancient sources that early Christians developed orthodox doctrines not out of abstract ideas but out of needs prompted by Christian practices and liturgy.[11] We may not have full trinitarian doctrine at the end of the Gospel of Matthew, but we can see already there that Christians were baptizing people "in the name of the father and of the son and of the holy spirit" (Matt 28:19). We may have another hint at the role of the three in baptism in 1 John 5:6–9: "This is the one who came by water and blood, Jesus Christ, not with the water only but with the water and the blood. And the spirit is the one that testifies, for the spirit is the truth. There are three that testify: the spirit and the water and the blood, and these three agree. If we receive human testimony, the testimony of God is greater; for this is the testimony of God that he has testified to his son."

The three also occur in situations of prayer and doxology, as at the beginning of 1 Peter: "To the exiles of the Dispersion . . . , who have been chosen and destined by God the father and sanctified by the spirit to be obedient to Jesus Christ and to be sprinkled with his blood" (1:1–2). Paul supplies a benediction at the end of his difficult or (probably) "tearful" letter (2 Cor 10–13; for likely references to this letter, see 2 Cor 2:4; 7:8): "The grace of the Lord Jesus Christ, the love of God, and the communion of the holy spirit be with all of you" (2 Cor 13:13). Incidentally, 2 Cor 13:13 is the only benediction in Paul's letters in which all three "persons" are named (if we take "holy spirit" here to *be* a "person," which is debatable; see the next chapter, "Spirit"). Much more commonly Paul names only God the father and Jesus in such contexts.

Once all three become important for prayer or liturgy, some attempt has to be made to understand their relation to one another. Once Jesus be-

10. See Martin, *New Testament*, 263–64; Ehrman, *Orthodox Corruption*, 56–57; Ehrman, *How Jesus Became God*, 218–25.
11. See the introduction above and the works there cited.

gins to be worshipped along with "God," which apparently happened not very long after his death, some account of why he deserved worship had to be given. The "higher" Christology of later Christianity and the trinitarian proposals of the nature of God grew not out of nitpicky philosophical debates but out of the actual liturgical practices of churches: if Christians were going to include Jesus and the holy spirit in worship and prayer, some account of their status vis-à-vis one another and of their divinity had to be given. And that had to be done in a way that could preserve, at least in the minds of Christians, the belief in "one God" they also valued.

What Jesus Is Not

Before getting to "what Jesus is," it may help to point out popular claims made for Jesus that are, in my view, at least theologically naïve and suspect, if not downright wrong. For example, many people like to say that Jesus was no doubt a "Great Moral Teacher"; here we are often talking about well-meaning non-Christians who wish to say something "nice" about Jesus without affirming Christian doctrines. I will address below what uses for theology we may and may not derive from "the historical Jesus," but even if we stick with the Jesus portrayed in our four Gospels it is hard to see why people so blandly claim that Jesus was what most of them would consider a "Great Moral Teacher." True, in some contexts Jesus taught a supreme ethic of love (Mark 12:28–34, and par.). But Jesus teaches much else in the Gospels. He pulls his disciples away from their families and households (there are many examples but see esp. Mark 1:16–20 and par.). He orders a man to follow him immediately, telling him not even to bury his father, an abandonment of loyalty to family almost unimaginable in ancient cultures (Matt 8:21–22; Luke 9:59–60). Would a "Great Moral Teacher" attempt to outlaw divorce for any situation?[12]

In all four Gospels Jesus commits some kind of violent action in the temple, overturning tables, driving people out (Mark 11:15–19, and par.). Most modern readers don't realize how radical such behavior would have been. In order for the Jewish sacrificial cult to take place, the business of buying and selling offerings was simply necessary. And for Jews to buy sacrificial materials, they had to change the different forms of money they may

---

12. See Mark 10:1–12; Matt 19:3–9. For a full argument that Jesus here completely forbids divorce without exception, see Martin, *Sex and the Single Savior*, 125–47; for Jesus on family and household, see 103–24.

have been carrying from far away. Jesus's action could be seen as a violent demonstration against the entire temple cult (as I will later argue that it was, historically constructed). To mention other radical aspects of his message, the Jesus of the Gospels advocates the overturning of all social hierarchies: the last must be first, and the first last. If someone went around today teaching and acting the way Jesus does in the Gospels, most people would want him arrested. They wouldn't call him a Great Moral Teacher.

Terry Eagleton drives the point home well: "Jesus, unlike most responsible American citizens, appears to do no work, and is accused of being a glutton and a drunkard. He is presented as homeless, propertyless, celibate, peripatetic, socially marginal, disdainful of kinsfolk, without a trade, a friend of outcasts and pariahs, averse to material possessions, without fear for his own safety, careless about purity regulations, critical of traditional authority, a thorn in the side of the Establishment, and a scourge of the rich and powerful." And about the kind of "morality" Jesus preached, Eagleton concludes, "The morality Jesus preaches is reckless, extravagant, improvident, over-the-top, a scandal to actuaries and a stumbling block to real estate agents: forgive your enemies, give away your cloak as well as your coat, turn the other cheek, love those who insult you, walk the extra mile, take no thought for tomorrow."[13] Christians certainly cannot be content to judge Jesus merely as a Great Moral Teacher, but even for others to do so betrays an ignorance of the actual texts or, more likely, an ideological misconstrual of them.

When he was running for president of the United States, George W. Bush was asked who his favorite philosopher was. I'm sure many conservatives, including conservative Christians, were pleased when he answered, "Jesus Christ." Bush certainly did not understand any more than most people how inappropriate the answer was, bordering on heresy. But, to contravene the assumptions of many people, Jesus was not a philosopher, and Christianity is not, rightly interpreted, a philosophy, as I argued more fully in the chapter "Knowledge" above. In the Gospels Jesus is presented as a prophet, in fact, as an apocalyptic Jewish prophet preaching and awaiting the imminent inbreaking of the Kingdom of God. Jesus is also a healer, an exorcist, a teacher, a rabbi, a miracle worker. But he is not a philosopher. For one thing, he is not presented as having much formal education, if any, which is probably historically correct.

13. Eagleton, *Reason*, 10, 14.

Moreover, while he does teach people how to live their lives, Jesus doesn't have a particular "program" in mind for that. He does not teach the kinds of things ancient philosophers were famous for, such as rigorous self-control over eating and sex or the nurturing of self-sufficiency and the avoidance of any kind of dependence on other human beings. Jesus doesn't teach what ancient philosophers did about divine beings: that it was impossible for them to be angry or harm human beings.[14] Jesus does not speculate on the material nature of the world or things within it. He doesn't lecture on arithmetic, mathematics, music, art, science—any of the topics one encounters among ancient philosophers.

And just as we should not look to Jesus for answers to ancient philosophical questions, so we should not expect from Jesus answers to the typical questions modern philosophers ask, such as: What is the nature of matter? How does language mean? Is mathematics true just because it works for some ends or purposes or because it corresponds in some metaphysical way to the very nature of nature? Are there laws of nature and, if so, what are they? There are legitimate questions people may have about the world, life, and human prospering, and modern philosophers raise them, but Jesus does not answer them. Jesus was and is not a philosopher in either the ancient sense or the modern.

Finally on this topic, I insist that another common notion about the identity of Jesus is wrong: Jesus is not the "founder of Christianity." This can certainly be demonstrated for "the historical Jesus." No properly constructed "historical Jesus" will present Jesus as intentionally "founding" a "new religion." The development of what we now may consider a religion separate from and alongside Judaism comes some time after the death of Jesus—and the precise time that happened is completely debatable. Though the Gospel of Matthew (and only Matthew among the Gospels) does have Jesus speaking of building his "church" (Matt 16:18), it would be a mistake, both historically and theologically, to consider Jesus mainly as the founder of Christianity. Theologically it is dangerous because Jesus is the central figure of veneration in Christianity, the second person of the trinity, God incarnate—not merely the founder of a religion.[15] Moving beyond these mistaken notions about who or what Jesus is, we may read the New Testament for more adequate ideas.

14. See Martin, *Inventing Superstition,* for this as a universal among Greek and Roman philosophers.
15. See Williams, *Resurrection,* 74, for warning against seeing Jesus as the "founding martyr" of the church.

Four Gospels, Four Jesuses

Some Christians through the ages have found it to be something of an em-
barrassment that the church has four different Gospels, four different portraits of Jesus. It is an interesting historical question as to why what later
came to be called catholic Christianity, and mainly in the second century,
decided to retain four different Gospels rather than choosing just one. Attempts were made early on, particularly in the second century by Tatian
in his *Diatessaron,* to blend the four different accounts into one. Christians
have tried many times to "harmonize" the four Gospels into one account, as
more conservative Christians continue to do. But rather than harmonizing
the Gospels or choosing one as offering our "favorite" portrait of Jesus, we
should see the variety as presenting opportunities for theology rather than
an embarrassing diversity and contradiction.

In premodern Christianity people often tried to "explain away" any
apparent discrepancies among the four Gospels. In "modernist" scholarship,
more liberal scholars sometimes even highlight the differences, sometimes
thereby insisting that the Gospels tell us much more about the people who
wrote and read them in their original "communities" than about Jesus. In
a "postmodern" Christian context, however, we may well use the variety of
presentations of Jesus as raw material for more creative Christology. I believe
we can legitimately read the four Gospels to present four different Jesuses
that need no harmonization but that each offer an account that is "true" in
its own way. Each of them, though different and even perhaps contradictory,
is true *in a sense.*

The Gospel of Matthew has sometimes ironically been read as the
most "anti-Jewish" Gospel. After all, it alone contains the sentence purport-
edly shouted by "the Jews" at Jesus's trial, "His blood be on us and on our
children" (Matt 27:25). In Matthew, Jesus conducts several arguments with
Pharisees, as he does in all the Gospels. But Matthew contains by far the
most outright, and outrageous, condemnations of the Pharisees. It is greatly
due to Matthew that English dictionaries list "hypocrite" as one definition
for "Pharisee," even though the historical Pharisees were certainly no more
hypocritical than any other people. The Pharisees were simply one (what we
would call "religious" as well as "political") "party" among several in Palestine in the first century.[16] We can think of them as the precursors of the Jewish rabbis represented in the Mishnah and the Babylonian and Palestinian

---

16. Pharisees seem to have lived also outside Palestine. Paul claims to be a Pharisee (or
perhaps "was"? but he seems to be speaking of the present; see Phil 3:5), and he, for all we

Talmuds. The fact that "Pharisee" became synonymous with "hypocrite" in later languages owes much, I would argue, to the influence of the Gospel of Matthew, especially chapter 23.[17]

The "antitheses" of the Sermon on the Mount, moreover, have often been read by Christians as Jesus's rejection of the Law of Moses and proposal of his own new law. But when Jesus says, "You have heard, 'You shall not murder,'" he does not then allow murder. He rather proceeds to include even being angry as forbidden. He is not rejecting the law of Moses but intensifying its requirements (Matt 5:21–26). In the next paragraph he does not reject the commandment against adultery in order to allow adultery; rather he teaches that even "lusting" after a woman breaks the commandment against adultery (5:27–30). In the Sermon on the Mount, Jesus is not setting aside the law of Moses and offering "another" law that is easier to fulfill. He is in fact making the laws of Moses more difficult to keep by intensifying and internalizing them. For Matthew's Jesus, not only "swearing falsely" is forbidden; swearing at all is (5:33–37).

Scholars in the past few decades have emphasized just how "Jewish" the Gospel of Matthew actually is. True, this is the only Gospel that presents Jesus precisely as "founding" a "church" (Matt 16:18). Much of Matt 18:15–35 reads like constitutional rules for the conduct of the later church; the word "church" (ἐκκλησία) occurs in Matthew on the lips of Jesus three times—quite anachronistically. None of the other canonical Gospels mentions it. So in spite of my claim above that it is a mistake, both historically and theologically, to see Jesus as "the founder of the new religion of Christianity," Matthew does portray Jesus as the founder of a "church."

But it is a Jewish church. In Matthew, Jesus *never* teaches that his followers need not follow the Mosaic Law. He in fact insists they must do so: "Do not think that I have come to abolish the law or the prophets; I have come not to abolish but to fulfill. For truly I tell you, until heaven and earth pass away, not one letter, not one stroke of a letter, will pass from the law until all is accomplished. Therefore, whoever breaks one of the least of these commandments, and teaches others to do the same, will be called least in the kingdom of heaven; but whoever does them and teaches them will be called great in the kingdom of heaven. For I tell you, unless your righteousness exceeds that of the scribes and Pharisees, you will never enter the kingdom

---

can tell from his letters, was a Greek-speaking Jew from the Diaspora. (I don't believe we can accept as historical Acts' account of Paul's education in Jerusalem.)

17. The connection of "hypocrite" with "Pharisee" is found most thickly in Matthew 23, but it occurs elsewhere in the Gospel also.

of heaven" (Matt 5:17–20; NRSV). It is clear that by exceeding the righteousness of the scribes and Pharisees, Jesus in Matthew means the righteousness taught by the law of Moses.

That this was the understanding of the author of the Gospel is shown by comparing how he edits the Gospel of Mark, which is one of his sources for Jesus's words and deeds. In a dispute with "the Pharisees and scribes" over hand washing, Mark tells a story in which Jesus teaches that certain Jewish traditions or requirements are not applicable to his followers. But then the author adds his own commentary, "Thus he declared all foods clean" (Mark 7:19). Matthew borrows the story from Mark but edits out that comment. In Matthew, the entire controversy is not over a commandment of the law of Moses at all but only over certain Jewish "traditions" (Matt 15:1–20). For Matthew, the story narrates a disagreement about how to *interpret* the Jewish law. In Matthew, Jesus never gets rid of Jewish dietary rules.

It may strike Christians as odd, but the first Gospel of our New Testament teaches that all followers of Jesus must keep all aspects of the Jewish law. The Gospel does end with Jesus commanding that his gospel be taken to gentiles ("the nations"; Matt 28:19). So the author of the Gospel obviously had in mind a church that included gentile along with Jewish believers. But we have no reason but to assume he expected those gentile converts to keep the law of Moses. He must have expected them to keep the Sabbath and to keep kosher food laws, at least as understood by himself, and for their males to be circumcised. The Jesus of the Gospel of Matthew is fully Jewish and law-abiding, teaching that all his followers will also adhere to the law of the Jews, at least as interpreted by himself.[18]

This is one case where I have left behind any postmodernist method of textual interpretation and adhered strictly to historical-critical readings. Indeed, reading Matthew by concentrating on its likely meaning in its original context rather than through the lens of later Christian orthodoxy is precisely what enables us to see just how Jewish the first Gospel is. But that in itself may supply useful theological fodder. Many Christians are nowadays working hard to free the church and Christians from our anti-Semitic past and current prejudices. As Matthew has been used against Jews in the "blood guilt" charges from ancient to modern times ("Let his blood be on us and on our children!"), so it is now time to recover just how Jewish our first

---

18. For a fuller account of the Jewish context and reading of Matthew, see Martin, *New Testament*, 93–107.

Gospel is and how Jewish Jesus is in it. I do not believe we ought thereby to attempt to put into practice its program of a Torah-abiding form of Christianity. Other parts of the New Testament, along with Christian doctrine and tradition, must also influence our Christian expectation of how we relate to the law of Moses and Judaism of our own day. But it would do us good to imagine ourselves as disciples of a fully Jewish Jesus. We must overcome centuries of Christian anti-Semitism and Christian supersessionism in relation to Judaism. By reminding ourselves that we venerate a Jewish teacher, we can never again join in oppressing and harming Jews or Judaism.

We may read the Gospel of Mark as portraying a very different Jesus. Jesus in Mark does not teach his followers to obey the law of Moses. Jesus in Mark, in fact, does not come across as a very good teacher at all. Regularly, people seem to miss Jesus's meaning entirely. The only figures who seem correctly to identify Jesus, at least at the beginning and in much of the narrative, are possessed people or the demons possessing them. The first character who correctly calls Jesus "the holy one of God" is "an unclean spirit" (Mark 1:24). Jesus regularly expresses frustration at the confusion and misunderstanding of people, including his closest disciples, while demons and crazy people alone seem to "get it" (see 6:51–52; 8:17–21; 5:19–20; but the theme occurs several times). And Jesus doesn't seem to help out much in Mark.

Most Christians assume that Jesus taught in parables in order to help "common people" understand his "great moral teaching." But Mark tells a completely different story. In fact, in Mark, Jesus explains that he teaches in parables *so that people won't* understand. When he is asked about his parables, Jesus explains that the "secret" he brings he will explain to his inner circle of disciples, but for "those outside," the parables are given so that they will *not* "perceive," will *not* "understand": "so that they may not turn again and be forgiven" (4:11–12). And even after Jesus offers an interpretation of his parable (which interpretation, incidentally, isn't very clear in *its* meaning), the rest of the Gospel repeatedly insists that even his "inner circle" keeps getting it wrong.

It is no wonder, then, that Mark's Gospel ends with a complete puzzle. Unlike the "longer endings" of Mark that are usually included after Mark 16:8, often in brackets and with footnotes explaining that these endings are not likely part of the "original Gospel," Mark actually ends with an absence. We are told that certain women make it to Jesus's tomb and find it empty. They are told by a "young man" (who may or may not be meant as an angel) to tell the other disciples that Jesus has been raised and that they should travel to

Galilee, where Jesus will appear to them. But no one, at the end of this Gospel, actually sees the risen Jesus. Furthermore, we are told that the women do *not* pass along the message. Are we to assume that the disciples somehow got the message later? Did Jesus appear to them at all? Did they even know to go to Galilee? The Gospel ends with the women afraid, too afraid apparently to say anything to the disciples, and running away. The Gospel of Mark ends not with a Jesus who is present after his death, but a Jesus who is absent—appropriate for the Jesus who spent most of this Gospel posing puzzles and ordering people to be silent.

The Jesus of Mark is therefore the silent, puzzling, even absent Jesus. But this is also true to our own experience of Jesus. In our lives we are sometimes frustrated by the absence of Jesus, at least as we sometimes experience it. Jesus as we know him is not always clear in instruction, is not always present in a "felt" way. Even when we affirm by faith belief in Jesus's presence, we may actually struggle with an experience of his absence. The Gospel of Mark prepares us for such experiences. We, like the women, run away from the empty tomb in fear rather than always in confidence. Jesus in Mark is a mystery and, in the end, absent. We must continually be trying to get ourselves to Galilee.

The Gospel of Luke presents still another portrait of Jesus. Most Christians, reflecting themes familiar from Paul, Mark, Hebrews, and several other New Testament books, can hardly think of the execution of Jesus without thinking of it as a "sacrifice" for sins, as a redeeming death. Perhaps surprisingly for many people, the author of Luke and Acts does not seem to consider Jesus's death to be a sacrifice. There is no "atonement" to speak of in Luke–Acts. Mark 10:45 ("For the Son of Man came not to be served but to serve, and to give his life as a ransom for many") is taken up by Matthew (Matt 20:28) but not by Luke. We might take the tearing of the temple veil that Mark has occurring right when Jesus dies as suggesting that Jesus's death is the sacrifice that now allows entrance for all people into the "holy of holies" (Mark 15:38). If so, it may be significant that Luke moves that detail to a time *before* Jesus dies, and then Luke presents Jesus not as dying in desperation but as willing his own death: "Father, into your hands I commend my spirit" (Luke 23:46). In fact, the death of Jesus is never depicted in Luke or Acts as a sacrifice or atoning ransom.

The closest Luke–Acts comes to interpreting Jesus's death as sacrifice or atonement is perhaps when Jesus, at the Last Supper, speaks of the bread as his body "given for you" and the wine as "this cup that is poured out for you" as "the new covenant in my blood" (Luke 22:19–20). But those words can be interpreted in several ways without bringing in any notion of a sacrificial death.[19]

Another passage in most Bibles that could be taken as alluding to Jesus's death as a sacrifice is Luke 22:43–44, the famous scene depicting Jesus in the garden agonizing over his impending suffering to the point of sweating "like great drops of blood." But the verses are, I believe, a later scribal interpolation. Apparently, some later Christian scribes didn't find the calm, composed Jesus of Luke's garden scene as compelling as the groaning, pleading, suffering Jesus of the same scene in the Gospels of Mark and Matthew (Matt 26:36–46; Mark 13:32–42). So someone added the verses to Luke's scene, making it harmonize better with the other Gospels.[20] Once we recognize the passage as an interpolation, its contrast to the presentation of Jesus's death in the rest of Luke and Acts becomes even sharper.

Luke's preferred way to portray Jesus's death is as a prophet martyred by his own people because of his message. Indeed, Luke's Christology centers on Jesus as prophet and martyr. Several prophets in Luke and Acts follow the model of Jesus himself. The first is John the Baptist, hailed as a prophet even before the birth of Jesus (Luke 1:76). In his first sermon in Luke, Jesus claims the mantle of the great prophets Elijah and Elisha (4:16–30). Other Jews call Jesus a "great prophet" (7:16), and Jesus claims the designation when he insists he is going to Jerusalem "because it is impossible for a prophet to be killed outside Jerusalem" (13:33).

In Acts, key disciples are also shown to be prophets. Stephen, by tradition the "first Christian martyr," aligns himself with the prophet Jesus, who is a latter-day version of the prophet Moses (Acts 7:35–43, 52). Throughout Acts, Paul is also depicted as a prophet. In all these cases the prophet preaches first to the Jews but upon being rejected by them goes to the "other nations" and eventually is killed (or so we may expect for Paul at the end of Acts). Jesus is the greatest prophet but is also a model for his followers.

---

19. Fitzmyer, in his commentary on Luke, insists that Jesus's words here do contain "a sacrificial nuance," but I am not convinced. *Gospel of Luke,* 1402. Since there is such a clear avoidance in the rest of Luke and Acts of interpreting Jesus's death as a sacrifice, I believe that reading it into these verses is just harmonizing with other texts of the New Testament.

20. Discussion of this issue can be found in many commentaries. In my opinion the best arguments are in Ehrman and Plunkett, "Angel and the Agony," and Ehrman, *Orthodox Corruption,* 220–27.

One of the most central themes of Jesus's prophecy in Luke is the reversal of the economic hierarchy of society. Mary's song at the beginning of the Gospel, the "Magnificat," predicts the scattering of the proud, the humbling of the powerful, the lifting up of the lowly, filling the bellies of the poor but sending the rich "empty away" (1:51–53). Whereas Jesus in Matthew says "blessed are the poor in spirit" (Matt 5:3), in Luke Jesus says simply, "Blessed are the poor" (Luke 6:20; see also 21). To his version of the beatitudes Luke adds "woes" directed against the rich (6:24–25). From his humble beginnings in a stable to his burial in a borrowed grave, Jesus in Luke is the prophet who preaches hope to the poor, social status reversal, and woes to the rich—and is killed because of his message. This is another Christology offered by our Gospels, different from Matthew's and Mark's but certainly relevant for Christians today.

Finally, with the Fourth Gospel we meet a Jesus closest to the Christology of the later creeds, a Jesus who seems fully divine, preexistent before his incarnation, fully incarnated in the flesh, and "equal" to the father (see especially John 1:1–18; 5:18). The father turns over the role of judge to the son (5:22), though Jesus later insists that he did not come to judge but to save the cosmos (12:47). At any rate, both the son and the father deserve equal honor (5:23). Jesus and the father are "one" (10:30; 17:21, 23).

In spite of being clear about his own divine status, however, Jesus in the Gospel of John often comes across as a riddler and a tease and as even pushing away those who would believe in him. Instead of answering Nicodemus's questions in anything like a straightforward manner, Jesus seems to pose riddles to him (John 3:1–21). One of the most famous is Jesus's saying that one must be "born again" / "from above" (3:3). The Greek can be taken in either sense, and in spite of Nicodemus's pleadings Jesus makes no attempt to clarify what he means. But this kind of thing happens repeatedly in John's Gospel. A dialogue between Jesus and a crowd, for instance, will begin with the people apparently wanting to understand and in some cases already "believing" in Jesus (see 8:31), only to be frustrated by Jesus's comments and accusations. "Dialogues" end up in confrontations in which the crowd tries to kill Jesus (8:31–59; see also 6:25–71). Rather than making it easier for people to believe in him, Jesus in the Fourth Gospel seems intentionally to push people away and make it *impossible* for them to accept him. The Gospel is full of such confrontations and riddles.[21] So in the Gospel of John we have a much more "orthodox" Jesus Christ that should better fit later creeds and

21. See a fuller exposition in Martin, *New Testament*, 159–65.

Christian theology, yet simultaneously a Jesus who seems to push us away. Can we use that Christology for our own imaginations also? We probably have ourselves experienced the "high" Christ of Nicea and Chalcedon as not always as accessible as we would expect or like. That too is Christ.

Historical Criticism and a Subordinate Christ

Throughout this section on the four Gospels I have mostly limited myself to what can be observed about Jesus in the Gospels when using purely historical-critical readings. My purpose is twofold: (1) to demonstrate how historical criticism can render good, orthodox readings of the Bible, and (2) to avoid the kind of harmonization of the different Gospels that often accompanies more "theological" readings of them. Yet I maintain my insistence, made repeatedly throughout this book, that Christians need not feel always constrained by modernist, historical-critical methods or conclusions. Indeed, I've argued that the New Testament, read historically rather than theologically, will not render Christologies that are sufficiently orthodox. We may certainly end up with a Christology that appears subordinationist, that is, that presents a Christ who is a subordinate being in relationship to "God." My point is that historical-critical readings are perfectly legitimate in their place, but sometimes historical readings must be submitted to theological critique.

When it comes to subordination, there are some statements about Christ and the father that may retain the sound of hierarchy. The problem with Paul's subordinationist statement in 1 Cor 11:3 is not that he says that the father may in some sense be the "head" of Christ. We could interpret such a statement as saying nothing more offensive to orthodoxy than that Christ is "begotten of the father," and not the other way around. Or that Christ is "obedient" to the father. The problem with Paul's statement is that Paul uses the term "God" for what most innocent readers would take to be a different being, and superior to, "Christ." Paul doesn't say "the father is head of the son," which may indeed be orthodox. He says rather "God" (in the entirety of the Godhead?) is "head" of "Christ," as if they are two different beings. That would be an unorthodox interpretation of the passage. Theological critique must trump historical criticism.[22]

22. Often in the New Testament we find the term "God" used over against "Christ" or "the spirit" (to cite only a few of the many instances: Acts 7:55–56; 10:38–42; Rom 1:1, 8; 1 Cor 15:57; 2 Cor 2:21; 1 Peter 1:21). From a more strictly orthodox perspective, we Christian readers supply the knowledge that here "God" is standing in for "the Father."

Yet our liturgical language does seem to require *some kind of* "subordination." The New Testament does speak of the son as being "sent by" the father (e.g., John 5:36–38; see also 3:17; the theme recurs often in John). Jesus is "obedient" to the father and sometimes simply to "God" (Phil 2:8).[23] The son "submits" or "is subjected" to the father (1 Cor 15:28). The beginning of the Epistle of Jude poses a cosmic hierarchy: God the father, Jesus Christ, and then the brothers of Jesus, James and Jude. We may take these passages as depicting perhaps some kind of "economic" submission of the Son to the Father—"economic" because it is an expression of the internal workings of the trinity done for the purposes of our salvation, but not thereby implying difference in being or essence among the three persons.

Thus, for example, John 1:18 states, "No one has ever seen God" but then proceeds to a rather confusing next statement: "It is God the only son, who is close to the father's heart, who had made him known." Though this is only one possible translation, it is a possibility (and there are other manuscripts that read simply, "It is the only son . . . ," not explicitly here calling "the son" "God"). The passage seems to imply some kind of ranking of hierarchy: Is the father unseeable because of superiority and therefore needs the son for mediation of knowledge of the father? The Fourth Gospel wants to make the son and the father "equals," but by nonetheless still using the labels "father" and "son" the Gospel cannot completely dispel a hierarchy of knowledge implicated in the hierarchy of familial statuses.

Yet Christian orthodoxy need not get rid of all such hierarchical language, whether in the Bible or otherwise. The so-called Creed of Athanasius, often called by its first words in Latin *Quicunque vult*, states that Christ is "equal to the Father, as touching his Godhead; and inferior to the Father, as touching his Manhood."[24] That is one way of dealing with such language. What Christian orthodoxy wants to avoid is taking Jesus to be some kind of "God Jr." or some kind of inferior divine being. Christians need to be able to defend both our worship of Jesus but also our insistence that we believe in "one God." Therefore, we can admit no "demigods" or beings that exist somehow "between" divinity and the universe.

As Tanner explains, Jesus cannot be a "creature elevated to a divine level, nor divine principle of a lesser sort. These other possibilities are ruled out just [because] there simply is nothing in between God and creatures—

---

23. Hebrews 5:7–9: Jesus learned obedience through suffering; obedience to whom? Presumably, God.

24. See the Book of Common Prayer, 865, from which this translation is taken.

no lesser divinities on the way to being creatures, no creatures that are themselves something approaching God. One has to be either one or the other, because creatures and God are all that the world divides into."[25] In another formulation from Tanner: "Jesus therefore mediates divinity and humanity because he unites both and not because he is something in between" (157). The combination of rigorous historical readings coupled with theological critique allows us to navigate the New Testament texts without using "bad" historical exegesis or ending up with "bad" theology.

The Suffering God

One reason it is important for Christians to be able to claim that Jesus is fully God and not some kind of junior deity, super angel, or secondary god, as I said above, is because we worship him and yet do not consider ourselves polytheists or idolaters. Another reason is because a robust divine Christology allows us to say things about God we might have difficulty otherwise claiming, for instance, that our God is a God who suffers, even to the point of pain and death.

I noted above that the author of Luke and Acts prefers to depict the death of Jesus as the voluntary, noble death of a martyr, and that author rigorously plays down the suffering of Jesus. There are a few exceptions. The very beginning of Acts does mention Jesus's "suffering": "After his suffering he presented himself alive to them by many convincing proofs" (Acts 1:3). But this is the barest of mentions. Repeatedly, Acts stresses the resurrection of Jesus over his death; the disciples are "witnesses" to the "resurrection" (1:22; 2:32). God "foreknew" that Jesus would be killed, but he is not really presented as the one who engineered it (2:23–36). The author admits that Jesus did "suffer," but it was as a "prophet," blame goes squarely on "the Jews," and God immediately overturns their action by vindicating Jesus in the resurrection (3:13–26; see also 10:39–43; 13:28–39).

The author of Acts does include a reference to Isa 53:7–8: Jesus is a "sheep . . . led to the slaughter," but there is no explicit language making his death a *sacrifice for sins*; the emphasis, again, is on Jesus's willing submission to an unjust death (8:32–33). Acts 17:3 notes that "it was necessary for the Messiah to suffer and to rise from the dead," but again what is lacking

---

25. Tanner, *Christ the Key*, 156. I have altered the wording slightly after consultation with Tanner. The original says, ". . . ruled out just in case there simply is nothing. . . ." Tanner confirms that she meant, "just because there simply is nothing. . . ."

is the *reason* for that "necessity" and any reference to sacrificial atonement. The one place in Luke and Acts that seems to hint at the idea is Acts 20:28: God "obtained" the "church of God . . . with the blood of his own son." I am tempted to suggest that this may be one of those instances when the author of Luke–Acts is drawing on a source: it seems to express a theological notion that he doesn't really "own."[26] At any rate, we don't get the idea from Luke and Acts that Jesus is a God who suffered or that his death is a sacrifice "for us."

But the theology is present in many other New Testament documents. I have already noted it in Mark, especially in his dramatic portrayal of the tearing of the curtain in the temple just at Jesus's death. Paul likewise, who reflects other interesting similarities to the Gospel of Mark, thinks of Jesus's crucifixion as a suffering sacrifice. God put Christ forward "as a sacrifice of atonement by his blood" (Rom 3:25).[27] Jesus "was handed over to death for our trespasses" (Rom 4:25). According to Gal 3:13, Christ became a "curse for us" in order to "redeem" us from the "curse of the law." These are only a few examples I could mention from many in Paul's letters.

According to the Letter to the Hebrews, Jesus is both the high priest who *performs* the sacrifice but also the sacrifice itself (7:26–27; 9:11–14). Jesus "tasted death for everyone" (2:9); his death effects "purification for sins" (1:3); by his death he destroyed "the one who has the power of death" and freed those enslaved by fear of death (2:14–15). The interpretation of Jesus's suffering as necessary for salvation and as making possible the redemption of human beings from sin pervades Hebrews (see also 2:17; 5:7–9; 9:15, 22, 26; 10:10, 12, 19–22; 12:24; 13:12).

The First Letter of Peter shares the theology. This document may indeed reveal influence from Paul's letters and theology; its Christology is similar to Paul's. Note how this formulation could easily have come from Paul's pen: "For Christ also suffered for sins once for all, the righteous for the unrighteous, in order to bring you to God. He was put to death in the flesh, but made alive in the spirit" (1 Pet 3:18). To cite a New Testament author much different in style and theology from Paul, we have John, the author of Revelation, which repeatedly emphasizes the suffering and death of Jesus

---

26. On the use of sources by the author of Luke–Acts, sources that seem to disagree somewhat with the theological tendencies of the rest of the books, see Martin, *New Testament,* 142–51.

27. As commentators and editors note, the term could be translated as "place of atonement," but the death as atoning sacrifice is present in either case.

and his followers: the bloody Lamb leading his bloody, prophetic, slaves and martyrs (see Rev 5:6, 12; 7:14; 14:1–5; 19:2, 13).

Thus we've already encountered different theological interpretations of Jesus's death available from the New Testament, and we've barely scratched the surface: Jesus's death as substitutionary atonement; as ransom; as example for the sufferings of his followers; as enabling a reconciliation between God and an estranged people. Later theologians offered others. As Alister McGrath points out, Gregory the Great and Rufinus of Aquileia interpreted the crucifixion as a "trick," "hook," or "trap" God laid to catch the devil unawares.[28]

I believe we have no need to settle on one "right" theory of the meaning of the death of Jesus. I also believe that all of them pose problems and are not completely acceptable. We today may find certain older explanations of Jesus's death to be less than satisfying and perhaps even unacceptable. When Augustine, for instance, interprets the crucifixion as the "true sacrifice . . . by which the principalities and powers lawfully detained us to pay the penalty," we may rightly balk at the mythological ideas there involved, as if personal, cosmic evil powers had the legitimacy to force God's hand and with justice demand a divine payment.[29] We may not want to allow such "legitimacy" to evil.

But this just points up the problem with all "theories of the atonement" and attempts at adequate "explanations" of Jesus's death. As Tanner argues, we must test all "theories" of Jesus's death by the values of theology and ethics we believe we have learned from the gospel. As she puts it, "The cross saves, not as a vicarious punishment or an atoning sacrifice or satisfaction of God's honor or as a perfectly obedient act—all those accounts of the cross that have become problematic for contemporary persons, especially since the lessons of white feminist, womanist, and liberation theology. The cross saves because in it sin and death have been assumed by the one, the Word, who cannot be conquered by them."[30] I like to remember a comment made once by George Lindbeck when I was a teaching assistant for one of his theology courses at Yale Divinity School. We were attempting to come up with good questions for the final examination. Lindbeck remarked, in his wry way, that he had always thought a good final exam question might be, "Explain why all theories of the atonement are offensive to pious ears." Indeed.

---

28. See McGrath, *Theology*, 85–86.
29. See ibid., 89, quoting Augustine, *Festal Letter VII*.
30. Tanner, *Jesus, Humanity, and the Trinity*, 29.

Finally on this topic, I want to stress that popular ideas about Christianity and Jesus's death have often wrongly focused too much on the aspect of humiliation endured by Jesus. Many people, not just Friedrich Nietzsche, have made the mistake of assuming that the gospel teaches some kind of abstract principle of value in humility in itself, as an end in itself. But that is not the role of humility in the New Testament. The Gospel of Mark, surely, emphasizes the necessity of suffering, both for Jesus and for his followers, but the suffering inevitably is to be followed by "glory" and celebration. As Paul writes, "We also boast in our suffering, knowing that suffering produces endurance, and endurance produces character, and character produces hope, and hope does not disappoint us, because God's love has been poured into our hearts through the Holy Spirit that has been given to us" (Rom 5:3–5, NRSV). We are united with Christ in his death in order to be united in his resurrection (6:5–11; see also 8:18). Paul says he became weak in order to share in the blessings of the gospel (1 Cor 9:22–23). The Corinthians share in sufferings and will share in consolation (2 Cor 1:7). Momentary affliction is followed by "weight of glory" (2 Cor 4:17). The famous section in Philippians, sometimes called the Christ Hymn, portrays Christ as "emptying himself," the "kenosis," to invoke the Greek word. He moves down, even to a shameful death in crucifixion. But the move down leads to a move up to glory (Phil 2:5–11). According to Hebrews, which does stress Jesus's humbling himself, Jesus achieved glory and honor through "the suffering of death" (Heb 2:9). Nowhere in the New Testament is humility, much less self-humiliation, taught as an abstract virtue in itself. It is a means to an end of salvation and even "fame," the more common translation of the term usually translated "glory," δόξα. Again to quote Tanner, humiliation is not an ultimate or final good but a "means to elevation." "The Son humbles himself, Jesus humbles himself, to be with us in the lowliness of our suffering and need, in order to save us from it, not to engrave that lowliness into the world as its final good."[31]

In the ancient world the emphasis on the suffering and death of Christ led to debates about "patripassianism," the idea not only that Jesus the son "suffered and died" but also that God the father did. To ancient philosophers, it was ridiculous to say that God could suffer. It was probably never seen as a problem to less educated people, as there were many myths of gods suffering and dying in ancient cultures. "Suffering" was assumed by philosophers to imply change and dense materiality, and to the kind of Platonism assumed by ancient philosophers—the time when church fathers were defending

31. Ibid., 77.

Christianity against non-Christian philosophical disdain and criticism—the apparently Christian idea that God had suffered and died, especially on a cross, seemed coarse, vulgar, uneducated, and literally impossible. In defense against this sort of anti-Christian attack, Christians condemned beliefs that God the father suffered and died as a heresy, labeling it "patripassianism."[32]

I can see the problems feared in the idea that the very Godhead, including God the Father, shared in the suffering of Jesus. That could be taken to do damage to doctrines I examined in the previous chapter, where I stressed the transcendence of God. If saying that all of God, the Godhead, the entire trinity, which would therefore include God the Father, "died" is taken to mean that the transcendent God has after all been caught in the universe as one more being in and of the universe, then the idea of "God dying" could lead to identifying the ineffable God with something in the universe.

But I don't believe we modern (or postmodern) Christians are nearly as concerned as ancient intellectuals about the ancient philosophical worry that only "matter" can change, that God cannot change at all, and that saying God "died" would be the same as making the impossible claim that God "changed" in some way. Thus several theologians in the twentieth century were indeed willing to talk about the Christian God, the God revealed in Jesus, as a God who died, in complete solidarity with the crucified Jesus and with us, who will also die.[33] At any rate, I do believe we must affirm the complete and full divinity of Jesus Christ, and hence we must see Jesus's death as portraying the "crucified God," the "God who died," united with us in our most human weakness and vulnerability.[34]

Jesus, the Human God

Whereas the last chapter focused in part on the distance between God and the universe—the transcendence of God, the fact that God is "wholly other" from what we are, God is "not us"—in this chapter we have the opportunity

32. The extent to which actual Christians taught that the Father also suffered is debatable; but at least some Christians *accused* others of the "heresy."

33. A famous such study is Moltmann, *Crucified God*; see the discussion of the history of the problem, as well as the state of the question in twentieth-century German theology, in Jüngel, *God as the Mystery*; see also the discussion in McGrath, *Making of Modern German Christology*, 186–210.

34. See Keul, "Inkarnation," 216–32. The incarnation renders God—in God's very self—"woundable." The German brings this out (*Verwundbarkeit*), as does the English when we remember its Latin etymology: subject to being wounded (*vulnerare*). In the incarnation, God joins the fragile world, including all the human beings throughout the strained world who are vulnerable to pain, hunger, thirst, and poverty.

to focus on the opposite fact, but one that is just as true. By confessing faith in the incarnation, that Jesus Christ as God took on flesh, *became* human flesh, we may stress the nearness of God to us. Christians sometimes do not take a robust enough view of the incarnation.[35] Too often we tend to emphasize the divinity of Christ at the expense of his humanity or, on the other hand, think of Jesus so much as a person "just like us" that we have difficulty thinking of him as "truly God." The doctrine of the incarnation is one of the things, along with the trinity, that makes Christianity seem so wrong and even irrational to many Jews and Muslims. Islam in particular emphasizes the transcendence of God. To most Muslims, God is so totally "other" than creation or human beings that it is ridiculous to believe in a human being actually being God. But with the doctrine of the incarnation, Christians get to have it both ways: God is certainly transcendent and utterly "other" than the universe, but in the person of Jesus Christ we believe in a human being who is also divine.

As Paul put it, Christ is the "icon of God" (2 Cor 4:4). The word "icon" here (εἰκών) is usually translated as "image." Christ is the "image of God." And that would be a translation less susceptible to anachronism. But it may also be helpful to engage in a bit of creative anachronism and think of the role of icons in later Eastern Orthodox churches. To Orthodox Christians, icons are not mere illustrations; they are not "pictures." They are sacred images that have some kind of participation in the archetype represented. To venerate an icon, therefore, is not to worship the picture or materials but to show proper veneration to the person represented. Icons are something like sacraments in materiality: they participate in what they represent and communicate the sacredness to the believer. Thus, taking Paul's "icon" in that way, we have him teaching that Christ is the "icon of God," the making present of God. Jesus is the "seeable God."

In another piece of creative exegesis, we may take the ubiquitous title for Jesus in the Gospels, "son of man," as emphasizing Jesus's humanity and

---

35. For a robust, and complicated, treatment of various difficult doctrines centered around the incarnation, see Gerald O'Collins, *Incarnation*. O'Collins, for example, deals with complex debates surrounding the orthodox doctrines of the incarnation, such as what precisely is meant by insisting on Christ "pre-existing his incarnation" without implying that there could be a before and after for Christ's personal, divine nature (15). I will not attempt in this chapter to address some of the most difficult problems in doctrines of the incarnation as found in late ancient and medieval theology. See also Crisp, "Incarnation," 160–75. As Crisp notes, "Classical theologians were not unaware of the problems associated with claiming the timeless Son assumed temporal human nature" (169).

therefore the incarnation. It is unlikely that the original authors intended "son of man" to be a reference to incarnation. More likely the title recalled for them the same phrase from Daniel (Dan 7:13). Often in the Gospels "son of man" occurs in contexts emphasizing the eschatological role Jesus is expected to play in the "end times," such as judge or leader of heavenly armies. The Gospel writers more likely had in mind that eschatological figure when they designate Jesus, or, more precisely, have Jesus designate himself, "son of man." That need not stop us postmodern Christians, however, from reading the title as communicating to us Jesus's radical incarnation in human flesh.

And indeed, I believe we should emphasize the "radical" nature of the Christian confession of the incarnation. Some church fathers resisted talking about "the Word" as itself fully becoming "flesh." They taught that the truly divine second person of the trinity, the "Word," did "take on" flesh, but they were sometimes uncomfortable fully embracing the idea that the Word actually *became* flesh, to the extent that one could say that the Word was actually crucified, suffered, and died. The Word perhaps "took on" humanity, but it was the human aspect of Jesus that suffered, not the divine aspect.[36] It seems they wanted to confess that Jesus truly suffered and died, but they were afraid of lapsing into the "patripassianism" mentioned above. The "Godhead" could not suffer and could not be flesh. The father did not take on flesh. So the aspect of Jesus Christ that was as fully divine as the father could not itself have experienced human ignorance or growth or suffering.

I think it better to live with the Christian paradox that Jesus really is a crucified God. Jesus is fully God and fully human, in spite of the fact that we sometimes cannot get our heads completely around that combination. But to confess the radical doctrine of the incarnation, we should confess that Jesus is the visible God, the seeable God, the God who willingly experienced human precarious existence, ignorance, frustration, anxiety, pain, and death. Jesus is the God who is like us. The God in whom we participate. The divinity we will eventually become, though by adoption not nature. Jesus is the son of God by essence and very nature. We are children of God by adoption and grace.

But in every other way except sin, Jesus is as human as we are. If we think of Jesus as simply some kind of "superman," as ancient Greeks thought a very special person might be a "divine man" (θεῖος ἀνήρ), a kind of different breed of being, we err on the other side of the doctrine of the incarnation.

36. Beeley provides much discussion and several examples from the church fathers in his *Unity of Christ,* esp. 39, 134, 164, 193.

We must remind ourselves that Jesus shared our human nature *in every way* apart from sin. Jesus's humanity must be understood as being just like our humanity. He may differ from us in his divine nature but not in his human nature. The definition of Chalcedon says this by using the same Greek word, ὁμοούσιος, to describe both Christ's "consubstantial" sharing with God of the being of God *and* his "consubstantial" sharing with human beings of the being of humans. Just as Christ is "consubstantial" (*homoousios*) with the Father with respect to divinity, he is "consubstantial" with us in his humanity. His humanity cannot be different from ours, except for lacking sin.

In spite of the fact that this kind of theological complexity certainly was not familiar to the authors of the New Testament documents, we may use them to think about God's incarnation for our theology. Besides so many of the "son of man" passages in the Gospels ("The son of man has no place to lay his head," Matt 8:20, and par.), the Gospels provide many other passages useful for teaching the humanity of Jesus. In fact, although the Fourth Gospel goes much further than the other three in portraying Jesus as divine, even as "equal" to the father, it also has no compunction about depicting a Jesus who is very human indeed. John highlights the close, loving relationship Jesus has with certain followers, the most obvious one being the unnamed "beloved disciple." In fact, because of one passage that describes the close, emotional relationship Jesus has with the sisters Mary and Martha and their brother Lazarus, some have suggested that the author is providing an obvious indication that the beloved disciple is Lazarus himself.

The scene begins by noting that Lazarus has fallen ill, and the sisters send a message to Jesus: "Lord, he whom you love is ill" (John 11:3).[37] Jesus delays, even though, as the narrator says, "Jesus loved Martha and her sister and Lazarus" (11:5). After Jesus arrives and finds a dead and buried Lazarus, we are told that Mary came out to see him, and then there is this description: "When Jesus saw her weeping, and the Jews who came with her also weeping, he was greatly disturbed in spirit and deeply moved" (11:33). After Jesus

---

37. This statement is the reason some people give for taking this passage as indicating that Lazarus is not just *a* person Jesus loved but *the* "beloved disciple." I accept that as a possibility but not as an exegetical certainty. The Greek used in 11:3 is not precisely like the Greek elsewhere when the author is referring to "the beloved disciple" ("the disciple whom Jesus loved"). In fact, the Greek of 11:3 could just as easily be translated, "Someone you love is ill." Moreover, the phrase is placed on the lips of disciples, not of the narrator himself. When "love" is next mentioned, the narrator says that Jesus loved Martha, her sister, and Lazarus. If the narrator took Lazarus to be *the* "beloved disciple," I'd expect his name to appear first here, not last. Nonetheless, I think it *possible though unlikely* that we are meant to take Lazarus to be the same "loved disciple" we find elsewhere in John.

asks where they had placed the body, we have the famously shortest verse in the Bible: "Jesus wept."[38] When Jesus comes to the tomb the narrator adds another detail, saying that Jesus was "again greatly disturbed" (11:38).

The story ends happily, as Jesus raises Lazarus from the dead and restores him to his sisters. But the portrait of Jesus is remarkably human, even as it shows he has divine powers. The Greek words here translated as "greatly disturbed" (11:33 and 38: ἐμβριάομαι) and "deeply moved" (33: ταράσσω) have many meanings. The first is a word that combines the preposition "in" with a word deriving from the Greek word for "nose," and it can refer to horses "snorting with rage."[39] It can also refer to human indignation, and it can mean "censure." The latter word, ταράσσω, can mean any kind of violent stirring up, whether literal or figurative. For both of these words there is at least the possibility that they invoke anger or indignity as much as grieving. In any case, both words show Jesus being extremely upset, certainly because of his sympathy for the grief of others and apparently in experiencing grief himself. This God is human enough to suffer and weep, and this, again, from the Gospel *most* concerned to depict Jesus as divine.

Another curiosity about the Gospel of John is its suggestion that Jesus is *absent* from the church after his departure at the end of the Gospel. John 13–17 contains a long speech by Jesus, interspersed at times by dialogue with his closest disciples, often called Jesus's Farewell Discourse. The speech does read at times like a "testament," a genre in which a famous character gives his last words and instructions to sons, family, or followers. Not far into the speech Jesus says, "Little children, I am with you only a little longer. You will look for me; and as I said to the Jews so now I say to you, 'Where I am going, you cannot come'" (John 13:33, NRSV). In contrast to Jesus's departing words in Matthew, "I am with you always" (Matt 28:20), Jesus in John insists that he will be *absent* from the church after his departure.

Jesus seems so serious about his absence that he promises a substitute for himself, in another detail unique to John's Gospel. He says he will send them "another Advocate," or, in what is a transliteration of the Greek, the "Paraclete" (παράκλητος; 14:16). Jesus promises that *that* figure, rather than Jesus himself, will "be with you forever." The Greek term is made up of the Greek word for "someone called" (κλητός) combined with a preposition meaning "to the side" (παρά): someone called to one's side as an aid or advocate. The English "advocate" is almost a transliteration of the equivalent

---

38. KJV and RSV. NRSV: "Jesus began to weep."
39. Thus one definition given by LSJ.

words in Latin: *ad* + *vocatus*. Though it is not immediately clear, "the Advocate" seems to be John's special term for the holy spirit (see 14:26). In fact, the
next verse says, "This is the spirit of truth" (14:17). The Paraclete or Advocate
is precisely like a lawyer representing the disciples to God or representing
Jesus to the disciples in his absence.

Jesus promises that his absence will not be permanent: "I will not leave
you orphaned; I am coming to you" (14:18). He seems to say he will be absent
for a while but then return: "In a little while the world will no longer see me,
but you will see me; because I live, you also will live. *On that day* you will
know that I am in my Father, and you in me, and I in you" (14:19–20; NRSV,
emphasis added). I highlight the words "on that day" because Jesus's meaning is otherwise not obvious: Jesus is not saying he will be "with" the disciples
also in some sense after his departure; he is rather promising merely that he
will return some "day" in the future. Thus he repeats the point a bit later:
"These things I have said to you while remaining with you. But the Paraclete,
the holy spirit, which the father will send in my name, that one will teach
you everything and remind you about everything I said to you" (14:25–26).
Later, in a long prayer that closes the Farewell Discourse, Jesus returns to the
theme of his absence. He speaks of his absence from "the world" although
his disciples are still "in the world" (17:11). Jesus speaks of a time when he is
with the Father, but his disciples are still, in a way, trapped "in the world,"
which for the Gospel of John is indeed a hostile place.

I have stressed this theme of Jesus's absence from the church because it
runs counter to much Christian teaching and liturgy that prefers to emphasize the *presence* of Jesus with the church. To Paul, remember, the church is
the very *body* of Christ, as I will explore more fully in the chapter below on
ecclesiology. As counterintuitive to Christian sensibilities as the idea is, I believe reflecting on the absence of Jesus, as I did also above in my discussion
of Mark, may be theologically useful. It makes sense of our own experiences
in which we do not immediately experience the presence of God or Jesus in
our prayers or devotions.

Most great Christian mystics have complained about the experience
of desertion and loneliness even when, perhaps especially when, they are
seeking some feeling of the *presence* of Jesus in their meditations. Bernard
of Clairvaux admits to his fellow monks, "Men with an urge to frequent
prayer will have experience of what I say. Often enough when we approach
the altar to pray our hearts are dry and lukewarm."[40] A biographer attempts

---

40. *Sermon on the Song of Songs* 9.5.7. Trans. Ilian Walsh, *On the Song of Songs*.

to imagine how Julian of Norwich may have experienced it: "Julian wanted to free her heart to love Christ. To learn true contrition. To feel and not just speak her prayers. Yet, if she was truthful, she still meditated on Christ's passion and felt cold. Barren. Dry. A thousand questions pricked her. Perhaps she did not understand what the friars meant by feelings. Perhaps she had not yet discovered Christ's true compassion. In the flickering wax light, the 'minde' of the Passion still seemed far away."[41]

The theme of the mystic bemoaning the absent Christ, missing the *feeling* of God's presence, is so common as to be stereotypical if not, by now, banal. But it does capture common experiences of believers. It is fitting to find it in the Fourth Gospel: the absence of Jesus. As Rowan Williams notes, reflecting on the fact that, according to the Gospel of John, the resurrected Jesus says both "do not touch me" and "touch me here" (see John 20:17, 27), the resurrection frees Jesus from the limitations of space and time—*and* from our "projections and expectations." Jesus is "not here."[42]

We may begin from the incarnation, the radical notion that God became fully human, to speak about other doctrines. Take, for example, the way we Christians should think about creation, about nature itself, the natural world. The fact that Christ as fully God took on human flesh means that divinity took on nature. God became creation in Jesus Christ. This does not mean the degradation of divinity; it means the raising up of creation to divine status. We may imagine that the doctrine of the incarnation makes of nature a sacrament: a physical, visible sign of the invisible grace of God. All creation, all our visible and invisible world, communicates to us divine grace and the presence of God in Christ. A better theological motivation for caring for the earth and everything in it can scarcely be found. A better motivation for marveling at our surroundings can hardly be imagined.

We may also take the incarnation as inspiration for thinking about soteriology, the doctrine of salvation. McGrath explains what he calls "one of the most controversial aspects" of the theology of Karl Barth: his application of radical incarnation to the salvation of human beings. As McGrath explains, summarizing Barth, the incarnation does not change anything about the relationship between God and human beings. It just discloses an already existing reality: "This point is confirmed by Barth's tendency towards a doctrine of universal salvation. Christ makes known the unilateral triumph of grace. It appears impossible for human beings to avoid being saved, whether they

41. Frykholm, *Julian of Norwich*, 14–15.
42. Williams, *Resurrection*, 81–82.

know it or not, whether they wish to be saved or not."[43] McGrath emphasizes the role of the incarnation, coupled with predestination, in soteriology: "Despite all appearances to the contrary, humanity cannot be condemned. In the end, grace will triumph, even over open unbelief. Barth's doctrine of predestination eliminates the possibility of the rejection of humanity. In that Christ has borne the penalty and pain of rejection by God, this can never again become the portion of humanity. Taken together with his characteristic emphasis upon the 'triumph of grace,' Barth's doctrine of predestination points to the universal restoration and salvation of humanity—a position which has occasioned a degree of criticism from others who would otherwise be sympathetic to his general position."[44] To many Christians, especially more conservative ones, this may sound impossibly radical, but it is a sensible extension of the doctrine of the incarnation. Rather than lowering divinity to the level of humanity, the incarnation raises humanity to the level of God. The incarnation makes the human divine. In the end, Christianity is not at all a rejection of "humanism" but its highest form.

Jesus in Hell

One statement about Christ, found in scripture as well as in credal formulations, offers an excellent opportunity for demonstrating the difference between historical interpretations and theological ones—and between historical truths and mythological ones (yes, "true myths" as opposed to false myths). According to 1 Pet 3:18–20, Jesus "was put to death in the flesh but made alive in the spirit." The author continues to say that Jesus, in the spirit, "went and preached to those spirits in prison" (3:19). The passage is none too clear about what event this refers to.[45] Even who these "spirits in prison" are is not clear, though the next verse implies that they are the persons (or angels? "sons of god" from Genesis 6?) who rebelled against God in the time of Noah. A bit later in the epistle the author again brings up "the living and

---

43. McGrath, *Making of Modern German Christology,* 137. McGrath is commenting on Barth's *Church Dogmatics* II/2, pp. 94–194. See further McGrath, "Barth als Aufklärer?"; and Stock, *Anthropologie der Verheissung,* 44–61.

44. McGrath, *Making,* 138.

45. For a recent discussion of the exegetical possibilities of 1 Pet 3:18–20, see Helyer, *The Life and Witness of Peter,* 148–56. I do not accept most of Helyer's conclusions, which are conservative and quite traditional, even to the extent of arguing that the historical Peter actually wrote the letter, but he does give references for different options, including some related to the interpretation of this passage.

the dead" as all having to account for their deeds: "That is why the gospel was preached to the dead, so that they might be judged on the one hand in a human way in the flesh, but also in a divine way in the spirit" (4:6).[46]

These verses seem to have provided the inspiration for the later Christian belief that Jesus, after his death but before his resurrection in the flesh, entered into hell, hades, or whatever the "place of the dead" was assumed to be and preached the gospel to the dead souls there, enabling those who had existed prior to the coming of Christ on earth to accept the gospel and have a chance at salvation. (See also Acts 2:31.) This was taken as the scriptural warrant for Christ's "harrowing of hell" that became such a popular theme of later literature and art.

The idea occurs in the so-called Creed of Athanasius, or *Quicunque Vult*: Christ "suffered for our salvation, descended into hell, rose again the third day from the dead" (trans. *Book of Common Prayer*). It is now perhaps most encountered by Christians in the Apostles' Creed: Christ "suffered under Pontius Pilate, was crucified, dead, and buried. He descended into hell." The implication from both creeds is that it was after his burial but before his resurrection that Jesus, perhaps only in "the spirit," entered hell. The creeds do not say that the purpose of his visit was to preach to the dead or save righteous souls, but that has been the story as found in literature and art for centuries.

What do Christians think they are confessing when they say these words—for Anglicans and Episcopalians, perhaps each day at Morning and Evening Prayer? Does anyone believe anymore that Jesus's soul or spirit actually left his grave and somehow physically journeyed to hades?[47] Does anyone actually still believe, as people certainly did in the ancient world, that hell is a region under our feet, in the physical earth, to which Jesus *could have* traveled simply by "going down"? No modern, Western person really believes such things anymore. But if those who confess this do not "believe"

---

46. These are my translations, and the Greek is a bit cryptic. The NRSV: "For this is the reason the gospel was proclaimed even to the dead, so that, though they had been judged in the flesh as everyone is judged, they might live in the spirit as God does." That is a rather expanded, interpretive translation that may indeed reflect the intended meaning, but it is far from certain. The main point, it seems to me, is that the dead, along with the living, will be judged in a human manner "in the flesh" and before God "in spirit."

47. Remember that for ancient Christians, at least in the first few centuries, the soul or spirit was thought of as what we would call a "physical" thing. That is, both were considered made up of very fine "matter" but were "physical" nonetheless. This is demonstrated more fully in the chapter below titled "Spirit."

it in any kind of historical or scientific or physical or literal way, what does it mean to believe it at all?

Jesus's descent into hell is a great example of a myth. It cannot be accepted as true in the same way a scientific or historical "fact" is true. The question therefore becomes one of whether it is a true myth or a false myth. It would be a false myth if we took it as a literal lesson in geography or history. But is there a way we may interpret it as a true myth?

I have always found the confession that Jesus descended into hell to express a valuable truth about the gospel. I take the words as indicating that we must remind ourselves, in our darkest of moods and depressions, that there is no place in the universe where Jesus cannot find us and save us. There is no place—whether in death, depression, sickness, even non-existence—where God in Christ cannot reach us. There is no place we can imagine where love cannot reach. And we may need to remind ourselves that this is true, given to us by a true myth, not only for ourselves but also for those we love. Our dead are not thereby bereft of the presence, comfort, and love of God. As Paul put it, "For I am convinced that neither death, nor life, nor angels, nor rulers, nor things present, nor things to come, nor powers, nor height, nor depth, nor anything else in all creation, will be able to separate us from the love of God in Christ Jesus our Lord" (Rom 8:38–39, NRSV). This is an excellent example of when theological interpretation must save a fact from the dustbin of outdated historical meanings. Though not historically or scientifically true, the confession may still be theologically (or mythologically) true. There is no place we can imagine that is off-limits to Christ.

The Resurrection of Christ

One of the central and often perceived as indispensable confessions of Christianity is a belief in the resurrection of Jesus. The Nicene Creed says simply that "the third day he rose again according to the Scriptures." The Apostles' Creed likewise contents itself with saying merely that Jesus "rose again from the dead" on the third day after his death. Many Christians, both individuals and various church bodies, have gone further to insist on the necessity for orthodoxy of belief in the resurrection of the "body" or of the "flesh." This was forcefully argued by church fathers, of whom Tertullian is an obvious example.[48] The Articles of Religion adopted in 1801 by the Episcopal Church

---

48. See esp. Tertullian, *On the Resurrection of the Flesh*.

in the United States say that in his resurrection Jesus "took again his body, with flesh, bones, and all things appertaining to the perfection of Man's nature; wherewith he ascended into Heaven" (Article IV). Various Roman Catholic statements and catechisms as well as confessions and statements of Protestant churches and organizations likewise affirm the resurrection of the flesh, the very flesh and blood that was buried.[49]

But what would it mean for modern or postmodern Christians to make such confessions? It is hard for us to accept quite literally and historically that Jesus rose in the very same flesh and blood from the tomb or ground and then zoomed up into space, where he sits now with that same physical, flesh, blood, and bones body. Where exactly is this spatial and physical "heaven"? If it is physical, why have scientists not found it? Why does Jesus's physical, flesh-and-blood body not show up in the by-now fairly extensive scientific visual and physical searches of the cosmos? Remember that according to the premodern doctrines, it must be a body *precisely like the one that was buried and precisely like ours,* at least to the extent of being flesh and blood or "physical." A postmodern Christian confession of the resurrection of Jesus will probably take a more theological rather than scientific, literal, or historical shape. The location of Jesus's flesh-and-blood body *physically present somewhere in the universe,* which is precisely what the ancient Christians meant when they insisted on the doctrine, poses a problem that demands theological interpretation for modern Christians.

One of the places to begin such a reinterpretation is actually with the very first surviving witness to the resurrected Jesus, the Apostle Paul. Paul not only gives the earliest testimony to the resurrection but also is the *only* person whose "eyewitness" testimony to the risen Jesus survives. Most critical scholars doubt that any of the Gospels were actually written by people who were disciples of Jesus during his lifetime. None of those authors, therefore, can claim to have seen the risen Lord. Critical scholars also don't believe Simon Peter was actually the author of the letters written in his name, or that Jude was actually written by Judas the brother of Jesus, or that the Epistle of James was written by Jesus's brother. We do accept the historical authenticity, though, of seven letters of Paul.[50] And one of those letters is 1 Corinthians, where Paul says more about the nature of the resurrected body than he does anywhere else.

49. *Catechism of the Catholic Church,* 2d ed., §990 (p. 258).
50. For defenses of these general statements, see the various relevant chapters in Martin, *New Testament.*

Paul begins his discussion by passing along a list of people who claimed to have seen the risen Jesus (1 Cor 15:1–7), and the list seems intended to express chronological order: Jesus appeared to Cephas (Peter), then to the twelve, then to more than five hundred "brothers" at the same time (I assume the Greek is not intended to exclude women), then to Jacob (James), then to "all the apostles," and finally to Paul himself. (Note that at this time in the history of the church "the apostles" are not equated with "the twelve.")

Paul considers his experience of seeing Jesus after his death, however we may later imagine the nature of that experience, to be exactly the same as that experienced by the others. We commonly imagine that the first disciples saw the actual risen flesh-and-blood body of Jesus, as some of the Gospels indeed insist, but that Paul saw "a vision," and he did so many years after the earthly appearances of the risen Lord had ceased. This is how the Acts of the Apostles presents Paul's experience (Acts 9:1–9; 22:4–16; 26:9–18; though we should not take Acts as being historically reliable). But that is not how Paul describes it. Indeed, it is absolutely necessary to his argument, both here and in Gal 1:12 and 16, that his "seeing" of the risen Jesus is *precisely the same phenomenon* as that experienced by all others who claimed to have seen Jesus's body. Whatever Paul "saw" was exactly the same as what they "saw," at least in Paul's mind.

But how does Paul describe the nature of that resurrected body? To answer that question we must also admit that Paul's argument assumes that the nature of Jesus's resurrected body is the same as the expected resurrected bodies of his followers. Paul argues that those who deny the future resurrection of believers, indeed, a *corporeal* resurrection, must themselves have no hope of a future existence after their own deaths: "If Christ has not been raised, then our preaching is in vain, and your faith in vain" (15:14); "If the dead are not raised, then Christ has not been raised" (15:16). However Paul describes the nature of the expected bodies of Jesus's followers must also therefore be how Paul envisions the resurrected body of Jesus.

And that is not as "flesh and blood." English translations have caused much confusion about the text and Paul's arguments in 1 Cor 15.[51] First, the actual composition of the resurrected body, that is, what kind of "matter" it is composed of, is different from the preresurrected body. Continuing an analogy to seeds and grain he began earlier, Paul explains, "What is sown in mortality, is raised in immortality; what is sown in dishonor, is raised in

---

51. For a larger contextualization of this topic in the ancient world and more supportive evidence for my thesis here, see Martin, *Corinthian Body*, 104–36.

glory; it is sown in weakness, it is raised in power" (15:42–44). The translation of the next several words is a bit more controversial. The NRSV renders
them, "It is sown a physical body, it is raised a spiritual body. If there is a
physical body, there is also a spiritual body. . . . But it is not the spiritual that
is first, but the physical, and then the spiritual" (15:44–46).

The problems with the translation are in the terms "physical" and
"spiritual," leading many modern readers to assume Paul is contrasting a
"physical" body with a body that is *not* "physical" but somehow "spiritual,"
and they read that as "not made of matter." The "spiritual body" is taken to
be "immaterial." But the word here translated as "physical" is not some form
of the Greek word that could reasonably be taken to refer to "matter" or
"nature" (φύσις, φυσικός). The word is one normally translated as "soul" or
"life" or as related in some way to "living" (ψυχή, ψυχικός). And the word
rendered here as "spiritual" would not have meant in Paul's day what later
Christians and philosophers would call "immaterial substance," which later
theologians took to be the nature of the Christian "soul" or "spirit." The word
is πνευματικός, related to the word πνεῦμα, which is indeed usually translated "spirit" but when taken as referring to a *substance* would not have meant
something *not* made of "matter" or something that was *not* "physical."

Pneuma in Paul's day was taken to be material indeed. It was normally
thought of as a thin, invisible kind of stuff. In medicine, science, and philosophy it was taken to be a very rarified form of air or fire. We might imagine
that ancient intellectuals thought of it the way we think of oxygen: invisible
perhaps but certainly "matter" and "physical." Pneuma was what the mind
used to communicate with the body's extremities. It raced through the body
to tell the limbs what to do, which way to move. It raced from the limbs to
the brain to enable touch, sensation, and pain. It was a very fast, very ener-
getic, very powerful material substance.

Uneducated people may not have had such sophisticated ideas, but
they also would have thought of pneuma as something like air or wind,
thus enabling the pun on "spirit" and "wind" in John 3:5–8: the same word,
pneuma, is translated in most English versions as *wind* in one place and *spirit*
in another. Moreover, pneuma was thought of as a "higher" form of matter.
It naturally wanted to rise, like helium or other gases lighter than thicker
or denser air. Thus pneuma could be considered the "stuff of the heavens,"
sometimes instead of and sometimes along with, another substance of ancient thought: ether.

When Paul says the preresurrected body is a *psychikos* body he probably means it is a body that is "merely alive," a body that has the substance and

nature that enable life (a normal meaning of ψυχή), that is, a "living body" rather than a dead body. He contrasts that with a body that is not merely living but also composed of the highest matter of the universe, at least in his cosmology. The "heavenly bodies" Paul mentions in 15:40–41 are assumed, therefore, to be composed of the substance of pneuma, in contrast to the "earthly bodies" composed of "flesh" but enlivened with *psychê* (15:39). As there is a descending hierarchy in Paul's list of different kinds of "flesh"—human, animals, birds, and fish (15:39)—so there is a hierarchy assumed in his list of "heavenly bodies" composed of pneuma (though whether this is a properly ordered list is not certain since the sun would normally be taken as "superior" to the moon): sun, moon, and stars of different levels of "glory" (15:41).

Paul later returns to his allusion to the difference between the body of Adam and that of the resurrected Christ. The former is earthy, made of dirt and dust, but Jesus's resurrected body is no longer "dusty" or "earthy," it is heavenly (15:46–47). Paul is talking here not just about status but also about material composition: as Adam's body was made of earthly matter, Christ's resurrected body is *no longer* composed of earthly matter but of "heavenly" matter. Then Paul arrives at a sentence that reads something like a punch line: "This is what I am saying, brothers: flesh and blood is not capable of inheriting the kingdom of God, nor does what is mortal inherit immortality" (15:50).

Paul is saying that the resurrected body of Christ was as different from his preresurrected body as a flower is from a seed. Not only is its appearance different; its very material substance is different—and superior. The flesh-and-blood body of Jesus before his resurrection was transformed into the pneumatic body of resurrection, a body whose flesh and blood have been transformed into pneuma. Paul then moves from his explanation of the body of the risen Jesus to explain that believers' bodies will also be transformed, in the resurrection if they die but suddenly even if they are living at the parousia: "We will not all sleep [Paul's euphemism for death], but we all will be transformed, in a moment, in the blink of an eye, at the last trumpet" (15:51–52).

This exegesis of the nature of the future resurrected bodies of believers has significance therefore with regard to what Paul thought he saw when he claims to have seen the resurrected body of Jesus—remembering that he believes his experience and what he saw was in no way different from what the other disciples had seen before him. He did not see the flesh-and-blood body of Jesus as it had been laid in a tomb. The body of Jesus he saw would be as different from his flesh-and-blood body as a flower is from a seed. It may not have been recognizable even to those who had known Jesus before his death. It may have looked entirely different. Paul had not known Jesus "in the flesh," so he would have had no way to reflect on the differences of the "before" and the "after" body of Jesus's resurrection.

Note that Paul never gives any indication that he knew anything about stories of the empty tomb. I think he would have assumed there was no need for someone to roll away a stone so Jesus's body could exit. If Jesus's body was at that time transformed into pneumatic substance, it could have easily passed through stone walls or doors, as easily as we imagine radio waves moving through the walls of buildings. This also means, though, that Paul would not have been able to imagine Jesus's resurrected body eating and drinking or being able to be touched by the finger of Thomas or held by Mary, unless by some additional miracle. And we should remember that Paul's is the earliest account we have of someone claiming to have seen the risen body of Jesus, and his is the *only* firsthand account we possess. The resurrected body of Jesus according to Paul, our earliest testimony and *only* surviving "eyewitness," doesn't fit with the later empty tomb and appearance stories of the Gospels.

But also of great importance is that the Gospel accounts do not agree with one another. Some Christian scholars are at pains to insist not only that the resurrection of Christ refers to *something* that "happened" in the past. They insist that it can be defended as a "historical fact."[52] The resurrection is not, to them, merely a theological confession, it is "history." And they extend their argument to the empty tomb: the empty tomb is not a theological, hortatory literary interpretation of the ancient belief in the resurrection but can be called a historical event.

In my view, their position makes two serious mistakes. In the first place, it makes the common error of confusing history with the past. What many scholars are doing when they say that the resurrection was a historical event is simply expressing their belief that "it really happened," that "it is an event in the past." There is nothing wrong with using the word "history" in everyday talk as referring to the past, but it brings with it problems when brought into more philosophical or technical discussion about the nature of history and historiography. Several philosophers of history have helpfully pointed out that, in order to be more precise with our claims, we should reserve the word "history" for *accounts* of the past produced by historians.[53]

---

52. See my references to and discussion of Ladd's view in the introduction above.
53. See my discussion of this in *Pedagogy*, esp. 41–44, and the references there cited.

After all, a history of the Civil War is neither the same as the Civil War nor a "reconstruction" of the Civil War, which would take the full four years or so the Civil War lasted. In fact, a history of the Civil War is not even a reconstruction at all, but a *construction,* something produced by a modern scholar or amateur. A history of the Civil War is a verbal account of the Civil War that is the result of at least one human being making countless choices about what to include and therefore what to exclude.

Moreover, the past does not exist. It is not some place a scholar can visit in order to collect data, or pieces of the past, that can then be transferred to the present and reconstructed. Many modern people cannot seem to get their heads around the very demonstrable fact that the past radically does not exist—at least for any of us. In other words, even if we imagine light rays emitted from persons or events in the past still zooming through space at the speed of light, there's no way historians could also zoom through space faster than the speed of light to be able to view them, at least as far as we know (taking contemporary physicists at their word). "History" refers to verbal artifacts created by human beings that are meant to convey some kind of "meaning" of past events, but they are not those events themselves, and they can never exhaust the entire "meaning" we may imagine for those events. So saying the resurrection of Jesus is "historical" is not saying merely that it "occurred in the past." It is claiming that modern historians, using the commonly acknowledged tools and criteria of modern historiography, can demonstrate that the resurrection of Jesus or, say, the empty tomb stories, should be accepted as "historical" by other professional historians, even those who are not Christian.

And that brings us to the second mistake. I argue that reasonable historians, viewing the data we have available in our sources, will agree that those sources are so problematic as historical sources that the historical value of their accounts must be denied. That is to say, the literary witnesses to the empty tomb taken as they are should convince any reputable historian that the empty tomb stories provide no historical data whatsoever. The Gospels themselves bear witness *against* the "historicity" of the empty tomb stories because of their very contradictions of one another.

We have no eyewitnesses at all of the empty tomb. Even if we admit Paul as a personal witness to the resurrection of Jesus, by all accounts he never saw the empty tomb. And none of the Gospels was written by an eyewitness. So the only "witnesses" to the empty tomb we have at all are secondary, tertiary, or even further removed. Furthermore, as I will demonstrate briefly here, the four accounts we have from our four canonical Gospels disagree with one another on almost all details. In fact, the only thing they agree on is *that* Jesus was raised. Paul shows no knowledge of an "empty tomb" at all. They differ on (1) who saw Jesus or any events; (2) what they saw; (3) where they saw it; (4) when they saw it; and (5) what Jesus looked like, that is, what the nature of the body was.

Who

According to Paul's list, which he apparently received from other believers before him, Peter was the first witness. Also significant is the absence of any named women on the list. Our earliest Gospel, Mark, has no resurrection appearances of Jesus at all. Three women, Mary Magdalene, Mary, the mother of James, and Salome discover the empty tomb and see a "young man" in the tomb itself, but they do not see Jesus. Though the young man instructs the women to tell the disciples "and Peter" to go to Galilee, where they will see Jesus, we are told that the women in fact *did not* tell the disciples. We have no reason to believe they later did or that the disciples later saw Jesus, whether in Galilee or elsewhere. Matthew follows Mark but with some changes: he calls one woman simply "the other Mary" and does not mention Salome (Matt 28:1); the women actually meet Jesus on the way back (28:9); and they apparently pass along the message because Matthew ends with a meeting between Jesus and "the eleven" in Galilee (Matt 28:16).

According to Luke, several other women are present. In addition to Mary Magdalene and Mary, the mother of James, Luke mentions Joanna and "other women" (Luke 24:10). They see the empty tomb but not Jesus. In Luke's account they *do* tell the other disciples. Peter is the first of the men to see the empty tomb (24:12), but he does not at that time see Jesus. Next, Luke narrates the episode of the "journey to Emmaus," during which Jesus appears to two disciples, one of whom is named Cleopas (24:13–32). After realizing it was Jesus speaking with them, they return to Jerusalem and report to "the eleven and their companions" (24:33) and are informed that in the meantime Jesus has also appeared to Peter (24:34). While they are talking, Jesus appears among them all (24:36). Jesus leads the group to Bethany and immediately ascends into heaven (24:50–51). The beginning of Acts tells a rather different story: after his resurrection, Jesus appears to many of his followers, even "staying" with them for a full period of forty days (Acts 1:3).

The Gospel of John has Mary Magdalene as the first to see the empty tomb, and she tells Peter and the beloved disciple. The latter two, after seeing the tomb, return home without seeing Jesus (John 20:1–10). While at the tomb Mary sees two angels and then sees Jesus, mistaking him for the gardener (20:14–16). Jesus lets himself be known to Mary and tells her to announce the resurrection to the disciples, which she does (20:18). That same evening Jesus appears to his disciples, except for Thomas, in a locked room in Jerusalem (20:19). Jesus then reappears to them one week later, with Thomas this time present (20:26). In what scholars sometimes treat as an epilogue to the main body of John's Gospel, Jesus appears in Galilee sometime later to Simon Peter, Thomas "the twin," Nathaniel, the sons of Zebedee, James and John, and "two others of his disciples" (21).

What

The accounts differ in their details, in some cases a great deal. According to Mark, the women see one "young man" *inside* the tomb, "sitting on the right side," who may or may not be intended to be an angel (Mark 16:5). According to Matthew, there is an earthquake, a descending angel who rolls away the stone, and a command by Jesus to tell the eleven to meet him in Galilee (28). According to Luke, the women see "two men in dazzling clothes" (24:10). Several details from Luke and Acts are unique to them: the Emmaus story and Jesus eating fish in the presence of his disciples, apparently to prove he is not a "ghost" (24:39). Jesus's forty-day stay in Jerusalem is unique to Acts. His ascension at Bethany is unique to Luke (Luke 24:50–51), and his ascension from Mount Olivet is unique to Acts (1:12). There is no explicit ascension in Matthew, but if the reader is supposed to imagine one, it must be in Galilee. The detail that the disciples are instructed by "two men" after the ascension is also unique to Acts (1:10–11).

The details of what people saw are different again in John. According to John, Mary sees two angels *in the tomb,* and they are sitting at the head and foot of the slab (20:11–12). The very presence of "the beloved disciple" is unique to John. The "footrace" between Peter and the beloved disciple (20:4) is only in John. Other details peculiar to John are Mary mistaking Jesus for the gardener; her dialogue then with Jesus; Jesus's appearance that night to the disciples in a locked room, without Thomas; Jesus appearing a week later, including the "doubting Thomas" incident; the later appearances on the shore of the lake of Galilee, including an account of their fishing, a fishing miracle, and a breakfast provided for them by Jesus (21:9–13); and finally Jesus's dialogue with Simon Peter (21:15–22). Indeed, John 21 is replete with details and narratives unique to the Gospel of John.

Where

According to Mark, no one saw the resurrected Jesus anywhere, though we may take from the young man's instructions that Jesus *intended* to appear to the disciples later in Galilee. Matthew apparently follows Mark, but he adds an appearance of Jesus to the women in Jerusalem and then an appearance later in Galilee, *but apparently only to "the eleven"* (Matt 28:16). According to Luke and Acts, *all* appearances of Jesus after his death took place in Jerusalem and its environs; *none at all took place in Galilee,* at least if the narrative is supposed to imply that the disciples obeyed Jesus's explicit instructions (Acts 1:4). According to John, Jesus appeared to several disciples twice in Jerusalem, and then sometime later to a select few male disciples beside the lake in Galilee. The author of John 21 tells us that this last appearance was the "third time that Jesus appeared to the disciples after he was raised from the dead" (21:14, NRSV), which would be accurate if we take the already narrated appearances in Jerusalem to constitute, in the author's mind, the only other appearances of Jesus to the disciples (not counting the first appearance to Mary apart from "the disciples"). Especially significant in all this is the direct contradiction between Luke–Acts and Matthew: according to the former, Jesus's appearances were in Jerusalem and *not* in Galilee; according to the latter, Jesus's sole appearance to the eleven took place in Galilee and *not* in Jerusalem.

When

According to Paul's understanding, the appearances of the resurrected body of Jesus took place over at least a few years' time. He gives the indication that the first was "on the third day" after Jesus's burial (1 Cor 15:4). And he counts Jesus's appearance to himself as the last of his list (15:8). If we estimate that Paul's experience of Jesus's appearance—and probably make that also the time of his "call" to be an apostle (Gal 1:15–16)—occurred around four or so years after the death of Jesus, as most scholars reckon, we are faced with the fact that Paul thought the resurrection appearances of Jesus went on over a few years' period of time. He apparently believed that Jesus appeared here and there and now and then from just after Jesus's death until his final appearance to Paul.

According to Mark's narrative, no appearances took place at all. If we are to assume that the author wants his readers to *assume* that a meeting later in Galilee actually took place, then the first time *anyone* saw the risen Jesus would not have been on the first day of the week but at some point after the disciples had time to travel to Galilee. Indeed, that is apparently what Matthew assumed: only the women saw Jesus on the first day; the eleven did not see him until they had traveled from Jerusalem to Galilee. According to estimates, walking distance from Jerusalem to Galilee would be about sixty-eight miles. That trip would almost certainly take a few days, maybe four. That would mean that, in Mark's assumptions, no one at all saw Jesus on the Sunday of his resurrection; they saw him only days later, in Galilee. According to Matthew, no one but the women saw Jesus on the first day, and the others did not see him until days later, in Galilee.

Luke and John are completely different in chronology from Mark and Matthew. As noted above, the resurrection appearances at the end of Luke seem to take place all at one time, namely, the same day and evening after the resurrection itself (see Luke 24:13, 33, 36). Even the walk to Bethany and the ascension there are narrated as if they happen at that same time (24:50). In Acts, that one day and evening period is expanded to a very explicit "forty days" (Acts 1:3). In John, one appearance happens first to Mary, then "that evening" to the disciples, then "one week later" to the disciples plus Thomas, and a third appearance to "disciples" some time later (weeks? months? years?) at the Sea of Galilee (John 21).

What Jesus Looked Like

The different accounts of the resurrected body of Jesus also do not agree about what Jesus looked like, what kind of body he bore. According to Paul, Jesus was embodied, but it was a body composed of pneuma, not flesh and blood. We don't really know what Paul "saw." Was it a gaseous-looking simulacrum of a "flesh-and-blood" body? It was probably a bright, luminous body, since Paul compares the resurrected body with the sun, moon, and stars. But one thing seems certain about Paul's notion of Jesus's resurrected body: it need have looked no more like his flesh-and-blood body than a flower looks like a seed.

There is no resurrected body on the scene in Mark's Gospel, but in both Luke and John we encounter "misrecognition scenes," scenes in which people at first do not recognize Jesus even though they had seen him as little as thirty-six to forty-eight hours before.[54] The two disciples walking

---

54. If Mary Magdalene was supposed to have seen Jesus's body when it was placed in the tomb on Friday evening (Matt 27:61; Luke 23:55) and she was the first or one of the first

from Jerusalem to Emmaus spend the entire trip without recognizing Jesus. They come to believe the man is Jesus only when he blesses and breaks the bread—and immediately vanishes (Luke 24:31).

In John 20:14–16, Mary Magdalene mistakes Jesus for the gardener until he speaks to her a second time, this time calling her by name. In John 21:4, Jesus appears by the Sea of Galilee ("Tiberias," in John's text) to several of his closest male disciples, and they don't recognize him. Later, even when Jesus is serving them a breakfast of broiled fish on shore, the text implies that Jesus doesn't look like himself. The narrator says, "Now none of the disciples dared to ask him, 'Who are you?' because they knew it was the Lord" (21:12). The statement makes no sense if Jesus was recognizable by normal means of observation. It again implies that Jesus's resurrected body didn't look like his preresurrected body—and this is true even though Luke insists that Jesus's resurrected body is "flesh and blood" (Luke 24:39–43), and John depicts Jesus's resurrected body as retaining the marks of the crucifixion (John 20:20, 27).

Admittedly, in the case of Luke 24:31 we are led to believe, perhaps, that the disciples' inability to recognize Jesus immediately is due to some kind of miracle because the narrator adds in the next verse, "Then their eyes were opened, and they recognized him" (24:32). But this sounds like a bit of editorializing added to explain why close disciples had not initially been able to recognize a strange figure as actually Jesus himself. It attempts to explain away known traditions that Jesus, in at least some of his resurrection appearances, had not looked like Jesus as his disciples had previously known him. At any rate, we have firm traditions embedded in the text and implied in Paul's account that the resurrected body of Jesus, at least in some early accounts, did not resemble in appearance his preresurrection body. The accounts do not agree on what Jesus's resurrected body looked like.

The four accounts of the empty tomb and Paul's account of Jesus's appearance to him disagree about everything except *that* Jesus was raised. All other details differ: *who* saw him, *where, when, what else* they saw, and *what the body looked like.* If we put five "witnesses" to an event in different rooms and asked them what happened, and the only thing they agreed on is *that* it happened, but they give different details about who, what, when, and where, we would have no reason to trust their testimony about what happened. There is no good reason to accept the historicity of the empty

_____

to see him on Sunday morning (Matt 28:9; John 20:11–16), that would imply an interval of about thirty-six hours.

tomb narratives. They count against one another by their contradictions and differences.

We can imagine how the different stories developed over time, growing in details and narrative elements. Written, let's say, some time around the year 50, Paul's account is the earliest and leanest, containing just his claim to have seen the risen Jesus a few years after the death and a list of other followers who are said to have seen him at some time in some place but no details of when or where. The earliest Gospel, Mark, written circa 70, has even less than Paul when it comes to people actually *seeing* Jesus. Mark mentions only an announcement that he has risen, but he does have an empty tomb, a new detail when compared to Paul.

If both Matthew and Luke knew Mark's account but did not know one another's, as most scholars believe to be the case, we can imagine why they differ so strikingly from one another, both embellishing Mark's account but in contradictory directions. Matthew has a bit more "information" than Mark or Paul, and the Gospel of Luke still more. Acts, which must have been written after Luke, adds forty days and more story. And finally, John has more again. In fact, if we assume that John knew the Synoptics or at least their traditions, his text could be read as an attempt to harmonize the Synoptic accounts with addition of some new materials. This growth in detail and "information" is precisely what we would expect in the development of religious stories and legends. I believe any unbiased, reputable historian must chalk up all the empty tomb stories to later invention and legend. In fact, Mark could have invented the empty tomb, and the other writers could have simply taken it from him, with their own embellishments, which is why they differ so much from one another. The empty tomb stories, in the end, have no claim to historicity.

Where Was the Tomb?

Another fact that works against the historicity of the empty tomb stories is that we hear nothing at all in early Christianity about any knowledge of where the tomb was located until the fourth century.[55] It was not uncommon

---

55. I have been unable to find any reference to the location of the presumed tomb of Jesus before the "discovery" of the tomb at the current site of the Holy Sepulchre in Jerusalem, which took place in 325 or 326. According to an expert on that site, Biddle, "It is not known why the rock-cut tomb now covered by the Edicule was identified in 325/6 as the tomb in which the body of Jesus was laid in the early evening of the day of crucifixion." *Tomb of Christ*, xi–xii; see also 19, 66. I take this to mean that, at least for Biddle, no testimony for the tomb, at least at this place, existed prior to this "identification." Raymond

in the ancient world for the tomb of a venerated person also to be venerated. People even customarily had memorial meetings and meals—picnics!—at the tombs of family members or people they held in honor. But we see nothing in the New Testament or anywhere else in early Christian literature that indicates that early followers of Jesus visited his tomb. We know from Acts as well as Paul's letters that there was an ongoing community of followers of Jesus in Jerusalem for many years after his death, probably until the outbreak of the war with Rome in 66 or so. Did they never visit the tomb site?

It is quite possible—I believe probable—that the body of Jesus was never buried or, if it was, in a mass or unmarked grave.[56] Part of the intended punishment of crucifixion, certainly in the intentions of the Romans, was to deprive the condemned of a proper burial. The body was left on the cross to be devoured by carrion or was thrown away in a mass grave. But even if we imagine that the corpse of Jesus was buried, we have no reason to believe his followers or family knew where that was. If the early followers of Jesus knew where his tomb had been, why did they not, as far as we know, ever meet there? Use it as a gathering place around Easter? Venerate it in any way? It seems it would have been a great place for an Easter sunrise service—if they had known where it was.

This is historical evidence that has been too quickly dismissed in debates about the empty tomb.[57] Yet given the common custom of tomb veneration

---

Brown too uncritically supposed it was possible that some idea of the tomb's location was known in the second century, but the evidence he cites doesn't support him. See Brown, *Death*, 1282. Brown said that Melito of Sardis claims to have had the location pointed out to him on a visit to Jerusalem. Brown's source is Harvey, "Melito and Jerusalem." But Harvey gives no citations that have Melito being shown the place of the *tomb*, just the place of the crucifixion. Since they all assumed that the tomb was near the place of crucifixion (based on John 19:40, which certainly should not be accepted uncritically as historical), Melito may have *assumed* that the tomb was also "in the middle of the city," as he says of the place of execution. But the passages cited do not have Melito saying he was shown the tomb site. They have him being shown the site of the crucifixion. See Melito of Sardis, *On Pascha and Fragments*, §§72, 93–94.

56. Several scholars agree that there was no veneration of the grave site because the disciples did not know where it was. They had no actual knowledge of it or of where Jesus's body was placed. See Crossan, *Historical Jesus*, 395; and Crossan, *Who Killed Jesus?* 160–88; Lüdemann, *Resurrection*, 45; Carnley, *Structure*, 58; Wedderburn, *Beyond*, 64–65; Betz, "Zum Problem," at 246. As early as 1958, Joachim Jeremias had remarked that it was "unthinkable" (*undenkbar*) that the early Christians would have let knowledge of the location of the tomb pass into oblivion had they possessed that knowledge to start with. See Jeremias, *Heiligengräber*, 145.

57. Perhaps the most extensive and vigorous defense of the historicity of the burial and empty tomb narratives is that of Craig, *Assessing*. Craig insists even that the lack of veneration of the tomb is evidence for the historicity of the empty tomb because, he insists, early

in the ancient Mediterranean, including among Jews, the absence of any indication of veneration of Jesus's tomb by Christians until the fourth century
is good evidence that the early disciples didn't know where the tomb was.
That would have been consistent with what we know about ancient crucifixion. It is historically much more likely that the body of Jesus was not buried,
or, if it was, the disciples didn't know where. The absence of knowledge of
the whereabouts of Jesus's tomb among the earliest Christians is one more
piece of evidence, added to all the mutual contradictions of the narratives,
that the empty tomb stories provide us with no history whatsoever.

What historians can affirm, I believe, is that at least Paul and some
other disciples of Jesus sincerely believed they saw him sometime, somewhere after his death. What exactly they saw is not ascertainable by historical methods. And I don't believe it is necessary to establish that for the
purposes of a confession of faith in the resurrection. What is necessary is
simply to believe that whatever those disciples experienced was caused by
God. One may assume they saw something indeed. Even skeptical historians
may imagine some disciples experienced a vision, or saw a figure from a distance they took to be Jesus, or saw a play of light they later decided was the
body of Jesus. It is not necessary, for faith or history, to settle the question of
what they actually experienced. Historians may content themselves with any
number of guesses or none at all. Christian faith necessitates only the belief
that whatever they experienced, God caused it. The introduction of God into
the story, however, means we have moved out of history and into faith.

This kind of faith in the resurrection is no more or less than the kind
of faith we have in God at all. To say that God "caused" the resurrection experiences of some of the earliest disciples requires no more belief in "the miraculous" or "the supernatural" (that most anachronistic of categories when
applied to ancient beliefs) than to say that God is the cause of the universe.
Both statements are confessions of faith, not of history or science. And one
is no more or no less unbelievable than the other.

Moreover, the way we imagine the resurrection "experiences" to have
occurred—was it a resuscitation of a flesh-and-blood body? a visionary ex-

---

Christians would have had no interest in an empty tomb. This is also the conclusion by
Dunn, *Evidence for Jesus,* 67–68. That is simply disproven by pointing out that *as soon
as Christians thought they knew the location of the tomb, they immediately began venerat-
ing it,* empty though it obviously was. Craig's and Dunn's arguments are easily refuted as
bad historiography or none at all. Perhaps the most thorough refutation is publications
by Lowder. See his "Historical Evidence"; a revised version appears as a chapter in Price
and Lowder, eds., *Empty Tomb.*

perience? a mass hallucination? the miraculous transformation and resurrection of a "pneumatic body"?—is in the end inessential for Christian faith.
To confess that God caused the resurrection of Jesus need not demand belief
that it happened in any particular physical way. This is akin to confessing that
God created the universe without needing to choose or specify any particular scientific theory of how the universe came to be. Christians, for example,
need not "believe in" a Ptolemaic universe or Newtonian mechanism or Ein-
steinian physics or quantum mechanics. Christians need not decide, as part
of Christian faith, whether the big bang theory is "how it really happened."
Christians need not reject evolutionary biology as an account of how species
came to exist in order still to believe that God created them. All we need to
confess is that "God did it." How God did it is, for faith, inessential.

Likewise, a confession that God raised Jesus from the dead needs no
particular historical or physical explanation of how it happened. We need
not believe that the empty tomb stories are "historical fact," or that the resurrected body was what we, in everyday language, would call a flesh-and-
blood body, or that it all happened "on the third day." We need not even believe, I argue, that what the earliest believers "saw" was the physical, fleshly
body of Jesus.[58] All we need to confess, in my opinion, is that whatever they
experienced, which is forever inaccessible to us as history or science, was
caused by God. And that confession cannot be submitted to the analysis of
history precisely because God cannot be historically analyzed.

Certainly historians may affirm that at least a few disciples of Jesus
thought they saw him after his death. Indeed, we may posit that experience
to be the earliest possible historical beginning of Christianity. What caused
Christianity, to be as simplistic as we may allow ourselves to be only for
the moment, was the shock that occurred when someone—we don't know
for certain who—first came to realize that a person he or she had thought

58. I disagree, therefore, with Denys Turner, who argues (I think he is here explicating
Thomas Aquinas) that the raised body must be "material" in precisely the same way as the
preraised body: "If in effect you strip the raised body of Jesus of all those properties that
belong to bodies as such, then your theology of resurrection in consequence entails the
denial of the resurrection of the human person who is Jesus. Human bodies are material
objects, and no two material objects can naturally occupy the same place at the same time
as one another." Turner, *Thomas Aquinas*, 247–48. Turner seems not to understand either
ancient notions about "bodies"—that *can* be "matter" though not "flesh and blood"—or
contemporary physics. Aquinas is arguing against his contemporary theologians who posited that a raised body likely could pass through stone walls. But, in spite of Turner's (and
Aquinas's?) arguments, in the ancient world (and in the postmodern?) the raised body
could be a pneumatic body that could, naturally, pass through other materials.

was a prophet, maybe even the Messiah, had been crucified but had then been raised from the dead. The fact of Jesus of Nazareth was nothing truly exceptional. There were many such prophets and teachers, even healers and miracle workers, in the world at the time. The fact that Jesus was executed was nothing exceptional. Anyone should have seen that coming. But then someone, we don't know who, saw "him" later alive. That shock was the beginning of Christianity.[59]

Christians who believe that their faith in the resurrection of Jesus must be propped up by modern historiography are putting their faith in the wrong place. Christians' faith is rightly not in modern historiography, but in God. The difference between a non-Christian account of the claims of our texts and a Christian one is simply that the Christian is willing to give God credit for whatever happened.[60]

What is more important to Christian theology than "what exactly happened" or "what physically they experienced" is what a confession of the resurrection means theologically and experientially for Christians. And that is not hard to discern. When we Christians confess faith in the resurrection of Jesus we are insisting that God did in fact vindicate the prophet Jesus as God's son and Messiah. In spite of the fact that Jews did not expect a messiah who would suffer and certainly not one who would be humiliated by Roman torture and crucifixion, God did actually prove them all wrong: this crucified Jewish apocalyptic prophet was in fact, in spite of all appearances, the Messiah. And even more, he was the son of God. And even more, he was and is fully divine, the second person of the trinity, the intercessor between God the father and all of humanity and the entire universe.

---

59. I should point out that stories about people seeing someone after his or her death were also not unusual in the ancient world. What made claims about Jesus's resurrection and deification unacceptable to those Greeks and Romans who ridiculed such claims (and some did) was that it was being claimed for a lower-class, manual laboring Jew who had been crucified like a slave or rebel. It was Jesus's *status* that would have challenged early Christians' claims about his resurrection, not simply that he was seen after death. For comparisons of the early Christian stories about Jesus to other "translation fables" of antiquity, see Miller, *Resurrection and Reception*.

60. To quote Gorringe, interspersed with his own quotations of Barth: "We cannot establish the 'how' of the resurrection. It takes place in 'sacred incomprehensibility.' The proper response to it is confession. 'We cannot try to go "behind" it, either behind the fact that it is given, or behind the way in which it is legitimate and possible for us to act in correspondence to this fact.' Our response to the resurrection is to 'act in correspondence with this fact.'" Gorringe, *Karl Barth,* 237 (Barth quotations from *Church Dogmatics* IV/2, p. 123).

To confess faith in the resurrection is a confession of faith in the gift of life after death, though we may have no idea of the exact nature of that life. Is it some kind of consciousness? Or perhaps it is simply the faith that we will rest eternally in the goodness and peace of God? But to confess the resurrection also affects our current lives. By confessing the resurrection, we insist also that we will live our lives as if death is not the last word, as if pain and evil cannot be the denouement of the story, as if death even for us is not an evil or a disaster but simply part of God's gracious will for us and for our loved ones. When we Christians confess the resurrection of Christ—which for us includes a confession also in human resurrection—we affirm that we live our lives constantly moving beyond a very natural fear of death into a confidence of living. We may accept death as a natural event for us and our loved ones precisely because we recognize it as part of the goodness of a world created and sustained by a loving God. Confessing faith in the resurrection of Christ means we live believing that God is still with us through all and that even the deaths of our friends, our families, and ourselves need not be the disaster we fear but part of the life we celebrate. Our natural deaths are not the last word. There is no threat from modern historiography or science that can take away that faith. It is not to be accepted because it is "a historical fact." It is to be repeatedly affirmed because it is a way of life.

The Historical Jesus

Debates about the historical Jesus have roiled scholars and churches for centuries now, at least from the publication by Gotthold E. Lessing of the "Fragments" of Hermann Samuel Reimarus from 1774 to 1778.[61] One part of these debates has been over the relevance of the historical Jesus with regard to Christian faith or theology. In popular talk one often hears the historical Jesus called the real Jesus or the authentic Jesus or some such terminology that ontologically elevates the Jesus constructed by modern historical methods over the Jesus of creeds, confessions, scripture, or piety. Other scholars have argued just as vociferously that the historical Jesus is a modern construction with probably little in common with the actual "Jesus of Nazareth" as he existed in the first part of the first century. Still others argue that the Jesus important for Christian theology is the Jesus Christ of faith, the

---

61. The full publication of Reimarus's manuscript came only in 1972: Reimarus, *Apologie*. For a selection and translation of some of the "Fragments," see Reimarus, *Fragments*, ed. Talbert.

Gospels, or the creeds and confessions. Are Christian confessions dependent on the establishment of the historical Jesus? Should modern or postmodern Christian theology be ruled by the results of modern historiography in its version of Jesus of Nazareth? If Christian faith or theology is not completely dependent on the historical Jesus, may Christians use aspects of historical Jesus research nonetheless to inform theological interpretations of Jesus?

I side with those who insist that the "real" Jesus for Christians who wish to remain in a relation of orthodoxy to Christian tradition and confession is Jesus Christ as interpreted through scripture and Christian tradition, including history of doctrine, the main creeds, and churches' confessions. The historical Jesus is a construction made by modern scholars who are attempting to use criteria derived from modern historiography. That construction of Jesus must reject any claim for Jesus of Nazareth that modern historians would be unwilling in principle to make about other historical persons. The historical Jesus cannot, therefore, be considered divine or someone who acted in ways not commonly understood as generically possible for other human beings. Since I have been attempting throughout this book to remain faithful to the primary doctrines of orthodox Christianity as I understand them, I insist that the historical Jesus cannot be determinative for Christology.

Yet I disagree with those scholars and Christians who argue that the historical Jesus is and must be completely irrelevant in any theology about Christ.[62] As I insist that we theologians are perfectly in our rights to use any and all resources for the "doing" of theology, so we may have access to modern constructions of the historical Jesus to inform our theology. We are perfectly within our rights to appropriate insights for theology from the "natural" sciences, history, social sciences, and philosophy. Though much modern rhetoric has depicted culture as something in opposition to Christ and to be avoided in speaking of Christian truths, I have argued that culture is everywhere human beings are. We can no more avoid being influenced by culture than we can avoid thinking or speaking. And though some particular philosophy may provide dangers for interpreting Christianity, if we have been exposed to any philosophical notions or tropes in any way, we can scarcely avoid being influenced by philosophy. Traditional rhetoric invoking some kind of pure Christian thought cleansed of any taint of philosophy or culture is false and misleading.[63]

62. See the positions, for example, of Kähler and Bultmann discussed in the introduction above.

63. See Mary McClintock Fulkerson's statements about "theology's inevitable entanglement with other signifiers." Theology is always "accommodated . . . to worldly media of communication." *Places of Redemption*, 235.

Thus I find that even the historical Jesus may furnish tools or inspiration with which to think theologically about Jesus Christ. Elsewhere, for example, I have argued that the historical Jesus, properly constructed, was not at all a "family man."[64] By all evidence, Jesus of Nazareth was never married, he left his own family behind and did not receive them when they may have attempted a visit, he called his followers away from their own families, probably even telling a man to neglect what was at that time a central assumed duty owed by a son to his parents, namely, proper burial and mourning (Mark 3:33–35 and par.; Luke 9:59–60 and par.). In sayings that may well be historical, again because they are shocking and fly in the face of values of Jesus's contemporaries, Jesus teaches that, if possible, people should be "eunuchs" and that in the resurrection they will be "like angels," probably meaning that they will experience no need or desire for marriage (Matt 19:12; Mark 12:25; Matt 22:30). Celibacy may have been taught by the historical Jesus as the only or at least the "higher" virtue. By all the evidence, in any case, the historical Jesus was no promoter of "traditional family values," either those of the modern nuclear family or the ancient extended household.

Another modern Christian bias against which a construction of the historical Jesus may be brought, although in this case it occupies a minority position among Christian theologians and ethicists, is Jesus's relationship to revolution and violence. For some Christians, again, only a minority certainly in the United States, a universal, abstract principle of pacifism and nonviolence is taken to be practically the sine qua non of the Christian gospel. For such Christians the gospel sometimes seems to cease being a narrative about God's work in Christ and becomes a container for a commitment to nonviolence in the absolute.[65]

I am not at all opposed to pacifism. I even believe that contemporary American Christians probably *should* be pacifists given the ready resort to warfare and violence so regularly undertaken by their government. Both conservative and liberal Americans far too quickly advocate violent responses

64. What follows is a brief summary of chapters from my book *Sex and the Single Savior,* esp. 103–47.

65. I was struck, for example, with this tendency in the treatment of Bonhoeffer's decision to join the plot to assassinate Hitler by Stephen Fowl and Gregory Jones, *Reading in Communion,* see esp. 157–59. They attribute what they take to be Bonhoeffer's *misreading* of scripture—to allow a violent act in an extreme case rather than absolute pacifism—to the fact that, while in prison, he was not "reading" scripture within a Christian community. That seems to me to *assume* that "the meaning" of the gospel is the principle of pacifism rather than entertaining the idea that the narrative of the gospel may not provide always applicable abstract rules of behavior.

as ultimately the only answer to both domestic and foreign problems. The huge military forces sapping desperately needed resources, the largest incarcerated population in the world, the power of organizations promoting possession and use of guns of unimaginable powers of destruction—faced with all that, American Christians would do well to advocate nonviolence more than most of them do. But still, making some abstract principle of nonviolence the *one* indispensable message of the gospel is, again, to practice idolatry. It also turns the narrative structure of the gospel into one abstract "principle."

And the historical Jesus may be used to make that point. People have tended to read the Jesus of the Gospels as something of a pacifist or at least as not advocating armed rebellion against the Romans or the Jewish priestly hierarchy. I agree that the Gospels go out of their way to depict just such a Jesus. But I believe there is more than sufficient evidence that the historical Jesus had his disciples arm themselves and that he led them to Jerusalem at Passover intending either to await or to provoke a battle between, on the one side, the Romans and their high-class Jewish clients and, on the other, Jesus, his disciples, and an angelic army. Perhaps the historical Jesus thought he was the "messiah" who would lead the armies of right. Or perhaps he thought of himself as a mere precursor to the Messiah. At any rate, the texts contain historical evidence that Jesus's disciples were armed in Jerusalem.

After all, our earliest account of the arrest of Jesus, from the Gospel of Mark, does not say that only one or two of his disciples were armed at his arrest. If all we had was that Gospel, we would assume that all of his disciples accompanying him that night were armed, and with swords at that. Furthermore, all our Gospel authors attempt to play down the fact that they were armed or that there was any intention of violent revolt by Jesus and his disciples against the Jerusalem authorities. Much evidence from our Gospels and other parts of the New Testament suggests that Jesus had his disciples arm themselves for their trip to Jerusalem and that he and they expected to join in an angelic and messianic overthrow of the Romans and their high priestly client-rulers in Judea.[66]

This "historical Jesus" is a construction, one made by a modern scholar using recognized historiographical methods and criteria. I repeat, no historical Jesus, however constructed, is the real Jesus. And I argue that modern (or postmodern) Christian theology need not feel it must accept any "historical

---

66. For the full historical treatment, see Martin, "Jesus in Jerusalem"; and Martin, "Response."

Jesus" or use it as a foundation for faith or doctrine. But imagining a historical Jesus who is not a strict pacifist may remind us that *no* single principle
provides *the* content of the gospel. In fact, a *principle* of nonviolence cannot
be found, as far as I know, in the ancient world. It is a modern invention.
For all ancient Christianity I know about, some assumption of violence was
very much retained. Sometimes a "strategic" adoption of nonviolence was
advocated, but it always, as far as we know from our sources, functioned as a
deferral of violence to the future or to divine prerogative. Christians did not
mount open rebellion against Rome, but only because they expected God to
destroy Rome in his good time. The earliest Christians didn't build armies
because they trusted that Christ would return with his own army, which
would necessarily be far superior to anything they could have built.

I believe we may use this historical Jesus to remind ourselves that
however much we may value ethical stances of nonviolence or pacifism, we
must not make the mistake of taking that principle or any principle to be *the*
meaning of the gospel. Nothing is the gospel except the gospel, even though
we are constantly trying to figure out what that means and what the gospel
precisely is. Although I do not believe the historical Jesus is *necessary* for
Christian faith, I insist that it may indeed be used as a resource for Christian
theology, just as all other products of science, nature, history, and culture
may be used as theological resources. We cannot tell the holy spirit what it
cannot use to teach us. We cannot limit what God will use for revelation.

There is much more that could be included in a chapter on Christology. One
topic I have not broached here is the important one about the centrality of
Christ for Christian reading of the Old Testament. I'm firmly convinced not
only that we Christians "may" read the Old Testament through the lens of
Christ but also that we must do so at least occasionally if we are to find in the
Old Testament useful and orthodox theology. I agree with other scholars who
make the same point, such as Todd Billings: "Christians do not receive the
Old Testament as a generic 'word of God' to be received apart from Christ;
it is because of Christ that Christians read the Old Testament as Scripture at
all. . . . Israel's Scripture is not 'someone else's mail' for gentile believers, but it
is the Old Testament inextricably connected to the New Testament because
it bears witness to Jesus Christ."[67]

I hasten to add that this is only a *Christian* way to read "Israel's Scripture." We must still guard against Christian imperialism or supersessionism.

67. Billings, *Word of God*, 168.

We must remind ourselves that Jews rightly read their scripture without recourse to Christ, and we must respect their readings of those scriptures that we still hope to share with them. But I would still insist that we Christians are quite within our rights to believe that what counts simply as text or even scripture for our Jewish sisters and brothers is the "Old Testament" of Christian Bibles and that those texts are patient, in a Christian context, of Christological readings.

That is only one topic in Christology I have left unexamined in this chapter. There are many others, including some I have not and perhaps cannot think of. As I said in the introduction about theology in general, so also Christology is always an ongoing, never ceasing activity for Christians. As Hans Frei said long ago, "The task of the redescription of Jesus will remain unfinished as long as history lasts."[68]

Orthodoxy allows us Christians to have our cake and eat it too: we insist that we are justified in worshipping Jesus, in seeing Jesus as God, and yet as retaining our belief in "one God." What may be contradiction to the critics of Christianity, even irrationality, is nonetheless what we confess. Jesus is what we think with or about when we want to think about God as a person with whom we can relate *as* a *person*. If we think of God as a friend, brother, comrade, we use Jesus. Jesus is God the manual laborer, a fisherman, a talker, a storyteller. Jesus is God we can imagine having a drink with, a dinner companion, a sharer of a train car. Jesus is God if God could be our brother. Jesus is God if God could be our friend. Jesus is God if God could be, dare I say it, our lover. Bernard of Clairvaux certainly dared to think so. Jesus is God fully incarnate, embodied.

Jesus is the radically human God—a version and vision of God unthinkable in many philosophies, theologies, and religions, but a version of God demanded by orthodox Christianity.

---

68. Frei, *Types of Christian Theology,* 146; see also DeHart, *Trial of Witnesses,* 147.

CHAPTER 5

Spirit

As in the last chapter, on Christology, I begin this one by pointing out that historical criticism is especially inept at deriving an orthodox theology of the holy spirit from the Bible.[1] As much as the Hebrew Bible talks about a divine "breath," "wind," or "spirit" (*ruach*), we must not imagine that any of the human authors of those texts intended to refer to *the* "Holy Spirit," the third person of the trinity. But even with the New Testament, problems of interpretation arise. As I demonstrate in this chapter, sometimes the authors use *pneuma* (πνεῦμα) as a reference to a human and universal substance, a form of "stuff."[2] Sometimes they seem to be using the word to refer to a part of the human self, of the body, mind, or "spirit." Sometimes they are clearly referring to some property of God or Jesus: the pneuma of Jesus or the divine pneuma in general. Sometimes they seem to be thinking of an impersonal substance or property, though in rarer cases they seem to be thinking of pneuma as a "person" or at least something that can serve as an "actor" in a narrative. Only in the most rare cases may we read their comments to imply

1. If readers need reminding of my reasons for using lowercase letters for the "holy spirit," see the introduction above.

2. In much of this chapter, instead of using the English translation "spirit," I use a transliterated "pneuma," even without italics in order to anglicize the term. Because my point is to insist that the Greek word almost always referred to a material substance, the technical term "pneuma" is more useful than constantly reminding readers that the ancient notion of "spirit" was *not* usually one of the modern Christian idea of spirit as "immaterial substance."

221

a "holy spirit" as the third name in a social group of three. And even in those cases we would be rash to read into those passages a full-blown reference to the trinity as defined in later Christian orthodoxy or creeds. If we limit ourselves to responsible historical criticism, we simply can't derive satisfactory trinitarian orthodoxy from the Bible. That said, in this chapter I will experiment with both historical criticism but also more creative theological interpretation to "read" the New Testament for a theology of the spirit.

The Material Spirit

In the chapter on Christology I briefly noted that the Greek word usually translated "spirit" is πνεῦμα, a word that in ancient Greek concepts almost never referred to "immaterial substance." I introduced the topic because I was advocating an interpretation of 1 Cor 15 in which the resurrected body of Jesus—and therefore also the expected resurrected bodies of believers—was assumed by Paul to be a "physical" or "material" body, one made up not of "flesh and blood" but of pneuma. Because this chapter concentrates on the spirit—the spirit of Jesus, of God, of human beings, of the cosmos, and the holy spirit—we need to look more expansively at the nature of ancient pneuma. And a good place to begin is to return to Paul's discussion in 1 Cor 15.

Recall that the issue in Corinth was probably not a denial by Corinthian believers of any afterlife at all.[3] What some members of the church were doubting was probably more specifically the Jewish notion of the resurrection of the body, as Paul had no doubt passed along to them in his own teaching. Especially believers with a bit of Greek education would have assumed that the body was composed of material substances that could not survive death into the afterlife. They were probably not questioning the possibility that the "soul" or "spirit" could survive death but the body could. And they probably equated the body with the "flesh and blood" of its earthly composition. Thus Paul may well be echoing their own questions when he says, "How will dead corpses be raised? With what kind of body will this occur?" (1 Cor 15:35). In fact, we could read the last question as something like, With what kind of body would this be physically possible? The remainder of Paul's argument therefore concentrates precisely on the *nature,* indeed, the physical nature, of the resurrected body.

---

3. For a fuller explication and defense of my interpretation here, see Martin, *Corinthian Body,* 104–36.

He first uses the analogy of seeds and plants. Everyone knows there is continuity between the seed and the plant, separated as they are in time but not in their essence. But, Paul insists, both the seed and the plant are "bodies." God gives one kind of body to the seed and another kind to the plant. The plant may look nothing like the seed, but it is a result of the seed. Paul in this first analogy even uses the word "flesh" to characterize the earthly bodies of seeds, plants, and human beings.

In the next verse, however, Paul changes his terminology. He leaves behind for the moment talk about "flesh" and reintroduces terminology of the "body" (σῶμα), precisely because he is now speaking not about "earthly" bodies but about "heavenly" bodies, and he assumes that heavenly bodies are *not* composed of flesh: "There are heavenly bodies and earthly bodies. But the 'glory' of the heavenly bodies is different from the 'glory' of earthly bodies" (15:40). Paul uses the term often translated as "glory" (δόξα), but we must remember that in the Greek this term was a reference to something's *appearance*. It connoted a shining, radiant, luminous physicality. So Paul is still speaking of the physical nature of these different bodies. Then he provides another list, which is also probably hierarchically arranged, as I explained in the previous chapter (15:41).[4]

Paul assumes, along with most people of the ancient Greco-Roman world, that pneuma, though a very thin, usually invisible, rarified substance, is still some kind of "stuff." In fact, the ancient notions of pneuma pervade ancient science, medicine, and even, apparently, common sense.

The greatest elaboration of the meaning and role of pneuma in the cosmos is found in the philosophy of the Stoics.[5] According to the Stoics, the entire universe is a hierarchy of materialism, with pneuma as the highest, most pure and refined, most mobile, most powerful substance. Sometimes it is named "aether," as in Cicero's Latin account. Pneuma results from the combination of the finest versions of fire and air. The sun, moon, and stars are all pneumatic bodies. Pneuma is also the material that enables

4. The hierarchical nature of the list is a bit confusing since most ancient science would have put the moon on the lowest level, the sun above it, and the stars highest of all. But Paul may be assuming a different hierarchy for his cosmos. I think both lists, in any case, are meant to reflect a hierarchy of the cosmos because physical hierarchy is precisely a driving concern of Paul's arguments in 1 Cor 15.

5. See Engberg-Pedersen, *Cosmology*, 19–22, for one summary, concentrating on the version provided by Cicero in his *De Natura Deorum*, book 2, composed around 50 BCE. In fact, my own title for this section was inspired by the subtitle of Engberg-Pedersen's book. For a similar treatment of Stoic pneuma theory, but in this case in an interpretation of the Gospel of John, see Buch-Hansen, *"It Is the Spirit."*

perception and thinking. So even the heavenly bodies are living, intelligent beings, in fact, gods. Pneuma extends throughout the universe, though its natural home is upward. Life, sensation, thinking all could not exist without the activity of pneuma in nature and human and animal bodies. All of nature is structured and held together by pneuma. Pneuma is what makes the mind work. In fact, we can say that if we separate the mind from the brain, the mind is pneuma itself and the brain is the organ that houses and refines pneuma from air. Throughout, however, we must remember that the Stoics nonetheless believed that pneuma was a material substance. It was "physical," if we may use that now somewhat problematic word.[6]

But the Stoics had no monopoly on pneuma. Indeed, it seems that the Stoics simply took over previous ideas about air, wind, and pneuma, some of these ideas coming from "science," medicine, or philosophy, and others simply common ideas. The Stoics took general ideas of pneuma and systematized them into philosophical physics and cosmology. We find, for example, teachings about both cosmic and human pneuma in Hippocratic texts, some of which may date from before the rise of Stoicism.[7] In the Hippocratic text *On Breaths* (περὶ φυσῶν), pneuma is discussed as one form of "air" or "breath."[8] After noting, "[Pneuma] is the most powerful of all and in all," the author ascribes storms and violent seas to the power of pneuma: "Such then is the power that it has in these things, but it is invisible to sight, though visible to reason. For what can take place without it? In what is it not present? What does it not accompany? For everything between earth and heaven is full of pneuma."[9]

6. I say "problematic" only because with the current state of science and physics in particular—with string theory; particles able to occupy more than one location at the same time, and even far, far apart; with ideas such as "dark matter" or the Higg's boson; with matter itself seeming to melt into energy; and all the other unbelievable ideas scientists keep telling us—it is none too clear any longer how we are to think of "matter" or "the physical." For some attempts by scientists to explain the current state of scientific thinking about "matter," see Davies and Gribbin, *Matter Myth*; Tegmark, *Mathematical Universe*.

7. I first pointed to medical and other ancient texts to demonstrate the materiality of pneuma in the ancient world and to argue for this reading in Paul also, in *Corinthian Body*, see 6–15 *et passim* (see the index under *pneuma*). Besides Engberg-Pedersen's book mentioned above, see also, especially for Hippocratic and other medical references besides Galen, Troy Martin, "Paul's Pneumatological Statements."

8. The editor of the LCL edition, W. H. S. Jones, dates the work to as early as the fifth century BCE, well before the Stoics.

9. Translation of W. H. S. Jones (*Hippocrates*, LCL, vol. 2), slightly modified: I have kept "pneuma" where he translates "wind."

The second-century CE medical writer Galen certainly did not consider himself a Stoic, though he obviously knew Stoic ideas, philosophy, and writings.[10] Yet he also has an elaborate theory of pneuma in his medical system.[11] For Galen, the human body takes in pneuma with the air it breathes. The lung has the largest role in refining pneuma from air, though the heart elaborates that pneuma a bit more, mixes it with specially refined blood, and sends that mixture to the lung for its nourishment.[12] Part of that heart-refined pneuma is then sent to what Galen believes is a netlike, complicated system of tiny arteries residing just at the base of the brain.[13]

This netlike complex refines the "psychic pneuma," that is, the form of pneuma necessary for basic living, into an extremely subtle, quick, powerful form of pneuma that resides mainly in the brain. That form of pneuma enables thought, sensation, and movement in the human body. It is sent throughout the body through the arteries (the veins carry most of the blood). Pneuma moves unbelievably rapidly through the nerves, telling the parts of the body to move and carrying back sensations from the body to the brain. The most elaborated, refined, powerful form of pneuma Galen labels the "logical" or "rational" pneuma (πνεῦμα λογικόν).[14] Galen takes mainly from Stoic theory these ideas of the cosmic and human centrality of pneuma; he combines them with Platonic notions also. But he shares with many others

10. Galen insisted that he was not a member of any school, either of philosophy or medicine. This seems, though, to be one expression of his rather egotistical tendency to make himself always the most correct, insightful, and wise "school of one." Though Galen harshly criticized Stoic writers, he never takes on Plato or Hippocrates in any negative way. Even if he disagrees with something we find in Plato or a Hippocratic text, he usually just explains that others have misinterpreted them. Galen is indeed more a Platonist than a follower of any other known philosophical school of thought. See Martin, *Inventing Superstition*, 109–24.

11. For one important treatment of pneuma in Galen's system, see Siegel, *Galen on Sense Perception*. See also Jaeger, "Pneuma im Lykeion"; the note by A. L. Peck in Aristotle, *Generation of Animals* (Loeb), appendix B, pp. 576–93; and for more on pre-Galenic theories of pneuma, Peck, "Connate Pneuma." For a meticulous exposé of some of the confusions and apparent contradictions in Galen's theories about pneuma, see Prioreschi, *History of Medicine*, 3:368–75.

12. *Use of Breathing* 3.8–9 (K 4.490–492); 4.6 (K 4.500); 5.5 (K 4.507); 5.8 (K 4.510). For a comparison of Galen's views with others, see *Galen on Respiration*, esp. the essay by Furley, "Theories of Respiration before Galen," 3–39. See also Debru, *Le corps respirant*.

13. Modern scholars explain that this "retiform plexus" or "rete mirabile" does not actually exist in human beings, suggesting that Galen must have seen such organs in animals and only supposed they existed also in human heads.

14. For elaboration of some of these ideas, see *On the Doctrines of Hippocrates and Plato* 3.19–36 (K 5.606–611). See also Woollam, "Concepts of the Brain," esp. 17.

in the ancient world the idea that pneuma is a most important material substance of the universe, one that even links human beings to the gods.

We need not limit such ideas to the rarified environs of philosophical schools and medical theorists. And Paul need not have gone much further afield to appropriate these ideas than common sense—or Jewish scripture, for that matter. The second verse of the Bible already introduces pneuma (in the Greek translation) as a powerful wind and perhaps even divine breath. The term used for the wind that blows over the chaos before creation is *pneuma,* indeed the "pneuma of God" (Gen 1:2). Pneuma refers to wind elsewhere in the Greek Bible, often as an especially powerful or violent wind (see Gen 8:1). It is the blast of God's breath, named alongside other forces of nature, such as lightning and sea floods (2 Kingdoms [2 Sam] 22:16; see also Ps 17 [LXX 18]: 15). Pneuma is the wind that, along with dark clouds, brings rain (3 Kingdoms [1 Kings] 18:45; see also 19:11–12). Throughout the Greek Bible "pneuma" refers to wind, breath, God's breath or spirit, good or evil "spirits," or the human pneuma or spirit. It is no surprise, therefore, that Paul uses pneuma in these ways also, and just as we would be rash to deny the materiality of pneuma in much of the Greek Bible, we shouldn't do so for Paul or the New Testament, at least most of it. Most people in the ancient world assumed pneuma referred to a kind of stuff, available in many forms and levels of refinement.

But how do we imagine they pictured the "stuffness" of pneuma? Ancient writers admit that generally it is invisible, but they also sometimes speak as if one can see it in some forms, like a particularly powerful, hot, bright fire. And though Paul believed the body of the resurrected Jesus was made of pneuma, he nonetheless claims to have seen that body. What did it look like? I think we may take the story of the transfiguration as giving some clue: Jesus's transfigured body shines like the brightest light (Mark 9:2–8; and par). We may imagine lightning shooting from it. Maybe it put off heat. However we allow our imaginations to be informed by ancient imaginations to construct for ourselves physical pneuma, we are much more at home in Paul's ancient cultural context if we read his use of pneuma as assuming material substance.

Which Pneuma?

"Pneuma" is used in the New Testament for what appear to us to be different entities, and it is not always clear what the intended reference is. I will argue, however, that our interpretations may take this ambiguity as a theological opportunity. We may use the very confusions of the text to teach us different doctrines of the holy spirit, the cosmic pneuma, and our own pneuma.

"Pneuma" is often used to refer to what we may call the natural pneuma of a human being. People have bodies, composed of flesh, and they have pneuma, which allows their bodies to move, perceive, and think. So authors and characters may refer to "my pneuma" (none of these lists is in any way exhaustive, but see Mark 2:8; Rom 1:9; 1 Cor 14:14; 16:18; Acts 7:59).

This natural pneuma is what the author of James means when he says that a body without pneuma is dead (James 2:26). A dead woman becomes alive again when her pneuma "returns" (Luke 8:55). Psychological anxiety or anger may be attributed to someone's pneuma being (physically!) "stirred up" or troubled in some way, which can happen even to Jesus (Mark 8:12; John 11:33; 13:21; see also Acts 17:16; 2 Cor 2:13). It is possible that one's pneuma, just like one's body, may be polluted, that is, "infected" (2 Cor 7:1). People can be "poor in [their own] pneuma" (Matt 5:3).[15] Conversely, the pneuma may be willing even if the flesh is weak (Mark 14:38; Matt 26:41). Paul may be absent in body but present in pneuma, though it is none too clear how he managed that (1 Cor 5:3; see also 5:4). As we have seen to be the case in non-Christian texts, the pneuma in the New Testament as well is the material in a person that thinks or knows, that is, one's internal thoughts or conditions (Mark 2:8; 1 Cor 2:11).

The individual person's pneuma may be what is meant when used by an author in a benediction: "The Lord be with your pneuma" (2 Tim 4:22). Here we may take it that the reference is to Timothy's own pneuma. But Paul has a similar benediction that combines "pneuma" in the singular with "you" in the plural. He closes his tempestuous letter to the Galatians with this: "The grace of our Lord Jesus Christ be with your [pl] pneuma [sg], brothers" (6:18). In the letter to Philemon, which careful reading shows was really intended to be heard by the entire house church, he has the same: "The grace of the Lord Jesus Christ be with your [pl] pneuma [sg]" (25).[16] It seems

15. That this must refer to their own pneuma, and not the holy pneuma, seems clear because Jesus says they are "blessed" when found in this condition, and presumably they wouldn't be "blessed" if they had a lack of the holy spirit.

16. I perhaps should point out that I am here "playing around" with the Greek for the purposes of playful theology. This combination of singular and plural is not at all unusual in classical Greek, though we English speakers do often take note of it. For an argument that the letter was intended to be read aloud to the entire house church, see Martin, New Testament, 213–17. It is possible that some scribes thought the second person plural pronoun at the end of the Letter to Philemon was a bit out of place. In a few rare cases the

unlikely that the meaning here is the shared holy spirit, the pneuma of God, or the pneuma of Jesus, which believers are also supposed to share. But how does Paul conceive of the different individuals of a church all sharing one pneuma *unless* that be a shared pneuma of God, Jesus, or the holy spirit? The usage, in any case, should spark our minds to imagine how an entire body of people could share even their "natural" pneuma collectively. Like breathing the same air? Sharing the same static electricity? Being influenced all by the same magnetic field? This is just one instance of how our ideas about the spirit may be stretched when we put ourselves more decidedly back into the ancient cosmos of the New Testament writers.

It is harder to discern in the New Testament when "pneuma" is supposed to refer to the cosmic pneuma, the universal pneuma that permeates the entire world and gives it unity and structure. It may be that the divine pneuma or the holy pneuma has to some extent taken over that meaning in Christian texts. Early Christian authors certainly would have known about the pneuma that hovers over the world before and during creation. They would most likely have taken that to be the cosmic pneuma. But there are rare glimpses of the cosmic pneuma in the New Testament, that is, a form of pneuma that cannot be simply identified with the holy pneuma in particular or limited to the pneuma possessed by individual bodies particularly. Thus, when Paul says he and other believers did not get their knowledge of God's gifts from "the pneuma of the cosmos" (1 Cor 2:12), I doubt he is thereby denying that the cosmos has pneuma entirely. I think he is assuming that there *is* a "cosmic pneuma" but that it differs from what he calls, in the same verse, "the pneuma that is from God." He seems to assume that both of these pneumata have something to do with knowledge. Even ordinary human knowledge, in ancient pneumatic theory, would not be possible without *some* form of pneuma.

The same notion may lie behind the words attributed to Paul in the Areopagus speech in Acts 17. As I mentioned briefly in the chapter "Knowledge" above, in that speech, the most "philosophical" one in Acts, Paul admits that even unbelieving Greeks have had *some* knowledge of the existence of God, quoting one philosopher and one poet to further his point (17:28). Thus when Paul says that God gives to everyone and every living being "life, breath, and everything" (17:25), the word for "breath" here (πνοή) may well invoke the cosmic pneuma that must be the source of any kind of knowl-

---

plural pronoun has been omitted or changed to "our." And in at least one manuscript of the Latin Vulgate, the plural pronoun is changed to singular.

edge, even a preliminary and therefore, in the end, insufficient knowledge of God's existence.

The "evil" or "unclean" pneumata that occur in many New Testament texts must have their origin somewhere also. These occur many times in the Synoptic Gospels (though not, surprisingly, in John: see also Acts 8:7; 19:12, 13, 15, 16). We may imagine that the "pythian pneuma" that enables the woman to prophesy and that Paul rebukes and silences (Acts 16:16) would have been taken by early believers to be a form of the kind of pneuma known to enable women to prophesy at Delphi, the classical site of the prophesying Pythia. As Plutarch and other authors assumed that some kind of natural vapor or wind could be responsible for the Delphic phenomenon, early Christians might assume that some form of the cosmic pneuma could inspire non-Christian prophets.[17] So the evil or corrupt pneumata recognized by most early Christians as realities could have been assumed to be one form of the "pneuma of this cosmos."

Then there is the pneuma of God the Father proper, or what we may think of as simply the "divine pneuma" in general. This need not be a reference to the holy spirit in anything like the later Christian sense. It would be evidence that early Christians thought of God as a person who possessed a special form of pneuma (see Acts 2:17–18; 1 Cor 2:11, 14; 3:16; 6:11; 12:3; 2 Cor 3:3; Phil 3:3). We have seen that Christians assumed that Jesus, as a human being, had his own personal pneuma, which he had to "give up" at his death if he experienced a real "death" at all. But even after his death Jesus can be attributed his own pneuma, which may be not exactly the same pneuma as that of the Father (see Acts 16:7; Gal 4:6; Phil 1:19). Indeed, it is difficult to discern when "pneuma" is a general reference or a reference to the pneuma of God or of Jesus proper.

Even when "pneuma" is accompanied by the adjective "holy," it is not always clear what exactly is being referred to or how we may imagine the ancient authors imagining this "holy pneuma." Often the texts speak of this pneuma not as a person but as a substance, something that can be "poured out" on people or that "fills" their bodies (Acts 2:4; 4:8, 31; 6:3, 5; 7:55; 12:24; 13:9, 52). The holy pneuma "falls" on Peter's audience (Acts 10:44; 11:15).

Acts is not consistent about *how* the pneuma comes upon people. In Luke, the pneuma had descended upon the baptized Jesus *bodily* in the form of a dove (Luke 3:22). The pneuma, famously, descends on the disciples at

---

17. See, for example, Plutarch, *On the Obsolescence of the Oracles* (*Moralia* 432D-E); Martin, *Corinthian Body*, 238–42.

Pentecost spontaneously and in the visible and physical form of fire. It may be that this spontaneous descent of the pneuma occurs again in the case of the household of Cornelius precisely to make the point that gentiles must be treated the same as Jewish believers (Acts 10:44; 11:15). These "first" gentile converts, therefore, experience a spontaneous pouring out of the pneuma in order to make their situation parallel to that of Acts 2. But even then, according to Acts 2:38, the pneuma is promised simply to accompany the baptism of other converts. On the other hand, in Acts 8, Philip is apparently unable to endow those he has baptized with the holy pneuma, so Peter and John go to Samaria. In this context it seems assumed that baptism alone is not sufficient, but the laying on of apostles' hands is necessary for the gift of the pneuma (Acts 8:17).

Paul's question to "certain disciples" in Ephesus initially implies that he would have expected them to receive the pneuma upon believing in the gospel: "Did you receive the holy pneuma when you believed?" (Acts 19:2). But when they show they know nothing of a holy pneuma, Paul's next question implies that he expects the pneuma to be given automatically at baptism: "Into what then were you baptized?" (19:3). Learning that they had experienced only the "baptism of John," Paul first baptizes them "into the name of the Lord Jesus," but even then it seems that Paul has to lay his hands on them for them finally to receive the pneuma. Why can Paul deliver the pneuma through the laying on of hands while Philip apparently could not? Surely not because Paul is ranked as an "apostle" in the sense "the twelve" are. It is well known that the author of Acts apparently believes an "apostle" must be someone who had been with Jesus from the baptism of John onward (Acts 1:21–22), and the author knows Paul was not. True, the author seems to slip up once and call Barnabas and Paul apostles (Acts 14:14), but that lapse seems to go against his more general tendency to reserve the term "apostle" for the twelve. It could also be evidence that the author is taking that scene from a prior written source, as we know he does for much of Luke and Acts. Taking all these narrative details into account, we must insist that the author of Acts is simply not consistent in *how* he assumed the holy pneuma was initially "poured out" on various believers. At any rate, in all the cases I've mentioned thus far the holy pneuma comes across not as a "person" but as a material substance that can be poured onto someone or fill bodies.

The Acts of the Apostles, however, goes further than most other New Testament texts toward depicting the holy pneuma as personal. God "speaks through" the holy pneuma (4:25). The pneuma "tells" Philip to approach the chariot in 8:29 (it is the "pneuma of the Lord" that later "snatches" Philip away after the baptism: 8:39). The holy pneuma speaks to Peter (10:19; 11:12). And in what I believe is the only such case in the New Testament, the holy pneuma speaks in the first person in Acts 13:2: "Set apart *for me* Barnabas and Saul" (emphasis added). This is the clearest depiction of the holy pneuma as a person, that is, as an actual character in a narrative, unless the "me" in this case is supposed to be God or Jesus, which is also possible; see also Acts 5:3; 15:28; 20:22–23.

There is still confusion, however, even if we confine ourselves merely to Acts. The author tells us that it was the holy pneuma that forbade Paul from preaching in the province of Asia (16:6). Yet the very next verse says it is the "pneuma of Jesus" that prohibits them from entering Bithynia (16:7). Later, the disciples reflect that it was "God" who was directing them through these signs (16:10). Are we to think of these as three different characters, who can act together and even through one another? Or should we take "holy pneuma" simply to *be* the pneuma of Jesus, which he shares with the pneuma of God? It is true, as Luke Timothy Johnson has put it, that "by establishing a narrative role for the Holy Spirit, Luke has taken a significant step towards the eventual theological recognition of the Holy Spirit as a 'person.'"[18] But the seeming inevitability of that step may be more easily seen in hindsight than simply in the text of Luke and Acts. The precise nature of the "holy pneuma" in Acts is actually confused and confusing.

The other New Testament book that seems clearly to speak of the holy pneuma as a person, at least in a couple of passages, is the Gospel of John when speaking of the Paraclete, the advocate, intercessor, or helper promised to the disciples after Jesus's departure, as we have already seen. Certainly the Paraclete is supposed to be a separate person from Jesus, since Jesus calls it "another advocate," apparently meaning "other than Jesus himself" (John 14:16). That this advocate is probably the "holy pneuma" is made clear in the next verse, when Jesus calls it "the pneuma of truth" (14:17), and it is called explicitly "the holy pneuma" in 14:26 (see also 15:26 and 16:13). It is given by "the Father" and so seems differentiated from both the Father and Jesus. This is perhaps the closest we get to a narrative depiction of the later trinity: Father, son, and holy spirit as Paraclete, another "advocate" on par with Jesus himself.

But things aren't so simple in the Gospel of John, as it turns out. Although the author tells us that the pneuma was "not yet" present to the disciples during the ministry of Jesus, not until Jesus was "glorified" (7:39), we

---

18. Johnson, *Acts of the Apostles*, 15; see also Edwards, *Breath*, 72.

first see the pneuma when the Baptist testified that he saw it descend "as a dove" from heaven and "remain" on Jesus (1:32, 33). Are we to assume, then, that the pneuma *was* present during Jesus's ministry but available only to Jesus and not yet to others? The pneuma is elsewhere spoken of as a substance, like wind or water (3:5, 6, 8). It is something God "does not give by measure" (3:34). People can worship God only by doing so "in pneuma and truth" (4:23–24). Are the disciples really never worshipping God or Jesus during his ministry? Toward the end of the Gospel, Jesus seems to dispense the pneuma to the disciples by breathing on them (20:21–22). This makes the pneuma sound like a kind of stuff, a stuff that comes from Jesus's (now "glorified") body. Does pneuma sometimes mean one sort of thing, and otherwise, even in the same Gospel, mean something different, such as a personal agent? The texts of the New Testament are never completely clear or consistent.

Finally, there are the very rare cases in which the text does *sound* "trinitarian." The Gospel of Matthew famously ends with Jesus "commissioning" his closest disciples to "make disciples of all the nations, baptizing them into the name of the father and of the son and of the holy pneuma" (Matt 28:19). Even if it would be a mistake from a historical-critical point of view to read a fully orthodox doctrine of the trinity into this text, this is at least one of the oldest surviving examples of trinitarian language, probably from one of the earliest liturgies of baptism. Another possible example is from Heb 9:14, where the author says that Jesus offered himself to "God," "through the eternal pneuma." Though "pneuma" perhaps should be taken here in an "impersonal" rather than "personal" sense, we do have the three in one context and interrelated to one another.

We should not force the biblical texts, however, into a false consistency. Too many unclear passages remain. When we are told that Paul "decided in the pneuma" (Acts 19:21), do we suppose it is Paul's pneuma or the holy pneuma? Was Apollos "boiling" with or in "his" pneuma or the pneuma of God (Acts 18:25)? At his death does Jesus give up *his* pneuma, as any dying person would, or does this imply that Jesus is being deprived of the "holy pneuma" (Matt 27:50; Luke 23:46; John 13:21)? Did John the Baptist "become strong" in *his* pneuma or is this a rather odd way of saying that the Baptist, though not a "Christian," nonetheless possessed the "holy pneuma" (Luke 1:80)? When Sapphira lied to the "pneuma of the Lord," is this God's or Jesus's pneuma (Acts 5:9)? My goal is to drive home the overwhelming impression that texts of the New Testament are remarkably *unclear* about the nature of pneuma and of *the* pneuma.

A great example of this lack of clarity is Paul's account of pneuma in the rich passage provided by the eighth chapter of Romans. The word "pneuma" occurs throughout the chapter but apparently has several meanings, functions, or references, and it is none too clear when it refers to what. Paul begins by insisting, "The law of the pneuma of life in Christ Jesus has freed you from the law of sin and death" (8:2). Pneuma is here like a *principle*, a system, a rationality, a structure, a way of being that can be contrasted to some "law of sin and death," another system or rationality. In the next several verses Paul continues this dichotomy by contrasting living κατὰ σάρκα (according to the flesh) with living κατὰ πνεῦμα (according to, by the lights of, pneuma; 8:4). Paul here reintroduces the idea that pneuma is the material with which human beings think and perceive, but apparently "sarx" is also a material with which one may think and perceive. "Those who exist *kata sarka* think 'sarkic' thoughts; those [who exist] *kata pneuma*, think 'pneumatic' thoughts" (8:5), with contrasting results: "The thinking of the sarx is death, but the thinking of the pneuma is life and peace" (8:6). This is complicated epistemology. Paul, though describing what he takes to be physiological facts, is also exhorting, "Think pneumatically! Think pneumatic thoughts!" Thus, although chapter 8 began with pneuma looking like an abstract principle (it has a "law"), Paul quickly moves into the significance of pneuma as the medium of thought and mind.

We must update Paul's language and our imaginations to come up with ways to make Paul's language and thinking relevant to us. Pneuma is, to Paul, something like what a combination of oxygen and electricity might be for us. Pneuma is the electricity-oxygen stuff-force of the body and the cosmos. It is a cosmic stuff of life, energy, movement, and thought. It can be experienced individually and shared, both with the persons of God and Jesus but also among ourselves with one another.

We encounter more confusion in 8:9: "You are not in sarx but in pneuma, since the pneuma *of God* lives in you. If anyone does not have the pneuma *of Christ*, that one is not of him." Note what may be different referents of pneuma, all woven together in one tight verse: a principle opposed to sarx; that which lives in people and gives life; that of God; that of Christ. And the next verse (8:10) is likewise ambiguous: "If the pneuma of Christ is in you, the body may be dead [a corpse] because of sin, but the pneuma alive because of justice [or righteousness]." Is it that *our personal* pneuma is enlivened, or do we possess "live" pneuma because it is Christ's pneuma that has replaced our merely human pneuma? It is impossible to answer these questions simply from the verse itself.

Then Paul brings *God's* pneuma back into the discussion: "If the pneuma of the one who raised Jesus from the dead lives in you, the one who raised Christ from the dead will make alive also your mortal bodies, through his pneuma that lives in you" (8:11). God's pneuma seems now to be living in the believers. Is it the same as Christ's pneuma? Has it replaced our mere human pneuma? Or is it just an addition, though a mightily important one? We do see here, as will be expanded in verses 12–14, the central function and activity of pneuma as what makes alive. There is no life without pneuma. So even unbelievers must have some kind of pneuma, and even that pneuma must ultimately have come from God, the source of all life and good things, even the life and good things enjoyed by unbelievers. I will return to this point below.

But there is a bad kind of pneuma in the cosmos also: "For you did not receive a pneuma of slavery again to fear, but you received the pneuma of sonship [adoption] in which we cry, 'Abba, Father!'" This could be considered again a form of the pneuma/sarx dichotomy. Paul uses the familiar (to them, if not to us) picture of the fearful slave cringing and cowering before a ruthless master; to that, he presents the contrasting image of adopted sons.

The questions with this chapter, though, keep coming: "This pneuma [which? God's?, recalling 8:14?] bears witness with our [pl.] pneuma [sg.] that we are offspring of God" (8:16). There must be two different "forms" or "kinds" of pneuma, but it is not clear what the relationship between them is or even which is the first pneuma mentioned ("this pneuma"). Finally, do we have hints of an independent pneuma, a pneuma distinguishable from our pneuma or the pneuma of God or Christ? "As also the pneuma helps in our weakness. For we do not even know what we should pray for. But that very pneuma intercedes with wordless groans" (8:26). This gives Paul the opportunity to reintroduce the epistemological function of pneuma: "The one who searches hearts knows what the thinking of the pneuma is, because it approaches for the holy ones according to God" (8:27).

We could have read just about all of Romans 8 up until this point without introducing the later Christian concept of the Holy Spirit. Finally here, though, we at least approach the concept of an independent agential pneuma, *the* "holy spirit." It is not exactly identified with us since it intercedes for us. Nor is it entirely identified with God because it intercedes *with God*. Yet taken in context it is still difficult to read this as a reference to the holy spirit as the third person of the trinity. The references are, admittedly, confusing. And they continue to be ambiguous. When Paul says in 9:1 that his conscience bears witness with (or to?) him in the "holy pneuma," what does that mean? What pneuma is meant? When he speaks of believers as "boiling in pneuma" (12:11), what does that mean? Is this the "holy pneuma"? Or do they "boil" in their *own* pneuma?

Romans 8 is indeed a rich resource, in spite of its many ambiguities, for thinking about the nature and function of pneuma. Pneuma is a principle of living, the material of thinking. It gives life to human bodies, even in their mortal state. It functions as a sign of possession of persons by Christ. It bears witness to our being adopted as children of God. It helps us pray and even prays for us when we cannot. It intercedes for us with the Father. It provides the epistemological link of our minds with God's. Above all, it is "the giver of life," the source and substance of life itself.

But is it trinitarian? The theologian Robert Jenson has called Romans 8 "the most remarkable trinitarian passage in the New Testament."[19] That is true only if it is read from a later, Christian, orthodox point of view. As we have seen, one can easily read the entire chapter without necessarily introducing the idea that the pneuma here presented was considered, by Paul or his historical audience, a "person" at all, much less in the robust sense of "the third person of the trinity."[20] Being familiar with much of Jenson's work, I imagine he believes he is just reading the text for its original meaning, that is, the meaning historical critics would also likely see there. This confirms my argument that if one finds references to the holy spirit of later orthodoxy or to the trinity throughout the New Testament, one may well be practicing good theology, but it is bad historiography. Romans 8 can be read as a remarkable trinitarian text, but it is better to do so realizing that we are thereby practicing *theological* interpretation, not just "reading the text" for its "original" or authorial meaning (that of the human author). Indeed, Romans 8 is such a fruitful text for thinking about the spirit precisely because it provides plenty of opportunities for different meanings of pneuma and therefore for different interpretations of spirit and "the holy spirit."

The Universal Pneuma

We've seen that one common use of "pneuma" in the ancient world, including early Christianity, is as a reference to the universal, cosmic pneuma believed to infuse the universe physically and materially, pervading the cosmos and

---

19. Jenson, *Triune Identity*, 44; see also Rogers, Jr., *After the Spirit*, 77, citing Jenson.

20. See Stowers, "Matter and Spirit"; originally published in *Redefining First-Century Jewish and Christian Identities*. Speaking of pneuma in Romans 8: "The divine pneuma is clearly not a 'person' as it becomes in later Christian Trinitarian theology. Paul agreed with the prevailing culture, including philosophers and medical doctors, that pneuma was the vital component of the living person and that there were various kinds and qualities of pneuma in the workings of the world." Rogers, *Holy Spirit*, 99.

giving it structure. The pneuma even provides the universe with its "meaning." Several recent theologies have urged a more robust Christian notion of pneuma in this universal and even material sense. Scriptural depictions of the pneuma certainly encourage this imagination of pneumatic materiality. The spirit is a bird hovering over a person or the universe, the oil of anointing, the water of baptism, the fire of Pentecost, the seed in the womb.[21] As the theologian Mark Wallace points out, in Genesis the spirit is wind, in the Gospels a dove, in Acts fire.[22] As Veli-Matti Kärkkäinon notes, John of the Cross called the spirit "spiced wine."[23] The Gospel of John famously depicts the pneuma as the "wind" or "breath" of God that "blows where it wills" (John 3:8), an image accepted by recent theologians with a material imagination.[24] As the theologian Eugene Rogers insists, "To think about the Spirit it will not do to think 'spiritually': to think about the Spirit you have to think materially."[25]

Thinking about the spirit as pneuma throughout the universe brings us back again to epistemology and how we "know" God. Elizabeth Johnson describes how we may imagine God acting in the world and in its and our histories: "Speaking about the Spirit signifies the presence of the living God active in this historical world. The Spirit is God who actually arrives in every moment, God drawing near and passing by in vivifying power in the midst of historical struggle."[26] Wallace insists that since the spirit pervades all nature, we must get beyond (as I have argued in the chapter above on epistemology) the twentieth-century debate over "natural theology" versus "revealed doctrine." Wallace joins Jürgen Moltmann in rejecting an earlier (Barthian?) opposition of "revealed" to "natural" sources of divine knowledge. Wallace writes,

> Note that a Spirit-centered theology of nature is not equivalent
> to a natural theology. I do not claim that one can have positive,
> independent knowledge of God apart from revelation, but rather
> that through the work of the Spirit in creation one can receive
> disclosures of the divine presence in communion with the earth

21. Rogers, *After the Spirit*, 54. For the spirit as seed filling the womb, see also the citation of Ambrose in Edwards, *Breath*, 43.

22. Wallace, *Fragments*, 4.

23. Kärkkäinen, *Holy Spirit*, 55; see *Spiritual Canticle* 25.7, in *Collected Works of St. John of the Cross*, 571–72.

24. See, for instance, Edwards, *Breath*, esp. 126.

25. Rogers, *After the Spirit*, 56.

26. Johnson, *Women, Earth, and Creator Spirit*, 41–42.

and its inhabitants. . . . But *if* the Spirit indwells all life, including the life of the mind within the body, *then* there can be no "pure" natural theology because all knowledge of God is mediated by the Spirit's omnipresence. From this perspective, the neoorthodox criticism that theologies of nature are fundamentally flawed because they are categorically distinct from, and thereby inferior to, so-called revealed theology trades on a false alternative.[27]

Referring approvingly to the same work by Moltmann, Kärkkäinon agrees: "Moltmann reminds us that in biblical understanding the word *spirit* does not denote something antithetical to matter and body; rather 'spirit' in the Bible refers to life-giving force and energy."[28]

Besides bringing in the historical and material, other theologians use these notions of spirit to emphasize the "everyday-ness" of God's communication with us, in "the ordinary." Mary Ann Fatula says, "Though we may not always realize it, we experience the Holy Spirit's closeness when we are near our loved ones and our life feels good and sweet to us. We feel the Spirit's joy, too, as we savor the perfumes of springtime, when nature all around us bursts into bloom."[29] As Clark Pinnock writes, "The Spirit meets people not only in religious spheres but everywhere—in the natural world, in the give-and-take of relationships, in the systems that structure human life. No nook or cranny is untouched by the finger of God. His warm breath streams toward humanity with energy and life."[30] William Atkinson argues that we must see the spirit not as contrary to nature but infusing it.[31]

Elizabeth Johnson gathers together several metaphors for or images of the spirit from the writings of Hildegard of Bingen, making the point that many such metaphors and images are needed so that we do not get trapped with the possible errors of any one:

The Spirit, she writes, is the life of the life of all creatures; the way in which everything is penetrated with connectedness and

---

27. Wallace, *Fragments*, 138. See Moltmann, *Spirit of Life*, at, for example, 6.

28. *Holy Spirit*, 87; pointing particularly to Moltmann, *Spirit of Life*, 40.

29. Fatula, *Holy Spirit*, 2.

30. Pinnock, *Flame*, 187. So also Pinnock: "The world reflects God's glory; therefore anything can mediate the sacred, where there are eyes to see and ears to hear. Since the Spirit pervades the universe, any event or experience can bring God to mind and mediate his presence" (120).

31. Atkinson, *Trinity After Pentecost*, 56.

relatedness; a burning fire who sparks, ignites, inflames, kindles
hearts; a guide in the fog; a balm for wounds; a shining seren-
ity; an overflowing fountain that spreads to all sides. She is life,
movement, color radiance, restorative stillness in the din. Her
power makes all withered sticks and souls green again with the
juice of life. She purifies, absolves, strengthens, heals, gathers the
perplexed, seeks the lost. She pours the juice of contrition into
hardened hearts. She plays music in the soul, being herself the
melody of praise and joy. She awakens mighty hope, blowing
everywhere the winds of renewal in creation.[32]

The point is that the spirit infuses all creation and is its life force.

Theologians have, moreover, shown how such ideas about God and
the material world make perfect sense in light of traditional sacramental
theology. Johnson recalls teachings by Thomas Aquinas to make the point:
"Catholic sacramental theology has always taught that simple material things
—bread and wine, water, oil, the sexual union of marriage—can be visible
bearers of the invisible healing grace of divine love. This is so, it once again
becomes clear, because to begin with the whole physical world itself is the
locale of the Spirit's gracious indwelling, a primordial sacrament of divine
presence."[33] Wallace agrees, coming at the point also from a Protestant perspective: "Christian thought has always maintained that nature and grace,
world and God, while not the same reality, are inseparably interrelated. The
eucharistic doctrine, for example, that Christ's body and blood are really
present in the Lord's Supper underscores the mutual indwelling of the Divine in and with everyday foodstuffs. Put simply, if God can become a loaf
of bread or a cup of wine, then why can God not become a bird or a beast or
a tree or a mountain or a river?"[34]

Wallace goes so far as to suggest that when we ponder the ongoing
destruction of our natural environment we think of it not only as "ecocide"
but even as "deicide."[35] For me, that may be going too far. After all, if we
really can kill God ourselves, as we are undoubtedly killing our livable environment, to whom or what can we look for salvation—salvation, that is,
from ourselves? Rogers recognizes the problem. Even though he has avowed

32. Johnson, *She Who Is,* 127–28. For the English translation of Hildegard used by Johnson, see Hildegard of Bingen, *Scivias.*
33. Johnson, "Creator Spirit," 28.
34. Wallace, *Fragments,* 143–44.
35. Ibid., 143.

that "the Spirit makes sense only when paired with bodies: the bodies of individuals, communities, sacraments," he nonetheless urges theological balance.[36] Though we must "think materially" when thinking about the spirit, we must never completely identify the spirit with the universe. "To reduce the Spirit to matter," Rogers writes, "breaks the rule of Christian speech that God is not to be *identified* with the world; to divorce the Spirit from matter breaks the rule of Christian speech that God is not to be identified by simple *contrast* with the world."[37]

Before leaving the topic of the universal pneuma, I want to note how some theologians have related the doctrine not only to materiality and epistemology but also to soteriology, or universal salvation. Some theologians quote from *Gaudium et Spes* (Joy and Hope), a document from the Second Vatican Council: "All this holds true not only for Christians, but for all men of good will in whose hearts grace works in an unseen way. For, since Christ died for all men, and since the ultimate vocation of man is in fact one, and divine, we ought to believe that the Holy Spirit in a manner known only to God offers to every man the possibility of being associated with this paschal mystery."[38] Another document from Vatican II teaches something similar: "Those also can attain to everlasting salvation who through no fault of their own do not know the gospel of Christ or his church yet sincerely seek God and, moved by grace, strive by their deeds to do his will as it is known to them through the dictates of conscience."[39] John Paul II later confirmed the sentiment: "The universality of salvation means that it is granted not only to those who explicitly believe in Christ and have entered the Church. Since salvation is offered to all, it must be made concretely available to all. . . . For such people [those without the opportunity to 'know or accept the Gospel'] salvation in Christ is accessible by the virtue of a grace which, while having a mysterious relationship to the Church, does not make them formally part of the Church but enlightens them in a way which is accommodated to their spiritual and material situation" (*Redemptoris Missio* 10).

In spite of the fact that most of the New Testament documents were produced by and within rather sectarian early Christian communities—that is, groups that saw themselves as a minority of "the elect" in a world that

---

36. The quotation is from Rogers, *Holy Spirit*, 3.

37. Rogers, *After the Spirit*, 58. See also Tanner, *God and Creation*, 46–48. In speaking of "rules of Christian speech," Rogers is alluding to a book by one of his teachers, George Lindbeck, *Nature of Doctrine*.

38. *Gaudium et Spes* 22. Quoted in Kärkkäinen, *Holy Spirit*, 81.

39. *Lumen Gentium* 16.

mostly did not know God and was probably destined for damnation and destruction—one can find resources even there for a more universal vision of knowledge of God and even salvation.[40] Many scholars, for instance, have come to read Paul's words in Rom 11:26, "And thus all Israel will be saved," as indicating that Paul believed or at least eventually came to believe that God would somehow, even miraculously, bring about the salvation of all Jews.[41]

Even an evangelical theologian such as Pinnock can read certain passages as allowing us at least to hope that God will save all people. He cites 1 Tim 4:10, for example: "For this we work and struggle, because we have hoped in the living God, who is the savior of all human beings, especially those of faith." God is here *especially* the savior of believers but ultimately the savior of "all human beings." Pinnock likewise reads 1 John 4:7 to teach that knowledge and love of God are not limited to the church: "Everyone who loves is born of God and knows God." Note that the text does not say, "everyone who loves God" but simply "everyone who loves." When human beings experience and express love, even in an ordinary, everyday sense, they do so only because of divine inspiration, divine "inbreathing." Their actions betray knowledge of God because of their love.

I view this as a theologically valuable reading of 1 John even though I would dispute that it is the meaning "intended" by the human author. Taking the whole of the First Letter of John, we should admit that the author and likely his original audience had a rather sectarian view of the church as being *opposed to* the world. The author seems to see most people outside his church as sinners in a dark and godless world that is destined for destruction. Pinnock was no postmodernist; he seemed to assume that texts have rather fixed meanings, and I suppose that he, as a self-described evangelical, believed that meaning should be ascertained by attempting to discern the "original," "author's" meaning.[42] I rather doubt that the author of 1 John or of 1 Timothy believed God was going about saving all humanity. But I don't believe we should be bound by the human author's intention, and texts such as these, taken in conjunction with the doctrine of the universality of the holy spirit, may allow Christians to hope and pray for and believe in the salvation of all humanity. As Ian Markham puts it, taking inspiration from John 16:

40. For early studies of the sectarian nature of much of early Christianity ("early" within the genre of social-historical or social-scientific scholarship), see Meeks, "Stranger from Heaven"; Meeks, *First Urban Christians,* esp. 84–105; Elliott, *Home.*

41. See, for example, Sanders, "Paul Between Judaism and Hellenism"; see also, from the same collection, Martin, "Promise of Teleology," 100–103.

42. See his comments on postmodernism and textual meaning at 230.

12–15, where Jesus says that the Paraclete will reveal things Jesus himself had not revealed, "It is because we believe in the Holy Spirit that we are required to be attentive to the witness of other faith traditions. The Holy Spirit seeks to guide the Church into a deeper knowledge of the truth. Given God is active in all human cultures, we should expect to learn of God from other religious cultures."[43]

There is no good without God. The holy spirit is the person of the trinity that especially pervades the universe in all its materiality. How do we imagine this universal and material spirit? The pneuma is the energy and life of the universe. All thought, including but not limited to "revelation," is pneumatic. We may imagine pneuma to furnish the stuff of everyday life— light, energy, magnetism, gravity—as well as those mystical things scientists tell us exist and impact our reality even though we can't understand them: dark matter, dark energy, stardust, invisible but powerful particles of matter. We may imagine pneuma to be the basis of information, DNA, genetic codes. Just as the ancients used materials of their world like wind, breath, light, fire, water, aether to imagine pneuma, we should use others that are closer to our imaginary worlds of modernity and postmodernity. It is no accident that the creeds speak of the spirit as the quintessentially "life-giving" person of the trinity: *vivificantem*. What are those things in our world that we see as especially life-giving? What in our world are the bases and origins of life?

Finally, we may look to the universal pneuma to bring knowledge of God and salvation also to those outside the church. This may need to remain an eschatological hope and mystery. We don't need to know how and when God will save the world. We may believe in hope. Indeed, a doctrine of the pneuma is a good place to combine three theological topics or "stances": epistemology, soteriology, and eschatology. The pneuma is the revealer of the divine to us and to all people. Since pneuma is universal, pervading all nature and the universe, we may hope that there is some knowledge of God throughout the universe and therefore some possibility for universal salvation. Yet we maintain this hope in eschatological reservation. The mystery of God's complete goodness will never be entirely graspable by us human

43. Markham, *Understanding*, 111. See D'Costa, "Christ." For another argument that the Holy Spirit is not confined to the church, see Sesboüé, "Spirit in the Church": "Finally, I remember that God's Spirit, which inhabits the entire universe, is present in [non-Christians] in the form of an invitation, an incitement to open themselves up to selflessness, to self-giving, to the acknowledgement of God in one form or another" (74–75).

beings, even in some beatific vision we may expect in some future world. But we wait for our salvation and the salvation of the world in hope.

The Third Person of the Trinity

As I have said, we must move beyond the constraints of historical criticism to read the New Testament, and even more so the entire Bible, as teaching about the holy spirit as the third person of the trinity. There is no reason we should not do that. As we have seen to be the case in discussing to what extent it is theologically valuable (or dangerous) to consider the "person-hood" of God, so we must not naively assume that the concept of person is without potential problems. God is not a "person" in the same sense we think of ourselves and our neighbors as persons. All this is true even more obviously for the spirit. In fact, as I will expand upon below, the spirit is the least "personable" person of the trinity. Yet there is a completely worthwhile way of speaking of God as person and the holy spirit as the third person of the trinity. As Rogers put it, if by "person" we mean something that can function as an actor or character in a narrative, the holy spirit certainly does that in at least some parts of the New Testament, and we may justifiably expand those places to read the person of the spirit "into" or "out of" the entire Bible.[44]

The Gospel of John contains one of the few references to the spirit that comes across clearly as personal, as we have seen, when Jesus refers to the spirit as the Paraclete, the "other advocate" (John 14:16, 26; 15:26; 16:7). These passages also raise the issue of the gender of the pneuma. Whereas most of the time in the New Testament the pneuma is referred to grammatically as neuter, because the Greek word *pneuma* is neuter, once Jesus in John gives the pneuma the label "Paraclete," that entity can then take a masculine pronoun. Thus, whereas most of the New Testament refers to the spirit as "it," when the word *paraklêtos* is assumed as the antecedent, it can be referred to as "he" (see John 14:26: ἐκεῖνος; see also 15:26; 16:7, which use masculine terms rather than neuter to refer to the Paraclete). In fact, in these various passages from John the author shifts back and forth: when the antecedent is *pneuma*, he uses neuter terms, and when it is Paraclete, he switches to masculine, sometimes in the same sentence. This is not at all surprising. As is well known, linguistic gender is seldom tied firmly to the gender of the entity itself but is simply an aspect of linguistics. As English speakers who

44. Rogers, *After the Spirit,* 53.

don't usually have to deal with the gender of particular things or words, it is interesting to note when New Testament texts regularly refer to the spirit using neuter pronouns and the rare cases when those texts refer to the spirit, in the form of the Paraclete, as masculine. At any rate, the Paraclete does come across in the Gospel of John as a person more than pneuma does throughout the New Testament.

Yet the Gospel of John's pneumatology poses a problem, as we have seen, about the dual presence of Jesus and the pneuma. Although Denis Edwards may be making a *theologically* true claim when he says, "We should not think of the Spirit as coming only after the death and resurrection of Jesus," that is exactly how John narrates it.[45] We have here another case in which good exegesis may lead to bad theology. As shown in the previous chapter, "Christ," according to John's Gospel, it *is* true that the spirit comes, at least onto the disciples, only after the death and resurrection of Jesus. The spirit in John is a substitute for the absent Jesus, or at least for the Jesus who is absent in body.

The same is true of the Acts of the Apostles. The spirit makes many appearances in Luke: making Mary pregnant (1:35), "filling" Elizabeth (1:41) and Zachariah (1:67), coming "onto" prophets (2:25). The spirit certainly interacts regularly with Jesus (4:1, 14; 10:21). But in the beginning of Acts, Jesus tells his disciples, after his resurrection, to remain in Jerusalem until the holy spirit comes upon them, which does take place several days later (Acts 1:5; 2:1–4). As we have seen, the spirit becomes virtually the main actor in Acts.

Scholars have noted, for instance, that the Acts of the Apostles is mistitled. For one thing, it isn't really about all the apostles but mainly, in the beginning, about Peter. Paul is the star character for the majority of the document, but Paul doesn't fit the criteria for being an "apostle" as set out by the author of Acts.[46] Thus scholars have often made the point that a more accurate title for the work would be the Acts of the Holy Spirit. Luke–Acts, like John, makes the spirit a major character in the book of Acts, taking the place of the now-absent Jesus. In most of Acts Jesus speaks only here and there and as if from "offstage." Or, to use a slightly different analogy, we may read the spirit in Acts as something like an offstage director of the onstage action. At any rate, it is notable that though we would be making a theological mistake if we emphasized too much that the spirit comes only after the death and resurrection of Jesus, that is precisely how both John and

45. Edwards, *Breath*, 27.
46. See Martin, *New Testament*, 8.

Acts present the story. I will return to this point below in an attempt to use it theologically.

We may indeed use the emphasis in the previous section on the materiality of pneuma as a theological resource for fresh ways of thinking about the holy spirit. According to my interpretation of the resurrected body of 1 Cor 15, as the body of Jesus during his earthly lifetime was flesh and blood, his resurrected body is one not of flesh and blood but of pneuma, the material spirit. Notice what this may mean for the holy spirit. The pneuma is what "embodies" transformed, saved bodies, including that of Jesus. Pneuma is in fact the quintessential corporeality. If Jesus is God Incarnate, God in the flesh, the holy spirit is God "corporeal," divinity embodied. As ironic as it may seem to say so, we may indeed note that the holy spirit is the most corporeal of the persons of the trinity, just as Jesus was the most fleshly person of the trinity. By means of the three persons of the trinity we see divinity completely transcending materiality (the father), divinity manifested in the flesh (Jesus), and divinity incorporated in body (the holy spirit).

Although many of us Christians are used to thinking of the holy spirit as the most hidden or mysterious or even absent person of the trinity— it takes up much less space in our creeds than either the father or Jesus, as I point out below—we may use these ancient notions of the universal and material pneuma to spark different imaginings of the third person of the trinity. The holy spirit is the most universal, physical, and material person of the trinity. Pneuma is what breathed over the universe at creation. Pneuma is what physically inspired the prophets. Pneuma is what physically settled on Jesus at his baptism. Pneuma is what "filled" Jesus in his ministry. Pneuma is what came down on the disciples at Pentecost *as fire.* Pneuma is the most natural and physical of the persons of the trinity: breath, dove, water, fire.

Yet we have not been wrong to think of the holy spirit also as the most mysterious or impersonal person of the trinity. While some Christians and theologians have bemoaned this common perception of the spirit, others more recently have turned the idea—the *absence* of the "personal" spirit—to theological advantage as a way of reflecting on how Christians do commonly experience the spirit. Bernard Sesboüé, for example, says, "The Spirit never seems to be a clear-cut individual over against us or someone whom we can address directly and intimately like the Father and the Son, who are, as it were, our partners in prayer. Instead, the Spirit might be said to be located at the heart of our personal subjectivity. . . . This tendency is so uniform that we might well ask whether the New Testament shows us the Holy Spirit as a personal subject, or merely as a kind of objective force derived from God."[47] We do tend to personalize the holy spirit less than the father and the son. The term "holy spirit" is, after all, not an actual *name*. "Holy" is not the spirit's first name but one description of its nature. Although many Christians speak of the spirit as "he," doctrinally speaking it is perfectly acceptable to use the pronoun "it." This is part of the mystery of this most nonpersonable person of the trinity.

The mystery of the spirit may have been both a contributor to and a result of the way the spirit is spoken of in the major creeds. In the Apostles' Creed, the holy spirit gets one line: "I believe in the Holy Spirit." The Father gets two substantial lines, and Jesus gets a whopping ten lines.[48] In the Nicene Creed, God the father gets four lines for himself, though he is mentioned in other places in the creed. Jesus gets twenty-one lines. The holy spirit gets four:

> We believe in the Holy Spirit, the Lord, the giver of life,
> who proceeds from the Father and the Son.
> With the Father and the Son he is worshipped and glorified.
> He has spoken through the Prophets.

Even here, where the holy spirit gets as many lines as the father, both the father and son are mentioned in two of those lines. The spirit just doesn't get comparable attention.

It may not be quite fair to bring in Chalcedon here since its purpose was clearly to define the nature of Christ and the relation of Christ to the father and to human beings, but this important early "definition" (451 CE) doesn't mention the holy spirit at all. It even talks of Mary as the "mother of God" and the prophets' prophecies about Jesus, in either of which contexts one might expect a mention of the spirit. After all, in the Bible and much church teaching and tradition the holy spirit was the person of the trinity par excellence who brought about both Mary's pregnancy and the prophecies of scripture. Yet Chalcedon remains silent on the spirit.

47. Sesboüé, "Spirit in the Church," 69–70. Sesboüé may be speaking here more particularly of the way we read the spirit in the Acts of the Apostles, but his point is more broadly applicable to much Christian experience.

48. My quotations of and line counts come from the current version of the Book of Common Prayer (1979).

This impersonal, nameless aspect of the spirit leads William Atkinson, following Tom Smail before him, to speak of the spirit as a "person without a face."[49] Sergius Bulgakov points to the New Testament as one reason for this characteristic of the spirit: "We cannot fail to be amazed by the fact that, with a single exception [Acts 13:2], nowhere does the Bible speak of the Third hypostasis in the first person. Rather, it always speaks of the Third hypostasis in the third person, i.e., impersonally. The person of the Holy Spirit remains enshrouded in mystery; He is unknown, unrevealed."[50] The seventeenth-century Anglican theologian John Owen said that "the imme-diate actings of the Spirit are the most hidden, curious, and mysterious, as those which contain the perfecting part of the works of God."[51]

We have seen how passages of the New Testament can reveal mystery or absence. As I noted in the chapter titled "Christ," in the Gospel of John the Paraclete as the holy spirit comes to the disciples only once Jesus is ab-sent or at least just about to be absent. The Gospel of John emphasizes more than the other Gospels the *absence* of Jesus from the church. We may take inspiration from John so that when we experience the absence of Jesus we must remind ourselves of the presence of the spirit, taking Jesus's place and continuing to reveal truths to the church that Jesus, in his lifetime on earth, did not reveal (John 16:12–15).

Such musings have occurred to me when the use of older liturgical forms takes us back to talking not about the holy spirit but about the holy ghost. I remember as a child having Sunday school teachers discourage us from using the term "ghost" for the spirit. I suppose they were afraid we children would think of ghost stories or other frightening or superstitious things, and they didn't want us thinking that way about the holy spirit. But as I have recited the creeds in the older forms, I have found a bit of inspiration in the term "ghost." There is something mysterious, perhaps even spooky, about the third person of the trinity. I say we embrace that interpretation of the spirit. In fact, we can think of the holy spirit as Jesus's "ghost," being present for us in his bodily absence. We are reminded that ghosts connect living people to dead people. And it is through the holy ghost that we are in communion in the body of Christ with all believers who have ever existed. We who still live, through the ministry of the holy ghost, remain connected

49. Atkinson, *Trinity*, 61, quoting Tom Smail, who appropriates the phrase from Yves Congar and uses it as the title of his second chapter: *Giving Gift*, 30; Congar, *I Believe*, 3.5.

50. Bulgakov, *Comforter* (original Russian: 1936), 174.

51. Owen, *ΠΝΕΥΜΑΤΟΛΟΓΙΑ* (originally published 1676), 98.

to all the saints, meaning that term in the broadest sense: all members of the body of Christ who have ever existed even if they are now dead. We can't see the ghost, but we can feel it. This must be a good ghost. But we've seen, in literature, film, and television shows, plenty of helpful, friendly ghosts. That doesn't mean, though, that they are necessarily less spooky. And that may be a good thing.

How, though, did we get from the "most embodied" person of the trinity to thinking of it as an invisible ghost? It shouldn't be taken to be a weakness of my points here that I was arguing above that the spirit is the most "corporeal" and "material" of the persons of the trinity. Throughout this book I am trying to illustrate that the truth of a theological statement lies not in some property inherent in the statement itself but in how it is interpreted. There are no theological statements that are true in all and every sense. Only "in *a* sense." And good theology may well hold together, side by side, theological images or claims that seem even mutually contradictory. In fact, I believe the only good Christian theologies are those that regularly say things that seem the opposite of one another. Good theology contains contradictions or at least statements that seem contradictory on their face. We would do well to imagine the holy spirit as, in one sense, the most corporeal and material of the persons of the trinity but at the same time as the most impersonal, hidden, and mysterious. This is to take the mysteries, ambiguities, and even contradictions of the New Testament itself as theological fodder.

Spirit in Trinity and Church

As we have seen, the spirit in the New Testament is often interwoven with God and Jesus, even to the extent that we can't really be sure when the reference of pneuma is to the holy spirit proper, the pneuma of God in general, or the pneuma of Jesus in particular. The pneuma seldom plays a role all its own in the New Testament apart from God or Jesus playing some role in the same context. Remarkably, this is not so true of either God or Jesus in the New Testament. Jesus occupies center stage for much of the Gospels, though God is usually not far off. But Jesus is so much the center of attention in especially some parts of the Gospels that readers sometimes make the mistake of thinking that the Gospels are more about Jesus than God. Theologically speaking, the Gospels present Jesus only to lead readers to the kingdom of God and God's own self, not to end with Jesus alone. But much of Christianity, especially in the West, has suffered from a sort of "Christomonism" or

"Christologism."[52] When it comes down to it, a truly "Christocentric" theology should be held in some suspicion. Jesus is God incarnate but not all that needs to be said about God. We confess the trinity for a reason, and no one person of the trinity should be the "center."

Some New Testament texts may be used to make the point. The entire Letter of James may be read without giving much thought to Jesus at all. Jesus is mentioned only twice in the letter, once in the greeting ("James, a slave of God and the Lord Jesus Christ") and again at 2:1 ("our glorious Lord Jesus Christ").[53] On the other hand, "God" occurs seventeen times, and "father" as a reference to God three times.[54] My point is that New Testament texts may focus mainly on Jesus as the central player or on God, but they seldom focus on the spirit alone, apart from the activities of God or Jesus, as *the* central figure.

I've already touched on some of these passages when talking about pneuma as one person of the trinity. Heb 9:14 speaks of "the blood of Christ, who through the eternal spirit offered himself without spot to God." In the Gospels, the spirit is regularly "on" or "with" or "leading" Jesus (Mark 1:10, 12 and par.). And, as we saw above, pneuma works its way in and out of the text of Rom 8 thoroughly, though, as I argued above, it is not always clear if Paul is thinking of a "person" of "the holy spirit" at all: "But you are not in flesh but in the spirit, since the spirit of God lives in you. If one does not have the spirit of Christ, he is not of him" (Rom 8:9); "If the spirit of the one who raised Jesus from the dead lives in you, the one who raised Jesus from the dead will make alive also your mortal bodies through his spirit living in you" (Rom 8:11). Again, we need not take this ambiguity and confusion as to the precise reference of "pneuma" as a problem. It is, rather, an opportunity.

The intermingling of holy pneuma, pneuma of God, or father, or son has led many theologians, from early patristic authors to theologians throughout the centuries, to teach that the spirit is the person of the trinity who especially "binds together" the trinity. The Latin term often encountered

---

52. This is a criticism of Western theologies usually made by Eastern theologians based on objections to the *filioque*. See, for example, Dumitri Staniloae, excerpt from "Trinitarian Relations and the Life of the Church," in *Holy Spirit*, ed. Rogers, 247–57, esp. 250; see the discussion of the controversy from an ecumenical perspective in Shults and Hollingsworth, *Holy Spirit*, 75–76.

53. The term "Lord" does occur, but usually, I think, as a reference to God the Father or simply "God." The one use of "Lord" that I think *may* be a reference to Jesus is in the term "the name of the Lord" in 5:14.

54. Pneuma occurs twice in James (2:26; 4:5), but in both cases it seems to be a reference to the pneuma of human beings, not the "holy spirit."

is *vinculum trinitatis,* often translated as the "bond" or "union" of the trinity. The Latin *vinculum* may refer to anything that binds or ties things together. But tourists to Rome may remember that one attractive pilgrimage site is the beautiful church San Pietro in Vincoli, which is usually translated as "Saint Peter in Chains." If we retain the connotations of firmness and permanence but avoid those of slavery or imprisonment, we could think of the term as "the chains of the trinity." The spirit is that which holds together the trinity.

Rogers, introducing an essay by Hans Urs von Balthasar on Christ's "descent into hell," notes that in the descent Christ is furthest from the father but still connected to the father by means of the spirit: "It is the Spirit that stretches to accommodate the distance of the Son from the Father when one is in hell and the other in heaven—and brings them back, a divine rubber band, at the Resurrection."[55] Picturing the holy spirit as a cosmic rubber band is concrete indeed, and it vividly portrays the spirit as what holds together the trinity.

This union, by grace, includes us human beings also. In introducing a text from St. John of the Cross, Rogers explains, "The Holy Spirit teaches the soul to breathe the divine atmosphere shared by the Father and the Son, which is itself the Holy Spirit." As John of the Cross put it, "That breathing is the Holy Spirit Himself."[56] The spirit is the "name," one might say, of the love that binds together the three persons of the trinity and is able to broaden and deepen to welcome us human beings to the communion as well.

Perhaps to avoid any implication that this "bondage" is involuntary or unfortunate, a common way of speaking of it is as *vinculum caritatis,* the bonds of love.[57] Even in our popular songs we can speak of the "chains of love," and that is the preferred way of referring to the function of the spirit in the trinity: the love that binds together the union of the three. Wallace, in his book *Fragments of the Spirit,* cites both terms, *vinculum trinitatis* and *vinculum caritatis,* but he uses the latter much more than the former. And he argues that all of creation, all materiality and nature, is included in that love because of the universality of the spirit.[58]

55. Rogers, ed., *Holy Spirit,* 205.

56. From *Spiritual Canticle,* anthologized and translated in Rogers, ed., *Holy Spirit,* 278–80; these words are on 278.

57. Williams, *Vinculum Amoris,* esp. 16 for Augustine's use of the term. See also Kariatlis, "'What Then?" See esp. 9, where Gregory speaks of "the golden chain of salvation." See also the discussion of the appropriation by Nicholas of Cusa of Augustine's notion of *nexus amoris,* "bond of love," in Hoff, *Analogical Turn,* 196.

58. Wallace, *Fragments,* see esp. 6 but also *passim.*

Of the church fathers, Augustine is most often cited as the main source of the idea that the spirit is "the communion of divine mutual love between the Father and the Son."[59] For Thomas Aquinas, as noted by Kärkkäinon, one of the "key designations" of the holy spirit is "love."[60] Female mystics and theologians sometimes especially emphasize love within the trinity and as the characteristic especially of the spirit.[61] According to Catherine of Siena, the holy spirit *is* the love that binds the persons of the trinity and the human soul to that community.[62] Richard of St. Victor focuses on love to describe the relation of the persons of the trinity to one another.[63] The trinity is, to quote a summation by Pinnock, "a circulation of love in the social context of the Trinity and the understanding of God as loving society."[64]

But the spirit is also the *vinculum caritatis* that binds members of the church together and the church to the trinity. As Paul says, "The love of God has been poured into our hearts through the holy spirit which has been given to us" (Rom 5:5). The spirit confirms our new identity and salvation: "This spirit bears witness to our spirit that we are children of God" (Rom 8:16). Though the church lives in and because of God the father and Jesus Christ, the spirit is the person of the trinity most associated with the indwelling and ongoing presence of God in the church, in every local congregation and the church universal.

Though everything the spirit does in and for the church cannot be rehearsed, precisely because that would include every good thing entirely, I will note a few benefits the spirit provides the church that are particularly notable. The spirit is especially active, for instance, in prayer. Indeed, we cannot pray at all without the spirit. As Jude says, we pray "in the holy spirit" (Jude 20). It is indeed the spirit that prays "in us." As Paul says, we don't even know how to pray or what to pray for: "But this same spirit intercedes with wordless groans . . . because it appeals to God for the saints" (Rom 8:26–27). When there are words, it has been the spirit that supplied the words: "For you did not receive the spirit of slavery again to fear, but you received the

---

59. Burgess, *Holy Spirit: Medieval*, 5. Bulgakov says that Augustine was the first to suggest that the trinity is "love," a notion Bulgakov says was "foreign to Eastern theology." See *Comforter*, 42 (he cites *De trin.* 8.10.14; 9.11; 15.19)

60. Kärkkäinen, *Holy Spirit*, 41; see also for citations of Anselm of Canterbury.

61. See the examples given by Burgess, *Holy Spirit: Medieval*, 5.

62. The theme of spirit as loving mother occurs many times in Catherine's writings, but for an example, see *Dialogue* 74: Catherine of Siena, *The Dialogue*, 136–37.

63. See Fortman, *The Triune God*, 193–94.

64. Pinnock, *Flame*, 33; see also Hill, *Three-Personed God*, 78–79, 225–32.

spirit of sonship in which we cry out, 'Abba, Father!'" According to Jesus's words in John 4:23–24, it is the spirit that enables us to worship at all.

We have seen how the spirit is especially associated with baptism. The spirit descends on Jesus at his baptism in the first three Gospels, and in the Gospel of John, the Baptist testifies to having seen the spirit descend on Jesus, though no actual baptism is narrated (John 1:32–34). I have also noted above the many ways in which the spirit participates in baptism in Acts. In some cases the spirit is promised with baptism, in others the spirit comes after baptism, and in still others the spirit is the medium of baptism itself. "You will be baptized in the holy spirit" (Acts 1:5). In fact, for John, Jesus is the one who "baptizes in the holy spirit" (John 1:33). The precise role of the spirit in baptism in 1 Cor 12:13 depends on the translation. The Greek is ambiguous. Are we baptized "in" the spirit or "by" the spirit? In the same verse, the spirit is what we "drink." According to the NRSV, "In the one Spirit we were all baptized into one body—Jews or Greeks, slaves or free—and we were all made to drink of one Spirit." The KJV interprets a bit differently: "For by one Spirit are we all baptized into one body, whether we be Jews or Gentiles, whether we be bond or free; and have been all made to drink into one Spirit."[65]

The ambiguity, here as in other topics, I argue, is fortuitous. The spirit is the medium in which we are baptized. The spirit is the agent who baptizes us into the body of Christ. The spirit is what we drink up. This effusion of or immersion in the spirit is what we often experience, therefore, when we witness a baptism. We often have a bit of a rush of joy, of hope. A chill often goes around a congregation and the space when a baptism is taking place. People smile during a baptism. That is the spirit enabling and binding together the church with God and Jesus, especially but certainly not only in baptism.

Another central role played by the spirit in Christian theology is as the one who inspired scripture. The spirit spoke through the prophets, both in the past (Acts 28:25) and in the living church (Acts 21:4; 1 Tim 4:1). Although the holy spirit sometimes used past human agents to speak truth, it is really the spirit speaking "through" the human being (Acts 1:16). Human agents spoke God's word not through their own will or agency, according to 2 Peter, but by "being carried along by the holy spirit" (2 Pet 1:20). I translate the Greek to emphasize its image of prophets being physically carried off by

---

65. Robert of Deutz provides a wonderful example of premodern exegesis when he takes the spirit "hovering over the waters" of Gen 1:2 to be a reference to the Holy Spirit and / in baptism. See the excerpt and translation in Rogers, ed., *Holy Spirit*, 178–79. Latin: Rupert of Deutz, *De divinis officiis*.

the spirit. Thus when we read the text of scripture correctly we are hearing not just the human author but the spirit speaking (Heb 3:7; 10:15; 1 Pet 1:11). The holy spirit is not named explicitly in 2 Tim 3:16 but is surely in the neighborhood when the author insists that "all scripture is god-breathed" (θεόπνευστος). The author of scripture and prophecy is the holy spirit.

The inclination of historical critics to concentrate almost exclusively on the "intentions" of the human author as providing the foundationalist basis for the meaning of the text, therefore, is far from both premodern Christian tradition, doctrine, and practice and also ironically far from the "literal" meaning of the texts themselves, which would surely be "normally" taken to make not the human author but the holy spirit or God the ultimate author of scripture.[66] If meaning has anything to do with "intention" (and it need not), the intention that ultimately matters is that of God or the holy spirit, not the "historical" intentions of the supposed human author constructed by means of modern historical criticism.

The spirit, however, did not leave behind its responsibilities for scripture when it inspired and wrote scripture. The holy spirit is also thoroughly necessary for Christian *interpretation* of scripture to take place in a faithful and fruitful way. There is no Christian interpretation of scripture apart from the inspiration and guidance of the holy spirit. Another wonderfully ambiguous text, as I briefly noted above, is 2 Pet 1:20–21, which I translate initially as, "Knowing this first, that every prophecy of scripture is not of private interpretation, for no prophecy was brought by the will of a human being, but being carried by the holy spirit, human beings spoke from God." I have taken the Greek word ἐπίλυσις to mean "interpretation" and have intentionally left open the possibility that this may be referring not to the "interpretation" of "things as they are" or "God's will" or "truth" by the prophet but to the interpretation of the prophecy by readers. Is the verse speaking only about the *inspiration* of the prophecy or does it include reference to the *interpretation* by readers?

The ambiguity can be seen in how different translations render 1 Pet 1:20. To compare only a few:

KJV: "no prophecy of the scripture is of any private interpretation";

NIV: "no prophecy of scripture came about by the prophet's own interpretation of things";

66. As Barth put it, for premodern Christians (and should be for us also), God or the holy spirit is scripture's "*autor primarius*": *Church Dogmatics* I/2, p. 523.

English Standard Version: "no prophecy of Scripture comes from
  someone's own interpretation";
NRSV: "no prophecy of scripture is a matter of one's own interpretation."

A couple of these translations seem to attempt to clarify the wording so that
the "interpretation" must be that of the prophet him or herself (NIV; English
Standard Version). The other two (KJV and NRSV) leave things a bit more
ambiguous. They could be read as implying that the interpretation of the
text must also not be a matter of "private" interpretation.

Some theologians argue that just as we believe in the spirit's inspiration
in the origin of scripture, so we must depend on the spirit's inspiration in the
proper reading of scripture. Stephen Fowl, for example, insists on the necessity of the spirit in interpreting the Bible and therefore on the necessity of
also "interpret[ing] the Spirit": "If Christians are to interpret with the Spirit,
they will also need to learn how to interpret the Spirit."[67] Fowl argues that
this dependence on the spirit for proper interpretation of scripture extends
also to how we interpret other people's lives as actions of the spirit, that is,
"the Spirit's work in the life of another." The spirit for Christians is not only
the origin of meaning. The spirit, when we are interpreting in a Christian
way, is also the interpreter of scripture and of all our world. The holy spirit is
both author and exegete for the church.

Finally, in this section on the role of the spirit in the church, I want to
point out that though the holy spirit is often the most hidden and mysterious
person of the trinity and though I will argue below that we should, at least at
times, think of the spirit as feminine rather than masculine or nongendered,
we should not be misled into thinking of the spirit as passive, weak, or subordinate. Christianity has sometimes given the false impression that lowliness and self-sacrifice are values in themselves. That is not true. An attitude
of required and resigned humility or self-sacrifice for their own sake will
usually be damaging, especially if taken on by girls or women because they
perceive that is what society demands of them. But also for men, assuming
a persona of forced humility or submitting oneself to a constant practice
of sacrificing the self will too often entail a personality disorder and is certainly not good for one's social skills. When the gospel, rightly understood,

67. This quotation from the anthologized version of Fowl's essay "How the Spirit
Reads," in *Holy Spirit*, ed. Rogers, 301–15, at 308. The essay is excerpted from Fowl, *Engaging Scripture*, 97–99, 113–27.

demands humility and self-sacrifice, it is only in certain circumstances and for a greater good. As I pointed out in the previous chapter, "Christ," when Paul and other authors in the New Testament urge self-lowering, it is for the final goal of sharing in the glory of Christ.[68] Humiliation of self should not be celebrated as some abstract principle of value in Christianity.

The spirit is the power that enables Christians to enjoy glory and power. And this spirit is ours: "For God has given us not a spirit of fear, but of power and love and self-control" (2 Tim 1:7). The spirit is our electricity, our oxygen, our magnetism, our gravity, our force, our muscle. But all, as we must constantly remind ourselves, only in the service of love and to the good of our fellow human beings and the planet.

Filioque

Before moving far from the issue of the role of the spirit in the trinity, I feel I must at least briefly address the controversy known by the term "filioque" in the Nicene Creed, though I do not want to dwell long on the problem. For one thing, the issue is not central to my own theology, one way or another. But I bring up the controversy because I believe it will allow me to illustrate a central theme of my theology: that the truth—or danger—of a theological statement lies not in the words themselves but in how they are interpreted and used.

When we Christians in the West recite the Nicene Creed, we say that the holy spirit "proceeds from the Father and the Son." The English "and the Son" is a translation of the Latin *filioque,* and thus a disagreement about the wording of the creed that has divided Western churches from Eastern Orthodox churches is known as the Filioque Controversy.

Most scholars are agreed that the ancient versions of the Nicene Creed had the spirit "proceeding" from the Father but not from the Son. No one knows when Christians in the West first began confessing that the spirit proceeded also "from the Son."[69] It may have been as early as the fifth century in Spain, with the addition spreading to France and Germany later. At any rate, scholars attached to the court of Charlemagne, Emperor of the Holy Roman Empire beginning in 800, accused Greek Christians of heresy for adhering to the older form of the creed and *not* adding "and the Son" to their version

68. This is one of the main themes of my books *Slavery as Salvation* and *The Corinthian Body.*

69. My historical description is dependent on those provided by Burgess, *Holy Spirit: Eastern,* 12–15; and Burgess, *Holy Spirit: Medieval,* 6–8.

of the creed. The disagreement came to something of a head when each side excommunicated church leaders on the other side in 1054.

The split between Western and Eastern churches was actually caused by many issues over many centuries. The attempt by the bishop of Rome to assert himself as pope and head of the entire Christian church, East and West, and the resistance to his absolute authority by leaders in the East was a bone of contention. And what we may today think of as completely political issues were also central, as both Constantinople and Rome vied for primacy as the ruling city of the Roman Empire. The Filioque Controversy, therefore, may be seen as a doctrinal symptom of a much larger, more complicated struggle between East and West encompassing language, politics, and military affairs as well as liturgical and doctrinal differences. At any rate, the churches of West and East are still divided by the acceptance of filioque in the West and the rejection of it in the East.

I believe it is difficult for those of us in the West to understand what about the wording so troubles Eastern Orthodox Christians, but there have been arguments advanced even by Western—and Protestant—theologians that point out theological problems with filioque. Some of them agree with the long-standing Eastern argument that having the spirit proceed from both the Father and the Son tends to separate the spirit too much from the "paired partnership" of Father and Son: the spirit ends up on one side of the action, and Father and Son together on the other. Moreover, many scholars agree with long-standing Eastern arguments that the filioque tends to subordinate the spirit to both the Father and the Son.[70] Arguments have also been made that emphasizing Christ over the spirit, as Eastern theologians accuse filioque of doing, has led to a certain "Christomonism" of Western Christianity and an overemphasis on "Christocentrism" in theology in the West, a tendency I recognize in much Western theology and practice.

Pinnock bemoans the *way* the Western Church attempted to force the change on the East, calling the insertion by the church in the West "a misuse of power." And he agrees that it tends to subordinate the spirit to Christ. Moreover, Pinnock argues that the "universality" of the spirit's activities (as I described above) is threatened by linking the spirit too much to Christ and therefore to the church. He insists it would be a great act of ecumenism for the Western churches, especially the Vatican, to remove filioque from the creed.[71]

70. Kärkkäinen, *Holy Spirit,* 89, attributing this view to Moltmann and Pannenberg.
71. Pinnock, *Flame,* 196–97.

On the other hand, advocates of filioque can point to some biblical support. True, in the Gospel of John, Jesus tells his disciples that "the Father" will send "the Paraclete" in Jesus's "name" (John 14:26). But in the very next chapter Jesus brings the "Paraclete" up again, but this time adds, "whom I will send to you from the Father" (15:26). In the next chapter Jesus again refers to the spirit and says, "I will send him to you" (John 16:7). And then there is the scene after the resurrection, where Jesus, in the presence of his disciples, "breathed on them and said, 'Receive the holy spirit'" (20:21–22). Both sides of this old debate can therefore cite biblical and patristic support for themselves.[72]

I agree that the history of the Filioque Controversy has been an unfortunate, even tragic one. I agree that the insertion of filioque into the creed by church leaders in the West was done in an arrogant and unloving way, often constituting hardly more than a doctrinal tool in a power struggle. I believe that Western churches should repent for those actions and ask forgiveness.

But I would be loath to remove the words from the creed entirely. I'm not in favor of tampering with the content of the scriptures or the major creeds. Even though the version of the creed containing filioque has been around for fewer centuries than the older version, it is a form of the creed Christians in many parts of the world have been confessing for centuries.

The Filioque Controversy, though, can offer an opportunity to reassert a recurring theme of this book: the indispensability of interpretation. The filioque *may* lead to subordination of the spirit to Christ, but it does not do so automatically, as proven by the fact that many of us who confess filioque reject the subordination of the spirit. As I have argued throughout, the *words* of doctrines and theologies are important, but they do not in themselves provide their *meaning*. The filioque *may have* led to "Christomonism" among many theologians in the West and in the assumptions and practices of many Christians, but that is not a *necessary* result of the confession— *because there are no necessary results of any confession or theological statement*. Its truth or not is decided by its use. The filioque is an illustration of how the mere wording of doctrines is not as important as the interpretation of them. So also with all things related to the holy spirit: we Christians must

72. See the lengthy history and analysis of the subject in Bulgakov, *Comforter*, 75–151. Bulgakov provides many patristic citations but insists that the patristic evidence is inconclusive because the fathers just were not thinking of the problem the way the later controversy framed the questions. He does show, however, that later polemicists could call on different fathers for both their own positions because of the lack of clear expression of the formulae in their writings.

be diligent so that we interpret the reality of the spirit and our relation to it in proper, orthodox, loving, Christian ways—just as we must with anything we say we believe.

The Gender of the Spirit

Toward the end of the chapter "God" I addressed the issue of the gender of God. I will do much the same in the chapter below titled "Church." The gender of the spirit is even more open, if we may imagine it, to various interpretations. As I have shown, the Greek word most often used for the spirit is *pneuma*. Since it is grammatically neuter, the spirit is most often referred to in the New Testament as "it" or with other neuter-gendered terminology. (When "that" or "this" is used in Greek, for instance, those words are gendered to reflect the gender of the antecedent.) The exception, as noted above, is when the Gospel of John speaks of the spirit as "the Paraclete" or advocate. In those few cases the Paraclete is referred to in masculine terms. The potential gendering of the spirit that may be imagined on the basis of the grammatical gender used is usually hidden in English translations. Often translators use a masculine pronoun or term to translate a neuter term because of their own theological bias toward referring to the holy spirit as "he" rather than "it." For example, Acts 5:32 is rendered by the NRSV as "And we are witnesses to these things, and so is the Holy Spirit, whom God has given to those who obey him." The Greek word translated here as "whom" is the neuter relative pronoun that normally would be translated as "that" or "which." The vast majority of versions, however, use the more personal word "whom," reflecting their assumption of the personal nature of the spirit ("he") rather than impersonal ("it").[73] As Pinnock notes, however, the use of masculine pronouns for the spirit comes from tradition, not from the Bible itself.[74]

Yet the Bible and some Christians have regularly used feminine images and language for the spirit, as we have seen in the citation of female mystical writers like Catherine of Siena. The Hebrew word for "spirit" most often found in the Hebrew Bible is *ruach*, which is feminine in gender most of the time.[75] The *ruach* hovering over the waters of Gen 1:2 is a feminine

73. The exception I've found, though I've not conducted an exhaustive search, is the translation by J. B. Phillips, which uses "which."

74. Pinnock, *Flame*, 15.

75. Gender in Hebrew is sometimes a bit more complicated. According to Manfred Dreytza, most of the 376 uses of *ruach* in the Hebrew Bible are feminine, about 63

being or force sweeping over the chaos of the primeval universe. Thus Basil
of Caesarea compared the spirit of God hovering over the water to a mother
bird covering her eggs.[76] Basil admits that the interpretation is not original
with him. He takes it from "a Syrian." Because of the Syriac words associated
with the spirit and their feminine gender in Syriac, such images become
especially vivid, as Basil recognized.

The feminine word for "spirit" in Syriac allowed Syriac Christians
more opportunity for using feminine language and imagery for the spirit.
In fact, in some early texts from Syriac Christianity, the holy spirit is called
"Mother," leading to a trinity of "Father, Mother, and Son."[77] Even leaving
aside a few early Christian texts whose orthodoxy may be questioned, other
quite orthodox Syriac authors speak of the spirit as being feminine, reflecting the grammar of the Syriac references.[78] The Syriac word for "hovering"
prompts Syriac authors to take the "hovering" spirit of Gen 1:2 as a mother
bird.[79] As Susan Ashbrook Harvey notes, the *Odes of Solomon,* probably
from the second century, use both masculine and feminine references for
the spirit, though those that depict the spirit as a loving mother are perhaps
the most striking to us. A bit later, probably from the early third century, the
Syriac church father Aphrarat speaks of people putting "her" on in baptism.
For the celibate man, who has therefore left behind any earthly "family," God
is his "father" and the holy spirit his "mother."[80] Ephrem regularly uses many
female images for the spirit, such as weaving cloth, as God's womb, etc., and
this even though he is writing at a time when Syriac authors are increasingly
insisting that the spirit is masculine, in spite of the confusion that makes of

---

are masculine, and the remaining ones are indeterminate by syntax: *Der theologische
Gebrauch,* 182–88.

76. *Hexaemeron* 2.6 (SC 26:168–70).

77. See Brock, "Holy Spirit as Feminine," 79. See also Winkler, *Studies in Early Christian Liturgy,* 66–80; Burgess, *Holy Spirit: Eastern Christian Traditions,* 172–73.

78. As for those of questionable orthodoxy, in the *Gospel of Philip,* the author disputes
the idea that Mary conceived "of the holy spirit." The author rejects the idea, asking "when
did a female every conceive by a female?" The author is no doubt assuming the feminine
gender of the word probably from Syriac or Aramaic influence. *Gospel of Philip* 55.23;
trans. of logion 14 in Layton, *The Gnostic Scriptures,* 331–32. Origen quotes a fragment
from the *Gospel of the Hebrews* that takes the spirit to be "mother": "My mother, the Holy
Spirit, took me just now by one of my hairs and carried me off to the great Mount Tabor."
Fragment 2 in Elliott, *Apocryphal New Testament,* 9.

79. This and several of these references to Syriac texts are taken from Harvey, "Feminine Imagery."

80. Ibid., 116–17.

their grammar.[81] The early Syriac traditions, therefore, as Harvey has urged, provide many resources for adjusting our imaginations about the gender of the holy spirit.

In the Greek translations of the Hebrew Bible, the Hebrew feminine *ruach* would be usually rendered by the neuter *pneuma*. But with the Greek, and especially in Jewish scripture from later dates, we encounter the feminine *sophia*, "wisdom." And *sophia* is often linked with spirit. Wisdom, Sophia, is depicted as "mothering" and "nursing."[82] As Marie-Theres Wacker points out, God's *ruach* becomes associated with *sophia* in the later Jewish text Wisdom of Solomon.[83] Wisdom (in the Greek, Sophia) sits beside God's throne (9:4). "Solomon" (the attribution is a pseudonym) addresses God: "With you is wisdom, she who knows your works . . . she understands what is pleasing in your sight. . . . Send her forth from the holy heavens . . . that she may labor at my side" (9:9–10). Throughout chapters 9 and 10 Wisdom is portrayed as a female consort of God, a special mediator between God and human beings. Later Christians read these as references to the holy spirit.

It should not be surprising, therefore, to find later Christian writers thinking of the spirit in terms of feminine imagery. Catherine calls the spirit the soul's "mother who nurses her at the breast of divine charity."[84] As Stanley Burgess emphasizes, "This imagery of the Holy Spirit as mother is repeated frequently in Catherine's writings."[85]

The spirit in the Bible and Christian tradition has therefore been feminine, neuter, and masculine. Indeed, we may use our imaginations to take the grammatical gender of the different words as expressing mystical realities of the spirit. As the Hebrew is *ruach,* so the spirit is feminine. As the Greek is *pneuma,* so the spirit is neuter. As the Latin is *spiritus,* so the spirit is masculine.[86]

---

81. Ibid, 133–39.

82. Especially noteworthy here is Johnson, *She Who Is,* 124–46; but see also Kärkkäinen, *Holy Spirit,* 95–96.

83. Wacker, "Spirit of God," 38.

84. Catherine, *Dialogue* 141 (p. 292 in Noffke).

85. Burgess, *Holy Spirit: Medieval,* 118n19.

86. Jerome noted the three different gendered terms for the spirit in Hebrew, Latin, and Greek but simply concluded that this proved that "God is without gender." *In Isa.* XI; on Isa 40:9–11, p. 459. For similar statements that God is "without" or "beyond" gender, see Gregory of Nazianzus, "God is not male although he is called Father," "Fifth Theological Oration—On the Spirit," *Christology of the Later Fathers,* 3:198; and Gregory of Nyssa, *Cant. Cant. Hom.* VII, 6:212–13; for English: McCambley, *Commentary on the Song of Songs,* 145–46.

Rogers notes the variety but does little with it. He says, "I follow Jerome's remark that this variety shows that God is beyond gender."[87] Addressing the fact that Father and Son language is "irredeemably male," Markham insists that we should be open to other labels. "God is beyond gender; the alternative language draws attention to that fact."[88] If by insisting that God is "beyond gender" such theologians are saying that God or any person of the trinity can be "defined" by gender, I am in agreement, though I have tried to point out that God cannot be "defined" at all, if by that we mean "delimited" or "delineated." But if by saying, "God is beyond gender" we imply that God has nothing to do with gender or doesn't care about the meaning of gender for us, that is wrong. As always, the theological claim, if true, is also untrue.

I prefer to use the multiple gender identities of God to incite our imaginations about God and our own gender identities. The spirit as mother, feminine, nurturer is helpful. But we may go further, taking feminist imagination into queer imagination. The classical doctrine of *perichoresis* (περιχώρησις) teaches that "each member of the Trinity participates in the work of the other members of the Trinity."[89] Markham uses the term "mutual interpenetration" as one description of *perichoresis*.[90] We may use classical theologies of *perichoresis* to inspire our imaginations about the interactions of the persons of the trinity with one another and with ourselves.

Christians have at least since medieval times thought about the interaction of the persons of the trinity in erotic terms. I suggest we take that further into queer terms. The persons of the trinity may be imagined as penetrating one another in a sublime and erotic love for one another. The holy spirit, then, may be seen as the "bond of love" that is always active in the mutual interpenetration of the persons of the trinity. The spirit also is the power that invites us to join in the love. For those who think this debases the persons of the trinity or is somehow "dirty" or "vulgar," I would answer that they must then have an unfortunately dirty or vulgar idea of sexuality and sex. Imagining the eroticism of God in the activities of the persons of the trinity does not debase God. It rather elevates sexuality.

And while I'm at it, we should not limit ourselves to two genders or even three (feminine, masculine, neuter). We should use the multiple genders of God to make sacred the multiple genders people experience. Not

87. Rogers, *After the Spirit*, 21n9.

88. Markham, *Understanding*, 84.

89. Ibid., 77; Barth, *Church Dogmatics* I/1, p. 396. See also Volf, *After Our Likeness*, 208–13.

90. Markham, *Understanding*, 77.

only male and female but also transgendered, transsexual, intersexed, and simultaneously multiple gendered roles or identities. The multiple gender of the spirit celebrates the multiple genders Christians find themselves being. Ambrose speaks of the spirit as that which filled the womb of Mary: "The fruit of the womb is the work of the Spirit."[91] So we may think of a feminine spirit filling the womb of Mary and indeed filling every womb. Janet Martin Soskice, citing ancient texts and medieval female mystics, speaks of "the baffling of gender literalism," as "the single most productive strategy for moving beyond overly masculinised conceptions."[92] Kathryn Tanner takes advantage of queer theology: "The potential here for a gender-bending use of gendered imagery—a Father with a womb—might very well present the best hope for avoiding theological reinforcement of male privilege."[93]

I have argued that we may imagine the spirit as the most material of the persons of the trinity, as the most universal, as the most corporeal, as the most hidden and mystical, as the most "ghostlike." We now arrive at the realization that the spirit may be the most queer of the persons of the trinity, the one that disrupts and baffles and then reinvigorates gender in multiple forms. At any rate, we should not ignore gender but baptize it and theologize it. There is nothing remotely heterodox in speaking of the holy spirit as "it" or "she." What definitely offends orthodoxy is insisting that the holy spirit or any of the persons of the trinity must be referred to exclusively in masculine terms. As in all other matters theological, we must continually open our minds and hearts to new understandings, trusting the holy spirit to guide us into truth and keep us from error.

91. Ambrose, *On the Holy Spirit*, 2.5.38; see discussion in Edwards, *Breath*, 43.
92. Soskice, "Trinity and Feminism," 146.
93. Tanner, *Christ the Key*, 215.

CHAPTER 6

Human

In this chapter I move even further into rough terrain for any kind of "theology of the New Testament." The New Testament has lots of explicit statements about God and obviously also about Jesus as both man and Christ. In the previous chapter, however, I noted that although the word *pneuma* occurs many times in the New Testament, it is often difficult to figure out precisely what the author had in mind when using it.

We are faced with an even more demanding challenge when we read the New Testament in search of theological anthropology. Just what is a human being? What are we made of? What is our end? Purpose? Nowhere in the New Testament does any author set out to define or describe in any kind of abstract, theoretical, philosophical, or scientific way what it means to be human. This does not mean we cannot read the New Testament to construct a Christian theological anthropology. It just means we have to read between the lines, take our cues from here and there, use our theological imagination even more than in the previous chapters of this book. But that is not a hindrance to good theology. It may even be its salvation. Imagination in the reading of scripture is a virtue we need to encourage and develop.

Constructed

Let us start with a claim about the human person, the self, that has become less and less controversial over the past few decades: we are constructed.

That is a poststructuralist, postmodernist, philosophical way of saying, as we do in Christian theological language, we are created. The "self-made man," from Andrew Carnegie to Ayn Rand to Ronald Reagan, is a fool or a liar. We are contingent, coagulations of physical, social, and cultural contexts. There is no "essence" somewhere inside us that is the true "us." We are each and all constructions of our surroundings and histories.[1] We indeed are "dust," though modern science would prefer to call us "stardust" than "dust of the earth." Scientists tell us that the stuff of which we are made, all the fundamental elements and particles of our bodies and lives, were themselves products of the forming and exploding of stars. We are, we may imagine, truly dust of the earth; but we are also dust of the stars, if we are to believe contemporary science.[2]

One theological way of speaking of this constructedness is that we are created. We may speak of that mythologically with Genesis: God is a person who physically molds dirt to make the human being, breathes pneuma into its nostrils to bring it to life, and then, later, splits an originally unified human being into male and female versions.

The scientific account is that we arise historically out of the physical and biological material of our environment and history. The matter in our bodies was formed in the making and unmaking of celestial matter. The fundamental point is that we didn't always exist. We were made, created, constructed. There is nothing about us, not a soul or spirit or mind, that is not a contingent, temporary coagulation of our environment—physical, biological, social, historical, cultural.

To recall a point I made in the chapter on God, God did not create the universe at some time in the past and then retire. God is constantly creating. The existence of everything that is depends on God's unceasing work of creating and upholding the universe and ourselves in every nanosecond. The big bang may have been a onetime event—we don't really know if there were others or there could be more or a recurrence—but for Christians God is always creating and maintaining the universe through love.

Even though "the construction of the self" may be more a product of recent postmodernist social and cultural theory, and the scientific theory of the construction of our bodies from stardust a product of recent physics and cosmology, we can find indications of this fact of our selves also in

1. See the excellent discussion by Cooper-White, "Reenactors."
2. The point is being made in much popular science writing, but for one recent discussion, see Tegmark, *Our Mathematical Universe*, 64–65.

scripture. The New Testament gives little indication of modern individualism. Throughout the Bible human beings are assumed to belong to larger
entities and to get their identities from those social or cosmic bodies of
which they are members. Scripture presents us not with "self-made men" or
"rugged individuals" but simply with "made human beings": "Who of you
by worrying can add a single foot to your height—or an hour to your life?"[3]
We are not our own, in a quite literal, physical sense: "What do you have that
you did not receive?" (1 Cor 4:7). As the people of God, we were "made" to
be such; we did not form ourselves: "Those formerly not a people are now
the people of God" (1 Pet 2:10).

The contingency of human bodies and identity finds expression in the
assumption frequently voiced in New Testament texts that we human beings
get our beingness, our identity, from some larger body of which we are part.
Paul famously insists that by being baptized into Christ's body, believers are
"in Christ" and therefore can no longer be "in sin" (Rom 6:1–14). Paul seems
unable to imagine that believers, who are members of Christ's body, could
also be members of the body of the cosmos or of a prostitute or of Sin (1 Cor
6:15–20).[4] Human beings are caught: they possess either the pneuma of the
cosmos or the pneuma of God—perhaps both, according to how one reads
different New Testament passages, but not neither (1 Cor 2:12). They can participate in either the table of demons or the table of the Lord (1 Cor 10:21).
But believers are in the body of Christ, and that is what furnishes their true
identity (1 Cor 12:13, 20, 27).

This "identity by location" is true for all human beings. We get our
identity from that body of which we are part: "I no longer live: Christ lives
in me" (Gal 2:20); "Those of Christ have crucified the flesh with its passions
and desires. If we live in the spirit, let us conform to the spirit" (Gal 5:24–25);
"You are dead with Christ" (Col 2:20); "You are risen with Christ" (Col 3:1);
"You died, and your life is hidden with Christ in God" (Col 3:3). According
to Paul and other New Testament writers, human beings *will* be "slaves" to
something, either to sin leading to death or to obedience leading to justice
and right (Rom 6:16–17).

This explains Paul's reasoning in Rom 1 about the rise of idolatry and
polytheism. Once "the nations" invented idols and thus turned away from
the true God, God "gave them up" to filth and dishonor (Rom 1:24). They

3. Matthew 6:27: I take liberties with the translation since the Greek can be legitimately
read as referring to height or time. I just let both readings stand.
4. See Martin, *Corinthian Body*, 176–79, for fuller discussion.

had to be "somewhere," under some kind of power. Once they left God's company, God had to turn them over to other powers. There is no real independence for human individuals. We are all part of something bigger than we are, whether we admit it or like it or not. Fortunately, in faith, "none of us lives for himself and no one dies for himself. If we live or we die, we belong to the Lord" (Rom 14:7–8). "You are not your own." Your body and pneuma are God's (1 Cor 6:19–20).

Body Parts

But if we are indeed "constructed," of what are we constructed? As I said, scientists tell us that our bodies are made up of many different materials of the universe, our matter having been produced in the production and explosion of stars. Texts of the New Testament answer the question by using ancient assumptions and perhaps even a bit of ancient "science," though I doubt any of these authors had any kind of sophisticated education in philosophy or medicine. And there is no uniform answer among the New Testament documents. Regularly they assume, as does Paul, that the human body was, first of all, dust or dirt, "earth" (1 Cor 15:40, 47–48). But they also mention other aspects of human existence that seem to go into making us human beings what we are.

Traditionally and in much popular assumption Christianity is all about "the salvation of the soul," and Christians are presumed to believe in an afterlife involving the immortality of the soul or spirit. Indeed, the soul is often thought to be, at least by people living in the West, the central concern of all religion, Christianity included. Christians themselves sometimes think they are supposed to accept an anthropology that proposes a dualism of body and soul or perhaps a tripartite humanity of body (or flesh), soul, and spirit. It sometimes comes as a surprise when they are told that such assumptions don't really seem to be supported by a historical reading of the Bible.

The word often translated as "soul," ψυχή, occurs much less, actually, than other terms for the human person or parts thereof. It is found about one hundred times in the New Testament.[5] That's actually a relatively low number compared, for example, to the words for "body" (σῶμα) and "spirit" (πνεῦμα). In my fifth edition of Moulton, Geden, and Moulton, *Concordance to the Greek Testament,* there are not quite three columns for psychē,

---

5. The precise number varies somewhat because of textual variability among manuscripts and editions.

whereas there are a full five columns for soma and nine for pneuma.[6] The concentration of attention to "the soul" is not nearly as dominant in the New Testament as is often assumed.

The meaning of "psychē" in the New Testament is seldom, if ever, what later Christianity would think of as the "immaterial substance" that exists alongside—or inside—but differentiated from the body. In fact, I was surprised to discover, when recently checking it, that the "Dictionary" included at the end of the fourth revised edition of *The Greek New Testament* (United Bible Society) does not give "soul" as even one of the meanings of the word, preferring instead "self, inner life, one's inmost being; (physical) life; that which has life, living creature, person, human being."[7] This is quite correct. Most of the time when a New Testament document has the word "psychē," the best modern English translation is simply "life," as many translations actually render it.[8] Sometimes it is translated as "soul" but in a way that even modern English would use it just to indicate a human life or person. When one says something like, "More than fifteen hundred souls were lost in the sinking of the *Titanic*," it doesn't mean that the "souls" of those persons were lost whereas their "bodies" were saved. It simply means that more than fifteen hundred *persons* were lost. This is the meaning in several New Testament texts (see Acts 2:41; 7:14; 27:37; 1 Pet 3:20). Most of the time the term does not refer to a *part* of the human person but simply to the human person.

Sometimes psychē does seem to be a reference to a part of the human person along with other essences or parts but in many cases in rather interchangeable ways. When Mark 12:30 (and par.) has Jesus say, "Love the Lord your God with your whole heart and your whole soul [psychē] and your whole mind and your whole strength," we should not take this as some kind of anatomy lesson about the makeup of the human person. It is simply a way of emphasizing "your whole person." Just as we wouldn't take "strength" here

---

6. Through much of this discussion I used the transliterated and even "anglicized" words for these bodily entities partly to make my text more accessible but also because I want to distance these terms from their traditional meanings as "soul" and "spirit" in the heavily Christianized and theologized senses.

7. See Newman, "Concise Greek–English Dictionary of the New Testament," 201.

8. The examples are too many to cite, but for some instances see Mark 8:35–37 = Matt 16:25 = Luke 9:24: most translations use "life"; the NEB has "self" and "true self"; see also Acts 15:26; 20:10; 27:10, 22; Rom 16:4; Phil 2:30; 1 Thess 2:8. These are only the fewest of possible examples.

to represent a "part" of the human person independent and separable from the body, so we should not take "psychē" here in that way either.

This is shown by the way modern translators take justifiable liberties in rendering "psychē" in different texts. According to the RSV, in Matt 26:38, Jesus says, "My soul is very sorrowful." But the NEB is perfectly justified in rendering the phrase as, "My heart is ready to break." Paul writes in Phil 1:27 that he wants the Philippians to strive together "with one psychē," which is rendered by most translations as "one mind." Heb 12:3 warns against growing "weary in your psychai," which various modern translations render something like "do not lose heart" (NEB) or do not "give up for want of courage" (JB) or "grow weary and lose heart" (NIV; similarly NRSV). These are all justifiable translations because in the vast majority of cases when "psychē" occurs in the New Testament, it just means "a living person," a human being, or whatever makes living beings alive. It does not refer to a "soul" as a nonmaterial "substance" that can exist independent from the body and that is the "real" essence of the person. That meaning rises not from a critical reading of the Bible, not even the New Testament, but from later Platonic and then Cartesian influences.

There are, granted, a very few passages that could be read as implying that psychē is different from the body or some other part of the body. When Matt 10:28 warns against those who can "kill the body but not the soul," we may imagine the author as differentiating in some way the simple body from the life force of the body. The author of Revelation twice uses the term "psychē" to speak of disembodied souls of the dead (Rev 6:9; 20:4, or are these people given new bodies as part of their resurrection?). 1 Pet 2:11 speaks of "passions of the flesh that war against the spirit." Heb 4:12 says that the word of God can pierce to "the division of soul and spirit," though it is none too clear what the author means.

And there are a few passages that could be read to assume a soul separable from the body, though without using the word "psychē." In Luke 23:43, Jesus promises the thief on the cross that he would be with Jesus that very day "in paradise." Is this in an "ensouled" existence apart from any body? We can't be sure. In Phil 1:22–24, Paul muses whether he would rather "remain in the flesh" or "depart and be with Christ." He carries on a similar meditation in 2 Cor 5:1–10. He compares being "at home in the body," which he also calls a "tent," with the better possibility of being "away from the body and at home with the Lord" (NRSV). Paul, however, expects any afterlife for human beings to be in resurrected *bodies* (1 Cor 15), and he is obviously uncomfortable speculating about what kind of existence we might have outside body, insisting in any case that God will not leave us to be "naked" (5:4). So Paul may leave open some possibility that Christians may experience some interim state in which they could experience a continued existence of their "selves" apart from their current bodies. Tellingly, he doesn't use the word "psychē" for whatever that state of existence could be.

These are the very few passages that could be read (but need not be) as implying some kind of human existence apart from body, but even then they don't seem to posit clear ideas of the precise nature of that existence or what "we" will consist of. It is certainly not a simple body–soul dualism. It would be misreading to take any New Testament passage as teaching the existence of a human "soul" that is a real, physical or immaterial "thing" separable from the other "parts" of the person and able to exist, as the essence of the person, apart from the body.

We may find in the New Testament, therefore, many passages that give us reason to accept the growing trend of philosophers and even of Christian theologians to dispense with a dualist or tripartite understanding of the human person in body and soul or body, soul, and spirit. Something of a consensus, I would argue, is developing among even Christian thinkers to join with scientists in describing the human person as a physicalist monism. Several have argued that we need not make that a "reductionist physicalism," meaning that we need not believe that the mind, say, does not exist or is "merely" the physical brain.[9] Using theories of "emergence" that have become popular among scientists, philosophers of science, philosophers of religion, and some theologians, we could think of mind as the complex system produced when the brain and body are at work.[10] The mind is more than a simple sum of the cells that make up the brain. The mind is what happens when all those cells, along with the rest of the body, which processes sensation and information data in innumerable ways, function to produce thoughts, emotions, desires, or meaning. And the mind can work by "downward causation" to alter even the material structure of the brain. Therefore, we may think of the mind (or the soul, if one prefers) as having its own ontological existence that cannot be simply collapsed into the material cells of the brain. But we would still need to insist that the mind does not, at least

9. Murphy, "Resurrection Body"; Murphy, *Bodies and Souls?*, 272

10. For a good introduction to "emergence" in both science and religious studies, see Clayton and Davies, eds., *Re-emergence*; Clayton, *Mind and Emergence*; for an excellent appropriation of emergence theories to analyze Paul and his notion(s) of "sin," see Croasmun, "Body of Sin" and *Emergence*.

for now and as far as we can tell, exist independently of the brain or body. The mind, or soul, is an emergent property—one could say an emergent ontological system—that arises from the material functioning of the brain and body. This is a monist, physicalist understanding of the human person that is still not reductionist to a position that would insist that the only thing we may think of as existing is "mere matter." It is also, remarkably, more cohesive with a critical, historical reading of the Bible, which generally depicts the human person as necessarily embodied.

Following a critical reading of the New Testament, we may affirm that we do not "have" an immortal soul. What we may call a soul is simply the fact that we are alive.[11] When the body dies, it is not as if the soul leaves and then exists somewhere else. When the body dies, the soul ceases to exist. Or, if we think of it as existing somewhere, say, in the mind of God, that would not really be "us." As Thomas Aquinas insisted, if the soul exists as some kind of substance apart from his body—a teaching he felt he had to accept in some way because it was orthodox dogma of the church of his day—that is still not truly "him." According to Thomas's teaching, and here he is certainly in concert with most of the New Testament, the "I" does not exist as the authentic "I" without body.[12] Or, as Denys Turner wonderfully puts it, "You just have to try and stop thinking of *any* soul, a cabbage's or a king's, as a sort of *thing*."[13]

Having affirmed the basic unity of the human person, I should now, though, follow the tendency of this entire book and show how that is true only "in a sense," and that we may well, in another sense, affirm that we experience our selves as *not* constrained to our physical bodies. We don't actually always experience the limits of our being at the surface of our skin: "Though absent in body, I am present in pneuma" (1 Cor 5:3); "Whether in body or outside the body, I do not know" (2 Cor 12:3). We must build into our theories of our selves both the fact that we are bodies (not that we just

11. As Denys Turner explains the views of Thomas Aquinas, "The 'I' that I am does not consist in the soul that I have, and a bodiless soul is no person." For Thomas, to say that someone "has a soul" is "no more than a synonym for 'is alive.'" See Turner, *Thomas Aquinas*, 56–57; see also 62.

12. Kerr, *Theology After Wittgenstein*, esp. 178–79; McCabe, *Good Life*, esp. 103. According to the *Quicunque Vult* (The Creed of Saint Athanasius), "soul and flesh is one man," said of Christ's incarnation but therefore true for us as well: we are not soul apart from flesh, or flesh apart from soul, but a living body, the combination, if we may put it in these terms (though we need not), of life and body (I quote the creed from the Book of Common Prayer, 865).

13. Turner, *Thomas Aquinas*, 61.

"have" bodies) but also that we, at least in our experiences, seem to be more than or more extended than our bodies. "We" transcend our bodies in our experience of our bodies, but we cannot demonstrate, at least at this time, that "we" actually exist independently from our bodies.

Technology increasingly renders us transcending our bodies. We are not physically limited to the space inhabited by our bodies. We see things that happen worlds away; we speak in real time with people around the world; we communicate directly, visually, audibly with our loved ones thousands of miles away. This human ability of transcendence happens to us not just spatially but in time also. Because of memory, our minds, though certainly "contained" here and now, travel in our sensibilities back in time. Through our imaginations we look forward in time. We may use New Testament texts that illustrate the transcendence of the human person through spirit, soul, or other mechanism to help think of our own quotidian experiences of transcendence from our bodies.

Moreover, though I have insisted that we *are* bodies and not "embodied souls," we may also take the partition of the human person depicted by biblical images of flesh, body, soul, spirit, and mind (to mention only the few perhaps most frequent) to express our experiences in which we sense our selves as not so united and unified after all. The traditional, biblical entities of flesh, soul, and spirit need no longer have the same ontological, physical existence for us that they certainly did for most ancient Christians, yet we may still use them and "experience" them. When we do not do the things which we ought to have done and do the things which we ought not to have done, we may think of such events in modernist terms such as ego, id, superego, conscious, unconscious, subconscious, or we may resort to "biblical" language of flesh, soul, spirit, or mind. We need to accept both the unity of the human person as body and the partition of the human person into different, sometimes cooperating, sometimes warring, parts.

The varied anthropological terms and models we read in the New Testament are just as jumbled and various as our experience of our own bodies and minds. In order to avoid rejecting or rebelling against contemporary science, which tends to insist on a monist, physicalist anthropology, we can easily accept the picture the New Testament offers that we "are" bodies, not that we "have" bodies. But we may also use the mythological anthropology that includes soul, flesh, spirit, body, and mind. The important thing to keep in mind is that there is not one orthodox version of the nature of the human person. We have many choices. And that is a good thing since we in fact experience "our" bodies in diverse, ambiguous, and contradictory ways.

The Social Self

I noted above that many passages of the New Testament construe the human person as gaining identity by being part of a larger whole. This extends further into the idea that the human body is not only constructed of the materials of its environment and history, but the human self is also a construction of its social and cultural environment.[14] The idea flies in the face of much modernism, with its ideology promoting the "rugged individual." As Fergus Kerr puts it, "We have a very powerful picture of the self as isolated will and autonomous individual, left in radical freedom to bring a moral universe out of surrounding chaos either by a gamble of faith or by a God-like act of creation."[15] Kerr argues, however, that such a notion is bad ideology and bad theology. We are selves "in nature and history."[16]

The modernist idea of the autonomous individual was never a majority view in the ancient world, in my view—though it is difficult to get at what would have been an ancient "common sense" since almost all our evidence derives from the tiny highest class of ancient people, and mainly men. Ancient upper-class ideologies often seem exaggerated by our sources. But there was a dominant ideology of "self-sufficiency" at least among these wealthy male members of the ruling class, and it expressed itself in Greek and Roman philosophy almost universally in our literary sources. These rich men could never have lived their lives or even existed in the absence of their complete dependence on all that was provided by women, slaves, lower-class workers, and "clients" of lesser status. But in order to mask this dependence, which they despised and feared as servile and effeminate, they developed an ideology that insisted that the "true gentleman" could train himself to be completely self-sufficient. A favorite Greek word for this "virtue" was αὐτάρκεια, and the self-sufficient man was αὐτάρκης. The ideology was expressed in the upper-class male's ideal to use only materials produced on his own land, to eat and drink from the produce of his farms and vineyards, to

---

14. For something of a short intellectual history of modern philosophy and scholarship on the "social nature of human beings" ("sozialen Natur des Menschen") and the different ways societies and cultures have tried to acknowledge both the social and the individual in human existence, see Noelle, "Die doppelte Natur"; for a fuller treatment of the topic, see the exhaustive theological and phenomenological anthropology by Wulf, *Der Mensch*.

15. Kerr, *Theology After Wittgenstein*, 22.

16. Ibid., 52; see also 69: "I discover myself, not in some pre-linguistic inner space of self-presence, but in the network of multifarious social and historical relationships in which I am willy-nilly involved."

have his properties as self-sufficient as possible.[17] He therefore also entertained the conceit that he was himself self-sufficient, in body and person. Needless to say, this was a complete ideological illusion that simply served to mask and maintain an immoral system of exploitation.

The ancient ideology of self-sufficiency is notably absent from most of the New Testament, which is not particularly surprising since we think most, if not all, the documents of the New Testament were written by people who were well below the highest level of the ancient class and status system. In fact, the New Testament provides a rare glimpse of what sort of "literature" could be produced by generally lower-class persons in antiquity. It is no surprise, therefore, that these texts sometimes do not share in the ideologies of the highest class of Greek and Roman societies. On the contrary, in the New Testament human beings are assumed to be quite dependent on other human beings and on God, nature, and all sorts of constructing and supporting environmental factors. It is true that Paul in one context depicts himself as *autarkês*. In thanking the Philippians for a gift they had given him, probably financial support, Paul insists, practically as an aside, that he didn't really *need* the help: in all circumstances he had learned to be "self-sufficient" (αὐτάρκης; Phil 4:11). But he cannot really bring this off in the manner of a true philosopher, one of the many signals that Paul probably did not have actual philosophical training or education. The rest of his very fond letter to the Philippians is filled with his ready admission of his and others' dependence on one another. In his imprisonment he depends on their prayers and the help of the spirit (1:19). He urges them to practice humility and to think of others as "better" than themselves, invoking an attitude that would never have been urged or practiced by ancient philosophers (2:3). They should follow Jesus's example of self-lowering for the benefit of others (2:4–11). He praises the longing and distress experienced by Epaphroditus in his absence from them, again, not something philosophers would have praised (2:26). And in the end Paul thanks them heartily for the many times they have come to his aid (4:15–18).

This readily acknowledged interdependence, the *lack* of the kind of self-sufficiency taught by the philosophers, occurs throughout the New Testament. This is part of the assumption, which didn't need to be "recognized" because it was simply their "common sense," that the human body is a social

17. I have further described, and critiqued, this ancient—and modern—ideology of self-sufficiency in Martin, *Sex and the Single Savior*, see esp. 74–76; see also Martin, "Contradictions."

body. Elsewhere, Paul, using a different word for "sufficient," says, "*Not* that we are sufficient [ἱκανοί] of ourselves so that we could consider anything as really ours; rather our sufficiency comes from God" (2 Cor 3:5; I have added the emphasis, but I think it justified because the negative does begin the sentence, which can be a sign of emphasis in Greek). Notice the thick interplay of mutual need Paul is willing to admit to the Corinthians: he asks them to "make room" in their hearts for him, as they reside in his heart; he admits their previous aid to him and his companions when he was in distress and need; he notes the consolation Titus derived from them; he confesses to having caused them grief, but for a good end. Indeed, Paul and the Corinthians are locked in mutual need, "to die together and to live together" (2 Cor 7: 2–13). To the Romans he says much the same thing: "We do not live for ourselves, and we do not die for ourselves" (Rom 14:7).

In letter after letter members of churches are addressed as a collective, a community, a body. 1 Pet 1:1 addresses its readers as "resident aliens" who must stick together because they are in a strange land, this cosmos. He later calls them an "elect common bloodline" (γένος ἐλεκτόν), a "royal priesthood" (βασίλειον ἱεράτευμα) a "holy ethnicity" (ἔθνος ἅγιον) a "people" (λαός) of God's possession (2:9).[18] "Once no people, now a people of God" (2:10).

As just illustrated by those passages from Paul and the First Letter of Peter, these identities of "peoples" are created by narratives. "Peter" tells a story of the creation of a new people by invoking social terms that derive their meaning from larger, commonly known narratives.[19] Many scholars have increasingly stressed the role of story or narrative in the construction and maintenance of identity.[20] We become a people by telling one another stories about ourselves. As Rowan Williams puts it, "The self at any given moment is a *made* self: it is not a solid, independent machine for deciding

18. I use the term "common bloodline" because the Greek does refer to the idea of a people of common ancestry, which makes them a unity by common inheritance. The word is often translated as "race," but I find that anachronistic. I don't believe the ancients had a notion that corresponds to the modern term "race," which is a broader (and "racialist") category assumed to be based on biological differences among only a few racial groups (white, black, Asian, Native American, Latino, or whatever list is currently used in practice). Inhabitants of the ancient Mediterranean world *did* think of people as belonging to different nations or ethnic groups (Greeks, Romans, Jews, Germans, Egyptians), but those better correspond to our own ideas of ethnicity (German, Italian, English, Chinese, Japanese), which are usually distinct from those we consider "race" (white, black, Asian).

19. "Peter" is in quotation marks here because I, along with most critical scholars, do not believe the "historical" Peter wrote the letter.

20. See, for example, Cortez, *Theological Anthropology*, 36–37.

and acting efficiently or rationally in response to stimuli, but is itself a process, fluid and elusive, whose present range of possible responses is part of a developing story."[21] And stories, after all, are social products, a fact stressed by David Kelsey: "Personal bodies are inherently relational beings, limited by their dependence on others and by others' dependencies on them."[22]

These writers emphasize that the human body or self is constantly an ongoing project. This certainly lays upon us much responsibility for who we are, since we can make different choices that will be part of forming our selves. But it can also be liberating and provide hope: if there are aspects of our selves we are unhappy with, we may be able to change them for the better. The social and individual practice of *habitus* provides a way of thinking about how we, as individuals and social bodies, come to be. As explained above in the chapter titled "Knowledge," habitus refers to how we human beings ingrain "ways of being" in and for ourselves by repetition and practice. This is possible precisely because we are social bodies, formed and re-formed by interacting with other human bodies, completely dependent on others, and responsible for the dependencies of others on us. Realizations such as this may be reinforced by careful reading of the New Testament, whose world was so unlike ours and whose "rationality" was so different from the rationality of modernist individualism out of which we are attempting to climb.

Finitude

Given the fact that we are bodies, we are also finite, which is an aspect of human reality often forgotten in the history of Christianity but lately re-asserted by various theologians. In fact, one of the important themes of the recent theological anthropology by Kelsey, *Eccentric Existence*, is its emphasis on the finitude of the body. Kelsey reminds us that as human bodies, we can "not be": "The integrity of human living bodies' personal identities is inherently capable of dis-integrating."[23] Kelsey is here in fact reclaiming a common ancient assumption. A few ancient Greek and Roman philosophers may have entertained the possibility of human possession of an immortal soul, and ancient literary sources could imagine a realm of the dead, such as Hades, where only faint "shades" of formerly full human lives might

---

21. Williams, *Resurrection*, 23.
22. Kelsey, *Eccentric Existence*, 315.
23. Ibid., 283.

survive in some kind of existence, though it is seldom depicted as a robust or happy existence. For the most part, though, ancient people seem not to have expected to outlive their embodied lives. The vast majority certainly did not expect to receive "eternal life" as a gift or reward from their gods.[24] In fact, the most common assumption was that the characteristic most obviously separating human beings from the gods was precisely that only the gods were "immortals." Moreover, the gods jealously guarded their perquisite of immortality. The gods were known for killing or otherwise punishing any human being who tried to become immortal or any other being, divine or human, who tried to grant immortality to human beings.[25]

We can see this assumption reflected in many uses of the Greek word ἄνθρωπος in the New Testament. Hebrews is an especially illustrative example because its author has particular concerns to contrast human beings not only with God and Jesus but also with angels. Heb 2:6–8 quotes Ps 8:4–6 to assert that human beings were created "a little lower than angels." In Heb 7:8, the word seems to emphasize the mortality of ordinary human beings because it is opposed to "one who lives." In fact, the NRSV translates ἄνθρωποι here as "mortals." In 7:28, it is paired with "weakness" and opposed to "the son who has been made perfect forever." In 9:27 we are told, "It is appointed to ἄνθρωποι to die once and after that face judgment." Heb 13:6 quotes Ps 117:6 (LXX; Hebrew Bible 118:6) in another implication that human beings are impotent compared to God or Jesus: "The Lord is my help. I will not be afraid. What can a human being [ἄνθρωπος] do to me?" Heb 8:2 speaks of the "liturgy" of Christ as being superior to the liturgy of Jewish priests and of the "true tabernacle" as being superior to that of Moses: it is "made by the Lord, not by any human being [ἄνθρωπος]". The word ἄνθρωπος occurs nine times in Hebrews. It is regularly contrasted to another kind of being, God, Jesus, or angels. It carries connotations of the lower, "normal" *human* status, including finitude, mortality, and relative weakness. It is the "mere human."

This idea is borne out by other passages. "Things of human beings," such as thoughts and ideas, are opposed to "things of God" (Matt 16:23; see Mark 8:33). Deeds impossible for human beings are not impossible for God

24. This is a major point of the book by MacMullen, *Paganism;* see also Martin, *Corinthian Body,* 108–10, and sources there cited.

25. Asclepius was famously killed by Zeus for bringing a man back to life, but there were other examples of the gods guarding divine immortality. For the best resource on Asclepius, including essays on various topics and primary sources, see Edelstein and Edelstein, *Asclepius.*

(Matt 19:26 and par.). The First Letter of Peter contrasts the "desires of human beings" to the "will of God" (4:2). In the same context we are told that
the dead heard the gospel preached so that "though they had been judged
in the flesh κατὰ ἀνθρώπους" (as "typically human"; NRSV: "as everyone is
judged"), "they might live in pneuma κατὰ θεόν" (as is the manner of God;
4:6). Again, ἄνθρωπος implies the contrast of mortal, finite, human life with
the eternal, immortal life of God, Jesus, or perhaps even angels.

The finitude of human beings means that all notions of a natural immortality are wrong. We do not have "by nature" an immortal soul or spirit.
We are made to die. If we receive some kind of eternal life, that is by the
miraculous work of God in the future, not a consequence of our creation by
God in this universe. Even when we affirm faith in the resurrection of the
body, that is a reference to an eschatological miracle that we cannot really
understand, and it should not be taken as a denial of finitude or as an affirmation of any "natural immortality" or to the "immortality of the soul."[26]

Moreover, we should embrace our finitude as a gift of the "good" creation of the universe. Finitude is part of creation, not a flaw within creation.
Edward Schillebeeckx explains: "The basic mistake of many conceptions
about creation lies in the fact that finitude is felt to be a flaw, a hurt which as
such should not really have been one of the features of this world . . . finitude
is thought to be improper, an ailment, even sinfulness or apostasy, a flaw in
the existence of mankind and the world. There is a feeling that . . . mortality,
failure, mistakes and ignorance should not be part of the normal condition
of our humanity."[27] We must learn to see our finitude as a gift, not a flaw.

Kelsey similarly argues that we must not see our finitude as an evil:
"It is not a problem to be solved, nor a predicament from which we need
to be saved."[28] Indeed, God declares us, even as created to die, to be good:
"Personal bodies who, precisely *in* their finitude, fragility, and vulnerability,
are deemed by God to be good."[29] Thus, when we encounter passages in the
Bible that speak of Death as a great enemy, something to be defeated and
overcome (see, for example, 1 Cor 15:54–55), we must read them as a reference not to our natural physical death, which need not be such a disaster,
but to the "mythological" Death that would separate us from God. That is
the Death from whose "sting" God saves us. We may indeed pray for deliv-

26. See Murphy, *Bodies and Souls*, 29.
27. Schillebeeckx, *God Among Us*, 92. See also Kerr, *Theology After Wittgenstein*, 184,
whose editing of the larger passage I here accept.
28. Kelsey, *Eccentric Existence*, 212.
29. Ibid., 308.

erance "from dying suddenly and unprepared"; we may pray for "eternal life and peace" for those of us already having died.[30] We pray for those who have died that "they may have rest in that place where there is no pain or grief, but life eternal."[31] In other words, what we ask God for is that we may experience normal, human death in a peaceful way and then to rest in God's being in some way after that. But our created finitude in itself we embrace as a good creation. As Williams puts it, "Being creatures is learning humility, not as submission to an alien will, but as the acceptance of limit and death; *for* that acceptance, with all that it means in terms of our moral imagination and action, we are equipped by learning through the grace of Christ and the concrete fellowship of the Spirit, that God is 'the desire by which all live.'"[32]

Sex and Desire

All this talk about our bodies, biology, and physical nature leads us to confront an issue we experience as central, if not compulsive: our nature as sexual beings, physically, psychologically, emotionally, and actively. For most of this chapter I have been relying on basic historical criticism in reading the New Testament. That is because we can derive perfectly orthodox and valuable Christian theology about the nature of the human via a discovery of the ancient meanings of these texts, the possible intentions of the original authors, and the possible understandings of the texts' ancient readers. Indeed, much of my case has urged a "return" to some key ancient understandings of the nature of human beings: our necessarily embodied existence; our fact as physical; our natural finitude. Now, however, I must use historical analysis to *criticize* the notions of desire, gender, and sex held by our ancient authors and readers. If I am to derive an orthodox and usable theology and ethics of sexuality, I will have to expose and criticize ancient Christian ideologies of sex and desire and use more creative exegesis to inform our own minds and lives about the erotic.

I have argued in several publications that a responsible use of historical criticism of the New Testament cannot produce a moral, usable theology or ethics of sex for our time. The historical Jesus in all likelihood taught some kind of ascetic celibacy or at least the dismissal of family and household. Jesus of Nazareth probably did teach that divorce of any kind was against

---

30. From "The Great Litany," Book of Common Prayer, 149, 152.

31. Book of Common Prayer, 391.

32. Williams, *On Christian Theology*, 78; the last six words, here in single quotation marks, are quoted from Moore, *Inner Loneliness*, 117.

the will of God, but if he did he did so not as advocating marriage but as simply forbidding divorce. In the ancient world the assumption would have been that a man divorced his wife only with the intention of marrying another. What Jesus was forbidding, therefore, was divorce *and remarriage.* That could be taught with complete consistency along with teaching that the avoidance of marriage was the higher ideal. That was certainly the position of the Apostle Paul, and I think it likely the position of the historical Jesus also: if his followers were not already married, they should leave the households of their parents, join the itinerant movement led by Jesus, and refrain from marrying and producing a family of their own.[33]

In the next chapter, titled "Church," I demonstrate in detail the "anti-family" or "antihousehold" messages of Jesus, Paul, and much of the New Testament and ancient Christianity. Only through a serious misreading of the ancient sources can modern Christians maintain their ideology that places marriage, family, and (at least heterosexual) sexuality as central and positive "values" of "biblical" or "traditional" Christianity. It should come as little surprise, however, that the texts of the New Testament do not celebrate the sensual. In popular imagination it has often been thought that Christianity basically invented the antierotic, antisexual asceticism long a part of Christian history. Many scholars of the past few decades have proven that to be a misconception.[34] Historians of antiquity as well as of Christianity and Judaism have in recent decades recognized that Christianity absorbed a kind of "cult of self-control" that sprang out of male upper-class cultures of discipline in Greece and, later, in Rome.[35] The idea that ancient Greece and Rome were boiling vats of sexual desire and activity was never really true for everyone in those societies. What has been more recently demonstrated is that the control of the body and even the emotions, especially as related to the control of passions, diet, and sexuality, had been, by the rise of Christianity, already a dominant cultural concern, at least of the philosophers and upper-class men who listened to them. Christianity inherited asceticism from at least a significant segment of the Greco-Roman Mediterranean culture surrounding it.

It is nonetheless a bit surprising that a main Greek word for erotic love, ἔρως, does not even occur in the New Testament, and neither does any verb or other form of that word group. Studies that have attempted to make

33. Evidence and arguments defending this interpretation may be found in Martin, *Corinthian Body,* 198–228; *Sex and the Single Savior,* 65–147; and *New Testament,* 278–84.

34. One of the seminal and best of such studies is Brown, *Body and Society.*

35. See especially Foucault, *History of Sexuality,* Vol. 3: *The Care of the Self.*

firm distinctions between three Greek words all translated into English by the term "love"—ἀγάπη, φιλία, and ἔρως and their corresponding verbal forms—perhaps sometimes exaggerated the differences among the three in meaning.[36] But some differences, at least in connotation, can be discerned in many contexts. "Agape" often refers to the kind of love experienced between husband and wife, in ways that might include the erotic but not necessarily. It also refers to the love of parents for their children and of children for their parents, the love of brothers for sisters and sisters for brothers. In the Bible it refers often to the love of God for human beings and of human beings for God. It seldom refers to erotic love. "Philia" may refer to any of those kinds of love, but quintessentially we may think of it as referring to love among friends. "Eros" also may have different meanings, but its most characteristic reference is to erotic love and sexual desire.

By far the word for love that occurs the most in the New Testament is of the *agap*-group, in noun and verbal forms mostly. The actual noun *philia* occurs, surprisingly, only once (James 4:4), referring to "friendship" with the world. But the verb form occurs often, though not nearly as often as ἀγάπη or ἀγαπάω. It refers to familial love (Matt 10:37), love between friends (John 11:3, 36), and God's love (John 5:20; 16:27). Words of the same word group, such as the verb φιλέω for "kiss," and the noun φίλημα, "kiss," also are used in the New Testament (verb "kiss": Matt 26:48 and par.; Luke 22:47; noun "kiss": Luke 7:45; 22:48; Rom 16:16; 1 Cor 16:20; 2 Cor 13:12; 1 Thess 5:26; 1 Pet 5:14; it is perhaps interesting that most of these are from Paul's letters and 1 Peter, a non-Pauline letter but much influenced by Pauline ideas and forms).

We must not make too much of a difference between "agape" and "philia." They can be used interchangeably. The two seem to be basically synonyms, at least in the Gospel of John. In John 11:3, 5, and 36, the love Jesus has for Mary, Martha, and Lazarus can be designated by agape or philia (in their verbal forms), apparently meaning exactly the same thing. The "beloved disciple" of the Fourth Gospel is usually called such by means of "agape," but

---

36. The classic, and very lengthy, study is Nygren, *Agape and Eros*. See now also Soble, ed., *Eros*, which provides, besides the contributions of Soble, an anthology of writings on the different meanings of "love" from ancient to modern, including an excerpt from Nygren. I agree with Johannes Hoff when he chides "Bishop Nygren's Lutheran attempt to expurgate the biblical concept of love from its Platonic-erotic connotations." Hoff points out that Nicholas of Cusa's use of "love" retains the aspects of erotic (eros, amor), friendship (philia, amicita), and charity (agape, dilectio caritas). See Hoff, *Analogical Turn*, 194. I argue below that we also should reintroduce the erotic to our faith and theology.

in John 20:2, it is "philia." Then there is the curious dialogue between Jesus and Peter at the end of the Gospel. Jesus asks Peter if he loves him more than the others (21:15; ἀγαπάω). Peter answers, "Yes, Lord, you know that I love you [φιλέω]." Jesus asks again, again using ἀγαπάω, and Peter answers again, again using φιλέω (21:16). Finally, Jesus asks a third time, this time using φιλέω, and Peter answers a third time, still using φιλέω (21:17).

What are we to make of this? Someone might be tempted to differentiate between the two terms. Perhaps Jesus began on the "higher plane" of agapic love, only to have Peter answer on the "lower plane" of mere friendship. According to such a reading, the third time Jesus asked, he realized he was not going to get Peter to answer with agapic love, and so he "settles" for friendship. I think such would be an imaginative interpretation but probably not very defensible by normal standards of modern exegesis. Since we've seen "agape" and "philia" used interchangeably in two other contexts of the Gospel of John, that is, with regard to the beloved disciple and Martha, Mary, and Lazarus, it is more likely that the author takes the two terms as simply synonyms.

In this book I have used "agape" as a technical term for the kind of love I see as *the* central Christian value, for theology and ethics alike. It does not include erotic love or romantic love, and it need not include the kind of affection or emotion we associate with friendship, though it may. "Agape" in my usage for this theology is an attitude of wishing and willing to do no harm to our neighbor. It is to wish for others the very best we can imagine. It is to treat others as we would be treated ourselves. It is to love God as the provider and sustainer of our lives and the universe. It is not an emotion but a way of living and a way of thinking and being. People often confuse "Christian love" with a *feeling,* but it is not. It is a way of thinking and living and willing.[37]

But when we turn to the New Testament for guidance about the realm of the erotic, it is notable that the very word most associated in the ancient Greek world with erotic love, "eros," does not occur even once.[38] That is testimony enough of the antierotic asceticism of most early Christianity and the authors who wrote the documents that make up our New Testament. They

---

37. "At its core, love is not a feeling at all, but an action, a way of being, in active care for others—for the integrity of their bodies and souls, as well as for their flourishing." Volf, *Against the Tide,* xi.

38. One would not expect to find in the New Testament one common Greek word for sexual pleasures: τὰ ἀφροδίσια; the corresponding verb is ἀφροδιάζω. Early Christians would avoid words so closely related to the name of the Greek goddess of the erotic.

simply did not consider sexual desire or erotic love something to be valued. If anything, they worked to suppress it or ignore it. Even those brief parts of the New Testament that talk about sex and marriage never connect either to erotic love explicitly.

But just as we must reject the inferiority of women and "feminized" men in the attitudes of many ancient Christians, so must we reject their sexual asceticism—if taught as any kind of "requirement" of all Christians or as validating the "higher virtue" of the ascetic over the "everyday" Christian. Yes, Paul was extremely suspicious of erotic desire (1 Cor 7). And the Gospels may be read historically as teaching sexual asceticism as well, though that is not nearly so obvious as is the case with Paul and could be debated. But we must reject the traditional Christian denigration of the natural human desires of sexuality. Only recently have churches come to reject as sinful the denigration of the "female" and the inequality of traditional gender roles. Yes, this is a new thing in churches. And it is also a good thing. Contemporary Christians rightly reject as sinful the church's traditional subordination of women and anything "feminine." We should rightly reject as well the ancient and premodern suspicion and fear of the erotic, sexuality, and sex.

How might we read scripture to discover new, *better* ways to be both Christian and sexual? We must keep in mind the thesis argued throughout this book that the meaning of the text is not a property existing in the text apart from human interpretation. In constructing proper Christian theological and ethical ideas about desire, sexuality, gender, and sexual activity, we cannot expect to "find" or "discover" the best Christian views just by "listening to the Bible." There is no "listening" involved apart from reading and interpreting. And as with every other theological and ethical topic, the rule for assessing the value of an interpretation of scripture is whether that interpretation promotes the love of God and the love of neighbor as well the proper understanding of our own biological and psychological realities. The love of self is as important as the love for others, precisely because a love for others divorced from a love of self leads to masochism and self-harm, and those are not Christian values either. How we construe our own erotic desires and actions in a Christian way must be informed by the centrality of love, of other and of self.

This book labels itself as "theology with the New Testament," but we would have perhaps more ready-to-hand texts for an affirmation of the good of erotic desire and sex were we to call on texts of the Old Testament. The texts of the Old Testament contain many references to sex, erotic desire, and even, in places, romance. This is to be expected precisely because these texts come out of an ancient Near Eastern context rather than the later Greco-Roman one, with its increasing valuation of asceticism. In fact, the most "ascetic" book of the Old Testament is no doubt Daniel, in which the hero carefully follows a strict dietary regimen and is rewarded for it in body and soul. It may be no coincidence that Daniel is almost certainly the latest book of the (Protestant) Old Testament, written as late as 164 BCE and therefore influenced by the Hellenism that by that time had pervaded at least the urban cultures of the eastern Mediterranean, including Judea and the rest of the region that came to be called Palestine. If we put aside Daniel, we find ready resources in much of the Old Testament for constructing a theology of sexuality.

The story of creation in Genesis itself is the obvious starting point. God creates the first human being as a sexual being. God creates human beings with built-in sexual desire and with built-in needs for companionship. God then commands them to "be fruitful and multiply" (Gen 1:28). A denial of our sexuality or passion is not entertained at the "beginning" of the scriptures.

The most obvious celebration of desire and sex in the Bible is the Song of Solomon or, as it names itself in its first verse, the Song of Songs. If we turn from the history of interpretation dominant among Christians and Jews that read the Song mostly as an allegory for the relationship between the church and Christ or Israel and God and return to how it was probably originally read as Near Eastern love poetry, we see it as an open celebration of sex and erotic love. It is also somewhat of a surprise to modern Christian readers, if they dare to read the text at all, that the relationship is not described as one between a married couple. This is a poem spoken at times by the man and at times by the woman. The man does, in a few instances, call his beloved his "bride" (4:8–12; 5:1), and we thus may imagine them as betrothed. But for most of the text there is no indication that they are already married. In fact, they obviously are not, since she has to go outside the home of her "mother" to seek him out (3:2), and he has to knock on her door to gain entry (5:2). They are presented simply as lovers.

Much of the language seems obviously to consist of euphemisms for the sex act—or at least can excusably be read as such (all translations of the Hebrew Bible NRSV unless otherwise noted):

> My beloved is mine and I am his;
>> he pastures his flock among the lilies. (2:16)
> I held him, and would not let him go
>> until I brought him into my mother's house,

> and into the chamber of her that conceived me. (3:4)
> Let my beloved come to his garden,
>> and eat its choicest fruits. (4:16)
> I come to my garden, my sister, my bride;
>> I gather my myrrh with my spice,
>> I eat my honeycomb with my honey,
>> I drink my wine with my milk.
> Eat, friends, and drink,
>> and be drunk with love. (5:1)
> My beloved thrust his hand into the opening,
>> and my inmost being yearned for him. (5:4)

The reclamation of the Song of Songs as a poetic celebration of erotic love and desire is one of the triumphs of modern historical criticism.[39] We can use it to construct better theologies and ethics of sexuality than those bequeathed to us by much Christian tradition.

There are other parts of the Old Testament that may welcome a more erotic interpretation than allowed by conservative, traditional Christianity. Many gay boys and men have not been able to ignore the erotic possibilities of the relationship between Jonathan and David. We're told more than once that Jonathan loved David more than his own life (1 Sam 18:1, 3). Jonathan saves David's life several times. Jonathan tells David, "Whatever you say, I will do for you" (20:4). Jonathan makes David swear an oath on his love for him (20:17; it is not clear whether this is Jonathan's love or David's). Jonathan and David kiss one another (20:41). After the deaths of Saul and Jonathan, David publishes a poem in their honor, calling them both beautiful. But it was only about Jonathan that David wrote those famous words, "Your love to me was wonderful, passing the love of women" (2 Sam 1:26). If David is referring here simply to "friendly love," he need not have brought up the "love of women." It is precisely because he is speaking of erotic love that the comparison with the female sex is relevant. There is nothing in the text itself that forbids us from interpreting this as an erotic, sexual relationship, and that should embolden gay Christians.[40]

---

39. An important impetus to the frankly sexual and erotic modern interpretation was given by Pope, *Song of Songs.* But see also Exum, *Song of Songs;* Bloch and Bloch, *Song of Songs;* Knust, *Unprotected Texts,* esp. 26–33.

40. Ackerman, *When Heroes Love;* Olyan, "'Surpassing'"; Knust, *Unprotected Texts,* 41–42.

We are not limited to the Old Testament, however, for inspiration for our gay male brothers in Christ. As I've shown elsewhere, the Gospel of John provides many scenes of male homoeroticism.[41] I know I was not the only closeted homosexual boy to take huge interest in the relationship between Jesus and "the disciple Jesus loved" in a special way. At his last supper Jesus has the young man lying practically on top of him (John 13:23–25). In the very last scene of the Gospel, Jesus seems reluctant to allow the young man even to die (21:20–22), reserving him perhaps in eternal youth for the time Jesus might return. In fact, in the older Jesus enamored with the apparently younger beloved disciple (think of Socrates and Alcibiades from Plato's *Symposium*) we have an example of the kind of autumn/spring erotic relationship known in gay circles as "dad/son."

And then there is Jesus's special relationship to Thomas. Though the risen Jesus will not allow a woman, Mary, to touch his resurrected body (the scene known in tradition and art by the Latin *noli me tangere*, "do not touch me!"), Jesus invites Thomas to penetrate his body (compare John 20:17 to 20:24 ff.). As I've pointed out before, there are several arguably erotic scenes in the Gospel of John, and most of them are homoerotic. Gay Christians, especially young, unsure, and closeted, should take inspiration from these scenes to learn how to act out their sexuality within their Christian faith and the church.

Given the proper freedom to interpret in creative, Christian ways, other texts of the New Testament may even challenge neat notions of sexuality or gender as always involving "male and female" in a dichotomous relationship. Following the lead of previous scholars, I have argued that Paul's words about there being "no male and female" in Christ (Gal 3:28) were, in their original contexts, a statement not about gender equality but about eschatological androgyny.[42] In the ancient world, including Paul's own assumptions, even in a body that was fully both male and female, masculinity would nonetheless still be superior to the femininity of that same body. Indeed, in some forms of ancient androgyny there was no difference between male and female because the female, characterized by absence, lack, imperfection, cold, would be "taken up into" the male, characterized by presence, possession, perfection, heat. Although Paul treated women in his churches with more respect and equality than they received in most ancient societies, Paul still assumed that "man" was the "head" of "woman" (1 Cor 11:3). Even

41. See Martin, *Sex and the Single Savior*, 99–100.
42. Ibid., 77–90.

eschatological androgyny did not, for Paul, include the equality of male and female; it just announced their reunion in one body.

Yet here, as in so many other cases, we may appropriate Paul's portrait of an androgynous body in Christ while rejecting his gender hierarchy. And thus we may imagine all of us as *not* neatly on one or the other side of a male/female dichotomy. We are all both male and female, or we are neither but some new, third "sex." Christians, once baptized into the body of Christ, are thereby created as a new gender. We are free to play at being women or men or something else of our imaginative invention. The Christian church should be the place where intersexed people, transgendered people, and people who reject either gender identity are the most welcome. The intersex, middlesex, or trans person is already well on the way to inhabiting the proper eschatological body of Christ: "no male and female" may mean "neither male nor female, but something else" or "both male and female."

In the same way, we may take as inspiration the Jesus movement and early Christian churches, which either rejected the traditional family and household or were adding to it experiments in wider, more diverse household structures, structures where slaves now were free and free men and women were now (formerly enslaved) "freed" people of Christ; where people who had been husbands and wives were now brothers and sisters; where the boundaries of either the nuclear or extended family were replaced by the mixed, diverse social structure of the church, a sojourner and alien social form while in "this world." The ancient church, as I will explore more fully in the next chapter, replaced the household with the *ekklêsia*, the "town meeting." I will argue further that we should use the ancient church and its replacement of the traditional family with its own eschatological body of Christ to criticize modern American ideology and idolatry of family and nation. The "family of God" does not just sit beside the traditional or modern family—either the heterosexual nuclear family or the extended family. It displaces those noneschatological forms of household, or at least it should.

We must use the strangeness of gender and sexuality we find in scripture to inspire our own imaginations to come up with new ways, Christian ways, to embody our sexual selves. And we must use the earliest Christian rejections of the traditional household to inspire our own Christian imaginations of our social structures. By rejecting the epistemological foundationalism of modernism, which insisted that we get our "meaning" from the Bible only via historical criticism, we may read scripture in new ways to reinject the erotic and the good sexual body into Christian doctrine and theology—without, however, reproducing the shame, guilt, and gender inequality surrounding sex and family so pervasive in Christian history.[43]

Sin

Our zeal to remove sex and sexual desire in themselves from the realm of sin should not lead us to dispense with the topic of sin altogether. Sin is a useful theological topic. Indeed, for Christians an indispensable one. Sin is obviously a big subject in the New Testament. In fact, most people would assume that Christianity and thus the Bible are obsessed with sin. And the New Testament's frequent use of words referring to sin or its connotations lend credence to that assumption. The most common word for "sin" in the New Testament, ἁμαρτία, occurs over 175 times. The related word for "sinner" (ἁμαρτωλός), 46 times. The verb form, ἁμαρτάνω, some 43 times. Add to these numbers the frequent occurrence of other terms that may be translated as "sin" or "transgression" (ἁμάρτημα, παράβασις, παραβάτης, παράπτωμα), and we can readily confirm that the fear and loathing of sin is a dominant theme of the New Testament.

But what is sin? In classical Greek the word often carries the connotation of a "mistake" rather than of some terribly guilt-inducing moral failure. Famously, it means more literally "to miss the mark," especially when thinking of casting a spear or shooting an arrow (many examples may be found in the *Iliad;* see, for example, 5.287, where it occurs in the form of epic dialect, ἤμβροτες). Something like this is the most common translation given in classical Greek lexicons. It can refer to failure in delivering a speech or just failing in whatever endeavor. I will return to this meaning later in an attempt to add nuance to our own understanding of mistakes and failures as well as of sin in our attempts to live well.

For much of the New Testament, "sin" occurs in the plural and refers simply to the misdeeds of individuals, the dominant meaning in Matthew, Mark, Luke–Acts, Hebrews, and James. They define certain acts as "sins" and speak of God through Christ as offering "forgiveness of sins." This fits the common way modern people think about the word "sin." The issue gets a bit more complicated in the Gospel of John and much more complicated, even confusing, in Paul's letters and the First Letter of John.

---

43. "To recognize desire and the erotic as ways in which the Divine is present as creativity in our lives is . . . a way of making theology come alive in human life." Henriksen, "The Erotic Self," 271.

In the Fourth Gospel the word occurs more often in the singular and seems to include a larger concept of sin as a force or even agent of the cosmos. John speaks of "the sin of the world" (1:29). A person can be a "slave of sin" (8:34). Or people may "have sin" (9:41; 15:22, 24). And there are degrees of sin. Jesus tells Pilate, "The one who handed me over to you is guilty of a greater sin" (19:11). "Sin" may refer in John, as it does more often in the other Gospels, to the misdeeds of individuals, but it has also in John taken on a larger, cosmic meaning and role.

This combination of meanings is more complex and even confusing in Paul's letters. Scholars of Paul have long debated the meaning of sin in Paul, some arguing that Paul is speaking merely of the misdeeds of particular human beings. Such scholars claim that when Paul's language sounds otherwise, as when he seems to speak of "Sin" as a cosmic force or even a personal agent, such statements should be understood as "mere personification." Other scholars, however, have countered that Paul says so many things about the power and deeds of Sin that we should take his language seriously. As Paul surely believed the devil or Satan was a real person of the cosmos, so, these scholars insist, he imagined Satan's partner or perhaps even consort was Sin. The word *hamartia* is feminine. Could Paul have imagined a relation between something like a demonic or angelic *person* or *force* that wielded great power in the world, with the name "Sin"?

The most compelling passages that sound like this are in Paul's Letter to the Romans. Paul says that "all are under the power of Sin" (Rom 3:9; I capitalize "Sin" to highlight the possibility of hypostatization). Chapter 6 of Romans repeatedly uses this kind of language. Paul writes, "So may Sin not rule in your mortal body resulting in obedience to its desires" (6:12); "Do not present your members to Sin as tools of injustice/unrighteousness" (6:13).[44] "For Sin will not lord it over you, for you are not under law, but under grace" (6:14). This is something like Paul saying to Sin, in a pop phrase current with young people, "You are not the boss of me!" Repeatedly, Paul invokes the notion of "slavery to Sin" as opposed to being a "slave of Christ" (6:16–23; 7:14; Gal 2:17).

Much of the debate about whether Paul is talking about "sins" or "Sin" focuses on his language in Romans 7. There, Paul says that Sin is something like a place we *used* to be in, perhaps as another body in horrible parallel

---

44. In many of these cases where Paul uses a word from the δικαιο-word-group, I use both terms "justice" and "righteousness" because the Greek most often includes connotations of both English words, though those two English terms mean different things in most modern English. We must keep both meanings in mind when reading Paul.

with the "body of Christ" (7:5). Paul says that Sin "grabbed an opportunity and produced evil desire in me" (7:8). Sin "worked death" in him, forcing him to obey its "law" (7:23). But Paul concludes with a triumph for Christ, Paul, and the Romans: "The law of the spirit of life in Christ Jesus has set you free from the law of Sin and death" (8:2). All this vivid imagery and language make it difficult to deny completely that Paul could have imagined Sin as an actual force or agent of the cosmos, one from whom or from which believers have been delivered and liberated.

The best study of sins or Sin now argues that we should retain both positions in our reading of Paul. In *The Emergence of Sin,* Matthew Croasmun draws from theories of emergence increasingly familiar to scientists, philosophers of science, and in theory and philosophy more generally.[45] As I mentioned above, emergence is the idea that complex systems are "things in themselves" that have properties (abilities to do things, characteristics) that arise from the properties of other entities that work on what we may think of as a "lower order" of ontology. Examples include the mind, which is made up of the combined activities of the different parts, even cells, of the brain. The mind is "the brain at work." Another popular example is a beehive, which collectively is able to do things that don't seem to be simply the abilities of the "sum of all the individual bees."

Croasmun argues that Paul's letters entertain the notion that "sin" refers to the particular misdeeds of individual human beings but also that the entire system of "sins" gives rise, at least in Paul's mind, to cosmic "Sin" that ends up being more than just the adding up of all the "sins" of individuals. Invoking another idea from emergence theory, Croasmun argues that "downward causation" also takes place in the activities of ancient sin/Sin.[46] The cosmic force or even agent "Sin" works by downward causation to affect human behavior to increase "sins."

In order to illustrate how this could work in the mind of an inhabitant of the ancient Mediterranean, Croasmun notes that "Roma" referred not only to the physical city of Rome but also to the goddess Roma, who was greater than the city or its component parts. But Roma was no doubt

---

45. Croasmun, "Body of Sin"; *Emergence of Sin.*

46. "Downward causation" refers to causal effect when an "emergent" entity that we might think of as possessing superior ontological status "causes" some "effect" in the entities "below," from which the superior emerged. These are all somewhat technical terms in the theory, but they are not difficult to understand. For example, scientists may argue that although the "mind" is the entity that "emerges" from the physical structures and activities of the brain, the mind may cause structural changes in the physical brain.

assumed to be, at least by most Romans and many others, an actual force and agent of the universe. The goddess Roma arose out of the reality of the city of Rome but then acted on the city and inhabitants of the Roman Empire in both frightening and beneficent ways. Croasmun goes so far as to suggest that Paul used the term "the body of Sin" in direct parallel with "the body of Christ." Human beings *must* inhabit one of those bodies, so they have to choose faith and behaviors that reinforced their roles as "members of the body of Christ" and *no longer* members of the body of Sin.

In fact, Paul often sounds as if he believed that those "in Christ" *could no longer sin*. Paul knows he has been accused of teaching believers that more sinning would lead to more grace. After all, he does say, "Where sin increased, grace abounded even more" (Rom 5:20). So he has to deny explicitly that he teaches, "Let us commit evil deeds in order that good will come." He quotes the phrase while condemning those people who accuse him of teaching it: "Their condemnation is justified!" (3:8). But how Paul gets out of the accusation is in itself rather confusing. Why doesn't he just say, as most Christians would, that, yes, we still sin. We're not perfect. As the bumper sticker says, "Christians aren't perfect, just forgiven." Paul could have admitted that believers continue to sin in spite of our best attempts to live up to the demands of the gospel. But he does not.

Instead, in Romans 6, Paul posits two realms that are mutually exclusive. On one side are Sin, death, the old self now crucified, slavery to Sin, wickedness, law, impurity, iniquity, and shame. On the other side are grace, Christ Jesus, God, resurrection, new life, freedom from sin, freedom from death, righteousness/justice, sanctification, and eternal life. Paul truly seems in Romans 6 simply to be insisting, all empirical evidence aside, that believers *cannot* sin because they *cannot* conceivably live "in Sin" and "in Christ" at the same time: "What are we saying? That we should remain in Sin so that grace may abound? Not at all! How could those of us who have died to Sin continue living in it?" (6:1–2); "Should we sin because we are no longer under law but under grace? Not at all! Don't you know that you are slaves to whomever you give yourself in obedience? You are slaves of the one you obey, whether of Sin leading to death, or of obedience leading to righteousness/justice" (6:15–16). Paul never admits that believers might continue to sin. It seems simply not to be an option in his imagination. As perplexing as this may be for modern Christians, Paul is radical in his either/or: you live in either the realm of Sin or the realm of Christ; there is no overlap. Therefore, Christians don't sin. I admit, this comes across more as an admonition than a proposition of empirical fact, and doubtless that is the best way to read

Romans 6. But it also gives us no reason to believe Paul admitted that believers could sin. That would be to twist Paul to meet *our* "common sense."

This stance also seems to be the position of the author of the Letter to the Hebrews, a letter not written by Paul but containing similarities to Pauline theology. Though this author clearly believes it is possible for believers to "fall away" and be lost (3:11), the writer also seems to believe that it is impossible for believers who have fallen again into sin to be forgiven (6:4–6). Christ was sacrificed, himself serving as both priest and victim, "once for all" for sins (9:12, 26): "We have been made holy by the offering of the body of Jesus Christ once for all. . . . one sacrifice for sins for all time" (10:10, 12). But once believers have been sanctified by Christ's sacrifice, they simply cannot intentionally sin thereafter and still be saved: "If we intentionally sin after receiving knowledge of the truth, there no longer remains any sacrifice for sins, just the expectation of judgment" (10:26–27).

Even more puzzling, perhaps, are statements in 1 John that appear initially to be simply self-contradictory. This author begins by insisting, "If we say we do not have sin, we deceive ourselves and the truth is not in us. If we confess our sins, the one who is faithful and just will forgive our sins and cleanse us from all injustice/unrighteousness. If we say we have not sinned, we make him a liar" (1 John 1:8–10). So far, so good: we Christians do not claim that we do not sin; we simply confess our sins and receive the grace of forgiveness. A bit later, the author says, "I write so you may not sin, but if anyone does sin, we have an advocate before the Father in Jesus Christ the Just One" (2:1).

Yet elsewhere in the letter the author seems to slide into a kind of either/or perfectionism resembling Romans 6: "Everyone who remains in [Christ] does not sin. And anyone who sins has not seen him or come to know him" (3:6). "The one who does justice/righteousness is just/righteous, as that one is just/righteous. The one who commits sin is from the devil, for the devil has sinned from the beginning. . . . Everyone who has been born of God does not commit sin, because his seed remains in him, and he is not able to sin because he has been born of God" (3:7–9). Is this just exaggeration for purposes of exhortation? Perhaps what sounded like a contradiction of this stance at the beginning of the letter was a reference to *prior* sin from which believers have been now delivered and for which they were forgiven. And perhaps the author assumed that believers *were* sinners, but now no longer. It is hard to get beyond the feeling that the author may not have sorted all these ideas out completely. But at least in parts of the New Testament, with

Paul, Hebrews, and 1 John, we see a kind of early Christianity toying with something like a perfectionist theology or anthropology.

This kind of theology of "perfectionism"—the idea that Christians simply *must not* sin—has recurred from time to time throughout Christian history, though usually in sects not part of the "mainstream" of the major churches. I believe we may read them as exhortation to avoid sinning as much as possible. But I also believe we must take other passages, for example, "Let the one who is without sin cast the first stone!" (John 8:7), as hindering any possible slide into Christian perfectionism. The fully Augustinian and Lutheran insistence that we are all simultaneously sinners and saved—*simul justus et peccator*—is certainly preferable. It is certainly more empirically verifiable. This is again a case in which we may explain how Christian doctrine is both false and yet may still be true *in a sense*.

Another Augustinian doctrine I believe should be reclaimed, again *in a sense*, is that of original sin. The classic inspiration from the New Testament for the later doctrine of original sin, which wasn't really developed until the writings of Irenaeus in the late second and early third centuries and then especially by Augustine in the fourth century, are in Paul's letters.[47] The most important passage is Rom 5:12–21: "Thus as sin came into the world through one human being and through sin death, so thus death came to all human beings because all sinned" (5:12); "For if, through the transgression of one, many died, by so much more the grace of God and the free gift in grace has abounded for the many through one human being, Jesus Christ" (15); "For if by the transgression of one death reigned through one, by much more those who receive the abundance of grace and the gift of righteousness will reign through the one Jesus Christ. Therefore as through the transgression of one condemnation [came] to all human beings, thus also through the righteousness of one [came the gift] to all human beings for the justification of life. For as through the disobedience of one human being the many were rendered sinners, thus also through the obedience of one the many were rendered justified" (17–19).[48]

47. For a brief but good narrative of the development, including references to ancient sources and modern scholarship, see "Original Sin" in *Oxford Dictionary of the Christian Church*; and Kelly, *Early Christian Doctrines*, 346–74; see also the more recent treatment, and from a post–Vatican II Roman Catholic perspective, in Brambilla, *Antropologia teologica*, 486–549.

48. As usual, this is my own translation, which I have rendered rather woodenly to highlight Paul's rhetoric of parallelism and balance. The words in brackets are added to

One can easily read these passages, as many Christians have over the centuries, as teaching that all human beings do in fact sin without also introducing any notion of *inherited* guilt or sin from Adam merely through birth. But Paul's carefully worded construction, repeated three times, of the Adam–Christ parallel may also be read to support a doctrine of original sin. After all, if we take Paul's language to mean that we gain justification through Christ without "earning it," as I think we must, we might as well take the similar language about sin as implying that we stand under guilt and condemnation without first individually earning that either. Just as we simply *are* justified by free gift and grace through Christ's faithfulness, so we simply *are* sinful by the fact that we are all children of Adam, that is, human beings. The same parallel occurs in 1 Cor 15:21–22: "For since death [is] through a human being, also resurrection of the dead [is] through a human being. For as in Adam all die, so also in Christ all will be made alive."

The doctrine of original sin may indeed be false if interpreted wrongly. For example, it is certainly not acceptable to imagine that unbaptized infants go to hell or some kind of limbo state due to their inheritance of sin through Adam. I also would want to argue against appropriating the Augustinian notion that connects the inheritance of sin to concupiscence or sexual desire or sex itself. Those ideas degrade the blessing of erotic desire and experience we should celebrate as God's creation and gift. In other words, this doctrine, *like all doctrines,* is false if used in ways not conducive to Christian health and love.

Yet I find the doctrine of original sin also useful in that it reminds us of something we already know deep down about ourselves and all human beings: we are seriously flawed from the first. To put it without using vulgar language that might make the point even better: if something is "screw-up-able," we human beings will screw it up. We find that in spite of our best intentions and efforts, we still make mistakes—really serious mistakes. In spite of our love for others, we *will* at some time hurt them, not to mention those we wouldn't count among our "loved ones." Even when we try our best, we cannot seem to avoid harming our world and our fellow human beings, at least much of the time. The doctrine of original sin keenly expresses a fundamental human truth: we cannot completely escape the fact of our fundamentally flawed nature.

The doctrine of original sin may also guard us against the kind of perfectionism that has plagued so much of Christianity, at least in some of its

---

make sense of the passage, which is somewhat elliptical in the Greek.

forms. This is captured in the fitting title of a book by James Alison: *The Joy of Being Wrong: Original Sin Through Easter Eyes*. When we harm ourselves, others, or our environment, we should not sink into despair or become paralyzed by guilt. Rather, we confess, ask for forgiveness, and try to do better next time. We know we will never be perfect, and we teach ourselves to be comfortable with that. Moreover, we remind ourselves constantly that other human beings will never be perfect either. In fact, they will do terrible things, as we have and will do. The answer for sin, original or otherwise, is honest admission and forgiveness. As Alison puts it, "The doctrine of original sin is not an accusation against humanity, and by keeping it alive the Church is not engaged in an accusation against humanity. What the Church is keeping alive is the possibility that even those who bear the tremendous burden of being 'right' may recognize their complicity with those who are not."[49]

Moreover, the doctrine of original sin is not an "explanation" for the existence of evil or sin. As I have argued already, Christianity does not provide any kind of "intellectual" or "philosophical" explanation for the existence in our world of evil and suffering. Neither does it provide any philosophically satisfying explanation for the existence of sin. As Alison says, in a statement about Roman Catholicism that I insist applies to Protestant faith also: "In the Catholic faith we have no available explanation for evil or sin as such, not because we may not have many insights into such things, but because we don't have an explanation of anything at all. We have a salvific revelation: what is revealed as something now operative is the mystery of God's plan of salvation for us."[50] That mystery is that we simply *are* imperfect sinners and *are* justified and saved by God's free gift through Jesus Christ.

These complex and even sometimes confusing statements about sin/ Sin—election, predestination, original sin—may indeed strike us modern Christians as "mythological," but perhaps we should reintroduce some good "mythology" to our theology. Even the category of "sin" sounds mythological. Yet if we are honest persons we must admit and confess that we are not perfect, that we make mistakes, and that some of those mistakes are serious enough to merit the label "sin." We do not always treat our loved ones, friends, fellow human beings, or especially strangers in loving ways. We are often selfish in ways that harm not only others but also ourselves. We are sometimes too hard on ourselves, leading to stress, frustration, even depression. We are certainly often too hard on others, making demands on people

49. Alison, *Joy*, 261.
50. Ibid., 262.

around us that are not warranted or are even wrong. As the Book of Common Prayer well puts it, "We have left undone those things which we ought to have done, and we have done those things which we ought not to have done."[51] These are our sins.

We also experience our universe, in spite of its wonder and beauty, as being terribly flawed. We have no decent explanation for why the earth, all its sentient beings, and innocent people suffer as much as they do. We worry about wars, torture, famines we seem to be able to do little or nothing about. We stand helpless before natural disasters as well as humanly engineered disasters. We are on the brink of worldwide ecocide for which we ourselves are largely responsible. This is the Sin we cannot seem totally to escape or avoid. The world, we recognize, just does not seem to be able to be what we feel it should be, and we are part of the problem. Sin arises from our sins, and cosmic Sin works on us also to threaten us with suffering, a death that may not be a "good death," self-harm, and harm of others, even those others we love. That is Sin. It is a Christian concept I believe is indispensable to our theology if we are to avoid deception and self-deception. The concept arises out of the mythological world of ancient Christianity, is preserved in scripture and tradition, and is nonetheless completely relevant to our postmodern Christian faith.

Yet we must not be too hard on ourselves—and certainly not on others. The more general classical meaning of *hamartia* as "missing the mark" could also be useful. When we fail, that does not mean we are completely "evil." And when others fail us, we should not exaggerate the harm. The failure does not mean people are "evil." It just means we and they are not perfect. It also means we are forgiven, and thus forgive others. A concept of sin allows us continually to love those we love but whom we fail as well as those we love but who regularly fail us.

Salvation

Christianity has always promised "salvation," though precisely what that means has varied and is not always clear or agreed upon. The Greek word most commonly used in the New Testament for "salvation," σωτηρία, did not usually mean the kind of "religious salvation" thought of by modern people when they hear the term. It had rather more ordinary or everyday

51. The prayer occurs in several contexts in the prayer book. Its first appearance is in Morning Prayer, Rite I, pp. 41–42.

meanings, such as "deliverance" or "preservation."[52] It could refer to a safe
return from a voyage, security, or safety in general. Quite often in classical
Greek it referred simply to health or general well-being. In fact, the word
occurs even as indicating a physician's fee.

Likewise, the Greek word for "savior," σωτήρ, usually referred not to
some divine being who accomplished a "salvation" from damnation for sins
but to anyone or anything that could deliver or rescue someone or something
from any kind of threat or harm. It could refer to something that healed or
prevented a disease. It was quite commonly used to indicate the emperor or
some other ruler praised for the public benefit of rescuing a people or pre-
serving the peace, clearly not here a reference to one who gives eschatological salvation or eternal life. The word is used for someone like a ruler, physician, or benefactor who delivers someone from death or danger or any other
manner of threat. It is actually rare, therefore, to find these words used in
non-Christian sources as a reference to afterlife, the salvation of one's "soul,"
or any other of the commonly imagined "religious" meanings familiar from
modern popular assumptions.

In the New Testament and other early Christian sources these Greek
words take on more specific meanings, though they still retain the broader,
more everyday meanings from classical and koine Greek. *Sôtêria* does, for
example, refer even in the New Testament to deliverance or rescue from
one's enemies (Luke 1:71). God, through Moses, liberates the Israelites from
Egyptian slavery, and *sôtêria* is the term used (Acts 7:25). The word refers
to "surviving" a shipwreck (Acts 27:34; see the NRSV). Similarly, the word
describes Noah's family's "surviving" the flood (Heb 11:7). Paul uses the
word when speaking of deliverance from hardship or release from prison
(Phil 1:19).

But much more often in the New Testament *sôtêria* refers to salvation
in the eschatological sense, providing the common "religious" meaning assumed by popular thought. Many examples could be given, including Rom
10:1, 10; 11:11; 13:11; John 4:22; Acts 4:12; Heb 1:14; 9:28; 1 Pet 1:5. Even here,
though, we should not forget the more everyday meanings of the word. For
instance, the translation "salvation of your souls" at 1 Pet 1:9 might be better
translated as the more ordinary "saving of your lives."

What, though, are people saved from? Or what is promised to them
as their salvation? Most of earliest Christianity, from the Jesus movement
well into the second century, was an apocalyptic Jewish sect, which is to say

52. These examples are gleaned simply from those given in LSJ, s.v.

that the salvation they expected was at least protection from eschatological divine anger, judgment, and punishment. So Paul talks about salvation from divine "wrath" (Rom 1:16; see 1:18 for the reference to wrath). He assures the Thessalonians that God has destined believers not for "wrath" but for the possession of "salvation" (5:9). Paul had begun the letter by praising the Thessalonians for having turned away from "images" to "become slaves to a living and true god, and to await his son from the heavens, whom he raised from the dead, Jesus, who is the one who delivers us from the wrath that is coming" (1:10). That the word for "deliver" here is ῥύομαι demonstrates that in this case it is a synonym for salvation (σωτηρία). The same complex of apocalyptic expectation is at work when salvation is depicted as the "forgiveness of sins" (Acts 13:26; see 13:37).

As for what "salvation" grants, early Christians were regularly promised "glory" (1 Thess 2:13; 2 Tim 2:10; Heb 2:10). We should remember, in our attempt to "defamiliarize" overly "theological" connotations of so much early Christian language, for example, seeing σωτηρία as meaning "health" and "safety" as well as "religious salvation," that the Greek word normally translated as "glory" in the New Testament, δόξα, more often would have been heard as something like "fame" in classical and koine Greek. Early converts were assured not only that they would "shine," another connotation of δόξα, and gain power at the eschaton but also that they would be "famous."

Part of the salvation promised to converts was "eternal life" (Acts 13:47). The same thing is probably meant by the use of the term in Hebrews: "eternal salvation" (Heb 5:9). Living and reigning with Jesus Christ in the hereafter was at least one thing early Christians seem to have expected. But at least in one case Paul seems to have preached his version of the gospel without even mentioning any kind of afterlife at all. Although he had promised the Thessalonian gentiles that they would be saved from "the wrath that is coming" (1 Thess 1:10), he must not have told them about what kind of afterlife existence they could expect. Thus, after Paul's departure and after at least a few of their number had died, they bemoan their situation, as they understood it, because they assumed their departed loved ones would completely miss out on the benefits promised by Paul. Those departed, after all, were now no longer in danger of the "wrath that is coming." So what benefit did they derive from the hardships that had followed their acceptance of Paul's gospel about Jesus the Jewish Messiah?[53]

---

53. For the hardships, see 1 Thess 2:14; 3:3–4.

Thus Paul has to write 1 Thessalonians in order to inform them, among other things, about the resurrection of the body. He assures them not only that their dead loved ones would not miss out on the party, so to speak. Those fellow believers, though dead, would be raised; they would even *precede* any living believers, who then would follow the raised dead to "meet the Lord in the air" (5:13–17). As remarkable as it seems to us now, Paul's initial missionary message promised deliverance from divine "wrath" but did not necessarily include information about any possible afterlife. Yet this should not really surprise us if we remember that Greek and Roman myths and speculations about the gods and divine matters almost never led anyone to expect immortality or deliverance from death by their gods. Thus even in Paul's initial message "salvation" meant something very much of this earth, not emphasizing, at least in Thessalonica and at the beginning, salvation from death or promise of an afterlife.

A few passages of the New Testament may pose puzzles surrounding "salvation." In spite of our normal expectations that salvation is something people are granted by God and granted through the work of Jesus Christ, one passage mentions salvation as something believers may "grow into." The author of the First Letter of Peter tells his readers they should long for "pure, spiritual milk," by means of which they "may grow into salvation" (2:2; NRSV). For the New Testament this is an unusual way of speaking of salvation. I might also mention language in Revelation which depicts people ascribing "salvation and glory and power" to God (19:1; see also 7:10). How could we possibly offer "salvation" to God? From what could God possibly be saved? The more likely way to read these references is as saying that salvation, like glory and power, belongs to God. These benefits are God's to give. It is, though, a rather unusual way, within the New Testament, to speak of salvation.

Before leaving this discussion of the words for salvation in the New Testament, I want to note a special, ancient meaning of the Greek word for savior, σωτήρ. I mentioned above that in normal Greek it is often associated with the emperor or other ruler. In fact, it was a common piece of imperial ideology and propaganda to advertise, in literature, poetry, inscriptions, and statuary, Caesar as the "Savior of the World."[54] Thus when John 4:42 has the Samaritan villagers designate Jesus "the Savior of the World," an ancient hearer would automatically imagine Jesus as at least a new emperor of the

---

54. For a good recent study of the imperial cult, its ideology and propaganda, and similar language in early Christianity, see Peppard, *Son of God*.

entire *oikoumene,* the whole inhabited earth. This could no doubt have been taken also as a challenge to the Roman emperor. What is being promised is the deliverance of everything normally thought to be provided by Caesar, certainly peace and "security," another meaning of σωτηρία, but also worldly and heavenly benefits of many kinds.

What, though, may we Christians today take from this admittedly brief and selective survey of salvation in the New Testament? I think one tack we must take is to steer away from traditional, premodern but pervasive ideas about God consigning all nonbelievers to eternal, conscious torture and punishment in some version of hell. It is understandable that premodern societies would assume the existence of such a place, and they would have no difficulty in picturing God, just as they would any human ruler they could imagine, as a jealous, demanding monarch who would torture those he deemed worthy of it and leave "sinners" in an eternal prison. The more grotesque notions of hell and divine or demonic torturers would have been natural within their societies and cultures precisely because they lived with such authorities, institutions, and practices as part of their everyday lives. It is hard for many of us modern people to imagine the kinds of violence and the ubiquity of pain and death experienced by almost all premodern peoples.

Even if our own world is far too full of pain, torture, and evils inflicted on human beings by other human beings, not to mention the sufferings that simply accompany natural existence, we must trust our hopes and desires to move beyond cultures of violence and torture and toward building societies of peace and human dignity. We should quite self-consciously turn away from and leave behind the ancient cultures of torture, execution, and constant violence. Therefore, we must also train our theological imaginations to reject traditional ideas of eternal punishment as part of the will of God. Our God must be the creator and sustainer of love, and it is impossible to construct a proper Christian imagination of a God of eternal love while retaining the image of God as the creator and sustainer of eternal pain and torture.

In this, as in all Christian theology, there may be times when we wish for some kind of punishment for people who in this life have inflicted so much pain and harm on others and yet seem to have suffered nothing for it. We may say, for instance, that we don't really "believe in" hell and yet still believe that corrupt, stubborn rulers who have caused astonishing suffering through wars, poverty, incarceration, and torture but who died peacefully in their own beds—well, those people must end up in some kind of hell or there is no justice in the world. Therefore I, like, I assume, many other Christians, have sometimes said I did not believe in hell, but I sure hope certain human beings I can think of are punished after death. I may not believe in hell, but I believe Hitler and Stalin (and a few American presidents!) should go to hell.

In the end, though, we should move away from connecting God to torture and hell and imagine God rather as the savior, not the torturer. And what are we saved from? Basically, from everything that causes us, all human beings, and nature itself destruction, pain, suffering, and distress. In "The Great Litany" many Christians pray for deliverance from all sorts of evil and suffering.[55] We cannot assume we will be saved from all pain and suffering, but we can pray for it. We pray that God will "strengthen" those "who suffer in mind, body, and spirit" and that God will "comfort . . . those who are failing and infirm" (BCP, 151). Neither will we be saved from death. But we can be saved from the fear and dread of death. In the Book of Common Prayer we do not pray that we be spared death entirely but that we may experience a good death: "That we may end our lives in faith and hope, without suffering and without reproach" (BCP, 385). We pray that God will "give to the departed eternal rest" (387), that God's "will for them may be fulfilled" (389).

This may be a good place to address common ideas that "heaven" or eternal life is just the extension into infinity of time as we experience it. Many of us long ago questioned the traditional idea that a good afterlife is just "time going on forever." I find the idea of simply "existing" forever to be dreadful. Won't we all get bored with the same old thing going on forever? But the proper Christian understanding of an eternal afterlife in God does not include enduring "time." We must rather understand that we will exit "time," just as God has never existed in time. God's eternity is not a line but a point, and a point of infinite presence.[56] There is no before or after in God's essence but the eternal now. Thus no one could possibly get "bored" in an eternal present in God. Resting in peace in eternal life should be imagined as shifting from constant "becoming" to simply "being" in constant presence. It is, though we can't completely conceive it, coming to rest and peace in God's eternal presence.

More important than thinking of salvation as an escape from death or hell or even as an eternal afterlife is the idea that we are saved *in the present*

55. See the Book of Common Prayer, 148–55.

56. As Johannes Hoff notes, here quoting Nicholas of Cusa, De aequalitate, "Time is not eternity; it is only a 'likeness of eternity' (*esse aeternitatis similitudinem*)." Hoff, *Analogical Turn*, 124.

from despair and meaninglessness. We must remind ourselves that we are saved, most of the time, from ourselves. We are saved when we can rest from worrying, anxiety, and depression. Immersing ourselves in the gospel with its steady liturgies and assurances, we gradually may learn to live lives of meaning, not of despair. Salvation is God teaching us, step by step, to trust God and to be at home in the imagined good universe of God's will and creation. Salvation is being at peace and harmony with the good universe—and hoping and praying for peace and deliverance from the evils and sufferings we do in fact experience in the universe as we know it today. Salvation is the habitus of believing and living in the promise Julian of Norwich repeated from her divine visions: "All shall be well, all shall be well, all manner of all thing shall be well."[57]

As we attempt to train ourselves to relax in the salvation promised by God, another controversial traditional doctrine, like the doctrine of original sin discussed above, may also be redeemed from the dismissal it so frequently gets from modern Christians: the doctrine of predestination or election. Like the doctrine of original sin, and for very similar reasons, the doctrine of predestination—the claim that God preordained or predestined people to be saved long before they could make their own decision or do anything to gain salvation—seems to modern people to be offensive. How is it "fair" that God "chose" some people or even all people? Doesn't that offend against any notion of free will? The modern investment in individualism and individual freedom is the main motivation for modern Christians to ignore or reject previous beliefs about predestination for salvation. But again, as I argue in many contexts, it is the modernist ideology of individualism that needs more critical examination.

It is not difficult to demonstrate that the doctrine of election or predestination is "biblical." Some kind of notion of election occurs throughout the Bible. And it is hardly surprising that it can be found in the New Testament. Early Christian writers took the concept from the well-known idea in the Old Testament that God had "chosen" the people of Israel to be his "elect" nation. Passages in the New Testament refer to Israel as God's elect people (Acts 13:17, for example). Thus early Christians who saw themselves as chosen by God were building on the prior idea that Israel, or sometimes a "remnant" within Israel, constituted a chosen people.

The theme is pervasive in the New Testament also, being found in each of the four Gospels as well as in Acts, the letters of Paul, James, Peter, John,

57. See the short, devotional biography of Julian: Frykholm, *Julian*, 55, 108.

and Revelation.[58] Paul often refers to believers as having been chosen by God (Rom 9:11; 11:5, 6, 28; 1 Thess 1:4), a practice followed by the author of 2 Peter, who seems to have used Paul's letters as a model (2 Pet 1:10). Authors claim that God chose specific classes of people: Paul insists that God chose the foolish, weak, low, and despised over the wise, powerful, strong, or highborn (1 Cor 1:27–28). James says that God chose the poor over the rich (2:5). The theme pervades the Bible, including the New Testament.

Particular passages elaborate on it. One of the most astonishing is Rom 9–11. As I explained in the introduction above, Romans should no longer be read simply as an abstract argument for the Protestant doctrine of justification by grace through faith alone apart from all human works. I believe it may indeed be taken that way, but I think we should also recognize that in its original context Paul's argument in Romans had a more specific meaning. Paul wrote to a predominantly gentile church in Rome in order to argue, at least in part, that gentile believers in Rome should not think they had displaced Jews or Israel in God's plan for the salvation of the world. Paul does spend much of the letter arguing that gentiles need not keep the Jewish Torah in order to be justified. They are justified by faith, just as Abraham was. Yet Paul wants them still to respect their fellow believers who are Jews and also to respect and honor the heritage that is Israel.

Thus in chapter 9 Paul addresses directly the relationship of "Israel" to those gentiles who have become believers in the Messiah of Israel. He admits that it is something of a mystery, but God does, after all, choose whom he will "love" and whom he will "hate." Before Jacob and Esau were even born God had chosen Jacob over Esau, before either had any opportunity to do good or evil: "so that the plan of God according to election might be sustained, not from works but from calling" (9:11–12). Being chosen by God happens "not through willing, nor through running, but through God practicing mercy" (9:16). Each of these three activities is described by means of a participle formed from a verb: willing, running, "mercying." These refer to the activities of God and indicate that having mercy, dispensing mercy, is a continually ongoing activity of God. Paul cites a second example in the way God chose Pharaoh, but only to defeat him in favor of Moses and the Israelites: "Therefore, on whom he wills, he has mercy, and on whom he wills, he hardens" (9:18). I translate the sentence woodenly in

---

58. The word ἐκλεκτός as referring to people, or particularly believers in Christ, as God's elect occurs many times in Matthew and Mark, and see also, among other examples, Rom 8:33; 16:13; Col 3:12; 2 Tim 2:10; Tit 1:1; several times in 1 Peter; Rev 17:14.

order to highlight its parallelism and its stark contrast of the chosen and the unchosen.

In the next section, Paul addresses expected objections. How can God find fault if he is the one who preordained the nature of what he has made? Paul gives no really satisfactory answer, except to say that God's prerogative is God's prerogative: as the creator, God has the right to create as he wishes. The conclusion, in chapter 11, is that the believing gentiles may take no credit for their own faith. They believe because God chose them. And there is no reason to believe that God has given up on those he *originally* chose, Israel. At least some of them are still "the elect" (11:7). Those who rejected Jesus show by that action simply that they were "hardened" because of a larger plan of God: the mission of the gospel to the gentiles. Some Jews were "broken off" in order to allow the "grafting in" of gentile believers. But if God broke them off, he can very well graft them in again. Paul believes, in spite of the unbelief of some of his fellow Jews, that "the gifts and calling of God are irreversible" (11:29), so he holds out hope that eventually "all Israel will be saved" (11:26).

Rom 9–11 offer the most explicit and sustained argument for election and predestination. But the topic is rehearsed elsewhere. Eph 1:4 claims that God "chose us before the foundation of the world." God "predestined [προορίζω] us for adoption" (1:5). The same Greek word occurs in 1:11: we have been "predestined" to receive an inheritance from God, purely by means of his will and plans. Even the good works we may do, we can take no credit for; those good works were themselves already "prepared beforehand" (προετοιμάζω) by God, a phrase that is echoed in the Book of Common Prayer: we pray that we may "do all such good works as thou hast prepared for us to walk in" (339). Many scholars believe that the author of Ephesians (not Paul, according to this theory) used Colossians as a model for his own letter. If so, this author added the emphasis on election and predestination; we don't find that same theme in Colossians. But we can say that by adding it to his appropriation of Colossians, the author of Ephesians was also bringing at least that part of his message closer to Paul's.

Another letter that emphasizes election is 1 Peter. The letter is addressed to "the chosen [or elect] resident aliens" (1:1). These are former gentile worshippers of idols (1:14, 18, 21; 2:1, 9–11, 25; 4:3), who have been chosen "according to the foreknowledge of God the father" (1:2; the NRSV translates by using instead of "foreknowledge" the phrase "chosen and destined"). Like Paul, this author teaches that God chose not only the elect but also those who do *not* believe: those who rejected Christ, the cornerstone, stumbled by disobeying the word, "unto which [end] they were appointed" (2:8; NRSV: "as they were destined to do"). The recipients of the letter, on the other hand, are an "elected nation" (2:9). Thus the author of 1 Peter takes (from Paul?) the doctrine of election and predestation and adds to it his own designation of gentile believers as "resident aliens."[59]

How do we, though, make sense of the doctrine of election or predestination? In fact, this is an excellent example of how any Christian doctrine may be both false and true. It is false if taken to mean we have no freedom to choose and act for ourselves. Even if we may doubt the kind of radical individualism and freedom of will promoted by much of modernism, we need not doubt that we can and do make choices. We may celebrate the freedoms we do have, even if we cannot completely understand what "free will" truly is. As I have argued, we need not expect Christianity to be a philosophy, providing intellectual answers to all sorts of intellectual questions. Simply from a pragmatic perspective, we may act and think as if we do have some kind of freedom.

The doctrine of election is false if it leads to pride. We may not look down on nonbelievers because we now "know" they were not "chosen," and we were. The doctrine of predestination, certainly in Paul and probably in later theologians also, was intended to work against pride and for humility: you did not earn your justification, you can take no credit even for your faith, you will be saved due to absolutely nothing you did or can do. You were chosen in spite of anything you did or can do. Ironically, a doctrine that seems to have been intended to help Christians live in humility but in the confidence of their salvation sometimes in history has led Christians to *doubt* their salvation. Some Puritans, apparently, were caught up in guilt and anxiety. "Am I *really* one of the elect? How can I know for sure?" Others were sometimes caught up in pride: "At least *I* am one of the elect!" If the doctrine of predestination leads us to look down on others, take pride in ourselves, or think we have confidence about "who is going to hell," it is a false doctrine indeed.

But I believe, especially given the individualism and capitalist ideology of modernism, which believes that those who have deserve what they have, they have earned it, election and predestination can do good work for our theology and faith. The doctrine teaches that faith is not an accomplishment. Certainly, we may accept that we are not justified by "works," whether works

59. For one treatment of the doctrine of predestination, including a history of it in the church, see Brambilla, *Antropologia teologica*, 157–254.

of the Torah, as Paul certainly argued, or works of any sort, as the Protestant reformers emphasized. But predestination insists that we are not justified even by faith if that faith is at all considered by us "our accomplishment."

By meditating on predestination, we find ourselves refusing to condemn anyone to hell. That simply is not our business, and it is something God tells us we may know nothing about. Rather, predestination teaches us humility, not pride. Interpreted rightly, election and predestination are designed to teach us to rest in the free gift of grace: if we find we still, in spite of all evidence to the contrary, have faith, we may not take credit for it. That also is a gift of God for which we may claim no merit or credit.

Resurrection

As I began this chapter by emphasizing our human experience as created, constructed selves and as bodies, so it is appropriate that I end it by addressing our salvation as the resurrection of the body. Actually, the most common way of referring to the resurrection in the New Testament is not explicitly of "the body" but as the resurrection "from the dead" (often ἐκ νεκρῶν). But we should assume that most early Christians, or at least those represented by our texts of the New Testament, assumed the resurrection of the *body*. As we saw in the chapter on Jesus and his resurrection, Paul took that to be a pneumatic body, not a body of flesh and blood, which is how he envisioned the resurrection of Jesus and thus also of believers.[60]

That other early Christians believed in the resurrection of the *flesh* is clear from how they go out of their way to portray the resurrected body of Jesus to be one of flesh (and bone!: see Luke 24:39–43; see also John 20:27). But nowhere in the New Testament do authors speak of a human "resurrection of the flesh." In fact, a resurrection of νεκροί would be heard to imply "corpses," νεκροί being a common term for dead people. It would have emphasized the "physicalness" of the resurrection—and perhaps how disgust-

60. Two passages exist that may suggest that the authors of Hebrews and 1 Peter may have shared Paul's view that the resurrected body is one of pneuma but not flesh. Heb 5:7 speaks of Jesus's existence previously "in the days of his flesh." Does this imply that Jesus, after his resurrection, *no longer* exists as "flesh"? 1 Pet 3:18 says that Jesus was "put to death in the flesh but made alive in the pneuma"; and later speaks of how human beings will be "judged in the flesh" but "live in the pneuma" (4:6). Both statements would make perfect sense in Paul's anthropology, by which current human existence is "in the flesh," but any future existence after a resurrection would be not "in flesh" but "in pneuma," a pneumatic body. This is not a far stretch exegetically precisely because both Hebrews and 1 Peter show theological affinities with Paul.

ing it would sound to many people. Who wants dead bodies to start coming to life? No doubt when many Greeks and Romans heard Christians talk about "resurrection of the dead," they heard it as "the rising of zombies." That was probably one reason educated Greeks and Romans so disdained any promise of the "resurrection of the body." In any case, it was not until the second century, with the likes of writers such as Tertullian, that some Christians began to insist that the proper, orthodox belief was in the resurrection of the "flesh."

But how do we—indeed, can we?—believe in it? Paul's theology certainly gives us an out so that we need not confess the resurrection of our very flesh-and-blood bodies in all their molecular materiality. We don't really know how to understand exactly what Paul thought a "pneumatic body" is. As I suggested in the chapter on Jesus, we might imagine that Paul's pneuma was something like the way we think of pure energy or oxygen or whatever might be the most rarified, supercharged, powerful substance we can imagine in our world. Can we imagine a universe in which we could be alive in a body of something like that? Something like a body of pure DNA or a body of pure information?[61]

We must remind ourselves that the "kingdom of God" promised in passages of the New Testament is not simply "this cosmos" continuing or just started over again. Rather, even though ancient Christians (and Jews who believed in such an eschatological kingdom) assumed the kingdom of God would undoubtedly be a physical kingdom, they mostly seemed to believe it would be a "new" world, recreated to be completely superior to "this" world. As far as the New Testament goes, they weren't looking for a reformation of "this cosmos" but for the miraculous replacement—or, better put, transformation—of this cosmos into a very different "new heaven and new earth."

How is it more unbelievable that God might create a new universe than to believe that God created this one? It seems to me completely incredible, on its face, to confess that God made this universe, but I still find myself willing to confess it on a regular basis. And if God could make *this* one, why could God not make *another* one? And if God could have made *this* body, why could God not make a *new* body for me? In other words, though I cannot get my mind around any distinct notion of a resurrection of the body,

---

61. Note how James Gleick plays with ideas that information is neither matter nor energy, but still "information is physical": *Information*, 241, 279. Tegmark's *Our Mathematical Universe* is an argument that our universe *is* a "mathematical structure."

neither can I get my mind around the notion of God creating the universe, including my body, out of nothing. There is no belief more farfetched, it seems to me, than to believe in God in the first place and that God created and continues to create the universe. The idea that God could do it again is certainly not more unbelievable than that.

After all, some scientists, and quite reputable ones at that, lately have been asking us to believe in the possible existence of other universes, even "multiverses," and perhaps even an infinity of universes.[62] If physicists, many of whom do not "believe in God," can entertain completely inscrutable and unbelievable ideas about other universes that may or may not work by the "laws of nature" or the same regularities ours operates by, why would it seem *more* unbelievable that some entity we can't grasp or understand—let's just call it god—is responsible for this one and for all the other possible ones?

The philosopher of religion Nancey Murphy suggests that any eschatological "nature" that may exist in the future won't be the same as "our" nature now. We can't know much of anything about the nature of any future resurrection because we know nothing about the "nature" of "nature" in an eschatological world: "We now know a great deal about how natural processes subserve human psychic life. While we can know that, in some manner, glorified bodies support the same (or enhanced) psychic and social capacities, we know that we cannot know *how* this will be in the future. This is because our knowledge of future physical processes is based on projections using current laws of nature. We also know, as argued above, that the laws of nature in the eschaton (whatever 'nature' would then designate) cannot be the same as we have now."[63] Whereas I myself demur at using language about "laws of nature" because I don't think they can be proven to exist and because the notion seems not to be scientifically necessary or philosophically defensible, I do think Murphy has a point: we may confess a belief in a new world and new bodies without having any idea whatsoever about the actual nature of either.[64]

It seems to me that one can very well be open to a belief in some kind of afterlife for human beings without having to put any kind of specificity on it at all. What seems to me to be important in order to remain faithful to

---

62. Again, there are several examples, but one recent book suggesting such things is Tegmark, *Our Mathematical Universe*.

63. Murphy, "Resurrection Body," 217; see also Murphy, *Bodies and Souls*.

64. For a critique of "laws of nature," see the arguments advanced by the philosopher of science Van Fraassen, *Laws and Symmetry*; for fuller treatment of how Fraassen imagines "nonfoundationalist" science, see his *Empirical Stance*.

traditional, orthodox Christianity is to have faith that whatever will exist for me or my loved ones must have some kind of continuity with our beingness now, but also to be *discontinuous enough* that whatever that future body is, it is freed from the failings, suffering, sin, and evils we experience in *these* bodies. As Timothy Gorginge puts it (with some quotations of Barth), "We cannot establish the 'how' of the resurrection. It takes place in 'sacred incomprehensibility.' The proper response to it is confession. 'We cannot try to go "behind" it, either behind the fact that it is given, or behind the way in which it is legitimate and possible for us to act in correspondence to this fact.' Our response to the resurrection is to 'act in correspondence with this fact.'"[65] When confessing faith in the resurrection of the body, ultimately what I'm saying, I think, is that "all will be well, and all manner of thing will be well."

Indeed, I believe the doctrine of the resurrection of the body is more important for what work it does for us now than for what information it may provide for the future. The resurrection of the body affirms, again, as much of this chapter has insisted, that we are bodies, we are physical, we are finite, we are bundles of desires, emotions, needs, and wants, and we should not seek to escape that but to learn the habitus of happiness in embodiment. We affirm that our bodies are good and even beautiful, even when we don't feel beautiful. We affirm the goodness of sex, eating, drinking, sleeping, working, and all the other things God uses to bless us. We share so much, almost everything, with the other embodied creatures of the earth, and we owe them as much. We share existence with all of nature and depend on the health of the earth for our existence and happiness—which is just one more reason we must be environmentalists.

Though Neil Gillman is speaking from the perspective of his *Jewish* faith, I quote his statements as relevant also for why the resurrection of the body—as opposed to the immortality of the soul—is important for Christian teaching about our present and not only our future. Calling the doctrine "indispensable," he continues, "If my body inserts me into history and society, then the affirmation of bodily resurrection is also an affirmation of history and society. If my bodily existence is insignificant, then so are history and society. To affirm that God has the power to reconstitute me in my bodily existence is to affirm that God also cares deeply about history and society."[66] Again, we're back to one of the main themes of this chapter: the particularity

65. Gorringe, *Karl Barth*, 237; *Church Dogmatics* IV/2, p. 123.
66. Gillman, *Death*, 262.

of our natures as social bodies and physical bodies and therefore historical bodies. Our embeddedness in history and society is not a flaw; it is not
something from which we should ask "religion" to save us. It is not what we
should attempt to escape or forget in meditation or by ignoring. It is something we must learn to be our habitus and for which we give thanks.

Becoming God

As much as I have been insisting that we must celebrate our humanness and
embodiedness, I want again to change tack radically and resuscitate another
old Christian doctrine, though one held in suspicion by much of Protestantism: human deification, theosis, the hope that we may indeed somehow and
in some way become truly one with God, not by becoming God—much less
by becoming "other gods" alongside God—but by being taken up into God.
The doctrine has been an important one to some branches of Christianity
since antiquity, more popular typically in Eastern Orthodox churches and
theology than in the West. Yet it has been there, and it may constitute one
small attempt at reconciliation for us Christians in Western traditions to
reclaim it.

The idea that human beings can conceivably unite with the highest divinity comes from, initially, the influence of Platonism on Christian theology
in late antiquity. But we need not fear that the original impulse for the late
ancient doctrine of human deification and radical unity with God took its inspiration from philosophy. And we may read the New Testament to support
it. Paul insists that we currently await "adoption" as God's children. How can
we really be part of his family if we do not share his nature? Col 3:3, moving
beyond the "reserved eschatology" found in those letters Paul actually wrote,
says, "[Our] lives are hidden with Christ in God." The authors of Ephesians
and Colossians move the timeline forward, insisting that believers *already*
enjoy at least some of the fundamental blessings and rewards Paul seemed to
reserve for the future.[67] The adoption of believers into God's intimate family
and the joining of believers through the Holy Spirit to God's very person lead
later theologians and mystics to meditate on whether or not believers may
actually experience some kind of "becoming God." Their answer is yes.

Basil of Caesarea believes that the aspiration of Christians will be "becoming like God, and, the highest of desires, becoming God."[68] Gregory of

---

67. These are points about Ephesians and Colossians commonly acknowledged by
scholars, but for one summary of the position, see Martin, *New Testament*, 247–60.
68. *On the Holy Spirit* 9.23 (p. 44). See also the discussion in Zizioulas, *Being*, 49–50.

Naziansus says that Christ was born as a human being "so that we might be made divine just as he was made human."[69] Augustine voiced what was by his time a common way of putting it: "God was made human that human beings might be made divine."[70] Church fathers were quick to point out that we should not aspire to be divine in precisely the way Christ, the father, and the spirit are divine. They regularly insist, as Cyril of Alexandria puts it, that Jesus is God "by nature," and believers "by grace" and "adoption."[71] John Calvin will echo the distinction: the sonship of Jesus is his "by nature." But Jesus is the *only begotten*. Our partaking in God's nature is merely "by adoption" (*Institutes*, 2.14.5–6).

If we take these qualifications to heart, differentiating any divinity we may be granted by grace from the essential divinity of the persons of the trinity, we may recover a sense of ultimate, eschatological unity with God, as has been attempted by recent, even Protestant, theologians. Eugene Rogers, for instance, provides several qualifications of what deification means for human beings; for example, we don't create worlds that we then rule. He explains how, though, the doctrine may be interpreted as being true and useful: "Deification does not mean the erasure of the boundary of the Creator and the creature; it means the crossing of that boundary. . . . Deification does not mean that human persons become trinitarian persons. They become deified human persons, not persons of deity."[72] Kathryn Tanner also notes the difference between any divinity Christians may hope for and the essential divinity of God: "Divinity is an ingredient of our nature through external impartation and not because it is what human nature essentially is."[73] The doctrine of human deification is often explained now, as it was among the church fathers, by connecting deification with the incarnation of Jesus. Eric L. Mascall says, "The Incarnation is not to be thought of as the compression of the divine Word within the limits of human nature but as the exaltation of human nature to the level of Godhead by its union with the Person of the divine Word."[74]

---

69. *Oration* 29.19. See Beeley, *Unity,* 184–85, for this quotation and discussion.

70. Sermon 128, "In natali Domini," no. 12, *Patrologia Latina* 39:1997. This translation quoted from Rogers, Jr., *After the Spirit,* 48.

71. *St Cyril of Alexandria on the Unity of Christ,*, esp. 35. Greek: *Quod Unus Sit Christus,* PG 75:1253–1361; Pusey, *Works of S. Cyril,* 7.334–424; de Durand, *Deux Dialogues Christologiques.*

72. Rogers, *After the Spirit,* 47.

73. Tanner, *Christ the Key,* 65; citing Gregory of Nyssa, "On the Soul and the Resurrection," 5.440.

74. Mascall, *Christ,* 48.

This doctrine, like every one, as I have been insisting, may be true, but it is necessarily false *in some sense.* As ancient and modern theologians have insisted, we are not gods alongside God. None such exist. And we are not divine in our natural existence or essential being. In fact, we have being, essence, or existence only because we are sustained by God. The doctrine is false if taken to render us proud or superior to other creatures or to our fellow human beings. That would be making idols out of our selves, which we are far too prone to do already. But the late ancient notion that by grace we may hope for the beatification of being absorbed into God is something to which we may aspire, something more graduated and greater than any imagination we may have about finally and peacefully "resting in the universe." Christ became human so that human beings may become divine.

Christianity, understood correctly, should be always an eschatological faith. We promote nothing like the ideology—and deceptive political ubiquity—of American "optimism." American "optimism" is an assumed attitude fed by false ideology.[75] On the contrary, Christian eschatology is empirical, as it has always been. This may seem counterintuitive, but it is true. The authors of eschatological texts, and all the documents of the New Testament are eschatological to some extent, look at the world around and try to make sense of things they see. When they predict the future, they do so with a firm eye on the actual, material, political world. And because they are open to the future in radical ways, they cannot help but be revisable. Note how many apocalyptic writers (Daniel, Matthew, Mark, Luke, Paul, John the Seer) take over prophecies from the past and alter them to fit the facts, even facts that have been created only in the interim between-time, for example, Mark's use of Daniel, Luke's use of Mark, 2 Peter's use of Paul. We are not deceived. We are not "optimists." We admit that our world is, and we are, terribly flawed. By looking at the world in all its tragedies and injustices and yet remaining open to a radical future, Christian eschatology—the hope of our faith—is empirical.

The work of the Christian gospel is to take admittedly sinful, fallen human nature—inclined by its very fallen nature to harm ourselves, others, and our world—and remake it, along with all other creatures and the entire universe, so that it may be saved and even eventually become one with God.

---

75. Christian "hope" is not "optimism." On the differences, see especially Moltmann, *Theology of Hope,* e.g., 58; and Volf, *Against the Tide,* 44–46.

CHAPTER 7

Church

Some theologians begin their discussions of ecclesiology by noting how odd it seems that we confess to believe "in the church." According to the Apostles' Creed, "I believe in the Holy Spirit, the holy catholic Church, the communion of saints." The Nicene Creed, as worded in Rite I of the Episcopal Book of Common Prayer, reads, "We believe in one holy catholic and apostolic Church." In an alternative form in the same prayer book: "And I believe one holy Catholic and Apostolic Church." Is it significant that in one version we confess to believe "in" the church, and in another we confess to "believe the church"? And what does it mean that we "believe in the church" at all?

It makes immediate sense, or so we usually think, to confess to have "faith in" the Father, Jesus Christ, or the holy spirit. We confess to "believe in" them precisely because we cannot see them. We put our faith "in" the resurrection of the body precisely because we have never experienced it, and by definition it is something in the unseen Christian future. But we can see "church" around us all the time—in signs before buildings all over town, in people gathered in public and private, in huge institutions and governing bodies. Why do we confess to "believe in" the church when it is so obvious that "church" exists? It is a bit like the old joke: a Baptist asks an Episcopal priest if he believes in infant baptism. The priest replies, "Believe in it? I've *seen* it." Why do we confess to believe in the church when the existence of church is obvious to all?

As throughout this book, I wish to point out the ways in which such a confession is *not* "true." We should not believe everything any particular congregation, denomination, or institutional church tells us to believe. No one but Roman Catholic Christians should believe (I insist, in any case) in papal infallibility, and I'm sure many Roman Catholics decline to accept the doctrine without reservation themselves. Christians in Eastern Orthodox churches need not confess that the spirit "proceeds from the Father *and the Son,*" even though the Western churches for the most part do make that confession. Though some Protestant churches insist that only "believers' baptism" is proper baptism, Christians in other churches need not believe that. So the fallibility and contingency of all human social institutions that designate themselves "church" must be acknowledged, I insist, or we become idolaters looking to some particular social institution as our god.[1]

What's more, we must not take the church, in any sense of the word, to be a god we worship. We don't ultimately put our faith in the church, but in God, who does indeed use the church as the vehicle and mediator of our salvation. We must not, in any case, confuse "faith in God" with "faith in the church." The church may be thought of as the mediator of divine knowledge and experience without itself being divine, at least not in the sense that God or the persons of the trinity are divine.

And that means that the survival or growth of the church is not a matter we need to worry about. As Christians, we may value the church, in its many different manifestations, but its survival or growth is not something about which we should be anxious. That is God's business. We should use what gifts the holy spirit gives us to benefit the church universal and our small piece of it locally. But that is not the same as worrying about the church's future. That is better left to the holy spirit, which is, after all, the life and power of the church.

In spite of the fact that we should not believe several possible meanings of "we believe in the church," there are ways in which it is true nonetheless. When we say we believe in the church, we are acknowledging that we owe our faith to the church, not ultimately, but intermediately. When we confess to believe in the church we are rejecting any notion that we could, as free and

---

1. See the variety of perspectives in the essays in Collins and Ensign-George, eds., *Denomination.* I agree with most of the authors here collected that denominations are an acceptable way of thinking of the church in both diversity and unity. I disagree with the Eastern Orthodox and Roman Catholic writers who insist that while they recognize Christians outside their own institutional churches, their own institutions are not "denominations" at all but are simply "the church."

nondependent individuals, come to faith completely on our own. Everyone who is a Christian came to be so because of gifts given by and in the context of some church. We may have learned the stories that make up the gospel from our parents or grandparents, but even in that case the holy spirit was using them *as church* to reach us. The church has been chosen by the holy spirit as the mediator of the gospel, as the place where baptism takes place, as the teacher and nurturer of all Christians. Therefore, the church truly is our mother or father in the faith.

This is true even if we imagine someone coming to faith merely by reading the Bible, something I don't think is actually possible. Even in that case the church is the mediator of the gospel because scripture exists only because the holy spirit used members of the church to dictate, write, copy, edit, translate, publish, and distribute the Bible. Scripture, as I argued in chapter 2 above, is the product and instrument of the church. For that reason alone, though there are others, *sola scriptura* is a misleading slogan. Scripture is not accessible apart from some activity of the church. This is not at all to say anything against the divine inspiration of scripture, only to make the empirical observation that the church, under the guidance of the holy spirit, was the creator and mediator of scripture. When we confess that we believe in the church—or that we believe the church—we are giving thanks for the church, in whatever form we encountered it and continue to experience it, for bringing us to faith itself.

The Kingdom of God

Before addressing what the church *is*, I should discuss what the church is *not*. For example, the church cannot be equated with the kingdom of God as we find it in the New Testament, mainly on the lips of Jesus in the Gospels and mostly in just the first three Gospels.[2] The church may aspire to live the values of the coming kingdom, but the unfettered reign of God we hope for must not be confused with the church as we experience it now. We can, however, learn by focusing on what scripture teaches us about the kingdom of God, or of "heaven," as Matthew prefers.

There are both dangers and possible benefits in speaking of the kingdom of God. I rehearsed some of the dangers in chapter 3 above, on "God as

---

2. Kingdom and church are not "synonymous": see Weigelt, "Nature and Identity," 17. James Alison reminds us of the Second Vatican Council's insistence that the church is not the Kingdom of God: "The Church is not the Kingdom of God, but is the sign or sacrament thereof." *Faith Beyond Resentment*, 162.

king or emperor." As is true of all theological statements or images, calling the expected eschatological community that will exist in the perfect love of God a "kingdom" is both true and false. In the New Testament the image functions positively if it is taken to be a rejection, displacement, and replacement of all other human kingdoms. If Jesus is bringing his own empire, it will have to be established on the ashes of the Roman Empire or any other human empire. Given how oppressive the Roman Empire was, as all empires are, we may interpret that as a good thing.

Empires do not generally have good reputations in our world. Obviously, some people in our power-worshipping culture still dream of something like an "American Empire" and would welcome American hegemony over the rest of the world, full equality be damned. But I hope those aspirations would be rejected by Christians, though given the nationalistic idolatry of most American Christianity, I know they are not. All language about the "kingdom" of God or, perhaps better translated, the "empire" of God must be taken warily by Christians of our age.

But how may we use scripture to imagine profitable ways of thinking about the "kingdom of God"? What may we learn about God's love from New Testament language about God's reign? Some of the best depictions of the kingdom come from the sayings and parables of Jesus. First, we have to face up to the mysteries of the kingdom. The coming of the kingdom is inevitable, but we cannot discern when or how it will come. We can see this from a close reading of the parable of the sower. The parable has been taken to mean many things, even within the texts of the Gospels themselves (Matt 13:1–9; and par.). It has been read as a parable of the different kinds of "soil" or "ground" that either receives the seed fruitfully or not, with the result that the parable quickly becomes an allegory for individuals' acceptance of the gospel or not. I believe this rather allegorical interpretation of the parable to be a later invention of the church or perhaps of Mark, copied by Matthew and Luke. I take the meaning of the parable itself, apart from its interpretation in the Gospels, to be mainly about how the kingdom of God should be expected to grow. We cannot know ahead of time where, when, and how the kingdom will come. Indeed, we are right to call it the parable of the *sower,* not the parable of the seed or ground. The parable is telling people they should plant the seeds of the coming kingdom and leave it at that: they shouldn't worry about what happens to the seeds, just plant them. God will take care of the rest. The arrival and growth of the kingdom are both mystical, that is, to some extent hidden from us, and inevitable. This is also, I take it, the main message of the parable of the mustard seed and the parable of the yeast (Matt 13:31–33; Mark 4:30–32; Luke 13:18–21). We also learn from the parable of the ten bridesmaids that we cannot know when the kingdom will arrive (Matt 25:1–13). So the first thing to confess is that we do not know and aren't supposed to know how, when, or where the kingdom will appear. We simply hope for it, prepare for it, and wait for it.

Other passages emphasize the supreme value of the kingdom. It is worth more than anything else we have or can have: it is the treasure in the field that we give up everything to obtain; it is the pearl of great price (Matt 13:44–45; Luke 12:31). These parables tell us we must wager everything on the hope of a promised divine community, even when all other evidence seems contrary.

Other passages teach not just about the *value* of the kingdom but also about the *values* of its society. Indeed, the ethics and political dynamics of the kingdom are the mirror opposite of those of our familiar world. The kingdom reverses all hierarchies of our common experience. Children are the greatest of all (Matt 18:1–4; Mark 9:33–37; Luke 9:46–48). The lowest become the highest. The last will be first, and the first will be last (Matt 20:16; Luke 13:30; see also Luke 18:16–17). We can also say, however, that the kingdom will be a universal community, including not just Israel but all people "from the east and from the west" (Matt 8:11; Luke 13:29).

The kingdom of God, however, is not very hospitable to the rich (Matt 19:23–24; Mark 10:23–27; Luke 18:23–25). This means that no one, unlike in our societies, can buy a way into it. The kingdom is primarily for the poor (Luke 6:20; James 2:5). But the kingdom is also a place where people get more than they deserve (Matt 20:1–16). The kingdom is a place of forgiveness and *reciprocal* grace (Matt 18:23–25). This society will be especially hospitable to sinners, outcasts, and prostitutes (Matt 21:31; see also Matt 22:1–10; Luke 14:15–24). The kingdom will rid the world of evil and suffering (Luke 11:20). The main marker of the kingdom is love (Mark 2:34).

We are also assured that the kingdom will be eternal (Luke 1:33; Rev 11:15). The kingdom is in our future. It is eschatological: the future "end" (1 Cor 15:24). But we will have important roles to play: in the kingdom, we believers will be the "priests" (Rev 1:6; 5:10).

Although we must not confuse the church with the kingdom of God, therefore, we should recognize that we, as church, are the "first fruits," the precursors and promise of the future community of love and justice God the Father through Christ will establish. We may aspire, as church, to embody and promote those values of justice and revolution: the first should be last, and the last first; the needs of the poor must take priority over the desires of the rich; forgiveness and reciprocal grace must be enacted both in the church and, when possible, in society. Aspiring to live out the values of the future kingdom, however, must not lead us to confuse the current church, in all its maculate embodiment, with the community we await with hope.

The Household of God

The church, in both scripture and history, has been described as the "household of God." The designation has often, however, done more harm than good in the long history of the church. Moreover, the different documents of the New Testament and its various authors and characters took quite diverse positions on whether the traditional household was something to be rejected or encouraged. I have addressed this diversity and the various ideologies of household and family in other publications, so what I provide here will be little more than a summary of historical and exegetical arguments I have made elsewhere.[3]

First, the dominant social unit for "family" in the ancient Mediterranean world was not the nuclear family of modern imagination—father, mother, and immediate children. There has been debate about just how prevalent the nuclear family structure was in comparison with the extended family during the period of the early Roman Empire.[4] It seems clear to me, at any rate, that whether or not the *number* of extended families equaled or surpassed the *number* of nuclear families in antiquity, the dominant assumption about households was that they were usually some form of partial, extended, or "open" household structure. The neat triad of the heterosexual nuclear family, composed of one man, one woman, and at least one child, probably did not dominate socially, but it certainly did not ideologically or culturally. When we see references in the New Testament to "house" (οἶκος; e.g., Acts 7:10; 10:2; 11:14; 16:15) as a reference to a social unit (they had no word that exactly fits the modern English word "family"), we should assume that the reference is, in most cases, to a "household" rather than to a nuclear family.[5]

3. The main publications include Martin, *Sex and the Single Savior,* esp. chaps. 5, 8, 9; and *New Testament,* chap. 20.

4. See my own treatment of the issue in Martin, "Construction," and "Slave Families."

5. This is common knowledge among scholars. The Latin *familia,* from which we get the word "family," referred not to the parents or the children but primarily to the slave

The Gospels have many stories in which Jesus calls people, especially young men, to desert their familial households in order to join his movement. In one story Jesus instructs a potential follower even to leave it to his elderly father to bury himself at his death, a suggestion that would have been considered radical and even immoral by most people of that society (Luke 9:59–60; Matt 8:21–22). One story quotes Jesus as telling a young man to "let the dead bury the dead," implying that the man's father, upon dying, will have to bury himself. According to a saying in Matthew, Jesus warns his followers against loving their families more than they love God (Matt 10:37). But in the version of the saying passed along by Luke, Jesus tells them they must "hate" or "despise" members of their households, *including their wives* (Luke 14:26). This is the version of the saying that may have a better claim to derive from the historical Jesus, partly because it is more "radical" than the version in Matthew (the author of Matthew would more likely have toned down a more radical rejection of the family, I think, if that is what he found in his source), but also because Luke's is the version also passed along in the *Gospel of Thomas* (§55; including the term "hate" and the mention of wives).

Indeed, I have elsewhere argued that whereas the Gospels of Mark and Matthew forbid divorce and remarriage, the versions of similar stories from Luke suggest that its author forbade only remarriage after divorce and actually encouraged Jesus's followers to leave their spouses.[6] In the New Testament, Jesus is not presented as a supporter of "traditional family values," either those of ancient societies or our own. Jesus is at best ambivalent toward marriage and family and in places actively opposes the traditional household. Instead, he works to build a movement that will offer an eschatological alternative to household (e.g., Mark 3:33–35; cf. Matt 12:46–50; Luke 8:19–21). It is highly ironic that the modern American idolatry of the family *purports* to be reflecting the values of Jesus, the Bible, and Christian tradition. Nothing could be further from the truth.

The Apostle Paul was ambivalent toward marriage. In the letters critical scholars take to be authentically from him, Paul nowhere shows any concern about children or procreation. When he does address the issue of marriage and sexual relations, he acknowledges that he would prefer all believers to be like himself, single and celibate (1 Cor 7). He permits marriage and

---

members of a household. The Greek word we usually translate as "household" or "family" was the word for "house" (οἶκος or οἰκία; in Latin *domus*).

6. *Sex and the Single Savior,* 134–38.

sexual relations only so believers may avoid "burning," that is, so they may avoid the "burning" pollution that Paul assumed constituted erotic desire (1 Cor 7:9).[7] Jesus, much of our Gospels, and Paul are all on record as harboring suspicions about marriage and the traditional household.[8] If we were to follow their examples, we would admit the church to be a "household" only in a strongly countercultural manner.

Other parts of the New Testament support marriage and the traditional household, and those are the texts that most readily portray the church as itself a household. The author of Colossians—not Paul but someone who saw himself as a follower of Paul—famously passes along "household codes" prescribing behavior of husbands and fathers, wives, children, and slaves (Col 3: 18–4:1). This is certainly not a rejection of the traditional household but its presupposition, complete with the subordination of women and the submission of slaves. The author of Ephesians, another follower of Paul who also used Colossians as a model for his own letter, goes even further. His version of the household code, which he builds upon the version from Colossians, is more elaborate, emphasizes even more the subordination of women, children, and slaves, and makes the male patriarch practically an earthly version of Christ: "As the church is subject to Christ, so also women should be, in everything, subject to their men" (Eph 5:24). The slave master is also made parallel to Christ: slaves are to obey their master not simply as a human master but as if he were Christ himself (6:5–6).

The author of the Pastoral Epistles, 1 and 2 Timothy and Titus, wrote even later, again imitating Paul. But whereas Paul showed disinterest in or even suspicion of the traditional household and marriage, this later author attempts to turn the church itself *into* a household, with patriarchs firmly in charge, women silent and submissive, and slaves properly "in their place." Even widows have to be assigned a place in the "household of God," either as older, registered widows or, for younger widows, in some kind of arranged remarriage, so they won't follow their natural female inclinations to gossip, be busybodies, and in general cause trouble (5:11–12).[9]

---

7. As counterintuitive as this may sound, I have shown that such a position and assumption were not at all impossible in the ancient world and are the most "natural" reading of Paul's language. See Martin, *Corinthian Body*, 198–228 and *Sex and the Single Savior*, 65–76.

8. I could add the Revelation of John as being similar. The author of that document imagines a community of male, celibate saints and priests "who have never polluted themselves" by contact with women (Rev 14:4; for further exegesis, see *Sex and the Single Savior*, 109–11).

9. See exegesis and elaboration in Martin, *New Testament*, 284–90.

We discover something of a pattern in these various attitudes toward marriage and the household. Those of Jesus, Paul, and some of the Gospels seem opposed to traditional household structures. They are also the sources in our New Testament that seem to allow a more active and central role for female disciples. Jesus has some important women followers with whom he seems to have trusting, close relationships. Paul recognizes women in leadership roles in his house churches (see especially Rom 16). This is not to imply that either Jesus or Paul advocated or practiced complete gender equality, but women do seem to have fared better in their communities than in later Christianity. Yet the other New Testament sources, those that promote the traditional household and marriage, are the same ones that insist on the traditional patriarchal, hierarchical structure of the household, with submissive women and obedient slaves. We find a pattern in much of early Christianity: the more the traditional household is advocated and supported, the less freedom and respect is accorded to women. Conversely, the more early Christians oppose the traditional household, the higher respect and greater activity are allowed for women. This is not a coincidence.

Thus when we experiment with thinking of the church as the "household of God," we must beware. If we take the church to be in some sense the household of God, we must supplement that image with other metaphors and social images that make sure we do not, by thinking of the church as household, continue the sins of patriarchal and sexist Christian history. The church may indeed be "family" and "household," but we must be active in making it an *alternative* to the traditional hierarchical, male-dominated household of premodern cultures or to the idealized, romanticized, cloying ideological family of modern American culture. The church must be a radical alternative to the traditional and modern household and family, not their reproduction.

The Body of Christ

Paul may have been the early Christian most responsible for bequeathing to the church the belief that the church is the body of Christ. At least, it is mainly in the Pauline literature that we most find the doctrine and its elaborations. Especially throughout 1 Corinthians we see the image, which makes sense given the letter's overall theme of unity in diversity: "Do you not know that your bodies are members of Christ?" Paul asks (1 Cor 6:15). He then uses one of his, to us, odd combinations of plural possessive pronoun accompanied by a singular noun: "Your [pl.] body [sg.] is a temple of the holy spirit which you have from God" (6:19). Whether or not this combination would have sounded odd to ancient hearers, it does strike us as strange. But we may use the combination to emphasize that we all, all believers, actually are just *one body*. The image gets a real workout in 1 Cor 12:12–27. Though you are many members, you are one body of Christ: "You are the body of Christ, and individually members of it" (12:27). Paul will repeat the theme, with a bit less emphasis, in Romans: "Though we are many, we are one body in Christ" (Rom 12:5).

Paul is able to elaborate the theme in other contexts and with other subjects. When discussing the eucharist, for example, he insists that it is precisely when we eat the bread of the eucharist that we experience a "participation," a "sharing" (κοινωνία) in the "body of Christ." Elsewhere, he implies that it is the body of Christ that saves us: "You have died with regard to the law through the body of Christ" (Rom 7:4). Would it be too much a liberty to take this as teaching that the church itself, as the body of Christ, is what, in some sense, "saves" us? As I mentioned at the beginning of this chapter, that certainly fits some of our experience: we do, in fact, "get saved," at least by the intermediary activity of the church.

Sharing in the body of Christ then works the other way around as, according to Paul, Jesus's life becomes "visible" in *our* bodies (2 Cor 4:10). The author of Hebrews, apparently influenced by Pauline theology, may even be telling his readers that we are supposed to *share the body* of people imprisoned or tortured (Heb 13:3), a frightening counsel. We are to be "one body" or "in body" with them, meaning that we are to share their tortured body?[10]

The authors of Ephesians and Colossians expand and alter somewhat Paul's depiction of the church as the body of Christ. Whereas Paul had spoken of the church as the entire body of Christ in all its parts, the author of Colossians innovates by making the Christ the "head" of the body and the church apparently merely the rest of the body: "He is the head of the body, the church" (Col 1:18, see also 24; 2:17; 3:15). The author then uses the Greek word ἀρχή, which could be translated as "beginning" (so the NRSV) or as "head," as in "ruler" or "authority." I tend to take the Greek here as implying both. The author of Colossians, after all, makes much of the authority of the male head of household later in his epistle (Col 3:18–4:1), as we have seen. In this reading, Christ is both the "origin" and the "head" of the church.

---

10. This is at least one (overly creative?) way of reading the Greek. The last two words of the verse are "in body," and may more likely be read, "since you are also embodied," but I think it could be read as "since you are in the body with them." Either way, something has to be added in English to make the translation sensible.

The author of Ephesians, apparently inspired by his reading of Colossians, which he doubtless assumed was written by Paul himself, elaborates the Pauline theme even more. Christ is "head over all things for the church, which is his body" (Eph 1:22–23). It is in Ephesians that we find that wonderfully liturgical-sounding sentence, "There is one body and one Spirit, just as you are called to the one hope of your calling, one Lord, one faith, one baptism, one God and Father of all, who is above all and through all and in all" (Eph 4:4–6, NRSV). This author speaks of believers as participating in "building up the body of Christ" (4:12; see also 4:16).

The most notable innovation of Ephesians in its application of the image of the church as the body of Christ is the rigid hierarchy and patriarchy the author brings to the body, as I pointed out above. Ephesians goes much beyond what he borrows from Paul and Colossians to insist that the patriarch is "head" of his woman, just as Christ is "head" of his body, the church (Eph 5:22–24). As Christ had "washed" and "cleansed" the dirty, feminine church, so men should similarly take care of the bodies of their women (5:25–33). This is a version of the "church as body of Christ" we certainly should treat warily today, given its sexism and misogyny.

But the image of the church as Christ's body can do much good work also, especially when we examine the way it expands the community of the redeemed. In the Apostles' Creed, for example, we confess, just after confessing that we believe "in the holy catholic Church," that we also believe "in the communion of saints." This means we place trust not just in the "officially" canonized "saints" of any of those churches which practice such canonization. It rather means that we "believe in the communion," that is, the loving and mutually assisting fellowship, of all believers who exist anywhere now in the universe and who have existed at all times in the past or will exist in the future. We "believe" that the "body of Christ" extends through space and time to include everyone God has joined to divine communion with all other saved persons and with the communion of the persons of the trinity.

This fellowship of all is again referred to in a beautiful postcommunion prayer from the Book of Common Prayer. In it, we thank God "that we are very members incorporate in the mystical body of thy Son, the blessed company of all faithful people; and are also heirs, through hope, of thy everlasting kingdom."[11] We are incorporated members of the body of Christ. But it is a "mystical" body.

---

11. The prayer is found more than once in the prayer book, but see, e.g., p. 339.

I have sometimes been pressed, when speaking about "the church," to define what, precisely, I mean. Which church? Can I point to it? What actual social group am I referring to when I invoke "church"? I respond that I am speaking about the entire "body of Christ," but I remind people that it is precisely a "mystical" body. That does not mean it is purely an "invisible" body, a topic I address below. It simply means that I cannot know the precise boundaries of the church. I cannot define it—in the sense, that is, of showing its *limits*—because that would be to delineate it, a task beyond any human reckoning. This is also why the confession to believe "in the communion of the saints" as the "body of Christ" is an expression of faith, not of knowledge that can be confirmed by normal empirical observation. We *confess* faith in the "communion of saints" as the "body of Christ" precisely because we cannot show where the boundaries of that body lie.[12]

I also believe, however, that we should not allow the fact that the body of Christ is "mystical" to advocate some doctrine of the "invisible" church as the "real" church. We must insist that the church *is* church and body of Christ in its physical, visible, and even local manifestations (though not exhaustively so). The church as body of Christ may not be entirely visible to us, but we should grant that what "church" is visible to us is nonetheless *truly* the visible body of Christ. Actual, humanly peopled churches and congregations *are* the body of Christ. Thus, as long as one does not insist that the visible body of Christ, that is, socially, physically extant organizations and congregations, is the *entire* body of Christ, thus excluding those saints we may not now be able to see, I find no problem in considering the body of Christ to include both visible and invisible saints. But the "invisible" church should not take priority over the "visible" church, either in ontology or honor.

On the other hand, we must not completely identify any empirical institution with the church as a whole. No one social group of Christians may claim to be "the" church alone. Thus we must resist the temptation to identify the Roman Catholic Church as "the" church, making all others who identify themselves as Christian but not Roman Catholic somehow "outside" the church. We must resist the temptation to make any particular Orthodox national or ethnic church—or even the combined fellowship of all

---

12. See Lash, *Holiness*, 28, quoting Evdokimov: "We know where the Church is; it is not for us to judge and say where the Church is not." This is the translation of Evdokimov's French found in Butler, *Theology of Vatican II*, 119. The French: "Nous savons oú est l'Eglise, mais il ne nous est pas donné de porter de jugement et de dire oú l'Eglise n'est pas": Evdokimov, *L'Orthdoxie*, 343. For a slightly different translation, one may consult the more recent English, in *Orthodoxy* (2011), 350. See also Lash, *Believing*, 86–88.

autocephalous "Orthodox" churches—"the" church, with all others being "merely" "denominations" or separated "brothers and sisters," or any other second-class designation. The mystical body of Christ does include those social, physical, empirical institutions, but it also includes all those believers past, present, and future whom only God knows as members of the body of Christ.

I do not want to leave this subject without noting how, in my view, the doctrine of the church as the body of Christ becomes an extension of the doctrine of the incarnation. If we seriously take "body of Christ" as a true representation of Christ's presence in the world, we will better appreciate the church as an extension of divine presence in our communities and our world. This leads to the recognition, made by various theologians over the ages, that the church is itself a sacrament: the church is both a sign of God's presence in the world and an actual enactment of the embodying of God in the world.[13] The church is a spiritual *and physical* instrument the holy spirit uses to bring grace and revelation to us and to the entire world. We encounter Christ's body in various ways. We see Christ's body through our faith in Christ's resurrected body mediated by story, art, architecture, and many other media. We see Christ's body in the physical eucharistic elements. And we see Christ's body in the church, also a living, physical sign and enactment of divine presence and grace. This is what it means to call the church a sacrament.

The Gender of the Church

Focusing on Christ's body offers an opportunity to address a controversial issue: what is the gender of the church? In certain Christian contexts, usually those that preserve patriarchal structures, language, and ideology, the church (and it is often capitalized, "Church," making it seem almost like a fourth person of the trinity) is nearly exclusively designated as female ("she," "her") while all three persons of the trinity are completely male, including the spirit—even though, as I explained in the chapter on the spirit above, the Greek word for "spirit" is actually neuter. Often this is done without explanation or defense and almost always without signaling that the language inevitably denigrates women. Robert W. Jenson, for example, consistently

13. See Mannion and Wilson, "Introduction," 3. Denys Turner reminds us, quoting the Latin of Thomas Aquinas, that a sacrament is a "sign that effects what it signifies" (*Sacramenta novae legis efficiunt quod signant;* quoting *Super Evangelium S. Matthaei lectura,* cap. 26, lectio 3); in Turner, *Thomas Aquinas,* 239.

designates the church, as he does Israel, as "she." This regularly, however, leads to depicting the church as helpless, passive, subordinate, and indeed infantilized.[14]

The issue is addressed directly by Boris Bobrinskoy in a surprisingly recent ecclesiology written from a Russian Orthodox perspective. From the very beginning of the book, the persons of the trinity are all male, and the church is always female and subordinate, even to the extent of describing "her" "immaculate robe torn by enmity and divisions."[15] Bobrinskoy provocatively leaves us with an image of a woman in a torn dress. He quotes St. Cyprian of Carthage: "We cannot have God as Father if we do not have the Church as Mother."[16] Note, however, how this gendering is ideologically dangerous. The gendering of the church as exclusively female and in an intimate relation to an exclusively male "Father" is bad enough. But it also makes us Christians *children* of the church, our "mother," rather than making us *the church itself*. It infantilizes Christians and degrades women.

At least Bobrinskoy is self-conscious about his gendering rhetoric and theology. He later notes that in Orthodox doctrine and polity the bishop is the husband of his diocese, which is his "wife" (192). In the eucharist the bishop faces the church as facing "his wife" in "a nuptial relationship." Bobrinskoy uses such gendering as a defense of the exclusively male priesthood and episcopacy: "That is why a bishop can only be a man. It is due to this analogy of Church-Bride of Christ that the priest, representing Christ, must be a man" (189, see also 230). That is also why, he explains, bishops cannot be transferred, in much of Orthodoxy, to another diocese: "The bishop is the husband of his Church, and she is a 'widow' at his death. A nuptial relationship does not allow for a change of husband or wife. We remain with the one whom God has given us" (192). I'm not sure whether Bobrinskoy intends the sexual meaning of his language, but it seems glaring to me: is the bishop planning to screw his church?

---

14. See Jenson, *Systematic Theology*, 1:23–24: "When the church accepted that her Lord had deposited her in history, that the time between Resurrection and fulfillment would not be a historical instant but had occupied and therefore might yet occupy a succession of generations, she might have confessed her hope refuted." The church is the passive woman acted upon but discouraged from acting.

15. Bobrinskoy, *Mystery*. These words are from the first paragraph of the introduction. The English translation is of the original French published in 2003, which I think, given the fact that second-wave feminism is usually dated to the 1970s, still makes this work rather surprisingly sexist.

16. *De ecclesia catholicae unitate* §5; quoted at *Mystery*, 15.

Later, Bobrinskoy extends this feminization, and its necessary subordinationism, to each individual Christian. Though he had just admitted that it is perfectly permissible to think of God as both father *and mother* (222, citing Isa 49:15), he quickly reverts to his stunning, consistent gender hierarchy: "Above all, I would like to stress the 'femininity' of the Church, her 'spiritual motherhood,' her 'virginity.' . . . Every human person that enters the Church as a living stone participates in this femininity in a nuptial encounter with the Lord" (224). It is certainly crude to point out that the image invokes "the Lord" screwing his wife, which is both the corporate church and, as Bobrinskoy says explicitly, "every" Christian, but my way of putting it is no more crude than his repeated use of such gendered language, especially invoking the marriage bed.

I should be clear: I have no problem with gendered language and imagery when thinking about the church or, for that matter, when thinking about God or any of the three persons of the trinity. In fact, I think using gender images is theologically fruitful if done rightly. But speaking of the church exclusively in female terms and of God and the persons of the trinity consistently in male terms is not just dangerous, it is downright immoral. It scripts women and girls (and effeminacy in totality, including men or boys deemed by others to be "effeminate") in a passive, subordinate, submissive role, dominated, even though "cared for," by male priests, bishops, and gods. If gendered language is to be used for God or the church, it must be mixed up and subverted enough so that the church does not simply reinforce the misogyny of traditional Christianity and history.

No person, church, or social institution must ever advocate or tolerate the subordination of women to men, female to male. To do so necessarily—regardless of the conscious intentions of persons or institutions—is sinful, unjust, and loveless. It commits the old sin of the idolatry of the phallos, the Christian elevation of the penis, which has always led to the greater evaluation of masculine over feminine, the oppression of women and girls and of males deemed "effeminate." The maleness of Christ's body does not give the church, exclusively, a penis. Neither does being the "bride" of Christ give the church, exclusively, a vagina. If the church, as Christ's body, needs genitalia, it must, as the androgynous or intersexed body of Christ, have both.[17] No Christian or church should ever tolerate gender subordinationism, much less promote it. Those who consistently take the church to be "she" and God

17. For the androgynous or intersexed body of Christ, see Martin, *Sex and the Single Savior*, 77–90.

and Christ to be "he," whether intentionally or not, encourage and prolong the hierarchy of male over female, of men over women. To do so is to sin against the church and God and women.

Ekklesia

The Greek word in the New Testament usually translated as "church" is ἐκκλησία. I will use the transliteration "ekklesia" as a loanword because I wish to retain the several different meanings the word had in ancient Greek rather than limit its meaning or connotations to "church."

There are two main sources from which Paul and other early Greek-speaking believers could have taken the word in order to refer to the small house churches they founded around the Mediterranean: the Jewish scriptures in Greek translation and the Greek political institution of the "town assembly," the gathered political body of adult male citizens of a city. (Though there were other Greek versions of Jewish scripture, unless otherwise noted, I will be citing the Septuagint, usually by its abbreviation LXX.) Some modern scholars have emphasized the influence of the LXX on the early Christian usage of "ekklesia," sometimes to the extent of denying outright that there could have been influence on early Christians from the Greek political ekklesiai.[18] This is part of a fallacious conservative theological bias of much scholarship on early Christianity, which regularly downplays influence on Christianity from "pagan" Greek and Roman sources and emphasizes instead influences from Judaism and Jewish scripture. It also probably was caused in early twentieth-century German scholarship by opposition to democracy at that time in Germany. I will argue that it is much more likely that early Christians would obviously have thought about the local public ekklesiai when they heard the term used of Christian groups. Early believers took their inspiration, almost certainly, from *both* Jewish scripture *and* Greek and Roman political institutions and terminology.

The referent of "ekklesia" in the LXX varies. Quite regularly, it refers to all of Israel, the entire "people of God" or "of YHWH." Several times in Deut 23:2–8, for example, it is a reference simply to the whole people of Israel. Likewise, that is apparently its referent in 3 Kingdoms (1 Kings) 8, where we find "the ekklesia of Israel." Sometimes, however, it refers to a spe-

---

18. See, for example, the downplaying of any Greek political influence in the article on the topic in *TDNT*, 3:514.

cial gathering of the people. So Deut 9:10 says, "on the day of the ekklesia," implying a special gathering on a designated day (see also Deut 18:16).

Usually, "ekklesia" occurs as a translation of the Hebrew *qahal*. "Ekklesia" also seems to be simply synonymous with συναγωγή, which in the New Testament we often translate as "synagogue." There is no doubt that the word "synagogue," later used as a reference to Jewish meetings and, later still, probably, to the meeting place, took its inspiration from the Greek scriptures. In the LXX, συναγωγή is usually a translation of the Hebrew '*edah*. At Prov 5:14, the two words occur together in what is obviously thought by most English translators to be simply a parallel of synonyms. The Hebrew translated by the KJV as "in the midst of the congregation and assembly" is rendered in the LXX as ἐν μέσῳ ἐκκλησίας καὶ συναγωγῆς. Yet the phrase is translated by the NRSV simply as "in the public assembly." Both the NIV and the New Jerusalem Bible also elide the two terms: "in the whole assembly." It could be, however, that the two terms occurring together here, though synonymous, may have been intended to mark this not simply as the entire "people of Israel" but as the people in particular assembly. Thus the RSV translates the phrase as "in the assembled congregation."[19]

These are only a few representative examples of the many occurrences of "ekklesia" in the LXX. It may refer to the entire people of Israel or to particular gatherings of the people. And it seems usually to be simply synonymous with συναγωγή. It even refers, in Sir 26:5, to an "assembly of a mob." There need be no doubt, therefore, that early Christian believers and groups took their use of the term to refer to their own small groups from the occurrence of "ekklesia" in Jewish scripture. By doing so, early followers of Jesus, even the non-Jewish ones, were claiming a lineage of continuity with the Israel they read about in Jewish scripture—scripture they now claimed as their own also.

But it would be foolish to insist that these Greek-speaking inhabitants of Greco-Roman cities and towns would not have entertained also meanings of "ekklesia" they inherited from classical Athens and other democracies.[20] Since I wish to capitalize on the democratic and political meanings of "ekklesia" in my discussion of the theology of the church, some basic introduction to the classical democracies will be helpful. Though we should keep in mind that there were democracies in many cities in the classical period (say, 500

19. See the comments of Toy, *Proverbs*, 110; Fox, *Proverbs 1–9*, 198, who suggests much the same.

20. An important recent contribution to the discussion of the applicability of the Greek *ekklesia* to Pauline churches is Miller, *Corinthian Democracy*.

to about 300 BCE), and there were other political structures and constitutions that imitated democracy to one degree or another, the democracy we have the most information about is the Athenian, not only because it was the largest and most influential democracy of the time but also because they left more records, and posterity preserved many of those records. I concentrate, therefore, on the classical Athenian ekklesia, though we should remember that ekklesiai existed in just about all Greek cities throughout the eastern Mediterranean and into late antiquity.[21]

Scholars estimate the population, including all inhabitants, of Athens during this time to have been probably 150,000 to 250,000, which would have made it huge by the standards of the normal Greek polis of the time.[22] All citizens were allowed to participate in the ekklesia. "Citizen," however, meant only adult, native-born Athenian men, probably numbering around 30,000, the rest of the inhabitants being women, children, "metics," or foreigners resident in Athens, and slaves. All classes of male citizens, from the poorest to the richest, were allowed to attend and participate. And all our evidence demonstrates that lower-class men, manual laborers, day laborers, and even the unemployed did in fact participate, though we cannot say how many eligible men actually attended, or how personally active in the proceedings they were other than making the typical audience noises like shouting someone down or cheering and voting. It is estimated that perhaps 6,000 men attended most of the time. Apparently for some meetings that voted on certain issues a quorum of 6,000 was required.

But also, apparently, the city sometimes had trouble getting *enough* men to attend. Thus, eventually, in order to encourage attendance, those who arrived early enough were paid by the state. Payment for attending the ekklesia began around 403–393 BCE. By the 340s, the pay had risen to 1–1 ½ drachmas, depending on what kind of ekklesia it was—some were longer than others. Because the ekklesia met usually for half a day, working-class men could supplement the payment for attendance with other wages even

21. For democracies other than the Athenian, including a very few that may predate the democracy at Athens, see O'Neil, *Origins*. O'Neil does call Athens "the earliest democracy" (55), but it seems he is including, by that designation, various reforms in Athens that took place in the sixth century. Most scholars date the beginning of the Athenian democracy proper to around 500 BCE, but O'Neil had already designated a few sixth-century polities as "democracies" in Megara, Chios, Cyrene, and a few other cities of Ionia (see 21–26).

22. The summary I provide here is derived mainly from Hansen, *Athenian Assembly*; Starr, *Birth*; and Ober, *Athenian Revolution*. There are many studies of the Athenian democracy, but these are highly respected by most scholars.

on days when the ekklesia was in session, with the result that such income would be sufficient to make up for lost wages for working men. Indeed, the pay, according to one scholar, was sufficient to support a family of four.[23]

The ekklesia met around forty times per year. There was also a council (βουλή) of five hundred men, selected not by voting but by lot from a pre-arranged roster of names. The council would propose the agenda, but it did not control the debate or how the vote went in the ekklesia. Anyone could speak, though it is doubtful that every man actually took advantage of that right. As noted, the council was selected by lot, as were many officers, from the "archons" on down (the word is often translated "magistrates," though it means just a "leader" or "ruler"). At the beginning of the meeting a "president of the day" who had also been selected by lot would announce the agenda through a "herald." Anyone wishing to speak could hold forth as long as he liked or until he was shouted down by the others. A vote was usually by a simple show of hands, up or down, unless it was a matter requiring a quorum, in which case ballots would be used. A simple majority decided the issue.

For classical Athens, and doubtless for other democracies also, the courts and juries were in some ways just as important as the ekklesiai to the nature of the democracy. Juries for court cases were selected from the citizens by random drawing, and jurists were paid for their service. There were no professional or permanent judges who presided over courts or the juries. The jurists were themselves the judges. Juries would usually be composed of two hundred or five hundred men. One difference from the ekklesia was that a jurist had to be over the age of thirty whereas any adult male citizen could participate in the ekklesia. The magistrates, also chosen by lot, assigned cases to the appropriate court, but any citizen could bring cases against other people. Time clocks limited the amount of time each side was allotted to make its case. There were no questions or cross-examination. And a simple majority decided the case in favor of either the prosecuting citizen or the accused.

It may seem counterintuitive to modern people that so much of the selection of participants for juries, the council, and many other offices was by random selection of drawing names or some other method of lottery (sortition). There may have been different reasons for relying so much on the lot rather than voting. Certainly the lot, especially when selecting as many as five hundred men for a jury, would be quicker than campaigning and voting. But it also seems that ancient Greeks perceived the lot as being more

---

23. These details and estimates are mainly from Hansen, *Athenian Assembly*, 47–48.

democratic than voting.[24] Since these offices were not permanent—some would be limited to a year, others were for one day or meeting only—and since the jobs did not require special expertise, it perhaps did not matter too much who did the honors. For those offices that did require expertise, military commanders especially, a vote was taken, as no one wanted to serve on a warship under someone who didn't know how to sail and fight. But by using the lot, the Athenians also made sure many of the offices and jobs of authority really did get passed around randomly from citizen to citizen, thus encouraging even more the active participation of many more citizens in the day-to-day workings of the democracy. Moreover, everyone knew, as we should remind ourselves today, that votes can be bought and certainly influenced by money. By decreasing the use of the vote and increasing the use of random selection, Athens could strike at least one significant blow against the power of the rich. This is just one way in which the Athenian democracy was a much more thorough, even "radical," form of government than any modern democracy.

Another is the fact that the Athenian democracy was a "direct," not a "representative," democracy. The citizens did not elect others to represent their interests in the government; they did so themselves. And they directly elected most of those men who would represent them to other cities or other governments. Laws and decrees were proposed, debated, and adopted directly by the citizens in ekklesia. Offices were usually filled by laymen, not specialists. This form of democracy, as ancient political theorists themselves realized, favored the poor and therefore much more the majority of inhabitants of an ancient Greek city.

Moreover, for much of its history the Athenian democracy *paid* people to participate. This favored the poor and nonelites much more than the rich. The amount of the payment was a significant boost to the average worker's income, whereas it would have made no difference to the welfare of the wealthy. The payment for participation in the ekklesia not only was compensation for missed wages but also served as a steady social safety net for much of the population. To understand just how radical this was, we need only attempt to imagine any modern democracy paying its citizens a substantial amount of money just to participate in democratic institutions or to vote. It is beyond imagination to picture the United States of America paying its poor people or the middle class to vote or attend political meetings. Though we must acknowledge that ancient democracies excluded women, resident

24. See O'Neil, *Origins*, 1.

foreigners, and slaves from direct political participation, nonetheless, compared to modern democracies the Athenian democracy was revolutionary and radical and heavily favored the poor over the rich.

Then, as now, democracies often make bad mistakes and oppressive, unjust decisions. In his *History of the Peloponnesian War,* Thucydides seems to delight in chronicling instances when the majority adopted positions that severely oppressed particular persons or entire populations. Thucydides writes, in my view, as an enemy of democracy itself, as did Plato and Aristotle and almost every other ancient author. That reflects their position as members of the very small upper class. But we need not doubt that ekklesiai did often behave in a fickle manner and sometimes voted for policies that were repressive and cruel, just as modern democratic populations do. That does not negate the observation that the ancient democracies, making policy in the ekklesia, were nonetheless egalitarian, revolutionary, and radical when compared to other forms of constitution in the ancient or modern worlds. From around 500 to 322, with a few brief interruptions, Athens was ruled by a radical democracy.

After 322, when their Macedonian overlords quashed the Athenian democracy and no doubt other democracies that may have survived until then, there were few democracies in the ancient world.[25] Yet that did not mean the extinction of the ekklesia. In local regions and cities and towns, male citizens continued for centuries to meet in ekklesiai to conduct debates on local matters and make at least some significant decisions. We can see how this functioned in literature as well as in other documentation. The ekklesiai survived even into the Roman imperial period, though only with a tiny fraction of the power of the classical ekklesia of Athens. We can see them at work to some extent, for instance, in the speeches of the orator and sometime philosopher Dio Chrysostom, whose professional career(s) extended through the end of the first century CE and into the second. His *Discourse* 43 seems to have been delivered before the ekklesia in his hometown of Prusa. In contrast, his *Discourse* 50 seems to have been delivered in the council. At this time the council of a city was presumed to represent more the interests of the small upper class, whereas the ekklesia was presumed to represent more the interests of the lower class.[26] Thus it is telling to contrast Dio's rhetorical strategies

25. At the end of the regime of Demetrius of Phalerum in 307, the Athenian democracy could be considered restored, though not with full independence. It lasted until the time of Sulla, who defeated Athens in 86 BCE. See Tracy, *Athenian Democracy,* 18.

26. See, for example, my discussion of these speeches in Martin, *Slavery as Salvation,* 101–3.

in these two speeches: in the one to the ekklesia he cajoles and caters to the lower class; in the one to the council he takes care to assure them that he is no traitor to the upper class. It is obvious, in any case, that though all this takes place during Roman imperial rule and not in a democracy, the ekklesia still exists as an important vestige of democratic times.

We get another glimpse of the continued functioning of the ekklesia in the New Testament. Acts 19:23–41 tells the story of a riotous gathering of an *unofficial* ekklesia in Ephesus, when the people, led by makers of images of the goddess Artemis, fill the theater, dragging along some of Paul's companions. Though the author calls this an ekklesia (19:32), we know it is not an official meeting of the ekklesia of Ephesus because the "town clerk" (γραμματεύς) intervenes, warns the mob, and says formal charges may be brought against Paul and his companions in the courts or before the proconsuls, and if there is anything else the workers want to do, it must be done in a "legal ekklesia" (ἔννομος ἐκκλησία; 19:39). The author, though, continues using the term also for this "illegal" one: the author ends the scene by noting that the town clerk finally "dismissed the ekklesia" (19:41).

This little scene demonstrates that also in the first century, and well-known to Christians, the Greek ekklesia was still a significant institution in cities and towns of the eastern Mediterranean. Obviously, it was not as important as in the Greek democracies, but it was highly visible and played important roles at least in local politics and social activities. It was far too obvious a social institution to be ignored by the early devotees of a Jew executed years before in Judea. It is certainly ironic that these early believers borrowed from Greek politics the term "ekklesia" also for their tiny, insignificant house churches. But it is telling that they chose that political term— rather than others that may have had a more obvious relevance to a voluntary association or religious group, such as *thiasos*—with which to label their groups and gatherings.

The Politics and Theology of Ekklesia

Emphasizing the democratic ideology and functioning of the ekklesia should also provide theological and ethical fodder for our own churches. Let us compare the ekklesia with other models for church we have already encountered. When we think of Jesus or God as "king," we thereby render the church a "kingdom." When we put "Empire of God" in the context of the Empire of Rome, we are stuck, more or less, with the dangers of patriarchy, hierarchy, and all the injustices of oppression and exploitation committed by all known empires. When we consider the church a "household," as I emphasized above, we tend to value the traditional family more than much early Christianity did and more than we should in the current American context of the "idolatry of family." As we have seen, those parts of Christianity that emphasize most the church as a "household" also, not coincidentally, recreate the patriarchy, hierarchy, inequality, and misogyny of the traditional household. In contrast to those models of the church, the church as ekklesia, fashioned on the equality and justice of radical ancient democracy, is a much healthier alternative.[27]

And we can take inspiration not just from the fact that ancient Christian communities *called* themselves ekklesia; they also at times and in certain ways mimicked democratic structures and practices. In its earliest stages, apparently, early house churches and their networks of connections with the churches of other houses, cities, and regions were more democratically than hierarchically structured. Acts portrays the church in Jerusalem as holding property in common, with those better-off believers selling property to establish a common purse in order to help poorer believers (Acts 2:44–45; 4:32–37). This is obviously a presentation of an ideal that may never have actually happened and certainly did not last, even through all of Acts, but it is nonetheless a depiction that encourages equality, even in resources for daily life.

In presenting the conduct of meetings of the early church, Acts also makes it look something like an ekklesia of more or less equal persons. James the brother of Jesus seems clearly to be the main leader of the Jerusalem church, along with Peter playing a central role (15:13). And there is some recognition that "the apostles and elders," as smaller collective bodies, share some kind of leadership (15:2, 22). But when the issue about gentiles and circumcision is debated in what scholars sometimes call the Jerusalem Council, the text emphasizes that the matter is basically decided by a process of consensus of "the whole assembly" (15:12; the word *ekklesia* is not here used). The "letter" composed at the end of the meeting says, "We have decided unanimously" (15:25) and states that their conclusion was what "seemed good to the holy spirit and to us" (15:28). This sounds much like a democratic process, as in an ekklesia, except that it is done by consensus rather than show of hands, but that does not diminish the democratic coloring of

---

27. For one good demonstration of the relationship between ecclesiology and ethics—in that a rigidly hierarchical model of the church renders problematic ethics—see Mannion, "Act and Being."

the scene. After all, we often see ekklesiai in literary texts coming to decisions more by consensus than by explicit mention of voting.

Another democratic signal in Acts is seldom noticed as such, but that is probably because so many modern Christians have been usually unaware of the importance and ubiquity of selection of officers by lot in ancient democracies. At the beginning of Acts, when the place of Judas Iscariot among the apostles needs to be filled, his replacement is not appointed by any specific leader or by the remaining apostles; it is done in a typically democratic way: the entire group (we're told they number at this time "about 120 people") gather and among themselves choose, on the basis of agreed-upon criteria, two men, Joseph Barsabbas Justus and Matthias (1:15–26) (it has to be someone who has been with the movement from its beginning with John's baptism). The church then casts lots to see which of these two will be the new apostle. The procedure imitates the way democracies would first select a roster of qualified candidates and then make the selection by lot or some other random manner of selection. It is true that the author of Acts presents this also as the way the disciples find out which one is the choice of "the Lord" (1:24–25): they pray that "the Lord" (Jesus? God?) will manipulate the "lot" to the divine desired ends. But the practice of selection by lot would nonetheless have been recognized as a common democratic means of selection. So it is not surprising that this group, presented as an ekklesia, would use common democratic means for the selection of "officers."

The early Pauline house churches seem to have been informally structured with a combination of "household" and also democratic structures and behaviors. Paul clearly sees himself as the ultimate human authority figure for them, and he does not hesitate to emphasize his role as their founding "apostle" and even "father" (e.g., Gal 1:1–9; 2 Cor 12:11–14). Yet we can see by his pleading and tortured rhetoric in several places that he cannot simply dictate and snap his fingers and expect immediate obedience: 2 Cor 10–13 is a prime example, as is all of Galatians. Though Paul claims authority to command believers, at least those of the churches he founded, to do what he asks, he seems to realize he will have greater success by using persuasive rhetoric, as would be the case in any ekklesia (Phlm 8–9).

Paul's house churches recognized to some extent the leadership of other figures as well, probably in most cases the person in whose house the church met. Prisca and Aquila look a bit like leaders, at least of "the church in their house" (Rom 16:3–5; and it may not be accidental that her name comes before his, probably indicating that she enjoyed higher status at least at the time of Paul's writing; compare 1 Cor 16:19, where Aquila and Prisca seem to be hosting a church in their house in, probably, Ephesus, from which

Paul apparently is writing). Gaius may be something of a leader since he is called a host to the entire church of Corinth, probably indicating that different house churches occasionally met all together in his house (Rom 16:23). Stephanus may be a leader; he is a householder also (1 Cor 16:15, 17). Paul also mentions "overseers and servants" (Phil 1:1; NRSV: "bishops and deacons"), but these terms certainly do not designate, at this early date, the important "offices" that would later take these titles. All these are informal leadership roles, what in Weberian sociological language would be called charismatic rather than formal or institutional. The early Christian house churches and likely their citywide gatherings as well seem to have been rather democratic in structure and behavior, as we would expect since they chose to call themselves ekklesia.

The church became much more hierarchical as time went on. Already in the Pastoral Epistles we encounter top-down establishment of church offices. The letters, written pseudonymously and, I believe, well into the second century, present Paul in a role not unlike that of a later monarchical bishop or even archbishop. He, along with some collection of "elders," had "ordained" Timothy (1 Tim 4:14; 2 Tim 1:6). Now Paul places Timothy also in something like a bishop's role since Timothy seems to have authority over more than one church (in 1 Timothy he may be in Ephesus [1:3], but in 2 Timothy he seems to be itinerant [4:9, 21]), and he is now doing the "ordaining" (1 Tim 5:22). Timothy is to appoint "bishops" (or "overseers") and "deacons" himself (and perhaps "elders"? or is this another name for the "overseers"?: 1 Tim 5:17). Titus likewise has been appointed by Paul to oversee several churches in Crete (Tit 1:5), and he also is given authority to appoint elders/overseers (1:5, 7). So even in the New Testament we see the development of the more formal "offices" that will develop into the three-tiered hierarchy of bishop, presbyter, and deacon of later Roman Catholicism and Orthodoxy.

Even in later Catholicism, however, some democratic practices were retained from the early days. It may surprise many modern Christians to learn that for centuries bishops were not selected by a pope or even other bishops but were elected by the people of their diocese. The bishop ordained priests (sometimes only after the people insisted on someone popular with them), but the bishop himself was elected by the people, a later practice that retained, even in the hierarchical church of late antiquity, a vestige of earlier, more democratic ecclesial practices.[28]

28. See Hippolytus, *Apostolic Tradition* 2.1; *Apostolic Constitutions* 8.4.2–6; *Canons of Hippolytus* 2; *Testamentum Domini* 1.20; found conveniently translated in parallel columns in Bradshaw et al., *Apostolic Tradition*, 24–25; and see commentary at p. 28. See also Bobrinskoy, *Mystery*, 212.

Some people insist that the church is *not* a "democracy," and that has certainly been true for most of its history except for rare radical Protestant movements and more recently developed denominations. And some people disdain invoking democratic values and structures because they are not, in their opinion, "inherent" in Christianity but "come from" Enlightenment influences. As in all cases of such arguments, I completely dismiss any argument that impugns an idea or value because it "came from" some supposed source not "indigenous" to Christianity. Everything in Christianity, even if we confess that we receive it via revelation, has some existence or home in some other cultural location. Everything we have we got from *somewhere*. After all, the episcopacy and church hierarchy that developed in the late Roman Empire were simply a mimicking in the church of Greco-Roman and imperial structures and ideology.[29] Even the word "diocese" was originally a Greek term for a Roman administrative unit, only much later making its way into ecclesial usage. "Basilica" originally referred to a Roman building used for public courts and was only later appropriated for churches. If we postmodern Christians value democracy and its related "goods" of equality, equal justice for all, and self-rule by the people for the people—and most of us, at least in the West, do—we should mine the New Testament for theological inspiration for making our churches and the whole church of Christ a less hierarchical, more democratic body.

Paul's rhetoric in 1 Corinthians alone supplies two examples: his use of the "body metaphor" for the church, and his appropriation of "democratic" rhetoric in describing his ministry, that is, his practice and rhetoric of "self-lowering." In 1 Corinthians, Paul's attention throughout is on the body, both individual human bodies and the church as the body of Christ. As part of his strategy encouraging more unity in the Corinthian church, Paul takes from political rhetoric before him the topos of society as "body."[30] Politicians and rhetoricians, in Greek as well as Latin contexts, had long compared the city to a body, the upper class represented by the head or belly and the lower classes represented by other parts of the body. Manual laborers could readily be imagined as the hands while slaves could be the feet. The genitals were also regularly taken to represent the laboring classes because the upper class imagined them to be as fecund as vermin.

29. A point obvious to anyone with knowledge of Roman imperial governing structures, but it is made helpfully explicit by Wondra, "Problems with Authority," 24.

30. What follows is a summary of the exegesis offered in Martin, *Corinthian Body*, see esp. 39–47, 92–94, for the politically conservative use of the body metaphor, and 94–103 for Paul's more radical disruptive appropriation of the metaphor.

It was natural for the upper class to make themselves the head. It is a bit ironic, though, when they imagined themselves to be the belly, precisely because it was the *laboring* class, not the upper class, that actually *produced* goods and food. But the upper class thought of themselves as supporting everyone else because they paid wages, bought and sold slaves and fed them, and gave "gifts" to those of lower status to insure their loyalty. The upper class represented themselves as the belly, which digests the food and sends it out to the other members of the body in the form of blood and nourishment. The main point of the more conservative use of the body metaphor was to stress the "natural" nature of the hierarchy of society and to discourage any disruption of that hierarchy. (We have many more surviving examples of the conservative use of the body metaphor than those that may have favored the lower-class majority because the upper class wrote, reproduced, and preserved the vast majority of ancient literature.) According to upper-class ideology, the city as a whole body was healthiest and most productive and happiest when everyone stayed in their "proper" and "natural" place in the social body.

What is remarkable about Paul's use of this traditional rhetoric of the "body politic" is that he completely disrupts the traditional hierarchy and in fact *turns the body on its head*. Unlike some of his later imitators, Paul did *not* make Christ the "head of the body" when he elaborates on the metaphor in 1 Cor 12. That better enabled him to turn the more conservative "social body" upside down. First, he makes the usual point that all members of the body need one another and so cannot separate themselves from the body or ignore other members of the body (12:14–21). But then Paul does something surprising—surprising if we are familiar with the usually conservative use of the body metaphor from ancient politics. "On the contrary" (12:22, NRSV), Paul says, those parts of the body we might normally think of as lower or "weaker" are actually those we depend on the most. He compares some "members" (pun intentional) to the genitals but rather than saying they are of lower status he says we actually show that we honor them the *most* because we cover them up out of respect (12:23). This is not just our doing: "God has arranged the body this way, providing greater honor to the 'inferior' member so that there will be no conflict in the body, but the members will have identical care for one another" (12:25–26).

As I have shown in my book *The Corinthian Body*, this is Paul's strategy throughout 1 Corinthians: he knows the church in Corinth is divided along lines of social status, with those of relatively higher status taking different positions on a variety of issues from the positions being assumed by those of lower status. (No one at Corinth, I believe, was of truly high status; I wouldn't even use the term "middle class." But we may imagine the church in Corinth comprising persons of somewhat varying status levels. Some had slaves and households, for example, whereas most probably did not.) In 1 Cor 12–14, Paul's immediate goal is to get those who "speak in tongues," a "gift" taken in their culture as a sign of higher status, to submit to those who did not. The "higher" submitting to the "lower."

Paul repeatedly claims a "higher" position for himself but then uses his own intentional "self-lowering," whether as one who has taken on manual labor or who makes himself a "slave" to those he leads, to name only two such examples. He does this to serve as an example for the higher-status Corinthians to lower themselves and to act as the "servants" of those lower than them socially. Paul does the same with the metaphor of the social body: the head is the foot, and thus the foot is the head. Paul turns the social body on its head. This was a reversal of the traditional upper-class, conservative topos of the political body, using it in what would certainly be perceived in an ancient political context for a "democratic" strategy and goal. Paul had no problem appropriating ancient democratic ideology and rhetoric to inform his own theology and ethics of the body of Christ.

Paul's strategy of self-lowering comes out in another of his borrowings from older democratic rhetoric: the way he portrays himself not only as a "slave of Christ" but also as a "slave of all," a slave to those he is also leading.[31] In 1 Cor 9:15–23, Paul admits what to a conservative politician would have been anathema: that he "becomes all things to all people." In ancient political rhetoric, as in modern, a political leader could get into trouble if accused of being fickle, a waffler, to use the modern American slang. So upper-class or conservative political orators almost never admit to much changing of behavior or positions.

But interestingly, more "democratic" politicians used this as a political and rhetorical strategy. There were many such politicians, though only a fraction of their speeches and writings survive because, as I noted, the upper class was responsible for almost all surviving ancient literature. An upper-class man might give up the perquisites of his class and his loyalties to it to take on lower-class traits, such as speaking, dressing, or acting like a common laborer. He also talked the talk of democracy: the poor should have more power, debts should be more readily forgiven, we should receive

---

31. This is a summary of the arguments and exegesis from Martin, *Slavery as Salvation*, see esp. 86–135.

pay for participating in the ekklesia or the courts. In fact, the democratic politician might go so far as to say he has "enslaved" himself to "the people," the *demos,* which meant "people" but was taken to mean the lower class particularly. He claimed to do this for their good. His upper-class opponents would say he did it for mere monetary "gain." But he countered that his only "gain" was the betterment of the entire city, which meant raising the well-being mainly of the poor. Democratic politicians, who might wear the term "demagogue" proudly since it simply meant "a leader of the common people," changed their behavior, enslaved themselves to the people, and lowered themselves socially in order to "gain" better conditions for the people, meaning mainly the lower class.

This is precisely the rhetorical topos Paul appropriates in 1 Corinthians, especially chapter 9. Paul voluntarily became a manual laborer in order to "gain" manual laborers "for Christ." He becomes a Jew to Jews and a gentile to gentiles. He becomes weak to win the weak. And he does it admittedly for "gain," not for money but to gain the people for Christ. This is also why Paul refuses to accept payment from the Corinthians: he wants to make it clear that he is aware his strategy of self-lowering could be depicted as the servile, changeable behavior of the demagogue. But he embraces the portrait, lowering himself even to the point of calling himself a "slave of all." He does so not for financial gain for himself but to win people to Christ so that eventually even he, Paul, will "share in the blessings" of the gospel (9:23).

Paul did not invent the demagogue topos, as I have identified it. He took it from democratic political rhetoric before him. This indicates, for one thing, that Paul probably had at least some rhetorical training: he uses the social body metaphor and the demagogue topos so knowledgeably but creatively that he must have been schooled in these rhetorical moves. But in both cases he uses them in ways that an antidemocratic, upper-class Greek or Roman, someone like Plato, Aristotle, Cicero, or Dio Chrysostom, would disdain. Paul uses these rhetorical tools to reject upper-class ideology and promote what in ancient urban contexts would be clearly recognized as democratic values and ideology: reversing the traditional hierarchies of antidemocratic conservatives. Paul is a democrat. His ekklesia is the ekklesia of a democratic polis, not a monarchy, oligarchy, or republic. We should take Paul as an example: we should use the fact that we are ekklesia to promote and defend the values of democracy: equality; preference for the poor; reversal of traditional hierarchies that benefit the rich; justice and compassion for the oppressed and outcast. Like Jesus and Paul, we should make the last first and the first last.

Church and Ideology

If the church follows the values commended in the previous section, as democratic ekklesia it will of necessity be a church working against central ideological commitments of modern societies and culture. American Christians and churches are in the grip of an ideological stranglehold by the modern ideologies of family, nationalism, and capitalism. Thus we must recall the etymology of *ekklesia*. The term comes from the Greek for "call" (καλέω) and "out" (ἐκ). The Greek assemblies used the term "ekklesia" to refer to those citizens "called out" to assemble together. They were called out, symbolically even by a "herald" at the beginning of their meetings: out from their homes, workplaces, fields, and the "agora," that is, the marketplace. When early Christian house churches claimed the label "ekklesia" also for their small, rather insignificant gatherings, usually comprising only as many people as could fit in an average-size dining room, those disciples of Christ were precociously appropriating for themselves a powerful political and social image. The modern church needs to follow their example: we must reform the church so that it is no longer the church imprisoned by false modern ideologies, no longer, to mix "epics," in the "Babylonian Captivity" of "Constantinian Christianity."[32] Rather, it must be the church "called out" of that captivity chained by the ideologies of family, nationalism, and capitalism. The church must return to being the called-out church, the "church militant": the church that battles the oppressive ideologies of modernity.

When the emperor Constantine became the patron of Christianity beginning in 312, even before he may have officially "converted," everything changed with regard to the relationship of the church and Christians to the empire and dominant culture. It was no longer a church in opposition to the Roman imperial cult, no longer willing to suffer and die resisting imperial propaganda and demands. The church did not become the "official" religion of the empire for about seventy years, but it did receive huge financial and institutional patronage from the official organs of the empire, not to mention the propagandistic benefit derived from being the cult now supported by the

---

32. John Howard Yoder and Stanley Hauerwas are the two most influential theologians on what has been called Constantinian Christianity, or, in the term used by Yoder himself, the "Constantinian shift." To cite merely a few relevant sources, see Yoder, *Politics of Jesus*, 135 *et passim*; Yoder, "Is There Such a Thing," esp. 65; Hauerwas, "Christian Critique," now conveniently found in *The Hauerwas Reader*, esp. 474–75; Hauerwas and Willimon, *Resident Aliens*, 17–18 *et passim* (see "Constantine, Constantinian" in the index). But also see now the fascinating study by Aers, *Beyond Reformation?*

emperor, his influential household, and all the trappings of imperial power. In evolving with that change, the church lost its previous stance of militancy against unjust and oppressive power. The church, to a great extent, became one more tool of the emperor and the upper class. For centuries after, many forms of the church were simply incorporated into the power structures of rulers and the ruling class. The church evolved to promote the interests of rulers and the powerful. The church became an instrument of governing powers. This is what scholars mean by "Constantinian Christianity."

This was a situation not foreseen by any of the authors of the documents of the New Testament. A few of them did urge their readers to pray for rulers, to obey the state as far as morally possible, to pay taxes, even to "honor" the emperor (e.g., Mark 12:13–17 and par.; 1 Pet 2:13–17). And some of them could imagine a time when they themselves would join with Christ in a government that would include the church, but their term for that was, as we have seen, the "kingdom of God." None of our New Testament authors would have imagined, much less condoned, that the church of Christ would become a ward and loyal promoter of the Roman Empire. Paul speaks of "principalities and powers" as evil, oppressive entities. He probably was thinking of evil angelic or superhuman powers, such as Satan and those cosmic powers who do his bidding (Rom 8:38; 1 Cor 2:8; 15:24). But I believe anyone hearing his letters read aloud in a city in the Mediterranean basin would not have been able to help but assume he was speaking also of the powers of Rome. The John who wrote Revelation portrayed Rome, the emperor, and all who profited from Roman rule as beasts, demons, dragons, and whores. He would have considered later Constantinian Christianity as bearing the "mark of the beast" (Rev 13:16–17). Thus even those New Testament writers who do not explicitly rail against the rich and powerful, against Rome and the emperor, would never have imagined that the church would slip into subservience to the state, as it certainly did.

Most modern American Christians assume that the two values held most centrally and universally by all churches are promotion of "family values" and patriotism. Conservative Christians may think of family values in terms of the "traditional family" of one man, one woman, and their children. Liberal Christians may be more open-minded to enlarging that portrait to include other configurations of "family," including same-sex marriage, extended families, and other forms. But American Christians of many different political persuasions still assume that family is one of the most important values promoted by Christianity, if not *the* most important. One can see this by simply observing that people not in more traditional families are much less likely to attend church than those in traditional families. Most churches are not very welcoming places, perhaps in spite of their intentions, to single people and people in "unusual" household formations. The problem with putting so much emphasis on the family is that it allows the command to "love thy neighbor" and the love of one's family to suck up all the "love oxygen" in society. Karl Barth therefore criticized the ideology of the nuclear family: "It is the concentration of neighbourly love on these persons [that is, one's family] which really means its denial. It is the indolent peace of a clannish warmth in relation to these persons, with its necessary implication of cold war against all others."[33] This fact can be observed in American politics: many of those people who most want the state to promote "traditional family values" are also those who do *not* want the state to help the poor. If the church is to love as it should, it must be "called out" to become the militant church in a post-Constantinian society, and it must radically question its worship of the family. That is not Christianity, it is idolatry. Churches need to be places where those without families may find *their* form of "family" as well as the social supports families certainly provide. That is what was taught and modeled by Jesus and Paul.

The other reigning modern ideology that keeps the church from living out the gospel is nationalism, expressed in the assumption of almost all American Christians that *not* being "patriotic" is to be un-Christian. Yet it should be clear that the church must never identify its well-being with the well-being of any nation or state. It is baffling why Christians so easily confuse the gospel with nationalism. All the evidence is against such identification. If colonialism and imperialism were the great sins, the bane, of the seventeenth and eighteenth centuries—and I think a good case can be made to support that thesis—then nationalism was the most harmful political sin of the twentieth. The First World War was caused, at least to a great extent, by a clash of imperial systems and their financial and economic suppliers and structures, most visibly the combined Austro-Hungarian and Ottoman Empires against the British and French Empires, joined at the beginning of the war by the Russian Empire. With the end of the First World War, the huge systems of empire began unraveling. The Second World War was caused, on the other hand, most obviously by the attempt to reassert German and Japanese nationalisms against all of Europe and Asia. The aftermath of the Second World War likewise exhibits the enthusiasms for and eventually sufferings caused by nationalism: the "decolonizing" of colonial territories; at-

---

33. *Church Dogmatics* IV/2, p. 551. See also Gorringe, *Karl Barth,* 245.

tempts to replace colonial territories by carving up areas into new "nations"; creating new "nations" around the globe, which were then "validated" by the United Nations. Think of the countless wars fought in the name of "nation": in Pakistan, India, Tibet, Korea, Vietnam, Algeria, Bosnia, Serbia, the list is endless. Think of all the fighting, dying, torturing, kidnapping, raping, and killing done now in order to create or maintain "nations": such brutal acts are being carried out in Africa, the Middle East, Iraq, Afghanistan, Russia, Georgia, Ukraine, Israel, Palestine. Again, the list seems endless because new conflicts seem to break out regularly. Throughout the twentieth century and during the first decades of the twenty-first, more millions of people have suffered and died in the name of "nation" than probably from any other human activity. People have been persuaded to commit the greatest crimes, sins, and brutalities against their fellow human beings for the promises of nationalism, and we see them doing so every day on the evening news. It baffles me how so many Christians assume that patriotism and nationalism are somehow consistent with the gospel preached by Jesus and promoted by the early apostles and disciples. In fact, many American Christians practically *identify* Christianity with patriotism.[34] That is the power of ideology, and the result is idolatry: *American* idolatry.

Finally, the church is "called out" to oppose the ideology of capitalism. The very structure and logic of capitalism are based on the necessity of inequality, including unemployment for at least a significant portion of the population. Capitalism requires and produces the toleration of at least a significant number of poor and suffering people.[35] By its very logic, capitalism cares only for the return on investment, for profit. If it cares at all about the well-being of the worker, it is only to the extent that the worker is able to work productively in return for as little wage as possible. Capitalism cares for the worker's family only to the extent that capitalists know that workers must be reproduced, and at a rate high enough that labor costs, meaning

34. This attitude at least *used* to rule also in England, though I suspect that the identification of the Church of England with British nationalism is today a bit less firm. See the account of "The Mothers' Union" of nineteenth-century Britain provided by Cordelia Moyse, "Mothers' Union." The Mothers' Union promoted, according to Moyse, "divine patriotism": "the inherent rightness of British identity as an imperial power. Like many Christians, MU leaders ascribed imperial rule to the providence of God, not to base motives of wealth or adventure" (119).

35. If the idea that capitalism both *needs* radical inequality and *produces* it was not obvious to brain-washed Westerners before, the thesis has recently received strong support with the large, meticulous study by an economist who insists that he is *not* a Marxist: Thomas Piketty, *Capital in the Twenty-First Century*.

wages and whatever else it costs to keep workers alive, will remain as low as possible. If capitalism cares anything at all for the survival of human beings, it is only as producers and consumers: it needs human beings to produce the goods that can be then sold to human beings at a profit for the capitalist. If capitalism cares at all for a health care system, it cares for it and will support it only to the extent that such a system keeps laborers, at the lowest possible cost, just healthy enough to be productive workers. Capitalism, by its very nature, cares for nothing but profit, that is, return on investment for a tiny fraction of the overall population of any country and the world. Any reasonable observer freed from the blinding ideology of capitalism—and certainly any Christian educated by the gospel of Jesus Christ—should see from the injustices *required* by the normal workings of capitalism that capitalism, as a system and an ideology, is radically antithetical to the Christian gospel. Barth, therefore, described capitalism as "almost unequivocally demonic."[36]

To cite another Karl, this time Marx, capitalism presupposes the necessity of inequality and institutional violence; it is, he said, borrowing from Hobbes, "the warfare of all against all."[37] The gospel according to most of the New Testament, and certainly of Paul, valued equality. When Paul urged the Corinthian believers to collect funds for the poorer church in Jerusalem, he termed it an exercise in equality: ἐξ ἰσότητος (2 Cor 8:13). The lack of some is met by the abundance of others. Although Marx penned this famous phrase, and Marx would probably not be pleased with my use of it in this context, it correctly sums up Paul's gospel: "From each according to ability, to each according to need."[38] The church is a place where equality should be sought. The gospel ideal is *antihierarchical,* which is one reason the antidemocratic polity of some churches is offensive to a proper modern or postmodern theology. This is expressed by Paul even in economic terms.

---

36. *Church Dogmatics* III/4, p. 531. See Gorringe, *Karl Barth,* 225.

37. The phrase *bellum omnium contra omnes,* in one form or another, occurs several times in Hobbes's writings, but for one example, see *Leviathan* (1651), part I, chapter 4. Whereas Hobbes had made the phrase a characterization of human nature in general and in "nature," Marx used it for "bourgeois society" more historically, characterized, that is, by capitalism. Marx's use is also influenced by that of Hegel, though, again, for Marx it is "historicized" more particularly in capitalism. See the introduction by Lucio Colletti to Marx, *Early Writings,* 30, see also 101–2 (from "Critique of Hegel's Doctrine of the State") and 294 (from "Economic and Philosophical Manuscripts"); Tabak, *Dialectics,* 102, 136–37, 161, 162.

38. Marx, "Critique of the Gotha Program," in *Marx–Engels Reader,* 531 (I have altered the translation slightly to render it gender inclusive).

Contemporary Christians must finally learn the lessons of the gospel of love, of preferential treatment for the poor, of the democratic egalitarianism of the ekklesia. That would mean acknowledging, finally, the evils of the ideology and idolatry of family, nationalism, and capitalism.

Church and Israel

Something of a revolution has occurred in biblical scholarship since the end of the Second World War. Until that time, most Christians were taught that the Christian church had replaced Israel as God's favored people. The idea that Christianity was superior to Judaism, that the church was the "new Israel," and that Jews had now been forsaken by God ruled much popular thought and Christian theology and scholarship through most of Christian history. This is known as Christian "supersessionism": the idea was that Christianity had "superseded" Judaism, the church had taken the place of Israel in God's favor. That Christian ideological prejudice, expressing itself in many cases as out-and-out anti-Semitism, has been challenged even by Christian scholars and theologians in the past few decades.

Much of this change has come about because of—or perhaps as an impetus for—a rereading of Paul, sometimes labeled the New Perspective on Paul and his theology, much of which I described in the introduction above. The point to be made here is to remind ourselves that Paul never saw himself as founding a new religion. He saw himself as bringing gentiles to inclusion in Israel through Jesus Christ. Paul never uses the term "Christian" or "Christianity," and many scholars now are convinced that had he known the term "Christianity," he likely would have rejected it. Paul never saw himself as part of a "new religion" but as doing God's will to increase Israel with the inclusion, by faith, of gentiles *into* Israel. This is not the supersession of Judaism by Christianity, but the inclusion of gentiles *into* Israel.

There are other parts of the New Testament that also assume the church is part of Israel. In fact, the author of the Gospel of Matthew apparently believed, unlike Paul, that gentiles would be included in the church, but as observers of Torah, as gentiles who nonetheless keep the Jewish law. Matthew likewise, therefore, would reject any kind of "Christian supersessionism" or rejection of Jewish legal observation.[39] But we should admit that there are parts of the New Testament that can more easily be read as supersessionist.

39. Again, for a defense of this interpretation and fuller treatment, see Martin, *New Testament*, 93–107.

The Acts of the Apostles, for instance, *does* use the term "Christian" to designate members of the church as separate from at least most Jews (Acts 11:26). Repeatedly in Acts, Paul or some other evangelist will preach first to Jews, but when the message is rejected by the majority of the Jews, the speakers explicitly point out that they are turning away from the synagogue and going instead to the gentiles. In fact, it is a theme of Luke and Acts that the rejection of the gospel by Jews leads to its success among gentiles (Luke 4:24–27; Acts 13:46–52; 14:19–20; 17:5–15; 18:4–8; 19:8–10; 22:21; 28:24–28; to cite only a few such examples). The church depicted in Acts is always one that includes believing Jews, but one can easily discern a shift from emphasis on Israel to emphasis on the church of Christ.

One could debate the extent to which the Letter to the Hebrews imagines the church as superseding Judaism. Hebrews does make several arguments that at least the "liturgy" of the church is superior to the "liturgy" prescribed in Jewish scripture. The priesthood represented by Jesus is superior to the Aaronic or Levitical priesthood (e.g., Heb 3:1; 4:14–5:10; 6:20; 7:1–28; 8:1–7). Jesus is superior to Moses (3:3–5). The liturgy brought by Christ takes place in a "greater and more perfect tent" than was the tabernacle described in Jewish scripture (9:11, 24). The sacrifice of Jesus is superior to previous Jewish sacrifices (9:12–14). The "new covenant" is superior to "the first covenant" (9:15). The Jewish law was "only a shadow of the good things to come" (10:1). One could find more such arguments throughout Hebrews. One could make the case that the climax of the "speech" (which it really is, rather than a "real" letter: see 13:22) comes at 13:13. The author notes that as Jesus suffered crucifixion "outside the gates of the city" of Jerusalem, likewise the writer and his readers should "go to him outside the camp." Given the way this author has juxtaposed and contrasted Christ and the church with the "first covenant," Moses, the tabernacle, and the liturgies of the Jews, should this be read as advocating leaving Israel or at least the actual ethnic Jews behind? At any rate, Hebrews can easily be read as approaching as close to Christian supersessionism as one finds in the New Testament.

In this topic, the church must side with Paul. The church must repent from the history of Christian anti-Semitism. Christians may use recent historical-critical scholarship to affirm the continuity of the church with Israel, including contemporary Jews and the synagogue. In newer, developing Christian theology, we remind ourselves that Israel remains the people of God. Gentile believers in the God of Israel are dependent on Jews, not superior to them, and Christianity derives from Judaism and owes its existence to Israel. In fact, we Christians need Jews to be the root of our faith in the

God of Israel. For God's promises to remain faithful, God's promises to Israel must remain in place. For that reason I and many other Christians do not advocate the conversion of Jews to Christianity. For Christians to remain faithful to the God of Israel, we need the ongoing presence of the Jews as chosen people of God. Finally, in the past few decades, Christians seem to have found a way, biblically and theologically, to reject Christian supersessionism and to advocate loving coexistence with Jews and the synagogue.

Yet this raises a difficult issue, one that can still cause friction and sometimes unfortunate division between some Christians and some Jews: what should we believe about the modern State of Israel in the land of Palestine? One may repent of Christian anti-Semitism and grieve for the suffering of Jews throughout Europe in the twentieth century without believing that the answer to that suffering is Zionism. To many of us, including at least some Jews, Zionism is a form of wider nationalism that has been a plague in the twentieth and twenty-first centuries. Zionism, regardless of its early intentions, has been a violent movement of European colonialism. One does not have to exculpate Palestinians or other Arabs or radical Muslims to agree nonetheless that the continued violent taking of land and property by Israelis from Palestinians is an injustice. Zionism has not been possible without great and unjust violence.

It is unfortunate that some Jews and some Christians insist that any opposition to Zionism is itself anti-Semitic.[40] In doing so, they simply make support for the continued existence of Israel—which indeed must be supported by Christians no matter how we got to the current state of affairs—more difficult for Christians and others who love Jews but reject the violence that has necessarily devolved from the nationalistic ideology of Zionism. The situation is not completely incomparable, in spite of obvious differences, from how we should think about white Europeans' treatment of Native Americans. We must repent and grieve for the white—and Christian!—oppression and murder of Native Americans without believing that a workable solution is for all white people to leave the western hemisphere. So no one can seriously support those who believe the State of Israel should cease to exist. The church must figure out how to love Israel and Jews

---

40. For one recent tendentious equation of lack of support for contemporary Zionism with anti-Semitism, see Stegeman, "Theologie im Schatten." If Christians are not allowed to be critical of ongoing and increasing Zionism in the State of Israel—meaning the taking and holding of Palestinian land, property, and persons—without being tarred with the charge of being anti-Semitic, there will be no civilized debate on these complicated issues. There are Jews who criticize ideological Zionism. They are right to do so.

while still rejecting the obvious injustices of the oppression of Palestinians by Israel. That is simply a difficult line Christians mindful of the demands of justice and love must attempt to walk.

Church as Refuge

As the immediately preceding paragraphs demonstrate, the church can never be a space of escape from controversy and struggle. Learning to love one another—including others very different from ourselves and including those outside the church, such as Jews, Muslims, others of whatever religion, agnostics, atheists, or just "indifferents"—is difficult. But the church must become a space where that learning can take place.

And that requires honesty. A Greek word that occurs in the New Testament signifying a kind of honesty of speech, a boldness of speech, is παρρησία (it occurs many times, but see especially 2 Cor 7:4; Phil 1:20; Phlm 8). Paul uses it in a context in which he is experiencing inner conflict because of a harsh letter he had sent to the Corinthians. (It may indeed have included the content that now makes up 2 Cor 10–13; scholars are uncertain, but it is a possibility.) Paul recognizes that his language may have grieved the Corinthians. He says, "If I grieved you with the letter, I do not repent. But if I do repent, [it is because] I see that the letter did indeed grieve you, at least for a while" (2 Cor 7:8). Paul is letting us know that he realizes the honesty demanded by the gospel and needed in the church can sometimes seem like harsh honesty.

Paul comes across to modern people as unlikable. It may well be possible that he *was* unlikable. As a scholar of Paul for my entire career, I'm sometimes asked by people, If there were anyone from the past you would most like to spend time with, would it be Paul? I say, Not at all. I think Paul is a fascinating and frustrating subject, but I don't think he was the kind of guy I want to have a beer with. We do have to remember that what counted as civil or polite behavior in ancient Greco-Roman culture was probably not the same as what we take to be "nice behavior." Paul may have been no more unlikable than other men of his social station in the ancient cityscape.

But another thing we have to remember is Paul's very real belief that his well-being depended on that of others. Paul was, to put it mildly, "invested" in the realities of his churches: "I am under daily pressure because of my anxiety for all the churches" (2 Cor 11:28, NRSV). Thus he believed that complete honesty, even when painful, was necessary. That is also possible only in a context of presumed love and sincere interest in the well-being of all others in the community. So the context of agape allows and even demands *parrhêsia*.[41] Perhaps we Christians sometimes lack Paul's kind of honesty and "boldness of speech" because our churches do not matter to us as much as Paul's meant to him. Or perhaps we don't trust that we've created communities loving enough that we can risk Paul's kind of honesty. But we should learn from Paul that the church must be built and nurtured to be a place of loving honesty.

Andrew McGrath recalls an old image of the church as a "walled garden": "rather like the original garden of Eden—in which believers could grow in grace and holiness, protected from the world around them."[42] He traces the image back to Ephrem the Syrian, who died in 373, and to Augustine, who cited the Song of Songs to describe the church as "an enclosed garden, my sister and bride, a sealed fountain, a well of living water, an orchard of choice fruit" (4:12–13; trans. quoted from McGrath). McGrath also quotes a little-known hymn by Isaac Watts, the first stanza of which reads,

> We are a garden walled around,
> Chosen and made peculiar ground;
> A little spot enclosed by grace
> Out of the world's wide wilderness.

Thus I wish to add to my discussion of the "church militant" and out in the world working for peace and justice also this image of the church as refuge from the vicissitudes of the world.

Sometimes when I am in church I think about medieval monasteries and cloisters. It may be a bit romantic, but we do have images in our minds of monasteries as small places of light and civilization among the darkness of violence. At least the educated monks, after all, did copy and illuminate manuscripts. They kept ancient "civilization" alive through what we used to call the Dark Ages. Studying their books, praying the hours, memorizing the psalms, and working with their hands, they provided, at least as we may imagine them, places of refuge in a dark and violent world. In the darkness of a Compline service at my church, therefore, I can barely avoid imagining myself within the safe, thick walls of a medieval monastery, hearing the chanting and singing around me. I am a monk in a monastery in the "dark

41. Steinkamp, "Parrhesia." Steinkamp attempts a theological appropriation of the theme of *parrhêsia* in Foucault as "truth-speaking" in ancient formation of the self.
42. McGrath, *Theology,* 142–43.

ages," surrounded by barbarians and working to keep the flame of civility, compassion, and peace alive.

Back in the 1980s when I was "coming out" as a gay man, society was not as welcoming as it is today for gay and lesbian people, not to mention bisexual and transgendered persons. Although I was not the kind of person who liked to hang out in bars, especially loud dance bars, I would regularly go to one or another of the gay bars in town. I was not very good-looking or young and a bit shy about meeting strangers, so I was something of a wallflower. When friends of mine, knowing my lack of enthusiasm for loud discos and bars, asked me why I went I found myself explaining that I sought out such places for at least one reason most of us did: surrounded by gay men, queers, drag queens, lesbians, and all the other sorts, we could relish the feeling, in that space, that what the world outside was telling us was not true. We weren't "perverted." We weren't the enemy. We weren't even "abnormal"—or, if we were, we were learning that "normal" was overrated, and we *liked* not being "normal." With the world back then such a hostile place for gay people, we escaped regularly to a place where we were surrounded by other people and a subculture that affirmed our existence and told us we didn't have to believe all the lies the world "out there" was shouting at us. We had an alternative culture, a more "true" culture in which we could remind ourselves not to believe "them" but to believe "us." Yes, gay bar as monastery.

I'm sure many people may find my comparison of the church to a gay bar somewhat bizarre. Others may find it offensive. But besides the "church militant," we should cherish images of the church as an enclosed, protected space for the growth of people of faith. Church as gay bar in the 1980s. There is room for thinking of the church as a refuge from the world as well as a mission to the world.

Eschaton and Future

Besides invoking the past, though, these images should not lose their vision of the eschaton, the "last things," God's future for us. Throughout this book I have raised the theological theme of eschatology. That is because if we expect to enjoy all the benefits and promises of the gospel now, we will be dangerously disappointed. I say "dangerously" because the problem of disappointment is that too much of it can lead to loss of faith, loss of hope, and finally despair—which, as I've already noted, is, in my mind, the opposite of faith. As I said above, the opposite of faith is not atheism but despair, arriving at the conclusion that there is nothing meaningful in our world after all. Reminding ourselves that the promises of the gospel are precisely that, *promises,* keeps us looking to God for the future. It also keeps us from the false identification of the present church with the promised reign of God, the true, final community of the saved. The church may be the "first fruits" of the final gifts of God, but it is not its fulfillment—yet.

In the present, though, the church does function as a sacrament, that is, as a material thing that represents salvation but also in some way enacts it: something that not only points to God but also makes God present in our world, although certainly in a mystical way.[43] The church both is and supplies sacraments. I believe we should not get too hung up on the precise number of the sacraments or on which ones are "really" sacraments and which not. I believe the Roman Catholic Church was too hasty to innovate, and it *was* an innovation, in numbering the sacraments at seven. Protestants, for their part, were too constrictive and inappropriately "biblicist" in limiting the sacraments to two: baptism and the eucharist. I have been happily surprised to learn that premodern, early medieval theologians recognized many sacraments, even failing to provide dependable, consistent limits to the number. Hugh of St. Victor (ca. 1096–1141), in his *De Sacramentis,* discusses some thirty sacraments, and, according to Gary Badcock, "even Hugh's thirty sacraments represent something of a 'conservative estimate' for the time in which he wrote."[44]

"Sacrament," after all, comes simply from the early church's Latin translation, *sacramentum,* of the Greek word μυστήριον, "secret" or "mystery," in the New Testament, used of something formerly unknown but now revealed (see Eph 1:9–10; 3:8–9; 5:32).[45] We must not limit the materials and

---

43. Or as Gary Badcock puts it: "A visible token of the possibility of such an encounter [i.e., with God], and a concrete means—perhaps even *the* means—of realizing this possibility. Like a sacrament, it is a physical 'element'; yet, also like a sacrament, its meaning lies beyond its worldly character in what it symbolizes and realizes in ways that are more than material." *House,* 9; see also 97, where he quotes Joseph Cardinal Ratzinger, *Principles of Catholic Theology,* 53: "The Eucharist is the *sacramentum Christi* and, because the Church is *Eucharistia,* she is therefore also *sacramentum*—the sacrament to which all the other sacraments are ordered."

44. Badcock, *House,* 261. For an English translation of *De Sacramentis,* see *On the Sacraments of the Christian Faith,* trans. Deferrai.

45. See the discussion in Butler, "Learning," 50–75, esp. 58; see Tertullian, *Adversus Macionem* 5.17.1; 5.18.2, 9; *De anima* 21.2; *De ieiunio adversus Psychicos* 3.2. For the many different and shifting meanings of *sacramentum* over the centuries, see Van Slyke, "Changing Meanings."

mechanisms the spirit may use to make God present to us and to render us more like God. As the church awaits the salvation of the universe promised by Jesus and foreshadowed by the spirit in the church, let us look with expectation for sacraments all around us and in the church itself: those materials and mechanisms chosen by the spirit not only to show us grace but also to cause grace among us in our world. The church is the present sacramental promise in the world—or at least one of them—of the coming peace, justice, and love we have faith will be provided to the world, all the world, by our God.

Bibliography

Achtemeier, Elizabeth. "Exchanging God for 'No Gods': A Discussion of Female Language for God." In *Speaking the Christian God*, ed. Kimel, Jr., 1–16.

Ackerman, Susan. *When Heroes Love: The Ambiguity of Eros in the Stories of Gilgamesh and David*. New York: Columbia University Press, 2005.

Adam, A. K. M. *Making Sense of New Testament Theology*. Macon: Mercer University Press, 1995.

Adeney, Walter F. *The Theology of the New Testament*. London: Hodder and Stoughton, 1894.

Aers, David. *Beyond Reformation? An Essay on William Langland's* Piers Plowman *and the End of Constantinian Christianity*. Notre Dame: University of Notre Dame Press, 2015.

Alcinous. *The Handbook of Platonism*. Trans. and intro. John Dillon. Oxford: Clarendon, 1993.

Alison, James. *Faith Beyond Resentment: Fragments Catholic and Gay*. New York: Crossroad, 2001.

———. *The Joy of Being Wrong: Original Sin Through Easter Eyes*. New York: Crossroad, 1998.

Ambrose. "On the Holy Spirit." *Theological and Dogmatic Works*. Trans. Roy J. Deferrari. Washington: Catholic University of America Press, 1963.

Atkinson, William P. *Trinity After Pentecost*. Eugene, OR: Pickwick, 2013.

Austin, J. L. *How to Do Things with Words*. Oxford: Oxford University Press, 1966.

Badcock, Gary D. *The House Where God Lives: Renewing the Doctrine of the Church for Today*. Grand Rapids: Eerdmans, 2009.

Barrett, C. K. *A Critical and Exegetical Commentary on the Acts of the Apostles*. Edinburgh: T & T Clark, 1998.

Barth, Karl. *Church Dogmatics*. Trans. G. W. Bromiley. Ed. G. W. Bromiley and T. F. Torrance, 2d ed. Peabody, MA: Hendrickson, 1975.

———. *The Epistle to the Romans*. Trans. from the 6th ed. by Edwin C. Hoskyns. London: Oxford University Press, 1933.

Basil. *St. Basil the Great on the Holy Spirit*. Trans. David Anderson. Crestwood, NY: St. Vladimir's Seminary Press, 1980.

Bauckham, Richard J. *Jude, 2 Peter*. Waco, TX: Word Books, 1983.

Bauerschmidt, Frederick Christian. *Holy Teaching: Introducing the* Summa Theologiae *of St. Thomas Aquinas*. Grand Rapids: Brazos Press, 2005.

Beckwith, Sarah. *Shakespeare and the Grammar of Forgiveness*. Ithaca: Cornell University Press, 2011.

Beeley, Christopher A. *The Unity of Christ: Continuity and Conflict in Patristic Tradition*. New Haven: Yale University Press, 2012.

Bernard of Clairvaux. *On the Song of Songs, Sermones super Cantica Canticorum.* Trans. Ilian Walsh. Intro. Corneille Halfants. 4 vols. Spencer, MA: Cistercian, 1971–80.

Betz, Hans Dieter. "Zum Problem der Auferstehung Jesu im Lichte der griechischen magischen Papyri" In Hans Dieter Betz, *Hellenismus und Urchristentum: Gesammelte Aufsätze* 1:230–61. Tübingen: Mohr-Siebeck, 1990.

Biddle, Martin. *The Tomb of Christ.* Gloucestershire, England: Sutton, 1999.

Billings, J. Todd. *The Word of God for the People of God: An Entryway to the Theological Interpretation of Scripture.* Grand Rapids: Eerdmans, 2010.

Bloch, Chana, and Ariel Bloch. *The Song of Songs.* Berkeley: University of California Press, 1998.

Bloom, Paul. "Is God an Accident?" *The Atlantic,* December 2005, accessed July 28, 2014: http://www.theatlantic.com/magazine/archive/2005/12/is-god-an-accident/304425/.

Bobrinskoy, Boris. *The Mystery of the Church: A Course in Orthodox Dogmatic Theology.* New York: St. Vladimir's Seminary Press, 2012.

Boers, Hendrikus. *What Is New Testament Theology?* Philadelphia: Fortress, 1979.

Boethius. *Consolatio Philosophiae.* Ed. E. K. Rand. In H. F. Stewart, E. K. Rand, and S. J. Tester, eds., *Boethius: The Theological Tractates and the Consolation of Philosophy.* LCL 74. Cambridge: Harvard University Press, 1973.

Bonsirven, Joseph. *Theology of the New Testament.* Trans. S. F. L. Tye. Westminster, MD: Newman, 1963.

Bourdieu, Pierre. *The Logic of Practice.* Stanford: Stanford University Press, 1980.

Bradshaw, Paul F., Maxwell E. Johnson, and L. Edward Phillips. *The Apostolic Tradition: A Commentary.* Ed. Harold W. Attridge. Minneapolis: Fortress, 2002.

Brambilla, Franco Giulio. *Antropologia teologica: Chi è l'uomo perché te ne curi?* Brescia: Queriniana, 2005.

Brock, Sebastian. "The Holy Spirit as Feminine in Early Syriac Literature." In *After Eve,* ed. Janet Martin Soskice, 73–88. London: Collins, 1990.

Brown, Peter. *Body and Society: Men, Women, and Sexual Renunciation in Early Christianity.* New York: Columbia University Press, 1988.

Brown, Raymond E. *The Death of the Messiah: From Gethsemane to the Grave: A Commentary on the Passion Narratives in the Four Gospels.* New York: Doubleday, 1994.

———. *The Epistles of John: Translated, with Introduction, Notes and Commentary.* Garden City: Doubleday, 1982.

———. *The Gospel According to John: Introduction, Translation, and Notes.* Garden City: Doubleday, 1966–70.

Brunner, Emil. *Natural Theology: Comprising "Nature and Grace" by Professor Dr. Emil Brunner and the Reply "No!" by Dr. Karl Barth.* Trans. Peter Fraenkel, with Introduction by John Baillie. London: Geoffrey Bles/Centenary, 1946.

Buch-Hansen, Gitte. *"It Is the Spirit that Gives Life": A Stoic Understanding of Pneuma in John's Gospel.* Berlin: Walter de Gruyter, 2010.

Bulgakov, Sergius. *The Comforter.* Grand Rapids: Eerdmans, 2004.

Bultmann, Rudolf. *Theology of the New Testament.* 2 vols. Trans. Kendrick Grobel. New York: Charles Scribner's Sons, 1951, 1955.

Burgess, Stanley M. *The Holy Spirit: Eastern Christian Traditions*. Peabody, MA: Hendrickson, 1989.

———. *The Holy Spirit: Medieval Roman Catholic and Reformation Traditions*. Peabody, MA: Hendrickson, 1997.

Burke, Kenneth. *A Rhetoric of Motives*. Berkeley: University of California Press, 1950.

Butler, Christopher. *The Theology of Vatican II, The Sarum Lectures 1966*. Rev. and enlarged ed. London: Darton, Longman, and Todd, 1981.

Butler, Judith. *Bodies That Matter: On the Discursive Limits of "Sex."* New York: Routledge, 1993.

———. *Gender Trouble: Feminism and the Subversion of Identity*. New York: Routledge, 1990.

Butler, Rex D. "Learning from Patristic Community Formation." In *The Contemporary Church and the Early Church: Case Studies in Ressourcement*, ed. Paul A. Hartog, 50–75. Eugene, OR: Pickwick, 2010.

Caputo, John D., and Linda Martin Alcoff, eds. *St. Paul Among the Philosophers*. Bloomington: Indiana University Press, 2009.

Carnley, Peter. *The Structure of Resurrection Belief*. Oxford: Clarendon, 1987.

Catechism of the Catholic Church. 2d ed. Revised in accordance with the official Latin text promulgated by Pope John Paul II. Vatican: Libreria Editrice Vaticana, 2000.

Catherine of Siena. *The Dialogue*. Trans. Suzanne Noffke. New York: Paulist, 1980.

Certeau, Michel de. *The Practice of Everyday Life*. Berkeley: University of California Press, 1984.

Chadwick, Henry. *Augustine of Hippo: A Life*. Oxford: Oxford University Press, 2009.

Chesterton, G. K. *G. K. C. as M. C.: Being a Collection of Thirty-Seven Introductions*. Selected and ed. J. P. de Fonseka. London: Methuen, 1929.

Childs, Brevard S. *Introduction to the Old Testament as Scripture*. Philadelphia: Fortress, 1979.

———. *New Testament as Canon: An Introduction*. Philadelphia: Fortress, 1984.

Clayton, Philip. *Mind and Emergence: From Quantum to Consciousness*. Oxford: Oxford University Press, 2004.

Clayton, Philip, and Paul Davies, eds. *The Re-emergence of Emergence: The Emergentist Hypothesis from Science to Religion*. Oxford: Oxford University Press, 2006.

Clement of Alexander. *Les Stromates: Stromate V*. Comm. Alain Le Boulluec. Paris: Éditions du Cerf, 1981.

Coll, Niall. *Christ in Eternity and Time: Modern Anglican Perspectives*. Dublin: Four Courts, 2001.

Collins, Paul M., and Barry Ensign-George, eds. *Denomination: Assessing an Ecclesiological Category*. London: T & T Clark, 2011.

Congar, Yves. *I Believe in the Holy Spirit*. London: Geoffrey Chapman, 1983.

Conzelmann, Hans. *A Commentary on the Acts of the Apostles*. Hermeneia. Philadelphia: Fortress, 1987.

Cooper-White, Pamela. "Reenactors: Theological and Psychological Reflections on 'Core Selves,' Multiplicity, and the Sense of Cohesion." In *In Search of Self: Interdisciplinary*

Perspectives on Personhood, ed. J. Wentzel van Huyssteen and Erik P. Wiebe, 141–62. Grand Rapids: Eerdmans, 2011.

Cortez, Marc. *Theological Anthropology: A Guide for the Perplexed.* London: T & T Clark, 2010.

Craig, William Lane. *Assessing the New Testament Evidence for the Historicity of the Resurrection of Jesus.* Lewiston, NY: Edwin Mellon, 1989.

Cranfield, C. E. B. *A Critical and Exegetical Commentary on the Epistle to the Romans.* Edinburgh: T & T Clark, 1975.

Crisp, Oliver D. "Incarnation." In *The Oxford Handbook of Systematic Theology,* ed. John Webster, Kathryn Tanner, and Iain Torrance, 160–75. Oxford: Oxford University Press, 2007.

Critchley, Simon. "You Are Not Your Own: On the Nature of Faith." In *Paul and the Philosophers,* ed. Ward Blanton and Hent de Vries, 224–55. New York: Fordham University Press, 2013.

Croasmun, Matthew. "The Body of Sin: An Emergent Account of Sin as a Cosmic Power in Romans 5–8." Ph.D. diss., Yale University, 2014.

———. *The Emergence of Sin.* New York: Oxford University Press, 2016.

Cross, F. L. *The Oxford Dictionary of the Christian Church.* 3rd rev. ed. E. A. Livingstone. Oxford: Oxford University Press, 2005.

Crossan, John Dominic. *The Historical Jesus: The Life of a Mediterranean Jewish Peasant.* New York: HarperCollins, 1991.

———. *Who Killed Jesus? Exposing the Roots of Anti-Semitism in the Gospel Story of the Death of Jesus.* San Francisco: HarperSanFranciso, 1995.

Cyril of Alexandria. *Deux Dialogues Christologiques.* Intro., critical text, trans., and notes by G. M. de Durand. Paris: Éditions du Cerf, 1964.

———. *St Cyril of Alexandria on the Unity of Christ.* Trans. and intro. John Anthony McGuckin. Crestwood, NY: St. Vladimir's Seminary Press, 1995.

D'Costa, Gavin. "Christ, the Trinity, and Religious Plurality." In *Christian Uniqueness Reconsidered: The Myth of a Pluralistic Theology of Religions,* ed. Gavin D'Costa, 16–29. Maryknoll, NY: Orbis, 1990.

Davies, Brian. *The Thought of Thomas Aquinas.* Oxford: Clarendon, 1992.

Davies, Paul, and John Gribbin. *The Matter Myth: Dramatic Discoveries that Challenge Our Understanding of Physical Reality.* New York: Simon and Schuster, 1992.

Debru, Armelle. *Le corps respirant: La pensée physiologique chez Galien.* Leiden: Brill, 1996.

DeHart, Paul J. *The Trial of Witnesses: The Rise and Decline of Postliberal Theology.* Oxford: Blackwell, 2006.

Dodd, C. H. *The Parables of the Kingdom.* New York: Charles Scribner's Sons, 1936.

Dreytza, Manfred. *Der theologische Gebrauch von RUAH im Alten Testament: Eine wort-und satzsemantische Studie.* Giessen: Brunnen, 1990.

Dudley, Jonathan. *Broken Words: The Abuse of Science and Faith in American Politics.* New York: Doubleday, 2011.

Dunn, James D. G. *The Evidence for Jesus: The Impact of Scholarship on Our Understanding of How Christianity Began.* London: SCM, 1985.

———. *The New Perspective on Paul.* Grand Rapids: Eerdmans, 2008.

———. *New Testament Theology: An Introduction.* Nashville: Abingdon, 2009.

Eagleton, Terry. *The Meaning of Life.* Oxford: Oxford University Press, 2007.

———. *Reason, Faith, and Revolution: Reflections on the God Debate.* New Haven: Yale University Press, 2009.

Edelstein, Emma J., and Ludwig Edelstein. *Asclepius: Collection and Interpretation of the Testimonies.* Paperback with new introduction. Baltimore: Johns Hopkins University Press, 1998.

Edwards, Denis. *Breath of Life: A Theology of the Creator Spirit.* Maryknoll, NY: Orbis, 2004.

Ehrman, Bart D. *How Jesus Became God: The Exaltation of a Jewish Preacher from Galilee.* New York: HarperCollins, 2014.

———. *Misquoting Jesus: The Story Behind Who Changed the Bible and Why.* New York: HarperCollins, 2005.

———. *The Orthodox Corruption of Scripture.* 2nd ed. New York: Oxford University Press, 2011.

Ehrman, Bart D., and Mark A. Plunkett. "The Angel and the Agony: The Textual Problem of Luke 22:43–44," *CBQ* 45 (1983): 401–16.

Elliott, J. K., ed. *The Apocryphal New Testament: A Collection of Apocryphal Christian Literature in an English Translation.* Oxford: Clarendon, 1993.

Elliott, John H. *A Home for the Homeless: A Sociological Exegesis of 1 Peter, Its Situation and Strategy.* Philadelphia: Fortress, 1981.

Engberg-Pedersen, Troels. *Cosmology and Self in the Apostle Paul: The Material Spirit.* Oxford: Oxford University Press, 2010.

Esler, Philip F. *New Testament Theology: Communion and Community.* Minneapolis: Fortress, 2005.

Evdokimov, Paul. *L'Orthodoxie.* Neuchâtel, Switzerland: Delachaux et Niestlé, 1959.

———. *Orthodoxy.* Trans. Jeremy Hummerstone, updated by Callan Slipper. Hyde Park, NY: New City, 2011,

Exum, J. Cheryl. *The Song of Songs: A Commentary.* Louisville: Westminster John Knox, 2006.

Fatula, Mary Ann. *The Holy Spirit: Unbounded Gift of Joy.* Collegeville, MN: Liturgical, 1998.

Ferguson, Duncan S. *Biblical Hermeneutics: An Introduction.* Atlanta: John Knox, 1986.

Fitzmyer, Joseph A. *The Acts of the Apostles: A New Translation with Introduction and Commentary.* New York: Doubleday, 1969.

———. *The Gospel of Luke (X–XXIV): Introduction, Translation, and Notes.* Garden City: Doubleday, 1985.

Florensky, Pavel. *The Pillar and Ground of the Truth.* Trans. Boris Jakin. Princeton: Princeton University Press, 1997.

Fortman, Edmund J. *The Triune God: A Historical Study of the Doctrine of the Trinity.* Philadelphia: Westminster, 1972.

Foster, Paul. "Marcion: His Life, Works, Beliefs, and Impact." *Expository Times* 121 (2010): 269–80.

Foucault, Michel. *The History of Sexuality.* Vol. 3: *The Care of the Self.* New York: Vintage Books, 1988.

Fowl, Stephen E. *Engaging Scripture: An Essay in Theological Interpretation.* Oxford: Black-well, 1998.

Fowl, Stephen E., and L. Gregory Jones. *Reading in Communion: Scripture and Ethics in Christian Life.* London: SPCK, 1991.

Fox, Michael V. *Proverbs 1–9: A New Translation with Introduction and Commentary.* New York: Doubleday, 2000.

Francis, Matthew W. G. "'Blessed Is the One Who Reads Aloud . . . ': The Book of Revelation in Orthodox Lectionary Traditions." In *Exegesis and Hermeneutics in the Churches of the East: Select Papers from the SBL Meeting in San Diego, 2007,* ed. Vahan S. Hovhavessian, 67–78. New York: Peter Lang, 2009.

Frei, Hans W. *The Eclipse of Biblical Narrative: A Study in Eighteenth- and Nineteenth-Century Hermeneutics.* New Haven: Yale University Press, 1974.

———. *The Identity of Jesus Christ: The Hermeneutical Bases of Dogmatic Theology.* Philadelphia: Fortress, 1975.

———. *Theology and Narrative: Selected Essays.* Ed. George Hunsinger and William C. Placher. New York: Oxford University Press, 1993.

———. *Types of Christian Theology.* Ed. George Hunsinger and William C. Placher. New Haven: Yale University Press, 1992.

Frye, Roland M. "Language for God and Feminist Language: Problems and Principles." In *Speaking the Christian God,* ed. Kimel, Jr., 17–43.

Frykholm, Amy. *Julian of Norwich: A Contemplative Biography.* Brewster, MA: Paraclete, 2010.

Fulkerson, Mary McClintock. *Places of Redemption: Theology for a Worldly Church.* New York: Oxford University Press, 2007.

Gager, John G. *Reinventing Paul.* Oxford: Oxford University Press, 2000.

Galen. *Galen on Respiration and the Arteries.* Ed., trans., and comm. David J. Furley and J. S. Wilkie. Princeton: Princeton University Press, 1984.

Gillman, Neil. *The Death of Death: Resurrection and Immortality in Jewish Thought.* Woodstock, VT: Jewish Lights, 1997.

Gleick, James. *The Information: A History, A Theory, A Flood.* New York: Pantheon, 2011.

Gorringe, Timothy. *Karl Barth: Against Hegemony.* Oxford: Oxford University Press, 1999.

Greer, Rowan A. *Anglican Approaches to Scripture: From the Reformation to the Present.* New York: Crossroad, 2006.

Greer, Rowan A., trans. and ed. *Origen.* Preface by Hans Urs von Balthasar. New York: Paulist, 1979.

Gregory of Nazianzus. "Fifth Theological Oration—On the Spirit." Trans. Edward Rochie Hardy. *Christology of the Later Fathers.* Vol. 3. Philadelphia: Westminster, 1954.

Gregory of Nyssa. "Answer to Eunomius' Second Book." In *Nicene and Post-Nicene Fathers,* Second Series. Ed. Philip Schaff and Henry Wace. Trans. M. Day. Vol. 5. Peabody, MA: Hendrickson, 1994.

———. *Cant. Cant. Hom.* VII (*Seventh Homily on the Song of Songs; on Song of Songs* 3:11. Ed.Werner Jaeger. *Gregorii Nyssseni Opera.* Vol 6. Leiden: Brill, 1960.

———. *Commentary on the Song of Songs.* Trans. and intro. Casimir McCambley. Preface by Panaglotes Chrestou. Brookline, MA: Hellenic College, 1987.

Grözinger, Albrecht, and Georg Pfleiderer, eds. *"Gelebte Religion" als Programmbegriff Systematischer und Praktischer Theologie.* Zürich: TVZ, 2002.

Guthrie, Donald. *New Testament Theology.* Downers Grove, IL: Intervarsity, 1981.

Haile, Getatchew. "Ethiopian Church." In *Encyclopedia of Religion,* ed. Lindsay Jones et al., 5:2858–62. 2d ed. New York: Thomson Gale, 2005.

Hammann, Konrad. *Rudolf Bultmann: A Biography.* Trans. Philip E. Devenish. Salem, OR: Polebridge, 2013.

Hansen, Mogens Herman. *The Athenian Assembly in the Age of Demosthenes.* Oxford: Basil Blackwell, 1987.

Harvey, A. E. "Melito and Jerusalem," *JTS* ns. 17 (1966): 401–4.

Harvey, Susan Ashbrook. "Feminine Imagery for the Divine: The Holy Spirit, the Odes of Solomon, and Early Syriac Tradition." *St. Vladimir's Seminary Quarterly* 37 (1993): 111–39.

Hauerwas, Stanley. "A Christian Critique of Christian America (1986)." In *The Hauerwas Reader,* ed. John Berkman and Michael Cartwright, 459–80. Durham: Duke University Press, 2001.

——. *Hannah's Child: A Theologian's Memoir.* Grand Rapids: Eerdmans, 2010.

Hauerwas, Stanley, and William H. Willimon. *Resident Aliens: Life in the Christian Colony.* Nashville: Abingdon, 1989.

Hayes, Richard B. *Echoes of Scripture in the Letters of Paul.* New Haven: Yale University Press, 1989.

Helyer, Larry R. *The Life and Witness of Peter.* Downers Grove, IL: IVP Academic, 2012.

Henriksen, Jan-Olav. "The Erotic Self and the Image of God." In *In Search of Self: Interdisciplinary Perspectives on Personhood,* ed. J. Wentzel van Huyssteen and Erik P. Wiebe, 256–72. Grand Rapids: Eerdmans, 2011.

Hildegard of Bingen. *Scivias.* Trans. Columba Hart and Jane Bishop. New York: Paulist, 1990.

Hill, William J. *The Three-Personed God: The Trinity as a Mystery of Salvation.* Washington: Catholic University of America Press, 1982.

Hirsch,, E. D., Jr. *Validity in Interpretation.* New Haven: Yale University Press, 1967.

Hoff, Johannes. "Dekonstruktive Metaphysik: Zur wissenschaftlichen Erschließung des Archivs Negativer 'nach' Derrida." In *Kreuzungen Jacques Derridas: Geistergespräche zwischen Philosophie und Theologie,* ed. Peter Zeillinger and Matthias Flatscher, 138–68. Vienna: Turia + Kant, 2004.

——. *Spiritualität und Sprachverlust: Theologie nach Foucault und Derrida.* Zürich: Schöningh 1999.

——. *The Analogical Turn: Rethinking Modernity with Nicholas of Cusa.* Grand Rapids: Eerdmans, 2013.

Hoff, Johannes, and Peter Hampson. "Cusa: A Pre-modern Postmodern Reader of Shakespeare." In *Theology and Literature after Postmodernity,* ed. Zoë Lehmann Imfeld, Peter Hampson, and Alison Milbank, 115–35. London: Bloomsbury T & T Clark, 2015.

Hudry, Françoise, ed. *Le Livre des XXIV Philosophes.* Latin text and French translation. Grenoble: Millon, 1989.

Hugh of St. Victor. *On the Sacraments of the Christian Faith.* Trans. Roy J. Deferrai. Cambridge, MA: Mediaeval Academy of America, 1951.

Hultin, Jeremy. *Jude and 2 Peter: A Commentary.* Hermeneia. Minneapolis: Augsburg Fortress, forthcoming.

———. "The Literary Relationship Between 1 Peter, 2 Peter, and Jude." In *Reading 1–2 Peter and Jude: A Resource for Students,* ed. Eric F. Mason and Troy W. Martin, 27–45. Resources for Biblical Study 77. Atlanta: Society of Biblical Literature, 2014.

Isaacson, Walter. *Einstein: His Life and Thought.* New York: Simon and Schuster, 2007.

Jaeger, Werner. "Das Pneuma im Lykeion." *Hermes* 48 (1913): 30–74.

Jenson, Robert W. *Systematic Theology.* Vol. 1: *The Triune God.* New York: Oxford University Press, 1997.

———. *The Triune Identity: God According to the Gospel.* Philadelphia: Fortress, 1982.

Jeremias, Joachim. *Heiligengräber in Jesu Umwelt (Mt. 23,29; Lk. 11,47): Eine Untersuchung zur Volksreligion der Zeit Jesu.* Göttingen: Vandenhoeck and Ruprecht, 1958.

———. *The Parables of Jesus.* New York: Scribner, 1955.

Jerome. *In Isa.* XI. Ed. Marcus Adriaen. Corpus Christianorum Series Latina 73.1. Turnhout, Belgium: Brepols, 1963.

Jewett, Robert. *Romans: A Commentary.* Minneapolis: Fortress, 2007.

Johnson, Elizabeth A. "Creator Spirit and Ecological Ethics: An Ancient Frontier." In *Lord and Life-Giver: Spirit Today (Concilium* 2011/14), ed. Paul Murray, Diego Irarrázaval, and Maria Clara Bingemer, 23–31. London: SCM, 2011.

———. *She Who Is: The Mystery of God in Feminist Discourse.* New York: Crossroad, 1992.

———. *Women, Earth, and Creator Spirit.* New York: Paulist, 1993.

Johnson, Luke Timothy. *The Acts of the Apostles.* Collegeville, MN: Liturgical, 1992.

Jones, W. H. S., ed. and trans. *Hippocrates.* Vol. 2. LCL 148. Cambridge: Harvard University Press, 1923.

Joseph Cardinal Ratzinger. *Principles of Catholic Theology: Building Stones for a Fundamental Theology.* San Francisco: Ignatius, 1987.

Jülicher, Adolf. *Die Gleichnisreden Jesu.* Tübingen: J. C. B. Mohr, 1888–99.

Jüngel, Eberhard. *God as the Mystery of the World: On the Foundation of the Theology of the Crucified One in the Dispute between Theism and Atheism.* Grand Rapids: Eerdmans, 1983.

Kähler, Martin. *The So-Called Historical Jesus and the Historic, Biblical Christ.* Foreword by Paul Tillich. Trans., ed., and intro. Carl E. Braaten.

Kamionkowski, S. Tamar, and Wonil Kim, eds. *Bodies, Embodiment, and Theology of the Hebrew Bible.* New York: T & T Clark, 2010.

Kariatlis, Philip. "'What Then? Is the Spirit God? Certainly!': St. Gregory's Teaching on the Holy Spirit as the Basis of the World's Salvation." Downloadable PDF at http://www.academia.edu/. Accessed September 2, 2014.

Kärkkäinen, Veli-Matti. *The Holy Spirit: A Guide to Christian Theology.* Louisville: Westminster John Knox, 2012.

Kelly, J. N. D. *Early Christian Doctrines.* 2nd ed. New York: Harper and Row, 1960.

Kelsey, David H. *Eccentric Existence: A Theological Anthropology.* Louisville: Westminster John Knox, 2009.

Ker, Ian. *G. K. Chesterton: A Biography.* Oxford: Oxford University Press, 2011.

Kerr, Fergus. *After Aquinas: Versions of Thomism.* Oxford: Blackwell, 2002.

———. *Theology After Wittgenstein*. Oxford: Basil Blackwell, 1986.

Kessler, Charles, ed. *The Diaries of Count Harry Kessler*. New York: Grove, 2002.

Keul, Hildegund. "Inkarnation— Gottes Wagnis der Verwundbarkeit." *Theologische Quartalschrift* 192 (2012): 216–32.

Kierkegaard, Søren. *Concluding Unscientific Postscript*. Trans. David F. Swenson. Princeton: Princeton University Press, 1944.

Kimel, Alvin F., Jr., ed. *Speaking the Christian God: The Holy Trinity and the Challenge of Feminism*. Grand Rapids: Eerdmans, 1992.

Knust, Jennifer Wright. *Unprotected Texts: The Bible's Surprising Contradictions About Sex and Desire*. New York: HarperOne, 2011.

Knust, Jennifer Wright, with Tommy Wasserman. *Jesus, an Adultress, and the Gospel of John*. Princeton: Princeton University Press, forthcoming.

Küng, Hans. *Does God Exist? An Answer for Today*. New York: Doubleday, 1980.

Kwok, Pui-Lan, Judith A. Berling, and Jenny Plane Te Paa, eds. *Anglican Women on Church and Mission*. New York: Morehouse, 2012.

Ladd, George Eldon. *A Theology of the New Testament*. Grand Rapids: Eerdmans, 1974.

Landy, Francis. "I and Eye in Isaiah, or Gazing at the Invisible." *JBL* 131 (2012): 85–97.

Lash, Nicholas. *Holiness, Speech, and Silence: Reflections on the Question of God*. Aldershot, UK: Ashgate, 2004.

———. *A Matter of Hope: A Theologian's Reflections on the Thought of Karl Marx*. Notre Dame: University of Notre Dame Press, 1982.

Latour, Bruno. *The Pasteurization of France*. Trans. Alan Sheridan and John Law. Cambridge: Harvard University Press, 1988.

———. *We Have Never Been Modern*. Trans. Catherine Porter. Cambridge: Harvard University Press, 1993.

Latour, Bruno, and Steve Woolgar. *Laboratory Life: The Construction of Scientific Facts*. Princeton: Princeton University Press, 1986.

Law, Timothy Michael. *When God Spoke Greek: The Septuagint and the Making of the Christian Bible*. New York: Oxford University Press, 2013.

Layton, Bentley. *The Gnostic Scriptures: A New Translation with Annotations and Introductions*. New York: Doubleday, 1987.

Lessing, G. E. "On the Proof of the Spirit and of Power." In *Lessing's Theological Writings*. Ed. and trans., Henry Chadwick. Stanford: Stanford University Press, 1957.

Licona, Michael R. *The Resurrection of Jesus: A New Historiographical Approach*. Downers Grove, IL: Intervarsity, 2010.

Lindbeck, George A. *The Nature of Doctrine: Religion and Theology in a Postliberal Age*. Philadelphia: Westminster, 1984.

Löhr, Winrich. "Did Marcion Distinguish Between a Just God and a Good God?" In *Marcion und seine kirchengeschichtliche Wirkung/Marcion and His Impact on Church History*, ed. Gerhard May and Katharina Greschat, with Martin Meiser, 131–46. Berlin: Walter de Gruyter, 2002.

Louth, Andrew. *Denys the Areopagite*. Wilton, CT: Morehouse-Barlow, 1989.

Lowder, Jeffrey Jay. "Historical Evidence and the Empty Tomb Story." *Journal of Higher Criticism* 8.2 (Fall 2001): 251–93.

Lüdemann, Gerd. *The Resurrection of Jesus: History, Experience, Theology.* London: SCM, 1994.

Ludlow, Morwenna. *Gregory of Nyssa, Ancient and (Post)modern.* Oxford: Oxford University Press, 2007.

Luibheid, Colm, ed. *Pseudo-Dionysius, The Complete Works.* Foreword, notes, and translation collaboration by Paul Rorem. Preface by Rene Roques. Introductions by Jaroslav Pelikan, Jean Leclercq, and Karlfried Froehlich. New York: Paulist, 1987.

MacMullen, Ramsay. *Paganism in the Roman Empire.* New Haven: Yale University Press, 1981.

Mannion, Gerard. "Act and Being in the Church: Comparative Explorations in Ecclesiology and Ethics." In *Christian Community Now: Ecclesiological Investigations,* ed. Paul M. Collins, Gerard Mannion, Gareth Powell, and Kenneth Wilson, 109–34. London: T & T Clark, 2008.

Mannion, Gerard, and Kenneth Wilson. "Introduction." In *Christian Community Now: Ecclesiological Investigations,* ed. Paul M. Collins, Gerard Mannion, Gareth Powell, and Kenneth Wilson, 1–6. London: T & T Clark, 2008.

Markham, Ian S. *Understanding Christian Doctrine.* Oxford: Blackwell, 2008.

Martin, Dale B. "The Construction of the Ancient Family: Methodological Considerations." *JRS* 86 (1996): 40–60.

———. "Contradictions of Masculinity: Ascetic Inseminators and Menstruating Men in Greco-Roman Culture." In *Generation and Degeneration: Literature and Tropes of Reproduction,* ed. Valeria Finucci and Kevin Brownlee, 81–108. Durham: Duke University Press, 2001.

———. *The Corinthian Body.* New Haven: Yale University Press, 1995.

———. *Inventing Superstition from the Hippocratics to the Christians.* New Haven: Yale University Press, 2004.

———. "Jesus in Jerusalem: Armed and Not Dangerous." *JSNT* 37 (2014): 3–24.

———. *New Testament History and Literature.* New Haven: Yale University Press, 2012.

———. *Pedagogy of the Bible.* Louisville: Westminster John Knox, 2008.

———. "The Promise of Teleology, the Constraints of Epistemology, and Universal Vision in Paul." In *St. Paul among the Philosophers,* ed. Caputo and Alcoff, 91–108.

———. "Response to Downing and Fredriksen." *JSNT* 37 (2015): 334–45.

———. *Sex and the Single Savior: Gender and Sexuality in Biblical Interpretation.* Louisville: Westminster John Knox, 2006.

———. "Slave Families and Slaves in Families." In *Early Christian Families in Context: An Interdisciplinary Dialogue,* ed. David L. Balch and Carolyn Osiek, 207–30. Grand Rapids: Eerdmans, 2003.

Martin, Troy W. "Paul's Pneumatological Statements and Ancient Medical Texts." In *The New Testament and Early Christian Literature in Greco-Roman Context: Studies in Honour of David E. Aune,* ed. John Fotopoulos, 105–26. Leiden: Brill, 2006.

Martyn, J. Louis. *History and Theology in the Fourth Gospel.* 2d ed., rev. and enl. Nashville: Abingdon, 1979.

Marx, Karl. *Early Writings.* Intro. Lucio Colletti. London: Penguin, 1975.

————. *The Marx–Engels Reader*. Ed. Robert C. Tucker. New York: W. W. Norton, 1978.

Mascall, Eric L. *Christ, the Christian, and the Church: A Study of the Incarnation and Its Consequences*. London: Longmans, Green, 1955.

Matera, Frank J. *New Testament Theology: Exploring Diversity and Unity*. Louisville: Westminster John Knox, 2007.

May, Gerhard, and Katharina Greschat, eds., with Martin Meiser. *Marcion und seine kirchengeschichtliche Wirkung/Marcion and His Impact on Church History*. Berlin: Walter de Gruyter, 2002.

McCabe, Herbert. *After Aquinas: Versions of Thomism*. Oxford: Blackwell, 2002.

————. *Faith Within Reason*. London: Continuum, 2007.

————. *God Matters*. London: Continuum, 2005.

————. *God Still Matters*. Ed. Brian Davies. London: Continuum, 2002.

————. *The Good Life: Ethics and the Pursuit of Happiness*. Ed. and intro. Brian Davies. London: Continuum, 2005.

————. *On Aquinas*. Ed. and intro. Brian Davies. London: Continuum, 2008.

McGrath, Alister E. *The Making of Modern German Christology, 1750–1990*. 2d ed. Grand Rapids: Zondervan, 1994.

————. *Theology: The Basics*. 2d ed. Oxford: Blackwell, 2008.

Meeks, Wayne A. *The First Urban Christians: The Social World of the Apostle Paul*. New Haven: Yale University Press, 1983.

————. "The Stranger from Heaven in Johannine Sectarianism." *JBL* 91 (1972): 44–72.

————. "Why Study the New Testament?" *NTS* 51 (2005): 155–70.

Melito of Sardis. *On Pascha and Fragments*. Ed. and trans. Stuart George Hall. Oxford: Clarendon, 1979.

Miller, Anna C. *Corinthian Democracy: Democratic Discourse in 1 Corinthians*. Eugene, OR: Pickwick, 2015.

Miller, Richard C. *Resurrection and Reception in Early Christianity*. New York: Routledge, 2015.

Moll, Sebastian. *The Arch-Heretic Marcion*. Tübingen: Mohr Siebeck, 2010.

————. "Marcion: A New Perspective on His Life, Theology, and Impact." *Expository Times* 121 (2010): 281–86.

Moltmann, Jürgen. *Crucified God: The Cross of Christ as the Foundation and Criticism of Christian Theology*. London: SCM, 2001.

————. *The Spirit of Life: A Universal Affirmation*. Minneapolis: Fortress, 2001.

————. *Theology of Hope: On the Ground and the Implications of a Christian Eschatology*. 5th ed. Trans. James W. Leitch. London: SCM, 2002.

Moore, Sebastian. *The Inner Loneliness*. New York: Crossroad, 1982.

Moore, Stephen D. *God's Gym: Divine Male Bodies of the Bible*. New York: Routledge, 1996.

Morgan, Robert. *The Nature of New Testament Theology: The Contribution of William Wrede and Adolf Schlatter*. Naperville, IL: Alec R. Allenson, 1973.

Morris, Leon. *New Testament Theology*. Grand Rapids: Zondervan, 1986.

Moyse, Cordelia. "Mothers' Union: From Victorian Village to Global Village." In *Anglican Women*, ed. Kwok Pui-Lan et al., 117–34.

Murphy, Nancey. *Bodies and Souls, or Spirited Bodies?* Cambridge: Cambridge University Press, 2006.

———. "The Resurrection Body and Personal Identity: Possibilities and Limits of Eschatological Knowledge." In *Resurrection: Theological and Scientific Assessments,* ed. Ted Peters, Robert John Russell, and Michael Welker, 202–18. Grand Rapids: Eerdmans, 2002.

Murray, Andrew. "The Spiritual and the Supernatural According to Thomas Aquinas." Paper delivered at the Biennial Conference in Philosophy, Religion, and Culture, "The Supernatural," Catholic Institute of Sydney, 3–4 October 1998. http://www.cis.catholic.edu.au/Files/Murray-SpiritualSupernatural.pdf. Accessed June 30, 2012.

Murray, Paul, Diego Irarrázaval, and Maria Clara Bingemer, eds. *Lord and Life-Giver: Spirit Today* (*Concilium* 2011/14). London: SCM, 2011.

Nadler, Steven. *Spinoza: A Life.* Cambridge: Cambridge University Press, 1999.

Newman, Barclay M., Jr. "A Concise Greek–English Dictionary of the New Testament." In *The Greek New Testament,* Barbara Aland et al., eds. 4th rev. ed. Stuttgart: Deutsche Bibelgesellschaft, 2001.

Noelle, Elisabeth. "Die doppelte Natur des Menschen." In *Bildung, Identität, Religion: Fragum zum Wesen des Menschen,* ed. Hans Poser and Bruno B. Reuer, 67–76. Berlin: Weidler, 2004.

Nongbri, Brent. *Before Religion: A History of a Modern Concept.* New Haven: Yale University Press, 2013.

Norris, Richard. "Trinity." In *The Holy Spirit,* ed. Rogers, Jr., 19–43.

Nygren, Anders. *Agape and Eros.* Trans. Philip S. Watson. Chicago: University of Chicago Press, 1982.

O'Collins, Gerald. *Incarnation.* New York: Continuum, 2002.

O'Neil, James L. *The Origins and Development of Ancient Greek Democracy.* Lanhan, MD: Rowman and Littlefield, 1995.

Ober, Josiah. *The Athenian Revolution: Essays on Ancient Greek Democracy and Political Theory.* Princeton: Princeton University Press, 1996.

Olyan, Saul M. "'Surpassing the Love of Women': Another Look at 2 Samuel and the Relationship of David and Jonathan." In *Authorizing Marriage? Canon, Tradition, and Critique in the Blessing of Same-Sex Unions,* ed. Mark D. Jordan, with Meghan T. Sweeney and David M. Mellott, 7–16, 165–70. Princeton: Princeton University Press, 2006.

Owen, John. *ΠΝΕΥΜΑΤΟΛΟΓΙΑ, Or, A Discourse Concerning the Holy Spirit.* Vol. 2: *The Works of John Owen.* Ed. Thomas Russell. London: Richard Baynes, 1826; originally 1676.

Paddison, Angus. *Scripture: A Very Thoughtful Proposal.* London: T & T Clark, 2009.

Peck, Arthur L. "The Connate Pneuma: An Essential Factor in Aristotle's Solutions to the Problems of Reproduction and Sensation." In *Science, Medicine and History: Essays on the Evolution of Scientific Thought and Medical Practice Written in Honour of Charles Singer,* ed. E. Ashworth Underwood, 1:111–21. London: Oxford University Press, 1953.

Peppard, Michael. *The Son of God in the Roman World: Divine Sonship in its Social and Political Context.* New York: Oxford University Press, 2011.

Piketty, Thomas. *Capital in the Twenty-First Century.* Cambridge: Harvard University Press, 2014.

Pinker, Steven. *The Blank Slate: The Modern Denial of Human Nature*. New York: Viking, 2002.

Pinnock, Clark H. *Flame of Love: A Theology of the Holy Spirit*. Downers Grove, IL: Intervarsity, 1996.

Pope, Marvin H. *Song of Songs: A New Translation with Introduction and Commentary*. New York: Doubleday, 1977.

Potter, Christopher. *You Are Here: A Portable History of the Universe*. New York: Harper, 2009.

Price, Robert M., and Jeffery Jay Lowder, eds. *The Empty Tomb: Jesus Beyond the Grave*. Buffalo: Prometheus, 2005.

Prioreschi, Plinio. *History of Medicine*. Vol. 3: *Roman Medicine*. Omaha: Horatius, 1998.

Pusey, P. E. *Works of S. Cyril*. 7 vols. Oxford: Oxford University Press, 1868.

Radde-Gallwitz, Andrew. *Basil of Caesarea, Gregory of Nyssa, and the Transformation of Divine Simplicity*. Oxford: Oxford University Press, 2009.

Reimarus, Hermann Samuel. *Apologie: Oder Schutzschrift für die vernünftigen Verehrer Gotts*. Ed. Gerhard Alexander. 2 vols. Frankfurt am Main: Insel, 1972.

———. *Fragments*. Ed. Charles H. Talbert. Trans. Ralph S. Fraser. Chico, CA: Scholars, 1970.

Reventlow, Henning Graf. *History of Biblical Interpretation*. Vol. 1: *From the Old Testament to Origen*. Atlanta: Society of Biblical Literature, 2009.

Richardson, Alan. *An Introduction to the Theology of the New Testament*. New York: Harper and Brothers, 1958.

Robinson, Marilynne. *Gilead*. New York: Farrar, Straus, and Giroux, 2004.

———. *When I Was a Child I Read Books*. New York: Farrar, Straus, and Giroux, 2012.

Rogers, Eugene F., Jr. *After the Spirit: A Constructive Pneumatology from Resources Outside the Modern West*. Grand Rapids: Eerdmans, 2005.

———, ed. *The Holy Spirit: Classic and Contemporary Readings*. Oxford: Wiley-Blackwell, 2009.

Rupert of Deutz. *De divinis officiis*. Ed. Hrabanus Haacke. Corpus christianorum continuatio medievalis. Vol. 7. Turnout: Brepols, 1967.

Sanday, William, and Arthur C. Headlam. *The Epistle to the Romans*. 14th ed. New York: Charles Scribner's Sons, 1913.

Sanders, E. P. "Paul Between Judaism and Hellenism." In *St. Paul Among the Philosophers*, ed. Caputo and Alcoff, 74–90.

———. *Paul and Palestinian Judaism: A Comparison of Patterns of Religion*. Philadelphia: Fortress, 1977.

Sandys-Wunsch, John, and Laurence Eldredge. "J. P. Gabler and the Distinction between Biblical and Dogmatic Theology: Translation, Commentary, and Discussion of His Originality." *Scottish Journal of Theology* 33 (1980): 133–58.

Schillebeeckx, Edward. *God Among Us: The Gospel Proclaimed*. New York: Crossroad, 1983.

Schnelle, Udo. *Theology of the New Testament*. Trans. M. Eugene Boring. Grand Rapids: Baker Academic, 2009.

Schoot, Henk J. M. *Christ the "Name" of God: Thomas Aquinas on Naming Christ*. Leuven: Peeters, 1993.

Schüssler Fiorenza, Elisabeth. *But She Said: Feminist Practices of Biblical Interpretation*. Boston: Beacon, 1992.

———. *Democratizing Biblical Studies: Toward an Emancipatory Educational Space*. Louisville: Westminster John Knox, 2009.

———. *Discipleship of Equals: A Critical Feminist Ekklesia-logy of Liberation*. New York: Crossroad, 1993.

———. *Jesus: Miriam's Child, Sophia's Prophet: Critical Issues in Feminist Christology*. New York: Continuum, 1994.

Sedgwick, Eve Kosofsky. *Epistemology of the Closet*. Berkeley: University of California Press, 1990.

Sedmak, Clemens. "Der Glaube ist praktisch— über die Erkennbarkeit der Orthodoxie." *ZKTh* 137 (2015): 86–103.

Sesboüé, Bernard. "The Spirit in the Church." In *Lord and Life-Giver*, ed. Murray et al., 68–77.

Shults, F. LeRon, and Andrea Hollingsworth. *The Holy Spirit*. Grand Rapids: Eerdmans, 2008.

Siegel, Rudolph E. *Galen on Sense Perception: His Doctrines, Observations and Experiments on Vision, Hearing, Smell, Taste and Pain, and Their Historical Sources*. Basel: S. Karger, 1970.

Siker, Jeffrey S. "Homosexual Christians, the Bible, and Gentile Inclusion: Confessions of a Repenting Heterosexist." In *Homosexuality in the Church: Both Sides of the Debate*, ed. Jeffrey S. Siker, 178–94. Louisville: Westminster John Knox, 1994.

Smail, Tom. *The Giving Gift: The Holy Spirit in Person*. London: Darton, Longman, and Todd, 1994.

Smith, Barbara Herrnstein. *Belief and Resistance: Dynamics of Contemporary Intellectual Controversy*. Cambridge: Harvard University Press, 1997.

Soble, Alan, ed. *Eros, Agape, and Philia: Readings in the Philosophy of Love*. New York: Paragon, 1989.

Soskice, Janet M. "Trinity and Feminism." In *The Cambridge Companion to Feminist Theology*, ed. Susan Frank Parsons, 135–50. Cambridge: Cambridge University Press, 2002.

St. John of the Cross. *The Collected Works of St. John of the Cross*. Trans. Kieran Kavanaugh and Otilio Rodriquez, with Revisions and Introductions by Kieran Kavanaugh. Washington: ICS Publications, 1991.

Starr, Chester G. *The Birth of Athenian Democracy: The Assembly in the Fifth Century B.C.* New York: Oxford University Press, 1990.

Stegeman, Wolfgang. "Theologie im Schatten des neuen Antisemitismus." *Theologische Zeitschrift* 69 (2013): 661–88.

Steinkamp, Hermann. "Parrhesia als 'Wahrheit zwischen uns': Praktisch-theologische Erwägungen zu einem Modus der Subjekt-Konstitution." In *Tods des Subjekts? Poststrukturalismus und christliches Denken*, ed. Michael Zichy and Heinrich Schmidinger, 139–55. Innsbruck-Vienna: Tyrolia, 2005.

Stendahl, Krister. "The Apostle Paul and the Introspective Conscience of the West." *HTR* 56 (1963): 199–215.

———. "Biblical Theology, Contemporary." In *Interpreter's Dictionary of the Bible,* ed. George Buttrick, 1:418–32. Nashville: Abingdon, 1962.

Stevens, George Barker. *The Theology of the New Testament.* New York: Charles Scribner's Sons, 1899.

Stock, Karl. *Anthropologie der Verheissung: Karl Barths Lehre vom Menschen als dogmatisches Problem.* Munich: Kaiser Verlag, 1980.

Stowers, Stanley. "Matter and Spirit, or What Is Pauline Participation in Christ?" In *The Holy Spirit,* ed. Rogers, Jr., 91–105.

———. *A Rereading of Romans: Justice, Jews, and Gentiles.* New Haven: Yale University Press, 1994.

Suchla, Beate Regina, ed. *Corpus Dionysiacum.* 2 vols. Berlin: Walter de Gruyter, 1990.

Tabak, Mehmet. *Dialectics of Human Nature in Marx's Philosophy.* New York: Palgrave Macmillan, 2012.

Tanner, Kathryn. *Christ the Key.* Cambridge: Cambridge University Press, 2010.

———. "Gender." In *The Oxford Handbook of Anglican Studies,* ed. Mark D. Chapman, Sathnianathan Clarke, and Martyn Percy, 400–411. Oxford: Oxford University Press, 2017.

———. *God and Creation in Christian Theology: Tyranny or Empowerment?* Oxford: Basil Blackwell, 1988.

———. *Jesus, Humanity, and the Trinity: A Brief Systematic Theology.* Edinburgh: T & T Clark, 2001.

———. *Theories of Culture: A New Agenda for Theology.* Minneapolis: Fortress, 1997.

Tegmark, Max. *Our Mathematical Universe: My Quest for the Ultimate Nature of Reality.* New York: Alfred A. Knopf, 2014.

Thomassen, Einar, ed. *Canon and Canonicity: The Formation and Use of Scripture.* Copenhagen: Museum Tusculanum, 2010.

Thompson, Marianne Meye. *The Promise of the Father: Jesus and God in the New Testament.* Louisville: Westminster John Knox, 2000.

Torrence, Thomas F. "The Christian Apprehension of God the Father." In *Speaking the Christian God,* ed. Kimel, Jr., 120–43.

Toy, Crawford H. *Proverbs.* New York: Charles Scribner's Sons, 1899.

Tracy, Stephen V. *Athenian Democracy in Transition: Attic Letter Cutters of 340 to 290 B.C.* Berkeley: University of California Press, 1995.

Turner, Denys. "On Denying the Right God: Aquinas on Atheism and Idolatry." *Modern Theology* 20 (2004): 141–61.

———. *Thomas Aquinas: A Portrait.* New Haven: Yale University Press, 2013.

Udoh, Fabian E., et al., eds. *Redefining First-Century Jewish and Christian Identities.* Notre Dame: University of Notre Dame Press, 2008.

Van Fraassen, Bas C. *The Empirical Stance.* New Haven: Yale University Press, 2002.

———. *Laws and Symmetry.* Oxford: Clarendon, 1989.

Van Slyke, Daniel G. "Changing Meanings of *sacramentum*: Historical Sketches." *Antiphon* 11 (2007): 245–79.

Volf, Miroslav. *After Our Likeness: The Church as the Image of the Trinity.* Grand Rapids: Eerdmans, 1998.

———. *Against the Tide: Love in a Time of Petty Dreams and Persisting Enmities.* Grand Rapids: Eerdmans, 2010.

———. *Captive to the Word of God: Engaging the Scriptures for Contemporary Theological Reflection.* Grand Rapids: Eerdmans, 2010.

———. "Theology for a Way of Life." In *Practicing Theology: Beliefs and Practices in Christian Life,* ed. Miroslav Volf and Dorothy C. Bass, 245–63. Grand Rapids: Eerdmans, 2002.

Wacker, Marie-Theres. "The Spirit of God in the Public Sphere of Christian Communities: The Inspiration of the Hebrew Bible." In *Lord and Life-Giver,* ed. Paul Murray et al., 32–42.

Wallace, Mark I. *Fragments of the Spirit: Nature, Violence, and the Renewal of Creation.* New York: Continuum, 1996.

Ward, Graham. *Barth, Derrida and the Language of Theology.* Cambridge: Cambridge University Press, 1995.

———. "Tradition and Traditions: Scripture, Christian Praxes, and Politics." In *Christian Theologies of Scripture: A Comparative Introduction,* ed. Justin Holcomb, 243–60. New York: New York University Press, 2006.

Wedderburn, A. J. M. *Beyond Resurrection.* Peabody, MA: Hendrickson, 1999.

Weigelt, Morris. "The Nature and Identity of the Church." In *A Community of Faith: Celebrating the Church of Jesus Christ and Its Mission to the World,* ed. H. Ray Dunning, 7–24. Kansas City, MO: Beacon Hill, 1997.

Williams, David T. *Vinculum Amoris: A Theology of the Holy Spirit.* New York: iUniverse, 2004.

Williams, Rowan. *On Christian Theology.* Oxford: Blackwell, 2000.

———. *Resurrection: Interpreting the Easter Gospel.* London: Darton, Longman, and Todd, 2002.

Wilson, David Sloan. *Darwin's Cathedral: Evolution, Religion, and the Nature of Society.* Chicago: University of Chicago Press, 2002.

Winkler, Gabriele. *Studies in Early Christian Liturgy and Its Context.* Aldershot, UK: Ashgate, 1997.

Wondra, Ellen K. "Problems with Authority in the Anglican Communion." In *Anglican Women,* ed. Kwok Pui-Lan et al., 21–36.

Woollam, D. H. M. "Concepts of the Brain and Its Functions in Classical Antiquity." In *The History and Philosophy of Knowledge of the Brain and Its Functions: An Anglo-American Symposium, London, July 15–17, 1957,* 5–18. Amsterdam: B. M. Israël, 1973.

Wrede, William. *Über Aufgabe und Methode der sogenannten neutestamentlichen Theologie.* Göttingen: Vandenhoeck and Ruprecht, 1897.

Wulf, Claudia Mariéle. *Der Mensch— ein Phänomen: Eine phänomenologische, theologische, und ethische Anthropologie.* Vallendar-Schönstatt: Patris, 2011.

Yoder, John Howard. "Is There Such a Thing as Being Ready for Another Millennium?" In *The Future of Theology: Essays in Honor of Jürgen Moltmann,* ed. Miroslav Volf, Carmen Krieg, and Thomas Kucharz, 63–69. Grand Rapids: Eerdmans, 1996.

———. *The Politics of Jesus: Vicit Agnus Noster.* 2d ed. Grand Rapids: Eerdmans, 1994.

Zizioulas, John D. *Being as Communion: Studies in Personhood and the Church.* London: Darton, Longman, and Todd, 2004.

Subject Index

Words that naturally occur many times are not included in the subject index unless substantial discussion about those topics accompanies the reference. Such words include "God," "Jesus," "Christ," "scripture," "faith," "holy spirit," and others.

Abraham: in Barth's Romans commentary, 13–14; faith of, 62; as father of the Jews, 43; hope of, 63; in interpretations of Paul and James, 104–5

Adam, 202

adoption, by God, 308

afterlife, 222, 295–99, 306–7

agape, 39, 279–80, 349; defined, 280

agnosticism, 154, 157

allegory: Barth's modern theological, 16, 17; in interpretations by orthodox church fathers, 113; parables interpreted as, 162–64; Paul's in Galatians, 89–90; in premodern interpretation, 2–3; rejected by Gabler, 8

anachronism: in Bultmann's interpretations, 21; creative, 31, 190; in interpreting parables as allegory, 163; in Matthew, 177; in postmodern interpretation, 126; "race" as category of ancient world, 273n18; "supernatural" in ancient world as, 212

androgyny, 284–86

angels: in contrast to mortal human beings, 275–76; in the empty tomb stories, 206; in a messianic army, 218; providing knowledge of God, 50, as "supernatural," 156; in the theology of Pseudo-Dionysius, 119

Anglican churches, 55, 76, 92–93

anti-Judaism, 19–22

anti-Semitism, 21n34, 81, 178–79, 345–48

Aphrarat (Syriac church father), 258

apocalyptic, 20, 132–33, 214; literature, 310

Apocrypha, 84

apologetics, 31, 68

apostles, 200

Aristotle, 64, 140, 152, 331, 338

asceticism, 277–78, 281–82

atheism, 154, 157, 350

Athens, 328–31

atonement, 186, 187; absent in Luke, 180

Augustine: on atonement, 187; on becoming divine, 309; on church as "enclosed garden," 349; on divine simplicity, 138, 140; on original sin, 291; as reader of Psalms, 1; on rule of love in interpretation, 70

authorial intention, 102–3; in conservative Christian interpretation, 58; interpretation not limited by, 240; in Ladd's interpretation, 24; as modernist, 3, 88, 101, 235, 252; not "the meaning" of the text, 96–99; a "text" as having, 25n37

baptism, 52, 87, 230; the role of the spirit in, 251

Barth, Karl, 11–18, 28

Basil of Caesarea, 258, 308–9

beloved disciple, the, 44, 45n4

Bernard of Clairvaux, 220

bishops, 87; elected by the people in early Christianity, 335

body, 267–68; of Christ, 264; of Christ as androgynous, 325; church as, 336–38; human, 270; as mystical, 321–22

Bonhoeffer, Dietrich, 217n65

Book of Common Prayer, 35
Bultmann, Rudolf, 11, 18–23, 28

Calvin, John, 309
Calvinism, 137
canon, 71, 75–78
canonical criticism, 78n11
capitalism, 34–35, 67, 303, 340, 343–45
Catherine of Siena, 257–58, 259
celibacy, 217
Chalcedon, definition of, 192
Christ: the body of, 289; church as the body
    of, 319–23
Christology, subordinationist, 183–85
Christomonism, 247–48, 255, 256
church, 13, 17; as feminine, 165; gender
    of, 323–26; visible and invisible,
    322–23
Cicero, 223, 339
class, 271–72, 341; ancient, 336–39; and
    conflict, 139
colonialism: modern, 342–43; Zionism as,
    347
communion of saints, 52, 91–92, 246–47,
    321–22
Constantine, 340
Constantinian Christianity, 340–41
contradiction, 247
conversion, 14, 21, 31–32, 65–66
council (*boulê*), in ancient cities, 329,
    331–32
courts, in ancient cities, 329
creatio ex nihilo, 131–32, 160–61
creation, 133–34, 136, 213, 263, 276, 282
Creed, the Apostles', 197, 198, 311, 321
Creed of Athanasius, 184, 197
Creed of Nicea, 169, 198–99, 254, 311
creeds: containing "filioque," 256; on
    creation, 161; "ecumenical," 36; in
    liturgy, 5, 152, 153; on the spirit, 241,
    245
crisis, 23
culture, 53–54, 68, 219; and Christ, 216
Cyril of Alexandria, 309

David: "author" of Psalms, 1–2; and Jona-
    than, 283
death, 198, 215, 276–77
deification (*theosis*), 308–10
demagogue, topos of, 338–39
democracy: ancient, 139, 326–32; as valued,
    117
demythologization, 22, 59, 147
denominations, of churches, 312n1
depression, 154n77
Descartes, René, 156
despair, as opposite of faith, 350–51
diocese, original meaning in Rome, 336
Dio Chrysostom, 331–32, 339
Dionysius, Pseudo-, 138
discourse theory, 60n24, 68–69
divorce, 88–89, 277–78; and remarriage,
    317–318

Eastern Orthodoxy, 36, 76, 190, 255–57, 308,
    322–23, 324
ecumenism, 36
Einstein, Albert, 157–58
ekklesia, 177, 285, 326–39; as "called out,"
    340
election, doctrine of, 45, 66, 156. *See also*
    predestination
emergence theory, 268–69, 288
emperor, Roman, 116–17, 297–98
empire, 314
empiricism, 84; Christian eschatology
    dependent on, 310; as evidence for faith,
    111–12; as evidence in interpretation
    theory, 96–97; in explanations for faith,
    69, 135, 153; in modern epistemology
    and theology, 50–55
empty tomb, 26–27, 203, 204–12
Enlightenment, 336
Ephrem, 349
epistemology, 38–70; reserved, 40, 69
equality: of gender, 166–67; impossible
    under capitalism, 343–44; in some early
    churches, 333; valued in the NT and by
    Paul, 344

erôs, 278–81

eschatology: Bultmann's version of, 20–21;
    and Christian alternatives to traditional
    household, 317; and the future "king-
    dom," 315; and future states of "nature,"
    306; and hope of universal salvation,
    241–42; and Jesus as "son of man," 191;
    as necessary for Christian theology,
    350–52; not "optimism," 310; in the
    NT, 132–33; in Paul's epistemology, 39;
    reserved, 133, 308; and salvation, 295–96

eternity, 127, 299

ethics, 161–62

Ethiopian Church, 76n8

ethnicity, 17

eucharist, 87, 320

evangelism, 31

experience: of Christian mystics, 194–95;
    of collective Christians as constituting
    "tradition," 108–9; of the divine, 162; of
    faith, 152; of Jesus as absent, 180; not a
    discrete "source" for knowledge, 56; not
    always reliable as source for knowledge,
    69–70; of resurrection appearances,
    200, 212–14; of selves, 270; and sexuality
    and gender, 260–61; teaching that all
    words for God are inadequate, 144

faith: in James and Paul, 105–6; the nature
    of, 13–14, 61–70, 135, 151–54; as preced-
    ing knowledge in John, 45–46; as social,
    45–46

family, 277–78, 316; and household, 285;
    ideology of, 333, 340, 341–42; and Jesus,
    217

filioque, 36, 254–57

finitude, 274–77

flesh, 222–23

forgiveness, 131

foundationalism: defined and described,
    33; and empiricism, 52; epistemologi-
    cal, 40–41; of modern historicism, 30;
    and a nonfoundationalist approach, 32;
    the rejection of, in reading scripture,

126–27; and simple "observation," 96; in
    "sources" for religious knowledge, 55

free will, 66n39, 300, 303

Gabler, Johann Philipp, 6–9

Galen (ancient medical writer), 157, 225–26

Gaudium et Spes, 239

gay erotic, 283–84

gender: and God, 260; of God, 162–167;
    hierarchy, 281; hierarchy in Paul,
    284–85; and sexism, 321

gentiles: as "grafted into" Israel in Paul's
    theology, 301–2, 345; and idolatry in
    Paul, 145; and the Jerusalem church in
    Acts, 51; as keeping the Law of Moses in
    Matthew, 178; and Law in Paul, 104–5;
    Paul as becoming, 339; in Paul's theol-
    ogy and Barth's commentary, 15–17;
    as "resident aliens" in 1 Peter, 303; as
    "without excuse" in their idolatry, 47

Gnosticism, 21, 22

God: the body of, 114–15; as crucified, 189;
    as father, 118, 142, 160, 164–66; the gen-
    der of, 118; as king, 115–17; the name of,
    122–23, 148–51, 164, 165n97; the nature
    of, 167–68; as one, 143; as personal,
    154–60, 165; as shepherd, 117–18; and
    spirit as "persons," 242; as transcendent,
    125–28

gospel, 65, 71, 78–80, 217–19, 300; "of pros-
    perity," 67

grace: as causing faith, 68–70, 152, 304; and
    predestination, 66; reciprocal in the
    kingdom, 315; the spirit causing, in the
    world, 352; and universal salvation, 234

Greek Orthodox Church, 76

Gregory of Naziansus, 308–9

habitus, 64, 91, 152–53, 274, 300, 307–8

hamartia, 286, 287, 294

heaven, 289

Hebrew Bible, 31, 81, 82–84

hell, 31, 35, 59, 61, 292, 298–99, 304; Jesus
    in, 196–98

Hellenism, 282

heresy, 19, 35, 113, 127, 135, 166, 174, 189, 254–55

hierarchy, 168, 171, 202, 223; in ancient political structures, 332–33; in early church structures, 335; in household and church, 321; reversal of, 182, 315

Hildegard of Bingen, 237–38

historical criticism, 2–37 passim; and anachronism, 126; and an "impersonal" God, 156; the limits of, 85; in NT theology, 100–103; and sexual ethics, 277, 285; and subordinationist Christology, 183–85; and the trinity, 169–70, 242

history, 2–37 passim; and ancient interpretation, 90; the nature of, 203–4; and resurrection, 212–15; and theological truths, 59–61, 87–88

holy ghost, 246–47

holy spirit: as absent, 244; as corporeal, 244; gender of, 257–61; impersonal, 244–47; as life of church, 312–13; as mother, 258, 259; as Paraclete in John, 194; and revelation, 219; as rubber band, 249

homoousios, 192

homosexuality, 51, 53, 54

honesty, 348–49

hope, 62–63, 69, 310

household: ancient, 333; church as, 316–19

humility, 253–54, 272, 277, 303, 304; and humiliation, 188

icons, in Eastern Orthodoxy, 190

ideology: ancient conservative, 139; ancient democratic, 338; of "bible-olatry," 95; capitalist, 35, 303; in Christology, 174; and the church, 340–45; democratic, 332–39; of gender, 324–26; as harmful, 118; imperial Roman, 297–98; of individual autonomy, 217–72, 300; of modern anti-Judaism, 21; of modern family, 278; of "optimism," 310; of pa-

triarchy, 165; of "purity," 140–41; of the Third Reich, 23

idolatry: of the Bible, 95; and divine simplicity, 141–42; of family, 285, 317, 342; and gentiles, 47; of institutional authorities, 56; of institutions, 312; nationalist, 314; and negative theology, 120; origin of, in Paul's thought, 264–65; of pantheism, 135; of patriarchy, 118, 164–66; of the phallos, 325–26; principle of nonviolence as potentially, 218; of the self, 310; and the trinity, 28; why dangerous, 144–48, 154

incarnation, 129, 190–93, 195–96, 309; in the church, 323

individualism, 23, 264, 271, 300, 303

immanence, of God, 128–38

immortality, of soul or spirit, 265

imperialism, modern, 342–43

inspiration, of scripture, 85–88

interpretation, necessity of, 256–57

intersex, 285

Irenaeus, 291

Israel: in allegorical interpretation of the Song of Songs, 282; in Barth's Commentary, 17; as chosen people, 300; Christian dependence on, 80–81; and Christian use of Jewish scripture, 82–84, 219–20; the church and, 107; as ekklesia in LXX, 326–27; gentiles in relation to, 145; modern, and the Christian church, 345–48; modern state of, 347; the salvation of, in Paul's theology, 24; supersession of, in Christian theology, 301–2; when portrayed as female, 165

James, 69

Jesus: absent, 180, 193–94, 243, 246; apocalyptic Jewish prophet, 174; arrest of, 218; birth of, 60; death of, 187; disciples' worship of, 28–29; as divine, 23; "founder of Christianity," 175; "Great Moral Teacher," 173–74; the historical, 10–11, 19, 22, 60, 75, 90, 100–101, 175,

277–78, 317; as "philosopher," 174–75; prophet and martyr, 181; shepherd, 117–18; son of God, 170–72; son of man, 190–91
Jews, as saved, 240
John (author of Revelation), and Rome, 341
John the Baptist, 232
Judaism: in Barth's Romans commentary, 16–17; in Bultmann's interpretation, 22; and the Christian Old Testament, 80–81; in the Gospel of Matthew, 178–79; and interpretation of the Tanakh, 84; and the love commandment, 167; and the name of God, 148–49; in recent scholarship on Paul, 15–16; and resurrection of the body, 307
Julian of Norwich, 195, 300

Kähler, Martin, 10–11, 18n30, 33–34
kenosis, 188
kerygma, 19, 78
King, Martin Luther, Jr., 62
kingdom of God, 20, 305, 313–16, 341, 351
knowledge, 143–44
krisis, 13, 16, 19

Ladd, George Eldon, 23–28
language, 57–58, 140–41; and "purity," 85, 149
Law of Moses: in the Gospel of Mark, 179; in the Gospel of Matthew, 177–78; in Paul's theology, 15–16; summed up in love, 167
Lindbeck, George, 187
liturgy, 29, 69, 79, 160, 166, 246, 300; in Hebrews, 346; and trinity, 172–73
lot, selection by, 329–30; in early churches, 334
love: and divine inspiration, 240; erotic, 260–61; and failure, 294; God as, 140, 155, 167–68; God maintaining the universe through, 263; Greek words for, 280; and hell, 298; marker of the kingdom of God, 315; nothing can separate

us from, 198; and the nuclear family, 342; in Paul's epistemology, 39; of self, 281; superior to faith and hope for Paul, 63; ultimate meaning of the universe, 69–70, 152
Lumen Gentium, 239
Luther, Martin, 19, 291

manual labor, Paul's, 338
Marcion, 31, 46, 80, 112–13, 115
Marxism, 34–35
Mary, 245; as begetting God, 166; womb of, filled by spirit, 261
mathematics, 57–58
medicine: ancient, 138, 143, 166n101, 223, 224–25; Hippocratic, 224, 225n10
mercy, 301
messianic secret, 42
Methodist churches, 55
mind, 268–69, 288
miracle, 158–60, 161, 212, 214, 276
misogyny, 165, 325, 333
modernism: and epistemology, 108; and faith as assenting to propositions, 64; and foundationalism, 41, 285; and historical criticism, 2–37 passim; and the historical Jesus, 215; and historicism, 110; and history, 61; and individualism, 271, 300, 303; and the "literal" meaning of texts, 88; in psychology, 270; rejection of allegory, 163; and rules of interpretation, 89–90; and "the supernatural," 160
monotheism, 165
Moses, 88–89
mystery, 351
myth, mythology: ancient Greek, 138; and the atonement, 187; in the Bible, 5; and biblical anthropology, 270; of creation in the Bible, 132; and "Death" in the Bible, 276; defined, 60–61, 152; false, 147; God's actions in Genesis as, 263; Jesus's descent into hell as, 198; modernist rejection of, 8, 24; a "personal God" as,

myth, mythology (*continued*)
    160; and sin in the Bible, 293–94; true,
    69, 196; true and false, 60–61, 197–98

narrative, in constructing the self, 273–74
nationalism: as ideology, 340, 342–43;
    Zionism as, 347
nature: versus culture, 53; as divine in
    pantheism, 156–60; eschatological,
    306; and faith, 68; "laws of," 157–60,
    306; as revelation, 92; as source for
    knowledge of God, 219; and "the su-
    pernatural," 126
Neoplatonism, 126
Nicholas of Cusa, 70n40, 279n36

Odes of Solomon, 258
Old Testament: alternate names for, 81–85;
    in Bultmann's interpretation, 21; Chris-
    tian embrace of, 31; Christian inter-
    pretation of, 219–20; and the election
    of Israel, 300; and the erotic, 281–83;
    interpreted by NT writers, 73; and
    "natural" theology, 46–47; relationship
    to NT, 80–85; theology of, 1
optimism, 310
Origen, 113–14
original text, of scripture, 72, 77
orthodoxy: in biblical interpretation, 115; of
    Christology in John, 182–83; and church
    fathers, 113; defined for the trinity,
    169–70; of divine immanence, 130; and
    God's relation to the universe, 155, 158;
    and historical criticism, 85, 277; his-
    torical development of, 28–29; and the
    historical Jesus, 216; and the humanity
    of Jesus, 220; of Jesus's divinity, 127; and
    the name of God, 150–51; and the Old
    Testament, 80, 219; and resurrection
    of the flesh, 59; and the soul, 269; as
    starting point, 35–36; and subordina-
    tionist Christology, 184; and theological
    anthropology, 270

pacifism, 217–19
Palestinians, 347
pantheism, 130
parables, 162–64; in Mark, 179
Paraclete, 51, 193–94, 231, 241, 242–43, 256
parousia, 132–133n46
parrhêsia, 348–49
patriarchy, 56, 165
patriotism, 341, 342–43
patripassianism, 188–89, 191
Paul, the Apostle: and adoptionist Christol-
    ogy, 171–72; and atonement, 186; in
    Barth's interpretation, 12–17; in Bult-
    mann's interpretation, 21–22; and celi-
    bacy, 278; as depicted in Acts, 48, 243,
    332; on knowledge, 38–40, 51; in Ladd's
    interpretation, 24–25; on marriage and
    family, 317–18; on the material spirit,
    222–26; in paradise, 121; as prophet, 181;
    as reader of scripture, 1–2, 89, 94–95,
    104–5, 112; on the resurrection, 199–203;
    and Rome, 341; and sin, 287–91; as
    "slave of all," 338; on terms such as
    "Christian" or "Christianity," 345; on the
    veiling of women, 8
peace, 161–62
perception, 52–53
perfectionism, 291, 292–93
perichoresis, 260
Pharisees, 88–89, 176–77
philia, 279–80
philosophy: in accounting for faith, 69;
    ancient, on afterlife, 274; ancient, in
    Bultmann's interpretation, 21–22;
    ancient, on divine simplicity, 138–39;
    ancient, on immaterial substance, 201;
    ancient, on self-control, 278; ancient,
    on self-sufficiency, 271–72; ancient, on
    the nature of God, 157; ancient, on the
    suffering of God, 188–89; Christianity
    as not, 64–65, 303; of history, 203–4;
    as influence on Christian doctrine,
    140–41; influence on church fathers,

122; as influencing the translation of the LXX, 74; of language, 57; modern, and emergence theory, 288; modern, on the human person, 268–69; Paul's reference to, in Acts, 48, 130, 228; on "rationalism" and "empiricism," 50

Plato, 138, 331, 339; Galen on, 225n10

Platonism, 122, 188–89, 225, 303

pneuma: in bodies and cosmos, 154–55; of Christ or of the cosmos, 264; cosmic, 228, 233; gender of, 257–59; of God, 129; as a neuter noun, 28; in Paul's notion of the resurrected body, 201–3; as physical, 114–15n7; as providing knowledge, 50; of resurrected body, 305

politics, 16, 20–21, 54; American, 342; ancient theory of, 138–39

polytheism, 151

pope, 53, 92, 93

postmodernism: and apophatic theology, 123; defined, 33–35; and historical criticism, 191; and premodern biblical interpretation, 110; and resurrection of the body, 199; 213n58; and social construction of the self, 263; and "the supernatural," 158–60; and "tradition," 103

prayer, 172; and the spirit, 250–51

predestination, 66–67, 156, 300–304; and universal salvation, 196

premodern: and allegorical interpretation, 163; assumptions about scripture, 1–2, 5; confrontation with four Gospels, 176; interpretation of scripture, 110, 252; notions of a violent God, 298; notions of sacraments, 351; postmodern is not, 34

Prisca, as church leader, 334–35

prophecy, 86–87, 229

prophets, carried by the spirit, 251–52

Protestantism: of Bultmann's interpretations, 19, 21, 22; and canon, 76; as cognitive belief in a supreme being, 49; and the doctrine of transcendence, 137; on interpretation of Romans, 301; on

justification by "works," 303–4; and the resurrection of the flesh, 199; and the sacraments, 351; and suspicion of doctrine of deification, 308; and suspicion of "natural theology," 50

pseudepigraphy, 25

psychê, 201–3, 265–67

Ptolemy (second century Valentinian author), 113, 115

queer theology, 260–61

queer theory, 284–86

race, 273n18

rationality, as relative, 274

reader response theory, 96–99

reason, 56

Reformation, 92

refuge, church as, 349–50

religion, 22–23, 49, 58: versus faith, 12–14; versus theology, 7

resurrection, 88; of believers, 297; of the body, 222–26, 276; faith in, 215; of the flesh, 59, 198–99, 304–5; of Jesus, 10–11, 26–27, 44, 195, 198–215, 226; as salvation for human beings, 304–8

revelation: according to Gabler, 8; of God's gender, 164; inadequate for full knowledge of God, 144; and "natural theology," 236–37; necessary for sufficient knowledge of Christ, 92; not limited, 219; as source of knowledge, 45–50; by the spirit, 241

revolution, 217–18

rhetoric: ancient democratic, 338–39; Paul's training in, 339; Paul's use of, 334

Roman Catholicism: and the Anglican Church, 92; the canon of, 76; caricatured in Protestant scholarship, 19; on divine immanence, 137; doctrines special to, 36; and epistemological "sources," 55; and explanations for evil, 293; in relation to other churches, 322;

Roman Catholicism (*continued*)
    on the resurrection of the flesh, 199; and
    the sacraments, 351
Roman Empire, 219, 340–41
Rome, and the goddess Roma, 288–89
ruach, 221, 257–59
Rule of Faith, 36

sabbath, 130
sacrament, 161, 190, 238; church as, 323,
    351–52
Sadducees, 88
salvation, 91, 294–300; universal, 24,
    195–96, 239–42
Satan, the devil, 22
science: account of "energy" in modern,
    155; ancient, on pneuma, 201, 223–24;
    on the beginning of the universe, 213;
    the construction of the human self
    in modern, 263; creation stories not,
    132; in Einstein's understanding, 157;
    and emergence theory, 268–69, 288;
    epistemological foundationalism in, 33;
    and the existence of "hell," 198; and ex-
    planations for existence of homosexual-
    ity, 54; in explanations for existence of
    "religion," 48–49; human transcendence
    in modern, 270; and Jesus's resurrec-
    tion, 199; and "laws of nature," 159;
    modern, and problems with the term
    "physical," 224; and modern cosmol-
    ogy, 139; "multiverses" in modern, 306;
    versus mythology, 5; not the subject of
    the Bible, 90; seeming impossibilities of
    modern, 144; as source for theology, 56,
    216, 219; "the supernatural" in modern,
    160; theology as, 53
scripture, 56, 58–61; authority of, 93–95; as
    inerrant or infallible, 87–88, 90–91; as
    nonreferential, 101–3; perspicuity of, 91
self-sufficiency, 271–74
sensus literalis, 91
Septuagint (LXX), 82–83n18, 326–27

sexuality, 260–61, 277–86, 307, 350; divine,
    138–44
sin, 264, 286–94; the body of, 289; as
    cosmic force or agent, 287–89; original,
    291–93
Slavonic Church, 76
sola scriptura, 91–93, 313
sophia, 259
soul, 265–70; immortality of, 274–76; salva-
    tion of, 265
Spinoza, Baruch, 156–58
spirit, 29; gender of, 242–43; in inspiration,
    251–52; in interpretation of scripture,
    252–53
"spiritual" interpretation, 12, 59n21. See also
    allegory
spiritus, gender of, 259
Stoicism, 157, 223–24, 225
supernatural, 126, 156–60, 160–61, 212
supersessionism, 81, 82, 179, 219–20, 345–47
synagogue, 327; in Acts, 346
Syriac Christianity, and the spirit's gender,
    258–59

Tatian, 176
temple, Jerusalem, 20; Jesus's actions in,
    173–74
theodicy, 65, 161, 293
theology: apophatic (negative), 14, 17, 32,
    120–25, 151; natural, 46–50, 92, 236–37;
    nature of, 32, 37; provisional, 37; system-
    atic, 5, 24, 30
Thomas, Gospel of, 317
Thomas Aquinas, 36, 138, 141–42n63, 142,
    152, 159, 168n105, 213n58
time, 127, 132
tradition: not cited as a discreet "source"
    for knowledge by NT writers, 107–9;
    and the "Old Testament," 85; in relation
    to scripture, 56; and spirit as masculine,
    257
transcendence, 135–36; of God, 189; of hu-
    man beings, 270

transgender, 285
Trent, Council of, 36
trinity: in Acts?, 231; bound together by
the spirit, 248–51; in community in
biblical interpretation, 87; and the
"death of God," 189; definition of, for
orthodoxy, 169–70; deified human beings not members of, 309; doctrine of,
derived from liturgy, 172–73; as erotic,
260–61; as historically developed,
29; Jesus as second person of, 214; in
Ladd's interpretation, 28; not in NT
read historically, 85; NT texts taken
as hinting at, 232; in the Old Testament, 114; in Romans 8?, 235; the spirit
in the, 221–22, 242–47; as taking on
"flesh," 191

vinculum caritatis, 249–50
vinculum trinitatis, 248–49
violence, and the historical Jesus, 217–19

"Watchers," 47
Wisdom, as feminine, 164, 166
Wittgenstein, Ludwig, 64
women, in the early church, 319
works, 13
Wrede, William, 9

Zionism, 347–48

Author Index

Achtemeier, Elizabeth, 164
Adehey, Walter F., 30
Alcinous, 141
Alison, James, 78, 132n44, 293, 313n2
Ambrose, 261
Aristotle, 64
Atkinson, William, 237, 246
Augustine, 1, 70, 122, 158n89, 187, 250, 309

Badcock, Gary, 351
Barth, Karl, 11–14, 16–19, 22, 27n38, 28,
    65n34, 124, 134n50, 135,168n105, 169n1,
    195, 252n66, 342, 344
Basil of Caesarea, 258, 308
Bauerschmidt, Frederick Christian, 152–53
Beckwith, Sarah, 168n105
Berkeley, George, 50
Bernard of Clairvaux, 194, 220
Biddle, Martin, 210n55
Billings, Todd, 219
Bloom, Paul, 49n10
Bobrinskoy, Boris, 324–25
Bourdieu, Pierre, 64
Braaten, Carl, 33–34
Brown, Raymond, 210n55
Bulgakov, Sergius, 246, 256n72
Bultmann, Rudolf, 11, 18–24, 28, 59
Burgess, Stanley, 256
Burke, Kenneth, 118n11

Calvin, John, 309
Catherine of Siena, 250, 257, 259
Certeau, Michel de, 64
Chadwick, Henry, 140
Clement of Alexandria, 122
Craig, William, 211n57
Crisp, Oliver D., 190m35

Critchley, Simon, 64
Croasmun, Matthew, 288–89
Cyril of Alexandria, 309

Davies, Brian, 128n36
DeHart, Paul J., 159
Derrida, Jacques, 124
Descartes, René, 50, 156
Dio Chrysostom, 331–32
Dunn, James, 100–101, 212n57

Eagleton, Terry, 63, 65, 174
Edwards, Denis, 243
Ehrman, Bart, 72n1

Fatula, Mary Ann, 237
Fitzmyer, Joseph A., 181n19
Florensky, Pavel, 53
Fowl, Stephen, 217n65, 253
Frei, Hans, 32n45, 80n14, 91, 220
Frye, Ronald M., 164
Frykholm, Amy, 195
Fulkerson, Mary McClintock, 53n15, 216n63

Gabler, Johann Philipp, 6–9
Galen, 157, 225
Gillman, Neil, 307
Gleick, James, 305
Gorringe, Timothy, 214n60, 307
Greer, Rowan, 136
Gregory of Nazianzus, 259n86, 308–9
Gregory of Nyssa, 122, 166

Hampson, Peter, 135n51
Harvey, Susan Ashbrook, 258
Hauerwas, Stanley, 141n63
Helyer, Larry R., 196n45

Henriksen, Jan-Olav, 286n43
Hippocrates, 224
Hoff, Johannes, 33n47, 135n51, 279n36, 299n56
Hume, David, 50

Jenson, Robert W. 165, 235, 323–24
Jeremias, Joachim, 211n56
Jerome, 259n86
John of Damascus, 123–24
John of the Cross, 249
John Paul II, 239
Johnson, Elizabeth, 236–38
Johnson, Luke Timothy, 231
Jones, Gregory, 217n65
Julian of Norwich, 300

Kähler, Martin, 10–11, 33–34
Kärkkäinon, Veli-Matti, 236–37
Kelsey, David, 46, 59n23, 274, 276
Kerr, Fergus, 36, 142n65, 271
Küng, Hans, 136–37

Ladd, George Eldon, 18, 23–28
Lash, Nicholas, 36, 146–47, 151, 322n12
Lessing, Gotthold E., 215
Lindbeck, George, 187
Locke, John, 50, 93n30

Markham, Ian, 132, 240, 260
Marx, Karl, 344
Mascall, Eric L., 309
McCabe, Herbert, 36, 63, 121n17, 124–25, 128, 133, 142, 151, 159, 167n104
McGrath, Alister, 62, 187, 195–96
McGrath, Andrew, 349
Moll, Sebastian, 113n1
Moltmann, Jürgen, 236–37
Moyse, Cordelia, 343n34
Murphy, Nancey, 306

Nietzsche, Friedrich, 188
Norris, Richard, 129

O'Collins, Gerald, 190n35
Origen, 59n21, 113–14
Owen, John, 246

Piketty, Thomas, 343n35
Pinnock, Clark, 237, 240, 250, 255, 257
Pseudo-Dionysius, 118–20, 123–24, 126–27, 138
Ptolemy, 113, 115

Radde-Gallwitz, Andrew, 151
Richard of St. Victor, 250
Richardson, Alan, 18
Robinson, Marilynne, 137, 144
Rogers, Eugene, 236, 238–39, 242, 249, 260, 309

Sandys-Wunsch, John, 8
Schillebeeckx, Edward, 276
Schoot, Henk J.M., 136
Schüssler Fiorenza, Elisabeth, 149
Sesboüé, Bernard, 241n43, 244
Smith, Barbara Herrnstein, 40
Soskice, Janet Martin, 261
Stendahl, Krister, 24
Stowers, Stanley, 235n20

Tanner, Kathryn, 124, 128–29, 141n62, 166–67, 169, 184–85, 187–88, 261, 309
Tertullian, 82
Thomas Aquinas 114n7, 123–24, 126n35, 128n36, 158, 250, 269
Turner, Denys, 36, 124, 213n58, 269, 323n13

Van Fraassen, Bas C., 159
Volf, Miroslav, 35n49, 96n32, 99n34, 280n37

Wacker, Marie-Theres, 259
Wallace, Mark, 236, 238, 249
Ward, Graham, 124
Williams, Rowan, 128n38, 195, 273, 277
Wrede, William, 9

Scriptural Citations Index

Genesis

1:2	226, 251n65, 257, 258
1:6–8	59
1:26	114
1:27	89
1:28	282
2:24	89
3:8	114
3:9	114
5:2	89
6	47
8:1	226
15:6	102, 104–105
32:22–32	114

Exodus

3:6	88
3:8	94
3:14	140
3:15	88
3:16	88
23:20–21	73

Leviticus

16:12	133

Deuteronomy

8:16	327
9:10	327
23: 2–8	326
24:1	89, 112
24:3	89
25:4	90, 112

1 Samuel

15:1–3	58
18:1	283
18:3	283
20:4	283
20:17	283
20:41	283

2 Samuel

1:26	283
22:16	226

1 Kings

18:45	226
19:11–12	226

Job

37:18	59

Psalms

8:4–6	275
17:15	226
23	118
69:25	75
118:6	275
118:22	62n25
137:9	114
148:4	59

Proverbs

5:14	327
6:6	46

Song of Solomon

2:16	282
3:2	282
3:4	283
4:8–12	282
4:12–13	349
4:16	283
5:1	282, 283
5:2	282
5:4	283

Isaiah

6:1	122
6:5	122
6:9–10	41, 122
7:14	83, 106
8:14	62n25
28:16	62
29:13	74–75
40:3	72
40:13	38
49:15	325
53:7–8	185

Jeremiah

31:15	106

Ezekiel

34:11–16	118
37:1–14	88n26

Daniel

7:13	191
12:2–3	88n26

Hosea

11:1	106

Micah

5:2	106

Zechariah

9:9	117
14:9	142

Malachi

3:1	73

Wisdom of Solomon

9:9–10	259

Sirach

26:5	327

Matthew

1:20–23	50
1:23	106
2:5–6	106
2:15	106
2:16–18	106
2:23	106
3:3	73
5:3	161, 182, 227
5:4	161
5:8	162
5:9	161, 162, 170n7
5:11	161
5:17–20	178
5:21–26	177
5:27–30	177
5:33–37	177
5:38–41	161
5:45	170n7
5:48	161
6:22–23	52

Matthew (*continued*)

6:22	143
6:25–34	134
6:27	264
8:2	192
8:11	315
8:21–22	173, 317
9:2	67
9:22	67
10:26	69
10:28	267
10:37	279, 317
12:8	130
11:13	86
12:46–50	317
13:1–9	314
13:12–13	42
13:13	162
13:14–15	122
13:31–33	315
13:44–45	315
15:1–20	178
16:18	175, 177
16:25	266n8
16:26	275
17:20	67
18:1–4	315
18:12–14	117
18:15–35	177
18:23–25	315
18:34	115
19:1–12	88
19:3–9	112, 173n12
19:12	217
19:16	127
19:17	127
19:23–24	315
19:26	276
20:1–16	315
20:16	315
20:28	180
21:31	315
21:42	62n25

22:1–10	315
22:11–14	115
22:23–33	88
22:30	217
23	177
25:1–13	315
25:14–30	115
26: 36–46	181
26:38	267
26:41	227
26:48	279
27:25	176
27:50	232
27:61	208n54
28	206
28:1	205
28:9	205, 209n54
28:16	205, 206
28:19	172, 178, 232
28:20	193

Mark

1:2–3	72
1:10	248
1:11	170n4
1:12	248
1:16–20	173
1:24	179
2:1–7	131
2:8	227
2:10	131
2:27	130
2:28	130
2:34	315
3:11	170n4
3:33–35	217, 317
4:9	41
4:11–12	41, 179
4:11	42
4:12	122
4:13–20	163
4:30–32	315

4:34	41	1:51–53	182
5:7	170n4	1:67	243
5:19–20	179	1:71	295
6:51–52	179	1:76	181
7:6–7	74	1:80	232
7:19	178	2:25	243
8:12	227	3:4–6	73
8:17–21	179	3:5	73n2
8:29	170	3:6	73n2
8:33	275	3:22	171, 229
8:35–37	266n8	4:1	243
9:2–8	50, 226	4:14	243
9:7	170n4	4:16–30	181
9:33–37	315	4:24–27	346
10:1–12	88, 173n12	6:5	130
10:2–9	112	6:20	182, 315
10:9	127	6:21	182
10:18	127, 171	6:24–25	182
10:23–27	315	6:36	161
10:27	127	7:16	181
10:40	127	7:45	279
10:45	180	8:10	122
11:15–19	173	8:19–21	317
12:10	62n25	8:55	227
12:13–17	341	9:24	266n8
12:18–27	88	9:46–48	315
12:25	88, 217	9:59–60	173, 217, 317
12:28–34	173	10:21	115, 243
12:29	142	11:20	315
12:30	266	11:33–34	52
13:32–42	181	11:34	143
14:38	227	12:2	69
14:61	170n4	12:48	70
15:38	180	13:18–21	315
16:5	206	13:21	162
16:8	179	13:29	315
		13:30	315
		13:33	181
Luke		14:15–24	315
		14:26	317
1:26–38	50	15:4–7	115
1:33	315	15:5	117–118
1:35	243	15:8–10,	163
1:41	243		

Luke (*continued*)

15:11–23	147
16:1–12	115
16:13	115
18:2–8	115
18:16–17	315
18:19	127
18:23–25	315
19:14	116
20:17	62n25
20:27–40	88
21:31	315
22:19–20	181
22:20	82n16
22:25–27	117
22:43–44	181
22:47	279
22:48	279
23:43	267
23:46	180, 232
23:55	208n54
24:10	205–206
24:12	205
24:13–32	205, 208
24:31	209
24:32	209
24:33	205, 208
24:34	205
24:36	205, 208
24:39–43	209, 304
24:39	206
24:50–51	205–206
24:50	208

John

1:1–18	182
1:1	155–156
1:14–18	50
1:18	42, 121, 130, 184
1:29	287
1:32–33	44n3
1:32–34	250

1:32	232
1:33	232, 251
1:39	45
3:1–10	43
3:1–21	182
3:3	44, 115n8, 182
3:5–8	201
3:5	115n8, 232
3:6	232
3:8	232, 236
3:13	44n3
3:16	78
3:17	184
3:31	44n3
3:34	232
4:22	295
4:23–24	232, 251
4:23	28
4:24	114n7
4:42	297
4:48	45
5:16	132n44
5:17	132n44
5:18	182
5:20	279
5:22	182
5:23	182
5:36–38	184
6:25–71	182
6:34	43
6:38	44n3
6:41–42	44n3
6:44	45
6:50–51	44n3
6:51–58	44n3
6:52–59	43
6:58	44
6:65	43
7:39	231
7:42	1n1, 94
7:53–8:11	77
8:7	291
8:26	43

8:28	43	14:25	28
8:31–59	182	14:26	194, 231, 242, 256
8:31	43, 182	15:22	51, 287
8:32	43	15:24	287
8:34	287	15:26	28, 51, 231, 242, 256
8:37	43	16:7	51, 242
8:40	43	16:11–15	240
8:41–44	43	16:12–15	246
8:48	43	16:13	28, 51, 231
8:58–59	43	16:7	256
8:58	140	16:27	279
9:3	131	17:11	194
9:6	132n44	17:21	182
9:7	42	17:23	182
9:11	42	19:11	287
9:15	42	19:15	116n10
9:18	42	19:34	44
9:19	42	19:37	1n1, 94
9:21	42	19:40	211
9:25	42	20:1–10	205
9:39	42	20:2	280
9:41	42, 287	20:4	206
10:1–16	117	20:11–12	206
10:30	143, 182	20:11–16	209n54
11:3	45n4, 192, 279	20:14–16	206, 209
11:5	192, 279	20:14	44n3
11:33	192–193, 227	20:17	44, 195, 284
11:36	279	20:18	206
11:38	193	20:19	206
12:13–15	117	20:20	209
12:40	45	20:21–22	232, 256
12:46	46	20:24	284
12:47	182	20:26	206
13:1	127	20:27	195, 209, 304
13:1–12	44	20:29	45
13:21	227, 232	20:30–31	45
13:23–25	284	21	208
13:33	193	21:4	44, 209
14:16	193, 231, 242	21:9–13	206
14:17	194, 231	21:12	44, 209
14:18	194	21:14	207
14:19–20	194	21:15–22	206
14:25–26	194	21:15	280

John (*continued*)

21:16	280
21:17	280
21:20–22	284
21:18	44

Acts

1:3	185, 205, 208
1:4	207
1:5	243, 251
1:10–11	206
1:12	206
1:15–26	334
1:16	1n1, 94, 251
1:20	75
1:21–22	230
1:22	185
1:24–25	334
2:1–4	243
2:4	229
2:17–18	229
2:23–36	185
2:25–31	86
2:31	197
2:32	185
2:36	171
2:38	230
2:41	266
2:44–45	333
3:13–26	185
4:8	229
4:11	62n25
4:12	295
4:25	230
4:31	229
4:32–37	333
5:3	231
5:9	232
5:32	257
6:3	229
6:5	229
7:10	316
7:14	266

7:25	295
7:35–43	181
7:37	86
7:52	181
7:55–56	183n22
7:55	229
7:59	227
8:7	229
8:17	230
8:29	230
8:32–33	185
8:39	231
9:1–9	200
9:5	45
9:15–18	45
10:2	316
10:9–16	50
10:19	231
10:38–42	183n22
10:39–43	185
10:44–48	45
10:44	229–230
11:12	231
11:14	316
11:15	229–230
11:17–18	51
11:18	45
11:26	346
12:24	229
13:2	231, 246
13:9	229
13:17	300
13:28–39	185
13:32–33	171
13:26	296
13:37	296
13:46–52	346
13:47	296
13:52	229
14:14	230
14:19–20	346
15:2	333
15:12	333
15:13	333

15:20	146	27:22	266n8
15:22	333	27:34	295
15:25	333	27:37	266
15:26	266n8	28:24–28	346
15:28	231, 333		
15:29	146	**Romans**	
16:6	231		
16:7	229, 231	1	92, 145
16:10	231	1:1	183n22
16:15	316	1:4	171
16:16	229	1:7	162
17	92	1:8	183n22
17:3	185	1:9	227
17:5–15	346	1:12	67
17:16	227	1:16	296
17:25	228	1:18–32	17, 47, 296
17:27	48	1:19–21	17
17:28	130, 228	1:19–23	48
17:34	118n12	1:23–25	12n24
18:4–8	346	1:24	264
18:25	232, 251	3:8	289
19:2	230	3:9	287
19:3	230	3:19–20	16–17
19:8–10	346	3:22–25	78
19:12	229	3:25	186
19:13	229	3:30	143
19:15	229	4:3	1n1, 94, 102
19:16	229	4:8	63
19:21	232	4:25	186
19:23–41	332	5:3–5	188
19:32	332	5:5	250
19:39	332	5:12–21	291
19:41	332	5:12	291
20:10	266n8	5:15	291
20:22–23	231	15:17–19	291
20:28	186	5:20	289
21:4	251	6:1–2	289
21:10–11	50	6:1–14	264
21:25	146	6:5–11	188
22:3	25	6:12	287
22:4–16	200	6:13	287
22:21	346	6:14	287
26:9–18	200	6:15–16	289
27:10	266n8	6:16–17	264

Romans (*continued*)

6:16–23	287
6:17	66
6:23	66n39
7:4	320
7:5	288
7:8	288
7:14–21	48n7
7:14	287
7:22–25	13
7:23	288
8	129
8:2	233, 288
8:4	233
8:5	233
8:6	233
8:9	233, 248
8:10	233
8:11	234, 248
8:12–14	234
8:14	234
8:16	234, 250
8:18	188
8:26–27	250
8:26	234
8:27	234
8:29–30	66
8:33	301n58
8:38–39	198
8:38	341
9:1–5	17
9:1	234
9:11–12	301
9:11–22	156
9:11	301
9:16	301
9:17	94
9:18	301
9:32	13
9:33	62n25
10:1	295
10:10	295
10:11	1n1, 94
10:14	45
11:2	1n1, 94

11:5	301
11:6	301
11:7	302
11:11	295
11:25–27	24
11:26	16–17, 240, 302
11:28	301
11:29	302
11:33	38, 121
11:34	38
12:5	320
12:8	143n66
12:11	234
13:10	167
13:11	295
14:7–8	265
14:7	273
14:17	115n8
15:4	107
15:13	63–64
16:3–5	334
16:4	266n8
16:13	301n58
16:16	279
16:23	335
16:26	66

1 Corinthians

1:3	162
1:3–7	50
1:27–28	301
2:8	341
2:10–16	50
2:11	227, 229
2:12	129, 228, 264
2:14	229
2:16	38
3:16	229
4:7	264
4:20	115n8
4:21	38
5:3	227, 269
5:4	227
5:11	145

6:9	115n8
6:10	115n8
6:11	229
6:15–20	264
6:15	319
6:19–20	265
6:19	319
7	281
7:9	318
7:10	108
7:29–31	153
8–10	146
8:2–3	39
8:4	143
8:6	143
8:8	146
9:8–10	90
9:8–11	107
9:9	112
9:15–23	338
9:17	62
9:2	15
9:22–23	188
9:23	339
10:14	145
10:19	146
10:21	264
11	8
11:3	171, 183
11:13	284
11:23	107
11:25	82n16
12–14	338
12:3	229
12:12–27	320
12:13	251, 264
12:14–21	337
12:20	264
12:22	337
12:23	337
12:25–26	337
12:27	264, 320
13	63, 168
13:1	39
13:2	39

13:8–9	39
13:12–13	39
13:13	63
14:14	227
14:27	50
15:1–7	200
15:1	107
15:4	107, 207
15:8	207
15:14	200
15:16	200
15:21–22	292
15:24–28	171
15:24	315, 341
15:28	133, 184
15:35	222
15:39	202
15:40–41	202
15:40	223, 265
15:41	202, 223
15:42–44	201
15:44–46	201
15:46–47	202
15:47–48	265
15:50	115n8, 202
15:51–52	202
15:54–55	276
15:57	183n22
16:15	335
16:17	335
16:18	227
16:19	334
16:20	279

2 Corinthians

1:2	162
1:7	188
2:4	172
2:13	227
2:21	183n22
3:3	229
3:5	273
3:6	81
3:14	82

2 Corinthians (*continued*)

4:4	190
4:10	320
4:17	188
5:1–10	267
5:4	268
5:19	79
6:16	133
7:1	227
7:2–13	273
7:4	348
7:8	172, 348
8:13	344
10–13	172, 334, 348
11:5	38
11:28	348
12:1–4	50
12:3	269
12:4	121
12:11–14	334
13:2	38
13:12	279
13:13	172

Galatians

1:1–9	334
1:3	162
1:12	108, 200
1:15–16	207
1:16	200
2:7, 62	287
2:20	264
3:2	51
3:6	104
3:8	94
3:10	105
3:13	105, 186
3:20	143
3:22	94
3:28	284
4:6	229
4:9	38–39
4:21–5:1	89

5:4	15
5:14	167
5:20	145
5:21	115n8
5:24–25	264
6:18	227

Ephesians

1:2	162
1:4–5	66, 127, 156
1:4	302
1:5	302
1:8	40
1:9–10	351
1:9	40
1:10	133
1:11	301
1:22–23	321
2:8	66
3:8–9	351
3:9	132
3:19	130
4:4–6	321
4:6	129, 143
4:12	321
4:16	321
5:5	115n8, 146
5:22–24	321
5:24	318
5:25–33	321
5:32	351
6:5–6	318
6:5	143n66

Philippians

1:1	335
1:2	162
1:18	51
1:19	229, 272, 295
1:20	348
1:22–24	267
1:27	267

1:29	66
2:3	272
2:4–11	272
2:5–11	171, 188
2:8	184
2:13	129
2:26	272
2:30	266n8
3:3	229
3:5	176n16
4:9	129
4:11	272
4:15–18	272

Colossians

1:2	162
1:9–10	39–40
1:15	121
1:17	156
1:18	320
1:24	320
2:17	320
2:20	264
3:1	264
3:3	129, 264, 308
3:5	146
3:12	301n58
3:15	320
3:18–4:1	318, 320
3:22	143n66
4:11	115n8

1 Thessalonians

1:1	162
1:4	301
1:9	145
1:10	115, 296
2:4	62
2:8	266n8
2:13	296
2:14	296n53
3:3–4	296n53

4–5	145
5:9	296
5:13–17	297
5:26	279

2 Thessalonians

1:2	162
1:5	115n8

1 Timothy

1:2	162
1:3	335
1:5	168
1:11	62
1:17	121
2:5	143
4:1	251
4:10	240
4:14	335
5:11–12	318
5:17	335
5:18	94
5:22	335
6:13	132
6:17	132

2 Timothy

1:6	335
1:7	254
2	162
2:10	296, 301n58
3:16	85, 252
4:9	335
4:21	335
4:22	227

Titus

1:1	301n58
1:3	62

Titus (*continued*)

1:4	162
1:5	335
1:7	335

Philemon

3	162
8	348
8–9	334
25	227

Hebrews

1:3	186
1:14	295
2:6–8	275
2:9	186, 188
2:10	132, 296
2:14–15	186
2:17	186
3:1	346
3:3–5	346
3:4	132
3:7	252
3:11	290
4:12	267
4:14–5:10	346
5:7–9	184n23, 186
5:7	304n60
5:9	296
6:4–6	290
6:20	346
7:1–28	346
7:8	275
7:22	82n16
7:26–27	186
7:28	275
8:1–7	346
8:2	275
8:8	82n16
9:11–14	186
9:11	346
9:12–14	346

9:12	290
9:14	232, 248
9:15	82n16, 186, 346
9:22	186
9:24	346
9:26	186, 290
9:27	275
9:28	295
10:1	346
10:10	186, 290
10:12	186, 290
10:15	252
10:19–22	186
10:26–27	290
11:1	62
11:6	62
11:7	62, 295
11:8–12	62
11:12	132
11:27	121
12:3	267
12:24	82n16, 186
13:3	320
13:6	275
13:12	186
13:13	346
13:22	346

James

2:1	248
2:5	301, 315
2:19	61, 105
2:21–24	105
2:22	105
2:24	105
2:26	105, 227, 248n54
4:4	279
4:5	248n54
5:14	248n52

1 Peter

1:1–2	172

1:1	273, 302	3:6	290
1:2	156, 162, 302	3:7–9	290
1:5	295	4:7	240
1:9	295	4:8	155
1:11	252	4:9–10	79
1:14	302	4:12	121
1:18	302	4:16	130
1:21	183n22, 302	5:6–9	172
2:1	302		
2:2	297	**2 John**	
2:6	62		
2:7	62n25	3	162
2:8	303		
2:9–11	302	**Jude**	
2:9	273, 303		
2:10	264, 273	1:2	162
2:11	267	1:9	76
2:13–17	341	1:14–15	76n8
2:13	116	1:20	250
2:17	116		
2:25	302	**Revelation**	
3:15	68		
3:18–20	196	1:6	315
3:18	186, 304n60	2:14	146
3:19	59, 196	2:20	146
3:20	266	4:2–3	114
4:2	276	4:2	121
4:3	145, 302	4:3	121
4:6	197, 276, 304n60	4:5	121–122
5:14	279	5:1	114, 122
		5:6	187
		5:10	315
2 Peter		5:12	187
		6:9	267
1:2	162	7	24
1:10	301	7:10	297
1:20–21	50, 86–87, 252	7:14	187
1:20	251	11:15	315
3:14–16	50	12:10	115n8
		13:16–17	341
		14:1–5	187
1 John		14:4	318n8
		15:3	115
1:5	155	17:14	301n58
1:8–10	290		
2:1	290		

Revelation (*continued*)   19:13   187
19:1   297   20:4   267
19:2   187
19:6   117